COMING OF AGE IN ANCIENT GREECE

COMING OF AGE

IN ANCIENT GREECE

Images of Childhood from the Classical Past

Jenifer Neils · John H. Oakley

WITH THE ASSISTANCE OF

Katherine Hart

AND CONTRIBUTIONS BY

Lesley A. Beaumont

Helene Foley

Mark Golden

Jill Korbin

Jeremy Rutter

H. A. Shapiro

Yale University Press
New Haven and London

IN ASSOCIATION WITH

Hood Museum of Art · Dartmouth College
Hanover, New Hampshire

Hood Museum of Art, Dartmouth College,
Hanover, NH 03755.
Co-published and distributed by Yale University
Press, New Haven, CT 06511.

This exhibition was organized by the Hood
Museum of Art, Dartmouth College, and supported in part by a grant from the National
Endowment for the Humanities. The Alexander
S. Onassis Public Benefit Foundation (USA) is
also a major supporter of the exhibition. The
mission of the Onassis Foundation is to dissemi-
nate Hellenic civilization throughout the United
States of America and Canada. By cooperating
with universities, colleges, and art institutions
in Greece, in the United States of America, and
in Canada, the Onassis Foundation (USA) promotes bilateral cultural relations. The presentation of this exhibition at the Hood Museum of
Art is generously supported by the Philip Fowler
1927 Memorial Fund, The Marie-Louise and
Samuel R. Rosenthal Fund, the William B. Jaffe
and Evelyn A. J. Hall Fund, the Friends of Hopkins
Center and Hood Museum of Art, and the Fannie
and Alan Leslie Center for the Humanities.

Exhibition Schedule

HOOD MUSEUM OF ART
Dartmouth College, Hanover, New Hampshire
August 23–December 14, 2003

ONASSIS CULTURAL CENTER
New York
January 19–April 1, 2004

CINCINNATI ART MUSEUM
Cincinnati
May 1–August 1, 2004

THE J. PAUL GETTY MUSEUM
Los Angeles
September 14–December 5, 2004

Designed by Leslie Thomas Fitch.
Printed in Singapore.

TITLE PAGE SPREAD: Cat. 44. School Scenes
(detail), Attic red-figure kylix, signed by Douris,
ca. 490–480 B.C.E. Berlin, Staatliche Museen,
Antikensammlung.

LIBRARY OF CONGRESS CATALOGING IN
  PUBLICATION DATA
Neils, Jenifer, 1950–
Coming of age in ancient Greece : images
    of childhood from the classical past / Jenifer
    Neils, John H. Oakley ; with the assistance of
    Katherine Hart and contributions by Lesley
    A. Beaumont . . . [et al.].
               p. cm.
Catalog of an exhibition held at Hood Museum
    of Art, Aug. 23–Dec. 14, 2003 and other
    locations.
Includes bibliographical references and index.
ISBN 0-300-09959-2 (cloth : alk. paper) —
ISBN 0-300-09960-6 (paper : alk. paper)
1. Art, Greek—Exhibitions. 2. Children in art—
Exhibitions. 3. Childhood in art—Exhibitions.
4. Children—Greece—Exhibitions. I. Oakley,
John Howard, 1949– II. Hart, Katherine.
III. Beaumont, Lesley A. IV. Hood Museum of
Art. V. Title.
N5633.N35 2003
704.9′425′09380747468—dc21
                        2003000028

Στά παιδιά μας

For Jamie

For Jacob and Nicholas

Contents

Lenders to the Exhibition

Ackland Art Museum, The University of North Carolina, Chapel Hill

Allard Pierson Museum, Amsterdam

The American Numismatic Society, New York

Antikensammlung-Kunsthalle, Kiel

Ashmolean Museum, The University of Oxford

Bowdoin College Museum of Art, Brunswick, Maine

The British Museum, London

Brooklyn Museum of Art

Bryn Mawr College, Bryn Mawr, Pennsylvania

Iris and B. Gerald Cantor Center for Visual Arts, Stanford University, Stanford, California

Carnegie Museum of Art, Pittsburgh

The Cleveland Museum of Art

Dallas Museum of Art

Fine Arts Museums of San Francisco

Joan Tarlow Haldenstein, Pennington, New Jersey

Harlan Hatcher Graduate Library, The University of Michigan, Ann Arbor

Haverford College, Haverford, Pennsylvania

Mr. and Mrs. John J. Herrmann, Jr.

Hood Museum of Art, Dartmouth College, Hanover, New Hampshire

Indiana University Art Museum, Bloomington

Indianapolis Museum of Art

The J. Paul Getty Museum, Los Angeles and Malibu, California

The Johns Hopkins University, Baltimore

Kimbell Art Museum, Fort Worth

The Metropolitan Museum of Art, New York

Michael C. Carlos Museum, Emory University, Atlanta

Leo Mildenberg Collection, Zurich

The Minneapolis Institute of Arts

Musée national des beaux-arts du Québec, Québec City

Musées royaux d'art et d'histoire, Brussels

Museum of Art, Rhode Island School of Design, Providence

Museum of Art and Archaeology, University of Missouri, Columbia

Museum of Fine Arts, Boston

The Museum of Fine Arts, Houston

The Newark Museum, Newark, New Jersey

The Nicholson Museum, University of Sydney

North Carolina Museum of Art, Raleigh

George Ortiz Collection

Princeton University Art Museum, Princeton, New Jersey

Private collection

Private collection, New England

Arthur M. Sackler Museum, Harvard University Art Museums, Cambridge, Massachusetts

The Saint Louis Art Museum

The Spurlock Museum, University of Illinois, Urbana-Champaign

Staatliche Antikensammlungen and Glyptothek, Munich

Staatliche Museen, Antikensammlung, Berlin

Tampa Museum of Art, Tampa, Florida

Toledo Museum of Art, Toledo, Ohio

The University of Mississippi, Oxford

University of Pennsylvania, Museum of Archaeology and Anthropology, Philadelphia

Virginia Museum of Fine Arts, Richmond

The Walters Art Museum, Baltimore

Malcolm H. Wiener

Worcester Art Museum, Worcester, Massachusetts

Yale University Art Gallery, New Haven, Connecticut

FOREWORD

DARTMOUTH COLLEGE has a strong tradition of the study of classical history, literature, art, and archaeology. The excellence of the programs in art history and classics—whose professors have trained dedicated art historians, classicists, and museum curators and directors—has inspired the Hood Museum of Art to undertake the organization of *Coming of Age in Ancient Greece: Images of Childhood from the Classical Past*. Ada Cohen, associate professor of art history, and Jeremy Rutter, professor of classics, have been closely involved with this project from its inception and have contributed to its shaping and implementation. It is a great privilege to have them as colleagues and to know that they will take full advantage of this groundbreaking book and exhibition in teaching their students at Dartmouth College. In addition, I would like to extend my thanks to Roger Ulrich and Margaret Williamson, Department of Classics, for their participation in the planning meeting, and to their departmental colleague Paul Christesen, who also has given advice on the development of the educational website.

Under the guidance of former director Timothy Rub (now director at the Cincinnati Art Museum), the museum sought for several years to identify a topic for an ancient Greek or Roman exhibition that could serve as a successor to the successful 1992 exhibition *Goddess and Polis: The Panathenaic Festival in Ancient Athens*. Six years ago, Jenifer Neils, curator of that exhibition and Ruth Coulter Heede Professor of Art History at Case Western Reserve University, and John H. Oakley, Chancellor Professor and Forrest D. Murden, Jr., Professor as well as chairman of the Department of Classical Studies at the College of William and Mary in Virginia, presented the idea of an exhibition on images of childhood in ancient Greece. From the beginning of this enterprise, the museum has been indebted to these two exemplary scholars for their creativity, expertise, deep-seated knowledge of their field, and dedication to every aspect of this project. They traveled extensively throughout the United States and Europe to examine the objects that the Hood Museum of Art borrowed for *Coming of Age* and wrote essays for the catalogue and the catalogue entries that form the core of this publication. They have been superb collaborators, and the staff of the Hood Museum of Art extends to them our sincere and heartfelt gratitude for their curatorial efforts on our behalf. They are model curators, and I thank them for their friendship and support during the years we have worked together on this project.

Lastly, I would like to thank my colleagues at the Hood Museum of Art for their crucial and invaluable contributions to this project. Their energy, enthusiasm, and professionalism have influenced this museum to foster exhibitions that inspire scholarly inquiry and lay the groundwork for future intellectual endeavors.

KATHERINE HART
Barbara C. and Harvey P. Hood
1918 Curator of Academic Programming
Hood Museum of Art, Dartmouth College

PREFACE

On behalf of the Onassis Foundation (USA), I would like to express warmest congratulations to the Hood Museum of Art, the curators, and all of those people who made this major catalogue and magnificent exhibition possible.

As we approach the Olympic Games of 2004 in Athens, Greece, the place of their origin, it is only appropriate to delve more deeply into the way children were raised and educated in the country that gave birth to the Olympic Spirit. After all, one of the greatest influences on Western ideals, government, and education has been that of Ancient Greece.

The Onassis Foundation (USA) is proud to be part of this worthy endeavor to know more about and understand better the origins of our civilization, especially in the most important field of education.

STELIO PAPADIMITRIOU
President
Alexander S. Onassis Public Benefit Foundation

ACKNOWLEDGMENTS

THE CAREFULLY conceived birth, youthful development, and successful maturation of *Coming of Age in Ancient Greece: Images of Childhood from the Classical Past* are cause for proud communal celebration. The project provides me, too, with this welcome occasion for expressions of deep gratitude. Not since antiquity, perhaps, has a broad public had the opportunity to study attitudes toward childrearing and the role of children in Greek culture with such sustained attention and through such a wide variety of marvelous objects. First and foremost, therefore, I thank the institutional and individual lenders for having shared so many important objects. I appreciate and admire the generous instinct that has allowed these lasting expressions of core human experiences—rare, fragile, and extremely precious to all of their owners, who are listed in another section of this text—to be shared with large audiences throughout the United States.

Support from the National Endowment for the Humanities has been essential to the evolution and execution of *Coming of Age in Ancient Greece*. Under the directorship of Bruce Cole, together with strong guidance provided by Nancy E. Rogers, director of the Division of Public Programs, and with the invaluable advice of Karen Mittelman, senior program officer, the Hood Museum of the Art was inspired to create an exhibition of lasting significance and highest interest for diverse publics. The Alexander S. Onassis Public Benefit Foundation (USA) deserves credit for generously supporting the exhibition. Stelio Papadimitriou, president of the Onassis Foundation, was visionary in his identification of this project and its celebration of Hellenic culture. I am grateful both to him and to the board of distinguished representatives over which he presides. In addition, I extend my heartfelt thanks to Ambassador Loucas Tsilas, executive director, and Amalia Cosmetatou, director of cultural events, for their steadfast support and enthusiastic reception of our proposal. Their commitment to this project has been impressive and has ensured its excellence. The Friends of Hopkins Center and Hood Museum of Art has been extremely generous in their funding of the educational area of the exhibition at the Hood Museum of Art venue and its accompanying pedagogic materials. The presentation of the exhibition has also been made possible through the support of several Hood endowments: The Philip Fowler 1927 Memorial Fund, The Marie-Louise and Samuel R. Rosenthal Fund, and the William B. Jaffe and Evelyn A. J. Hall Fund. The interactive educational website for the exhibition was in turn partially funded by abovementioned Hood resources.

This project first took shape as a result of a National Endowment for the Humanities planning grant in 2000, which led to fruitful discussions between curators Jenifer Neils and John H. Oakley, Hood staff, Dartmouth professors Ada Cohen, Jeremy Rutter, Roger Ulrich, and Margaret Williamson, and seven outside scholars, four of whom (Helene Foley, Mark Golden, Jill Korbin, and Alan Shapiro) later produced essays for this catalogue. We are also extremely appreciative for the advice of the two other consultants, George Mason University professor Carol Mattusch and Emory University professor Cynthia B. Patterson. In addition, Dr. Mattusch, as coorganizer of the International Congress of Classical Archaeology held in Boston in August 2003, helped the curators organize a special panel on Greek childhood from archaeological and other perspectives.

Professors Neils and Oakley then served as editors of the catalogue essays, selected objects for the exhibition, and crafted informed, engaging entries about these objects. Collectively, their efforts ensure the long-term value of this publication and its academic excellence. When Timothy Rub left the Hood Museum of Art in 1999 to direct the Cincinnati Art Museum, the project was guided by my extraordinary colleague Katherine Hart, who deserves more credit than will ever fit on these pages for the realization of this complex, scholarly, and ultimately breathtaking enterprise. I seize this opportunity to express sincerest thanks to her and to record my gratitude for her selfless dedication to the project and the many gifts she brings to all of the museum's work.

Any exhibition of this nature is both transformed and enhanced by the contributions made by the museums that serve as partners. We have been particularly fortunate in having the Cincinnati Art Museum, the J. Paul Getty Museum, and the Onassis Cultural Center in New York serve as venues for *Coming of Age in Ancient Greece*. We thank Timothy Rub and Glenn Markoe at Cincinnati; Deborah Gribbon, Marion True, Karol Wight, Janet Grossman, K. Quincy Houghton, Amber Keller, and Jennifer Tracy of the Getty; and Ambassador Loucas Tsilas and Amalia Cosmetatou—as well as their colleagues from The Metropolitan Museum of Art—of the Onassis Foundation's Cultural Center. We are proud to have such distinguished venues for this landmark project, and I thank these colleagues for their appreciation of this topic and their recognition of its significance for their unique communities.

The guest curators wish to thank those who assisted in their research, and I am happy to convey their appreciation here. For valuable help in libraries throughout the world, they express thanks to Jim Edmundson of the Dittrick Museum (Case Western Reserve University); Jean Wellington and Mike Braunlin of the Blegen Library (University of Cincinnati); and the staff of the Beazley Archive at Oxford University. In addition, Jenifer Neils is extremely grateful for the award of a Margo Tytus Fellowship from the University of Cincinnati, which enabled her to use the Blegen Library. Professor Neils would like to recognize further her own graduate students at Case Western Reserve University: Tamara Dunn, Lindsay Ash, and Lori Weinke. Professor Oakley is indebted to Leslie Ashbrook, an undergraduate at the College of William and Mary in Virginia, and to Daryl Tress of Fordham University. At the Hood Museum of Art, Dartmouth undergraduates have been involved in a direct way with this project since its conception. Among the students who have made important contributions, I wish to acknowledge Amanda Herring, Amelia Kahl, James Parker, Katherine Reibel, Alison Schmauch, and Anne Wadlow. Anne Wadlow and Amanda Herring were particularly helpful in making the initial compilation of the glossary at the end of this volume.

The Hood curatorial staff has relied on advice from many other museum professionals throughout the planning and implementation of *Coming of Age in Ancient Greece*. We thank the following individuals for their expertise and patience: Nancy Edwards, Timothy Potts, Malcolm Warner (Kimbell Art Museum); Philippe de Montebello, Sean Hemingway, Joan Mertens, Carlos Picón (The Metropolitan Museum of Art); Mary Comstock, John Herrmann, Christine Kondoleon, Malcolm Rogers, George Shackelford (Museum of Fine Arts, Boston); Michael Padgett, Susan Taylor (Princeton University Art Museum); Michael Bennett, Katherine Lee Reid, Rachel Rosenzweig (The Cleveland Museum of Art); Carol Campbell (Bryn Mawr College); Renée Dreyfus, Harry S. Parker III (Fine Arts Museums of San Francisco); Amy Brauer, Marjorie Cohn, James Cuno, Karen Manning, David G. Mitten (Harvard University Art Museums); Aaron Paul (Tampa Museum of Art); Gina Borromeo (Rhode Island School of Design); Adriana Calinescu (Indiana University Art Museums); Brent Benjamin, Sid Goldstein (The Saint Louis Art Museum); Regina Schultz, Gary Vikan (The Walters Art Museum); Susan Matheson, Jock Reynolds (Yale University Art Gallery); Katy Kline (Bowdoin College Museum of Art); Gerald Bolas (Ackland Art Museum); William Griffith, Albert Sperath (The University of Mississippi); Michael Brand, Maggie Mayo, Kathleen Schrader (Virginia Museum of Fine Arts); Sandra Knudsen (Toledo Museum of Art); Thorolf Christensen, Traianos Gagos, Lauren Talalay (University of Michigan); Jaspar Gaunt (Emory University); Eunice Maguire (The Johns Hopkins University); Edward Bleiberg (Brooklyn Museum of Art); Diana Franzusoff Peterson (Haverford College); Anne Bromberg (Dallas Museum of Art); Edgar Peters Bowron, Peter Marzio (The Museum of Fine Arts, Houston); Anthony Hirschel, Martin Krause (Indianapolis Museum of Art); Evan Maurer (The Minneapolis Institute of Arts); Marlene Perchinske, Jeffrey Wilcox (University of Missouri, Columbia); Susan Auth, Mary Sue Sweeny (The Newark Museum); Sebastian Heath, Elena Stolyarik (The American Numismatic Society); Mary Ellen Soles, Lawrence Wheeler (North Carolina Museum of Art); Bernard Barryte, Thomas Seligman (Stanford University); James Welu (Worcester Art Museum); Douglas Brewer, James Dengate (University of

Illinois, Urbana-Champaign); Ann Blair Brownlee (University of Pennsylvania); René van Beek, Geralda Jurraiaans-Helle (Allard Pierson Museum); Arthur MacGregor, Michael Vickers (Ashmolean Museum); W. D. Heilmeyer, Ursula Kästner (Staatliche Museen, Antikensammlung, Berlin); Irene Boesel, Vinzenz Brinkman, Florian Knauss, Martin Schulz, Raimund Wunsche (Staatliche Antikensammlungen und Glyptothek, Munich); Dyfri Williams, Evelyn Wood (The British Museum); Joachim Raeder, Bernhard Schmaltz (Antikensammlung, Kiel); Karl van Dyke (Macquarie University, New South Wales, Australia); Christiane Tytgat (Musées royaux, Brussels); Thomas Brunner, Elena Mango (Leo Mildenberg Collection); Karin Sowada (The Nicholson Museum); and the generous private collectors who have lent invaluable works, including Joan Tarlow Haldenstein, Mr. and Mrs. John J. Herrmann, Jr., George Ortiz, and Malcolm H. Wiener.

The intellectual and aesthetic promise of *Coming of Age in Ancient Greece* was embraced and supported immediately by colleagues at Dartmouth College with customary enthusiasm and rigor. Thanks begin at the highest level of the institution with President James Wright, who has articulated a strong vision for the arts on campus. Provost Barry Scherr has also been committed to the work of the museum in both public and private arenas. This project has been enriched by the intellectual engagement and moral support of Professors Ada Cohen and Jeremy Rutter in their coorganization of the symposium and their contributions as advisers to this project. Robert Donin, general counsel at Dartmouth College, was, as always, a valued consultant to this project. In our fund-raising efforts, we were indebted to Lu Martin and Peter Knox. The look of the installation at the Hood Museum of Art was created through the collaborative work of architect Andrew Garthwaite and case builder Josh Metcalf, the graphic design expertise of Joanna Bodenweber and Glenn Suokko, and the in-house exhibition design team of Evelyn Marcus, Richard Gombar, and John Nyberg.

In writing acknowledgements such as these, I am always reminded of how privileged I am to work every day with colleagues as talented and hardworking as those I have at the Hood Museum of Art itself. Once again, it is appropriate to recognize Katherine Hart as exemplary in this regard. After Katherine, Juliette Bianco took first responsibility for the execution of this project in her key role as exhibitions manager. Nils Nadeau, editor and publications coordinator, was a skillful, deliberate editor of this volume. Mary Ann Hankel, exhibitions assistant, and Sharon Reed, public relations coordinator, made many important contributions along the way. Kellen Haak, Kathleen O'Malley, Cynthia Gilliland, Deborah Haynes, and Rebecca Fawcett participated in arrangements for the shipping of works to Hanover and other venues, as well as oversight of the couriers and the well-being of the objects while under their care. Nancy McLain, business manager, and N. Norman Rawlins, assistant to the director, each gave energy to the administration of the project on an almost daily basis. Lesley Wellman, curator of education, and her colleagues Amy Driscoll, Kris Bergquist, Linda Ide, and Amanda Potter made public outreach beyond the Dartmouth campus a focus of the exhibition in Hanover and provided program material to other venues. Mary Ellen Rigby, museum shop manager, developed related educational products in consultation with the curators and other colleagues at the J. Paul Getty Museum.

Lastly, I want to convey thanks to Patricia J. Fidler, publisher; Michelle Komie, assistant editor; Mary Mayer, production manager; John Long, photo editor; Dan Heaton, senior manuscript editor; and Leslie Thomas Fitch, designer, at Yale University Press. Their faith in, and attention to, this book ensures that *Coming of Age in Ancient Greece: Images of Childhood from the Classical Past* will have a long, useful life. I have to believe that their professional dedication to its production and its design was a well-placed effort. This book is both a lasting contribution to the literature on children in the world of the ancient Mediterranean and a touchstone for future research on this subject. In the same way that the antiquities gathered together in these pages inspired Greek society to consider the role of children in their culture, this book demonstrates the promise of scholarship for and about youth at a critical moment in our own history. We can all take pride and interest in that.

DERRICK R. CARTWRIGHT
Director

Jenifer Neils and John H. Oakley

INTRODUCTION

Anticipating Wordsworth, who wrote "The child is father of the man," the Greek philosopher Aristotle stated: "From day comes night, and from the boy comes the man."[1] While we know a great deal about the lives of adult Greek males in antiquity, and now to a certain extent something about the more secluded existence of women, the missing narratives of children's lives represent a major gap in our understanding of ancient Greece. Certainly the emotional and familial environment in which Greek children were raised, their activities from play to schooling, and their various religious and ceremonial rites of passage were key factors in the formation of those adult Greeks to whom Western civilization is so indebted. Yet Socrates told a friend, "Nobody cares about your birth or upbringing or education or about any other Athenian's—except maybe some lover."[2] As a result of this apparent lack of interest on the part of ancient historians and commentators, written information about Greek childhood is slight and widely diffuse. The types and reliability of the ancient evidence vary considerably. Snippets from literary texts have been collected and studied in an effort to produce some account of the lives of children in ancient Greece, but the resulting picture is incomplete. Learning more about Greek childhood offers a tangible link to the past, especially in an age such as ours, in which practitioners of many disciplines and professions—including

CAT. 124 Gravestone of the Girl Melisto, Attic marble grave stele, ca. 340 B.C.E. Cambridge, Harvard University Art Museums, Arthur M. Sackler Museum, Alpheus Hyatt Purchasing and Gifts for Special Uses Funds in memory of Katherine Brewster Taylor, as a tribute to her many years at the Fogg Museum

novelists, therapists, philosophers, social workers, and medical doctors—have examined contemporary childhood in all its dimensions.

THE STUDY OF CHILDHOOD

Childhood studies is a relatively modern field of research. It essentially began with the publication in 1960 of Phillipe Ariès's groundbreaking book *L'enfant et la vie familiale sous l'ancien régime* (translated as *Centuries of Childhood*, 1962).[3] Although he established the history of childhood as an academic discipline, Ariès has been roundly criticized for claiming that there was no concept of childhood in premodern Europe. Taking a literalist approach to art, he made the mistake of assuming that because children were represented as miniature adults in ancient and medieval art, there was little, if any, recognition of the difference between children and adults. Today our readings of Greek art reveal subtle distinctions, such as hairdos and garments, among children of various ages beginning already in the Bronze Age.[4] Another influential scholar was the psychohistorian Lloyd DeMause, who found little to admire in the treatment of children in premodern Europe, claiming that "the further back in history one goes, the lower the level of child care, and the more likely children are to be killed, abandoned, beaten, terrorized, and sexually abused."[5] While these abuses of children certainly took place in the past, and may even have been regular practice, there is plentiful evidence for positive attitudes and treatment of children in classical antiquity. We know that the ancient Greeks greatly valued children as a vehicle for perpetuating the family.[6] They frowned upon the celibate and childless as useless to society, and established a social system that provided for orphans' welfare.[7]

Looking farther back in intellectual history, modern philosophical interest in the child begins with the Enlightenment thought of Jean-Jacques Rousseau, whose eighteenth-century inquiries continue to influence Western historical studies of the subject. More recently the cross-cultural anthropological research of Margaret Mead (*Coming of Age in Samoa*, 1928) similarly represents a fundamental contribution to the current discourse on childhood, which has been continued in recent historical studies of childhood emphasizing cross-cultural perspectives.[8] Psychological perspectives fostered by Sigmund Freud have been continued by such followers as Erik Erikson (*Childhood and Society*, 1950). Still more recent approaches have attempted to examine childhood from the child's point of view.[9] Despite such intense scholarly effort, many debates relating to childhood—such as the overriding question of nature versus nurture—have yet to be resolved.[10]

While the history of childhood is a burgeoning field in interdisciplinary scholarship, thus far little scholarly interest has focused on children in ancient Greece. This is somewhat surprising, since the topic lies at the intersection of social history; family, gender, and women's studies; history of education; classics; history of art; history of medicine and health; folklore studies; linguistics; anthropology; and sociology. One talented social historian who has contributed greatly to our understanding of Greek childhood is Mark Golden, whose book *Children and Childhood in Classical Athens* (1990), as well as his many influential articles, has reshaped our ideas about the roles of youth in Greek society. Likewise, Robert Garland, in his various books on daily life in ancient Greece, has presented a synthetic portrayal of Greek childhood.[11] While the study of children in Greece will not resolve current debates in childhood studies, it can flesh out the picture from a historical perspective. For instance, it is clear that children's rights were not as important an issue in Greek antiquity as they are today. The *kyrios*, or male head of household, made all major decisions regarding his household's offspring (including slave children)—first, whether they should live or die, and later, the extent of their education, the timing of their marriage, and their inheritance.

Were the ancient Greeks "just like us," or is the past a foreign country, as implied by the lack of rights of children? One approach to this still unresolved issue is to examine the ways in which adults reached maturity in ancient Greece. While coming of age is a universal experience, its specifics vary from culture to culture and so shed light on the values and norms of any given society. Thus the study of childhood in ancient Greece can illuminate both what is universal as well as what is specific about childrearing, and what effects this might have had on Greek civilization. We lack any ancient treatise that describes an individual's maturation process from birth to adolescence and have no "hard" data, such as infant mortality rates or the length of time committed to schooling, that can be subjected to statistical analysis. The sources of evidence are primarily casual remarks scattered throughout Greek history, poetry, tragedy, and comedy. As for the subjective experience of childhood, we probably know next to nothing, for all texts are written and most art produced by adult males.

VISUAL EVIDENCE

One source that has tremendous potential for providing information about children's lives in ancient Greece is visual evidence, namely vase paintings, terracotta figurines, bronze and stone sculpture, and marble grave monuments. The last are timeless memorials to children who died prematurely, as

FIG. 1 Grandmother and Grandchild, Attic gravestone of Ampharete, late fifth century B.C.E. Athens, Kerameikos Museum, P695

thousand images of children painted on small clay vessels that were made specifically for children (*choes*). Though not photographs, they are realistic portrayals of boys and girls, infants and toddlers at play that illuminate the lighter side of childhood in ancient Greece. In 1975 Frederick Beck brought together a wide variety of images of Greek education in a book that had only limited circulation. It was not until 1984 that attention was again focused on such material, this time by a German scholar, Hilde Rühfel, whose two copiously illustrated books have collated a wider range of images of children in Greek antiquity than ever before and significantly helped to contextualize them.[12] Because her books are published only in German, their contents are not accessible to most nonspecialists in North America. In the area of field archaeology, interest is now shifting to the "invisible" people, of which children are perhaps the most invisible.[13] The study of the relation of children to material culture, whether it be toys, feeding bottles, or jewelry, is helping to expand our understanding of children's roles as consumers in Greek society.[14]

The aim of this book, and the exhibition that inspired it, is to bring together the literary evidence and the rich repertoire of representations of Greek childhood with a view toward posing questions from a contemporary perspective about the realities of a child's existence in ancient Greece. Although the visual material will not necessarily answer all questions, this important body of evidence has yet to be examined in light of such issues. Compelling works of Greek art, such as children's marble grave monuments or the terracotta statuettes of nurses and infants, belie the commonly held notion that there was little parent-child bonding in a society with a high infant mortality rate. Because of Attic drama and the greater rate of survival of Athenian painted vases, we know a great deal more about the lives of children in this city than in, say, Sparta. Contributors to this book have attempted to address regional variation in the upbringing of children as well as changes over time, to the extent possible.

One of the most revelatory contributions of this project is the development of the imagery of children in Greek art. It is not well known that the Greeks were the first culture to represent children and their activities naturalistically in their artworks. Although in the earliest phases (Geometric and Archaic) children resemble miniature adults, in the Classical period and later they are portrayed correctly anatomically for the first time in ancient art. In fact, this important perception on the part of Greek artists is the essence of the "Greek miracle"—an ability to depict what they saw as opposed to what they knew—and this distinguishes their artistic endeavors

was often the case in ancient societies. An example from fifth-century B.C.E. Athens serves to illustrate how art can reveal much about the ancient Greek view of children (fig. 1). It shows in high relief a seated woman named Ampharete gazing intently at an infant wrapped in part of her mantle and cradled on her knees. The baby reaches out to the woman, who holds a bird in her right hand. One would expect the relationship to be that of mother and child, but the inscription states:

> I hold this my daughter's dear child,
> whom I held on my lap, when we were alive
> and looked at the rays of the sun with our eyes,
> and now being dead, I hold it dead.

This monument provides invaluable evidence for the role of the grandmother in childrearing as well as possible unwritten testimony to the death in childbirth of a young mother. Its moving epigram documents the strong attachment between family members and across generations. While admittedly this scene is an idealized construct, its emotive quality can inform the viewer, more than any text, about the value of children and family life in ancient Greece.

In 1932 the classicist Anita Klein collected a great variety of images of children for her book *Child Life in Greek Art*. Not coincidentally, some twenty of these objects are included in the present exhibition. Fifty years ago these objects were simply collected and identified, and little could be said about their original contexts or relevance to children's lives. In 1951 the Dutch scholar G. van Hoorn collected more than a

from those of their predecessors. Another important aspect that the book addresses is the extent to which this imagery of children at different stages of their development was already formulated in the second millennium B.C.E. The recently discovered frescoes from the Bronze Age site on the island of Thera that show both girls and boys involved in ritual acts have opened up an entirely new chapter in the history of childhood studies. Classical imagery (fifth and fourth centuries B.C.E.) suggests that there was less emotional interaction between parents and children than there was in the later Hellenistic period (third to first centuries B.C.E.), when more realistic images show a great deal of intimacy between adults and children. However, in all periods of Greek art, artists demonstrate a remarkably keen awareness of the typical gestures, poses, and affects of young children.

It is evident that these often charming but little-known images of children in antiquity, many of which are strikingly similar to our own, can resonate with contemporary audiences. It is the intent of our exhibition to highlight differences as well as similarities, so that viewers will come away with a more informed sense of the past. In other words, viewers who are initially attracted by familiar images will then be led to the perception of difference: to what extent are the Greeks just like us, and in what way is their culture alien? The ancient Greeks used baby bottles and potty chairs, gave their children toys, sent them to school, taught them games and sports, and mourned their early deaths, just as parents do today. They also exposed unfit newborns, meted out excessive corporeal punishment, put slave children to work at an early age, indulged in pederasty, and married off girls in their teens—all activities we would consider criminal today. Within the context of Greek society these actions were deemed acceptable and often necessary, and they do not indicate that the ancients cherished their children less than we do today. Thus there are significant aspects of continuity as well as change from antiquity to the present.

The essays in this book purposefully do not deal with well-defined topics that have been much studied in the past, such as education in ancient Greece. Rather, they attempt to address overarching issues that have received little attention, such as interpersonal relationships between adults and children, as revealed by art and literature. These chapters are also the first broad syntheses of widely dispersed material evidence, which we hope will prove useful to readers from other disciplines who wish to understand children in ancient Greece. In her prologue Jill Korbin discusses the perspective that an expert in childhood studies brings to this material, as well as the contribution of this study on ancient Greek childhood to her field. Mark Golden's introductory essay frames questions on children and child life in ancient Greece, such as the relative status of children, the extent of stereotyping in their upbringing, and the issue of when childhood ends. Jeremy Rutter discusses representations of children in the prehistoric Bronze Age, incorporating many of the important new archaeological discoveries of the past two decades. Building on her earlier articles, Lesley Beaumont addresses the changing attitudes toward children over time from the Archaic to the Hellenistic periods as documented by literature and art. She concludes that political change had a direct impact on the changing constructions of childhood. H. A. Shapiro explores the relationship of fathers and sons in Greek society, as well as the complex social and sexual relationships between men and boys. Helene Foley investigates the emotional relationships between mothers and daughters, for which that of Demeter and Persephone is the mythological paradigm, and relationships between women and girls more generally. An overview of the multifarious roles of children in cult practice is the subject of Jenifer Neils's essay, which stresses their importance for the proper functioning of rituals as diverse as marriage and animal sacrifice. Finally, John Oakley addresses the experience of death vis à vis children, from their role as mourners for their relatives to the archaeological facts of their own burials. Each of these synthetic essays deals with important issues never before approached from the specific point of view of Greek childhood, and each incorporates a variety of evidence including myth, inscriptions, texts, topography, and monuments.

More specific topics like writing, toys, feeding vessels, and so on are discussed in the catalogue that follows, along with individual entries on each object. These objects have been chosen primarily from North American collections, which contain a wealth of material, often little known or unpublished. When North American collections lacked objects needed for the elucidation of certain themes, we have turned to European collections to round out the exhibition. We hope that this anthology will serve for decades to come as a useful resource for the history of childhood in ancient Greece.

If we have learned anything from this study, it is that in antiquity as today children exerted a significant influence on society. Though often invisible in the archaeological and literary record, their centrality is nonetheless evident in the artifacts and works of art that have survived. We can learn much from the *realia* of their lives and their representations in art. We trust that this project is just the beginning of renewed and continuing interest in *ta paidia*.

NOTES

1 Aristotle, *Generation of Animals* 724a.22.

2 Socrates speaking to Alcibiades, quoted in Plato, *Life of Alcibiades* I 122B.

3 Ariès 1962. This English version of Ariès contains the statement that "in medieval society the idea of childhood did not exist" (125). The word *idea* is a translation of the French term *sentiment*, which has a very different meaning, as pointed out in Cunningham 1998, 1197.

4 See the essay by J. Rutter in this volume.

5 DeMause 1974, 1.

6 Plato, *Laws* 773E.

7 Plato, *Laws* 926E.

8 For example, J. M. Hawes and N. Ray Hines, *Children in Historical and Comparative Perspective: An International Handbook and Research Guide* (New York, 1991).

9 For example, C. Heywood, *A History of Childhood: Children and Childhood in the West from Medieval to Modern Times* (Cambridge, 2001).

10 Some recent studies include H. Cunningham, *Children and Childhood in Western Society since 1500* (London, 1995); R. Cox, *Shaping Childhood: Themes of Uncertainty in the History of Adult-Child Relationships* (London, 1996); Colón and Colón 2001.

11 Garland 1985 and 1990, and R. Garland, *Daily Life of the Ancient Greeks* (Westport, Conn., 1998).

12 Rühfel 1984a and 1984b.

13 See J. Moore and E. Scott, eds., *Invisible People and Processes: Writing Gender and Children into European Archaeology* (London, 1997).

14 For a cross-cultural study of children and material culture, see Sofaer Derevenski 2000.

Jill Korbin

Prologue

A Perspective from Contemporary Childhood Studies

IN THIS book, figurines, statues, and pottery give us a glimpse of childhood in antiquity. As we gaze at artifacts that we are accustomed to viewing for their artistic and historical value, the children gaze back, challenging us to understand their lives. Although the ancient Greeks are far removed from us in time and space, we are nevertheless struck by the familiarity of the depictions of children and families. This is one of the most beguiling aspects of looking across time and cultures—how like us others seem, and yet how different.

Almost seventy-five years ago the anthropologist Margaret Mead published her landmark account of adolescence, asking whether childhood and adolescence were everywhere the same. The title of her book, *Coming of Age in Samoa*, is echoed in the title of this book and its exhibition, *Coming of Age in Ancient Greece*. Mead, as a young woman in the 1920s, undertook her fieldwork in Samoa to explore whether adolescence was always a time of storm and stress, as it was portrayed in the West, or whether adolescence, and childhood, were more contextual. She believed that in the United States and many other Western societies teens were held back from adulthood, prohibited from premarital sex, and generally repressed in their desires for freedom. In Mead's depiction of Samoa, in contrast, teens had far more freedom than was customary in the West. If adults would give teens little to rebel against, she wrote, conflict should be vastly diminished. Mead asserted that childhood and adolescence were indeed

CAT. 102 Girl on Swing, Apulian red-figure lekythos, associated with the work of the Lecce Painter, ca. 400–375 B.C.E. New York, The Metropolitan Museum of Art, Rogers Fund, 1913

not universally experienced but varied according to the culture in which children were raised. Following John Locke, she saw children as a tabula rasa, a blank slate upon which culture could write whatever it wanted its children to become. Mead's work has come under scrutiny, and ideas about culture's impact upon children have become more sophisticated in the intervening years. Nevertheless, she set a new standard for viewing children cross-culturally, growing up in a variety of contexts. *Coming of Age in Samoa* opened the eyes of those interested in child development to the fact that children and the experience of childhood varied substantially around the world, and that Western conceptions of children and childhood were not necessarily the only ones.

Children are now no longer seen as mere passive recipients of culture passed on by their elders. Children are seen as having agency, and their own perspective on the world around them, as shapers of the forces in turn shaping them. Just as this exhibition and these essays can help us to understand children in ancient Greece, they also can help us to better comprehend the questions about childhood that are relevant not only in antiquity but also in the diverse cultures of the contemporary world.

Along with the contribution that childhood varies across cultures, *Coming of Age in Samoa* set forth the idea that children, like others we seek to understand, are the best informants on their own lives. But how does one seek the perspective of children in the far distant past? It is a difficult task to reconstruct the lives of children from the archaeological record, and historical analyses more often address concepts of childhood than the actual lives of children.[1] Yet the ancient Greeks left us a treasure in their realistic depictions of children and their families. This exhibition and the essays in this volume, then, provide a fascinating perspective on the lives of children both through these depictions and through the objects that children themselves used.

A critical question that this exhibition brings forth is how to view the lives of children in a society so far removed from us in time. How do the lives of children in ancient Greece compare with the lives of contemporary children around the world, and how should we view this comparison? Are these ancient Greek children merely a curiosity, and trying to understand them only an intellectual exercise, or do their lives have something to say about children and the experience of childhood today?

Childhood is something that we all take for granted. Everyone was once a child and has ideas about the nature of childhood. Those who layer over their own childhood experiences with those of their children have even more opinions about the essence of childhood. Thus everyone is an expert in

some sense. The similarities between contemporary children and ancient Greek children point to a more universalistic view of childhood. Yet what does one make of a Greek childhood in which conduct occurred that in contemporary Western society would be severely disapproved of, if not illegal?

There are striking similarities between the contemporary West and ancient Greece. That the Greeks were the first to portray children realistically offers us a window on childhood in antiquity. In these works of art, we see children (almost always boys) going to school, playing with hoops and tops, getting new sandals, and participating in a range of culturally important rituals. These similarities resonate with what we know of children and childhood. Who would not be fascinated seeing a potty chair used in antiquity? If the toys are somewhat different, they are still variations on the familiar theme of childhood play. We may even recognize some of these as toys that persisted into our grandparents' or great-grandparents' childhoods. If only some children—that is, boys—went to school, or if the kind of schooling was different, there are still children carrying writing materials to classes. In many parts of the contemporary developing world, it is still common for boys to attend school while their sisters remain at home. These objects, then, reassure us about commonalities among peoples.

Even in unhappy or difficult circumstances, the ancient Greeks point to our common humanity. Numerous gravestones portray Greek parents mourning their children. Greek parents, like parents today, grieved when a child died prematurely. We see, too, that siblings of deceased children were depicted by the ancient Greeks as sharing in that mourning and grief. Parents in ancient Greece, like parents of today, tried to protect their children. The exhibition contains many depictions of rituals to prevent children from coming to harm. In one striking example young girls ritually swing to reduce the risk of suicide and suicide contagion (see cat. 102). This suggests to us that, as is true today, some youths took their own lives. The ancient Greeks show us that they felt the need to protect against the phenomenon of youth suicide that continues to devastate contemporary families.

The similarities do not end with behaviors that we would regard as familiar. The ancient Greeks practiced infanticide by exposing newborns, and men engaged in sexual relationships with boys. In the United States and other contemporary Western societies, young children also die from parental abuse and neglect, and young children also are sexually engaged by adults. In ancient Greece, exposure and pederasty were neither hidden nor criminal. In contrast, in the contemporary United States and many other countries, these acts have been criminalized or medicalized—though this does not prevent them from occurring. Parental abuse or neglect is among the leading causes of trauma-related death among children under four years of age. While estimates vary, it appears that one-third of girls and one-fifth of boys under eighteen years of age in the United States are sexually abused by a family member or someone well known to them, with similar estimates in most Western nations. Yet we do not think of contemporary Western society as either infanticidal or pedophilial. In neither contemporary nor ancient society do these acts present the whole picture. [2]

Although child abuse and neglect are not new problems, increased public and professional attention to child maltreatment over the past thirty years or so has forced the recognition that all parents do not always act in their children's best interests. Child abuse was first recognized as a clinical entity in Western nations. Questions inevitably arose as to whether child abuse existed in other cultures, and whether child abuse was the same across cultures. [3] While it may seem a commonsense conclusion that child abuse is the same everywhere, the question of how children are treated across time and space is complex, and this exhibition on children in antiquity is a case in point.

A range of disciplines have tackled the question of how to look at the treatment of children across space and time. One approach is to take an advocacy position and promote universal standards for child well-being. This view usually holds the West as a model and sees conditions for children improving across historical time. This approach, however, raises the difficult issue of ethnocentrism versus relativism. Ethnocentrism is the belief that one's own culture is preferable, and indeed superior, to all others. Cultural relativism, on the other hand, argues that each society needs to be seen in its own historical and cultural context and insists that one culture or historical period cannot pass judgment on another. Each view, in its extreme form, has its own set of dangers. Ethnocentrism precludes being able to understand other cultures that are different, because they are always being seen through a single lens. Relativism precludes work toward trying to ensure equitable standards for child well-being in the contemporary world because standards are entirely contextualized and therefore variable. The challenge is to establish a level of standards for how children should be treated while also respecting cultural differences. A historical perspective, including one told through objects, lets us stand back and look without the same pressure of working with contemporary children potentially in need of protection. A particular opportunity is provided for thinking through these issues when conduct that would be condemned in one time and place is taken as unremarkable in another context.

Regardless of how a behavior is regarded in cultural or historical context, however, the views of children are rarely considered. Child slaves or children who are beaten, for example, may have their own narratives of suffering independent of how the wider adult society views their plight.

An approach that provides insights into the quandaries involved in looking at children across time and place is the perspective afforded by an emerging discipline termed childhood studies. The primary advantage of childhood studies in the current discussion is that it contextualizes childhood. In addition to helping us understand children and childhood in one time and place, ancient Greece, this book contributes to an emerging field of study.

The emergence of childhood studies does not imply that scholarly interest in children is new, however. Children have for many years been the subject of work in the humanities and arts, the social sciences, law, the health sciences, and many other disciplines. What is new is a reorientation about how children and childhood are regarded in terms of some of the most basic assumptions about the lifestage and lifespace of childhood. How can this exhibition and these essays on ancient Greek childhood enlighten and inform childhood studies, and vice versa?

WHAT IS CHILDHOOD?

How we define children and childhood is a core issue in childhood studies about which the ancient Greek context is informative. When does childhood start? When does it end? Current conventional wisdom is that childhood extends from birth through adolescence. Certainly, as we can see in the United States, the timing of the beginning of life can be controversial. The end of childhood is no less problematic. Is adolescence included in childhood? With puberty beginning at earlier ages, the beginning of adolescence has been pushed back to the ages of nine or ten. And with dependence on parents extending longer and longer, the end of adolescence is being pushed forward into the early twenties. By the time individuals reach their early twenties in many other societies, they are likely to be married with children of their own.

The ancient Greek context, as portrayed in the objects of this exhibition and in these essays, suggests that Greek parents in antiquity, like contemporary parents in the United States, had conceptions of children's development and maturation. We may not know precisely when they viewed childhood as beginning and ending, but the Greek archaeological record contains *choes* that increased in size and changed the age-appropriate activities portrayed as children matured.

Is Childhood a Universal Experience?

A basic premise of childhood studies is that childhood is contextualized, and that there are multiple childhoods rather than a universal lifestage experienced similarly across time and place.[4] In this book and the exhibition it accompanies, we see Greek children doing what children do—playing with toys, going to school, performing tasks, engaging in family activities, and participating in rituals. In some of these depictions, we recognize things that children anywhere might be doing; in others, these activities seem unique to time and place.

We also learn that childhood is not a universal experience even within one society. The materials challenge us to think not of a unitary "Greek child" but of a variety of Greek childhoods in antiquity. Just as in other societies, including our own, children vary in their experiences by age, gender, and class. In ancient Greece, as in many cultures, boys went to school, girls did not. Boys and girls differed in their activities, rituals, and games. Class also played a role in the experience of children in antiquity. Some children were sons and daughters of the wealthy, while other children were slaves. Some were children of citizens, and some not.

Sadly, some children in all societies fare less well than others. Although the ancient Greeks are sometimes portrayed as a society in which parents cared so little for children that they exposed unwanted newborns, *Coming of Age in Ancient Greece* gives a more nuanced picture.[5] Certainly, some newborns were exposed, and some children were slaves. The works of art, however, also tell us of the efforts that Greek parents and society undertook to protect their children through many religious rites—for example, the ritual described above to protect adolescent girls against suicides and suicide contagion.

Not Blank Slates or Empty Vessels: Children's Agency

A hallmark of childhood studies is its departure from conceptualizations of children solely as recipients of socialization and culture. Children interpret and shape their surroundings just as they are being shaped by society and culture. In many fields, children's perspectives can be gathered directly from children. In others, like the endeavor of this volume, children's viewpoints must be interpreted and gleaned from objects and records.[6] As is the case for the study of contemporary childhood, children cannot be seen simply as inseparable from family.[7]

Recognizing the agency of children does not necessitate separation of the world of children from the world of adults. We cannot look at children as completely divorced from the world of adults—what adults make for children and how adults portray children signify their ideas about and relationships with children. But, one presumes, adults are motivated to create objects for children that children will like and use. Artifacts may tell us what adults created for and about children, but they also tell us what children used and received.

A fundamental shift has been occurring in the scholarship of children and childhood, and this book contributes to this effort. A major challenge in research and work with children, contemporary and ancient, is to comprehend the world from their viewpoint. As much as we are enlightened by this exhibition and volume of essays, we are encouraged by this work to question. The exhibition presents us with objects whose meanings and implications are not clear. We are encouraged to hypothesize about what objects mean and what they might tell us about the children we see depicted. The exhibition also addresses itself to children and not only adult viewers. Children who visit this exhibition are encouraged to look at objects from Greek childhood, perhaps thinking about their relevance to their own lives. From a childhood studies point of view, then, this exhibition moves us forward in our efforts to understand the multifaceted nature of children and childhood. A book such as this could easily have stopped, and made an important contribution, with the depiction of ancient Greek children and the parallels that could be drawn to contemporary childhood. Instead, the contributors have gone further to open the door for asking the questions that need to be asked in understanding how children in ancient Greece can contribute to our understanding of the lifestage of childhood across time and place.

NOTES

1 Sofaer Derevenski 2000; Cunningham 1998; H. Hendrick, "The Child as Social Actor in Historical Sources: Problems of Identification and Interpretation," in P. Christensen and A. James, eds., *Research with Children: Perspectives and Practices* (London, 2000), 36–61.

2 See Golden 1990 for a perspective on the caring of Greek parents for their children.

3 See J. E. Korbin, ed., *Child Abuse and Neglect: Cross-Cultural Perspectives* (Berkeley, 1981); and J. E. Korbin, "Culture and Child Maltreatment," in M. E. Helfer, R. Kempe, and R. Krugman, eds., *The Battered Child,* 5th ed. (Chicago, 1997), 29–48.

4 A. James and A. Prout, eds., *Constructing and Reconstructing Childhood: Contemporary Issues in the Sociological Study of Childhood,* 2d ed. (London, 1997).

5 See also Golden 1988 and 1990.

6 Cunningham 1998; Hendrick (supra n. 1).

7 J. Qvortrup, "A Voice for Children in Statistical and Social Accounting: A Plea for Children's Right to Be Heard," in James and Prout (supra n. 4), 85–106.

Mark Golden

Childhood in Ancient Greece

In the course of a political attack in 330 b.c.e., the Athenian orator Aeschines impugns his opponent Demosthenes' grasp of the proprieties.[1] "Though his daughter had been dead just six days, before he had mourned and done what is customary he put on a wreath and white clothes and began making sacrifices, going against the law—even though he had lost the first and only one to call him 'father.'" Then Aeschines drives his point home: "The man who hates children, the bad father, would never be a reliable leader of the people." Five hundred years later, Plutarch, a Greek citizen of the Roman Empire, refers to this attack in his *Life of Demosthenes*.[2] The facts are not in dispute, but Plutarch takes issue with Aeschines' treatment of them. It is the sign of a weak and ungenerous nature, he says, to think mourning the mark of an affectionate spirit and to condemn a man who bears misfortune moderately and without causing pain for himself or others. Demosthenes left tears and lamentations for this personal tragedy to women and did what he thought would benefit the city—and in so doing, he was right. Yet there are many, Plutarch concludes, whom Aeschines has inclined to pity and made womanish by his speech.

Taken together, these two texts illustrate major (and interrelated) themes in the study of childhood in Archaic and Classical Greece—and of any other place and time: gender, diversity within and across communities, continuity and change over time, sentiment, power, and conflict. These categories will organize what follows. First, however, a preliminary question: who were children for the Greeks?

Nothing would be more welcome here than the views of children themselves. They have occasionally left traces in the historical record elsewhere: fingerprint analyses may show that children were among the makers of tablets used by scribes at Bronze Age Knossos and of crudely shaped clay figurines of animals buried with Puebloan people of Northern Arizona.[3] But their voices are rarely audible. Baby talk in our sources represents what adults said to children and what they wanted and expected to hear in return.[4] Almost unique, a fourth-century lead tablet found in the Athenian Agora in 1972 bears a letter from a young foundry apprentice to his mother and a man named Xenocles.[5] Lesis, apparently not a member of a citizen family, complains about his treatment: "I have been handed over to a man thoroughly wicked; I am perishing from being whipped; I am tied up; I am treated like dirt—more and more!" Unfortunately for Lesis, his letter (found in a well) was never delivered. It is our bad luck that the feelings and thoughts of other Greek children have likewise been lost.

The most common Greek word for child, *pais* (plural *paides*), was used for boys before they came of age and for unmarried girls. At Athens, the city for which we are best informed, boys were introduced to their father's deme, the local body that recognized them as citizens, at seventeen or eighteen. (All Athenian boys born in the same year were introduced on the same date, which fell before the birthdays of the youngest.)[6] Girls usually married in their mid- to late teens. *Pais* had other meanings as well, however. It described the members of two other subordinate groups, slaves and the junior partners in a homosexual pair, *eromenoi* (beloved). Slaves, rarely freed, still less liable to become citizens, were generally regarded as utterly unlike free Greeks. But the situation for children (as for eromenoi) was more complicated. They were expected to change their status, to become adults. Consequently, they were thought to share some of the characteristics of the grown-ups they would be (less fully developed to be sure) and also to display some of their own.[7]

Children, then, look much like adults and enjoy the same senses—hearing, sight, and so on—but are as yet weaker in body and mind. Herakles' strangling of the snakes sent to kill him in his cradle (cat. 11), baby Hermes' theft of Apollo's cattle—these are the deeds of gods and demigods. But when Herakles murders his music teacher and Hermes carelessly kills a tortoise to make a lyre from his shell, their amorality is childlike: it was the mark of an adult male citizen to distinguish right and wrong.[8] Aristotle thought children lacked *prohairesis* (resolve, purpose) and so could not be truly

happy or moral.[9] The gods mature and only rarely (Orphic Dionysos, Cretan Zeus) receive worship as children; those who remained children forever—Eros, Adonis—were dangerous, subversive.[10] Mortal children too were expected to grow into adult capacities and roles; as Aristotle puts it, they are not yet complete and whole.[11] In so doing, however, they will lose something as well—playfulness, for example. *Pais* is etymologically linked to a group of words for play, and *paidia*, child's play, is often contrasted with *spoude*, the serious activity proper to adults.[12] The philosopher Heraclitus is said to have shown his scorn for grown-up games, the politics of his native city, Ephesus, by playing *astragaloi*, knucklebones, with local boys.[13] As for girls, when they ceased to be paides, at marriage, they offered female divinities their hair, their clothing, and their dolls (cat. 73)—often called *nymphai* (brides) and shaped to resemble young women rather than babies.[14]

Children, it seems, are not merely adults in waiting; their distance from that goal may be so great as to make them creatures of their own kind: sweet-smelling, soft, moist, hot of temperature and temper, prone to bawl, bleat, and bellow like storms and beasts. This gulf between appearance and ability, between potential and power, makes children cute. As a boy, Cyrus, destined conqueror and king, was like a pet puppy.[15] But children could rise above adult limitations as well as fall short. Baby Hermes lied when Apollo asked where his cattle were, but for mortals there was a proverb: "Wine and children tell the truth."[16] More than innocence is in play here: otherness may produce priests and prophets as well as puppy dogs, lend children's advice or chance comments oracular force, suggest their use as mediums.[17] It was allegedly a remark by his daughter Gorgo, a girl of eight or nine, that dissuaded King Cleomenes of Sparta from helping

CAT. 11 Herakles Strangling the Snakes, silver stater from Croton, Bruttium, mid-fourth century B.C.E. New York, The American Numismatic Society

CAT. 73 Corinthian terracotta doll, early fifth century, New York, The Metropolitan Museum of Art, Rogers Fund, 1944

for older children too. But babies could not speak, unlike their more developed brothers and sisters. Our most finely drawn sketch of the stages of childhood is provided by the Hellenistic scholar Aristophanes of Byzantium.[21] The sequence for males includes *brephos*, the newborn; *paidion*, the nurseling; *paidarion*, the child who can walk and talk; *paidiskos*; *pais*, the educable child—and goes on to cover adolescence, maturity, and old age. How much this owes to Aristophanes' extensive reading in earlier authors (most now partially or totally lost) and how much to his own time and the academic tendency toward theory, it is impossible to say. Some evidence is awkward: *pais* and *paidion* are sometimes synonyms, as are *paidion* and *paidarion*, and children in Greek tragedy can shift between helpless infants and pallbearers (Sophocles' Eurysaces), between blank incomprehension of direct threats and eloquent invocations of the future (Euripides' Astyanax), from scene to scene as dramatists demand.[22]

Plato and Aristotle too vary at times (with each other and in their own works) but basically seem to operate with a fivefold division, each with its own physical and psychological traits: babyhood (until about two, when a child is weaned and able to talk); early preschool (until three or even five, a time of increased physical activity and independent play); real preschool (until six or seven—children form their own social networks); school (until puberty at fourteen); and adolescence.[23] One modern commentator is struck by the similarity of this progression to contemporary paradigms, noting, however, that the Greeks apparently didn't experience the "terrible twos."[24] We might equally note another modern parallel: those of higher status (adult males, professionals) study and so stake a claim on childhood at the same time as they leave the care of real children to women and low-wage workers.

Meanwhile, Greeks introduced their children to their families and their communities through a series of rituals, not always closely connected to the stages that philologists and philosophers see. Athenian children entered the household at the Amphidromia (on their fifth or seventh day) and were named then or at the *dekate* (tenth day). Boys might be presented to their fathers' *gene* as babies, and to their *phratries*—another family-based social group—as toddlers and perhaps again at sixteen. Their civic debut may have occurred at the Anthesteria festival during their third year, a custom marked by gifts of *choes* (small vases) decorated with depictions of children (cat. 97).[25] Girls moved through their own ritual calendar. Some seven-year-old girls served Athena and Aphrodite as *arrhephoroi*, while *aletrides* ground meal for ritual cakes at ten years old and *arktoi* (bears) honored Artemis in a cult meant to prepare them for marriage.

the Greeks of Asia Minor to revolt against the Persians.[18] Less wary, the Athenians and Eretrians sent aid and bore the brunt of the Persians' revenge. Sophocles plays on these associations in *Oedipus the King*: a son unwittingly kills his father and becomes the embodiment of the gods' knowledge. Early on, other children are both victims and vectors of the plague that afflicts Thebes.[19] The irony of innocence that brings harm as well as good also informs a modern poet, the classicist Anne Carson:

> The Yamana too, he read, were extinct
> by the beginning of the twentieth century—
> wiped out by measles contracted from the children of English
>   missionaries.[20]

As children might share many attributes with adults but were also defined by distinctions of their own, so too there were cleavages as well as continuities within childhood. For example, while newborns and small children were thought to be especially smooth-skinned, this was true to a lesser degree

CAT. 97 Boy and Cart, Attic red-figure chous with added color, ca. 400 B.C.E. Bryn Mawr, Bryn Mawr College, Ella Riegel Memorial Study Collection, Gift of Charles K. Williams, 1975

If this seems complicated, it is not just because of our evidence, taken as it is from such diverse areas as the study of vocabulary, drama, and cult practices, and often lacunose or hard to interpret at that. On the stages of childhood, Greeks were inconsistent. What can we conclude? The father of childhood history, Philippe Ariès, opened his influential *Centuries of Childhood* with a discussion of the wide range of meaning of the word *enfant* in early modern France and the corresponding lack of terms for *baby* and *adolescent*. This played an important part in his argument that the concepts of infancy and adolescence as separate stages with their own positive characteristics were also late to develop.[26] By this logic—like much of Ariès's work, it is not beyond dispute—the Greeks, with their well-stocked lexicon, discovered childhood and its stages long before modern academics.[27] It might be objected that the diversity of opinion on the number of stages, their terminology, and their natures testifies to a lack of clear understanding that in turn stems from disregard. On the contrary: in this respect, Greece looks remarkably like the world around us. Today too theories of development differ. Fashions in how to apply them have led to a welter of options even within local school systems, with elementary schools from kindergarten to grade six next to those that reach to grade eight; with junior highs—where they are available at all—including grades seven and eight or seven to nine; with high school students from age twelve to age twenty. Even the age of majority varies: in my home province of Manitoba, children may be tried in adult court at

twelve, drive at sixteen, and vote and run for office at eighteen—long after they have begun earning wages and paying taxes on everything from candy to $100 video games. No one would seriously suggest that childhood for Archaic and Classical Greeks was terrain that ought to be and was contested by as many competing professional and political interests as it has become. But even the disagreements that still remain in our records bespeak anything but ignorance and indifference.

We will return to adults' attitudes later. Now, let us explore some markers of difference other than age: gender, social class and status, place, time.

GENDER

"I am so seriously glad that I didn't live in ancient Athens. All those athletic competitions must have been such a drag."

"It didn't seem to be the girls who had to do it. They just had to be virgins all the time, to get in those big parades, presenting *peplos* to the statues or whatever."

In some ways, all children in Archaic and Classical Greece were women.[28] At Athens, both were excluded from an active role in the courts and political process of the democracy and restricted in their economic capacity; both, unlike men, might wear the Persian *kandys* (or adaptations of it).[29] On vases, both might be distinguished by the use of added white, and boys could replace women in genre scenes—for example, holding a man's head while he vomits (fig. 1). In delicate medical operations, the best assistant is a woman or a child with soft hands.[30] Women and children are enslaved (while men may be massacred or ransomed) in the sack of cities. And both may escape their bonds in special circumstances. "They formed wax images and burned them while they uttered these words"—so runs the tradition of the founding of Cyrene in North Africa—"men and women, boys and girls."[31] Still, the two teenagers quoted above get it right (despite their mistaking *peplos* for a plural): Greek boys and girls lived different lives.

At Athens differences affected both divine and mortal realms. Red-figure vases show many gods and heroes as infants and children, but their female counterparts very seldom; Athena and Aphrodite are fully formed, Helen drawn as a young woman, though literary sources say she was abducted at seven.[32] Humans' houses sported olive wreaths at the birth of a boy—an aspiration for an Olympic victor—wool, emblematic of women's work, for a girl.[33] Such birth announcements appeared only after an earlier choice, whether or not to accept the newborn into the household, a decision that probably favored boys.[34] (Those refused were

FIG. 1 Boy Assisting Sick Man, Attic red-figure kylix, attributed to the Brygos Painter, ca. 490 B.C.E. Berlin, Staatliche Museen, Antikensammlung, F 2309

"exposed," put out in some public place.) Females outnumber males in all compositional formations on Classical Athenian tombstones except when reliefs depict children on their own. In such cases, boys are far more frequent than girls—to be sure, evidence not of demographic realities but of the attitudes that helped shape them.[35] Gods and heroes grew up quickly, nourished on nectar and ambrosia.[36] Whatever the diet of real children, girls got less.[37] Boys often went to school, while girls were rarely if ever educated outside the home (though some learned to read and write within it); a father would choose a guardian to educate his boys or protect his girls.[38] Schooling, of course, was a less central element in children's lives in ancient Greece than it is today, some of its socializing functions being filled by regular religious festivals. Here boys and girls alike had roles to play. Boys' roles featured competition—musical, athletic, equestrian—sometimes in teams with members of their own civic tribes. The ten tribes formed the basis of the organization of Athens's army: the feeling of fellowship formed with their young tribesmen contributed to cohesion and morale on campaign later on.

No Athenian girl could be unaware of the importance of warfare to the city's success or survival. Few, I expect, kept weapons in their bedroom, as Euripides' Iphigenia does the spear Pelops used to slay Oenomaus.[39] But their names frequently incorporated elements referring to war: *strat-* (army) is the most common root of all. When the comic poet

Philemon lists typical women's names, he chooses Hipponice, Nausistrate, Nausinice—all martial in meaning.[40] Such names, however, do not include indications of the kinds of qualities warriors need: ferocity, boldness, lack of fear. These are inappropriate for girls.[41] If their festival involvements also prepare them for adult life, these (like that life itself) must be unlike boys' involvements, and certainly not competition—girls did not openly vie for public prominence, liable as this usually was to come from real or imagined sexual misbehavior. (We hear of Harmodius's sister only because she was deemed unfit to be a *kanephoros* in a festival procession—a slur on her chastity avenged when her brother killed the man who rejected her.[42] Even then, as befits a girl from a good citizen family, we never learn her name.) Suitable girls carried infants or their images, prepared food, cleaned, wove clothing (like the peplos, the cloak that covered Athena's old statue in the Erechtheum), paraded, often adorned with the makeup and jewelry that enhanced their attraction for the divinities they served and the citizens who watched. These mundane tasks were thus enrolled among those essential for the gods' worship and the city's welfare, a source of pride for the girls who did them and for all the others who would throughout their lives. Boys who won or placed in events at the quadrennial Panathenaea, greatest of Athens's festivals, were given hefty prizes and exalted to a level approaching the gods. For girls, to take part as they were was reward enough. We do not know whether they agreed.

SOCIAL CLASS AND STATUS

Abundant though it is, our evidence for ancient Athens is skewed. Literary texts were mainly written by and for well-off adult males whose interest in children and childhood (when it is evident at all) coexists with many other interests. Durable grave monuments and the inscriptions on them were too expensive for most; besides, virtually all the dead, who were clearly identified as citizens (by the use of the patronymic and demotic), were adults, and we cannot always distinguish Athenian children from others whose tombstones have survived.[43] Painted pottery was more affordable and features domestic scenes of real importance to students of Greek childhood; painters, however—and presumably purchasers too—have a preference for the lifestyles of the rich and famous.[44] Yet despite these difficulties, we can still say something about the impact of class distinctions on Athenian children and childhood through a closer look at two important sites of socialization mentioned above, schooling and festivals.

Athens had no public education system. Schools were private enterprises, established and run for profit by individual entrepreneurs who followed their own curricula and methods. As a consequence, though most boys probably got some taste of school, those better off attended longer and only the elite could afford the most advanced instruction, in rhetoric and philosophy. Fees were one reason: few families would want to budget even a half-drachma to hear Prodicus speak at a time when laborers earned a drachma a day, let alone the ten thousand drachmas Protagoras is said to have charged for a course.[45] Perhaps more important, most would want sons to help out in the family business or even bring in wages from work elsewhere. Phrynichus (says an unsympathetic client of the speechwriter Lysias) was poor and tended sheep in the fields while a richer boy was being educated in town.[46] Potters' sons served an apprenticeship in their father's workshop and then set up for themselves.[47] Cooks and physicians learned their trade from childhood.[48] How young might such assistance start? Plato's Socrates says a potter's apprenticeship is a long one and recommends that the citizens of his utopian Magnesia go into the fields at ten.[49] This probably has their education in view rather than their labor, but in fact even younger children could contribute to agriculture, the most important sector of the ancient economy. (Young children in other peasant societies clear stones, break up clods of earth, cut fodder, mind animals.) Their availability for these and other simple chores (fetching water, running errands, housecleaning, child care) would not only be valuable in itself but also free up their elders for more demanding work.

As for festivals, there were probably no more than two or four arrhephoroi at any time, and not every girl could become a kanephoros, perhaps not an arktos either. Sexual impropriety was the grounds for the rejection of Harmodius's sister. There were other grounds too: late sources say *aletrides*—grinders of grain for Athena's sacred cakes—must be of noble birth.[50] Even in democratic Athens, some important priesthoods were hereditary, the preserve of old families among the elite. It would not be surprising to find such considerations entering into the selection of girls for their prominent cult positions. Sons of the elite may have been overrepresented in the tribal choruses at Athenian festivals.[51] That well-off boys had an advantage in athletic festival competition is equally probable: their resources could support the special diets, trainers, time for exercise, and travel to competition demanded for success. It was a long and arduous trip to Olympia, say; athletes had to spend thirty days at the site before the games began, and, eager though they were to reward victors on their return, cities did not offer subsidies to ease their way.[52] The real question is whether some poorer

FIG. 2 Skiaphoros and Kanephoros, Attic red-figure lekythos, attributed to the Brygos Painter, ca. 480 B.C.E. Paestum, Museo Archeologico

boys had a chance to win as well. It is attractive to think of competition as a path of upward mobility for some at least of the many boys who competed during the crowded festival calendar, paved at the start by victories and their prizes.[53] Certainly natural ability ought to matter most at earlier ages; besides, promising competitors might well attract the patronage of a prosperous admirer. On the other hand, few prizes were as generous as the Panathenaea's, themselves available only every four years. Moreover, the greater the prize, the more it brought in competitors from abroad too—many Panathenaic vases, distinctive containers for the valuable oil that winners took away, have been found in foreign graves. Most crucially, perhaps, though we know of many Athenian athletes, none definitely ran or wrestled his way from rags to riches. Whatever the theoretical possibility of success, in the end, a boy's background made a big difference.

Many children at Athens were not citizens, of course. Some lived comfortably—the children of Cephalus, a wealthy Syracusan who enjoyed metic status as a long-term free resident of the city, appear among the gilded youth of Plato's dialogues. Metics' daughters could carry water jars or sun shades in the Panathenaic procession (fig. 2).[54] However, we have the foundry apprentice Lesis's letter to remind us that some were less fortunate. Slaves' lives might be still worse. A prosecutor reviews the early career of the famous courtesan Neaera for an Athenian jury:

> Now, Nicarete—the freedwoman of Charisius of Elis and the wife of his cook—owned these seven girls from when they were small children. She was an expert in recognizing beauty in small children and understood how to rear and train them from long experience: this was her trade and she earned her living from them. . . . When she had reaped the profit of their prime, she sold their bodies, each and every one of the seven . . . this Neaera too.[55]

Exposed children who did not die were often raised as slave prostitutes.

Local and Regional Variation

Perhaps poorer Athenian boys were shut out from athletic competition. A sentiment attributed to Alcibiades, one of the wealthiest of Athenians, suggests this was a local peculiarity: he took to horseracing rather than other events because these included lowly born, poorly educated athletes from small cities.[56] The Greeks, after all, called some 750 states home; however much they had in common, diversity too is easy to demonstrate, in childhood as in other areas. For example, at

Athens the sons of those killed in battle (or in defense of the democracy) were supported until majority; daughters too received recognition at Thasos, a dowry from the state.[57] For another, paides are younger than paidiskoi at Sparta.[58] If I concentrate on Spartan childhood here, it is because it affords the greatest contrast with Athens and so illustrates the range of Greek practices. It is also the next best attested. But this evidence is as problematic as it is plentiful. We can rarely be confident that the contrasts it delineates are not (in part at least) illusory. Greek writers' accounts are shaped by the long-standing political rivalry and military conflict between the two states, their evident cultural differences— Athenians and Spartans spoke different dialects of Greek— and the barrier Spartan secrecy erected against even unbiased inquiry by others. Not that our elite authors are in fact unbiased, preferring as they do Spartan order to the openness of democratic Athens. Finally, later authors have a tendency to project contemporary institutions into the distant past.[59] In the brief sketch that follows, I will of necessity avoid entering into the debates these realities normally require, therefore presenting a portrait that may appear to some specialists to need retouching and to others to be an outright forgery.[60]

At Athens, the kyrios (the adult male citizen who headed the household) had the right to accept children born into it. Spartan fathers yielded this authority to the elders of the tribesmen, who met at a place called Lesche and consigned newborns they rejected to the Apothetae, a chasm at the foot of Mount Taygetus.[61] Much of this remains obscure. Where did Plutarch (our only source) derive his information?[62] Who were the elders of the tribesmen? Did they examine boy babies only?[63] Did their involvement reduce the number of the exposed—they had to consider Sparta's pressing need for military manpower—or increase it (since they lacked the emotional interest of individual fathers)?[64] Whatever the answers, Plutarch consistently notes ways in which Spartan childhood differed from others from its start. (Spartan women washed newborns with wine rather than water—to test their constitutions—and didn't swaddle them.) His description is also consistent with other evidence for the unusual prominence of the state and its collective institutions, a source of inspiration for both Plato and Aristotle.

When Pericles called Athens "the school of Greece" in his famous funeral speech, he meant that it offered a model others were free to follow.[65] The metaphor depends on the opportunity for individual choice that informs much of Pericles' praise of his polis: Athenian kyrioi (as we have seen) decided which of their children to send to school, where, and for how long. At Sparta, however, this too was out of a father's hands. All Spartan boys underwent a long, arduous, and collective upbringing, the *agoge*, supervised not by individuals of low status (slaves, hirelings, foreigners) but by citizens who held the most prestigious offices of the state. The two kings' heirs were the only exceptions: this signaled their special status and preserved it from the risk of poor performance.

From the age of seven, Spartan boys spent at least part of the day in the company of their agemates. Basic literacy and the choral singing and dancing that was as central to their religious observance as in other Greek cities may have been taught in this context or elsewhere. In any case, our accounts of the agoge ignore these pursuits to focus on physical training and its consequences. This was perhaps in keeping with the assimilation of children to animals that tinged Greek ideas everywhere (we may think of Athens's "bears") but was especially explicit at Sparta. The groupings of the agoge were called "herds" and "flocks," the official immediately responsible for it the *paidonomos* (boyherd). Boys lived close to the land—going shoeless, stealing from the fields to supplement scant rations, making their own beds with river rushes cut by hand. Recalcitrance or failure met brutal punishment, beating or a distinctive form of discipline, biting of the thumb. At twelve—an age when most other Greek boys had left school or were about to—the agoge became more demanding still: boys lived in barracks under the constant watch of leaders they chose themselves and of the community's elders as well as of the paidonomos and his whip bearers. In addition, each was encouraged, perhaps required, to take an older youth as a lover, a mentor who was himself answerable for his partner's progress.[66] Here again the Spartans may have made compulsory what was merely permitted elsewhere and used their own distinctive terms as if to underscore their singularity. These make their motives clear: the older youth was called *eispnelas* (inspirer), the young *eromenos, aïtas* (hearer). Besides this everyday scrutiny, boys faced frequent tests, from massed brawls and dancing under the midsummer sun at the Gymnopaediae festival to stealing cheeses from the altar of the goddess Orthia, in order to pass from one stage of the agoge to the next. Only those who proved their fitness could eventually earn election to one of the common messes where Spartan males lived from the ages of twenty to thirty and ate their main meal for thirty years more.

The agoge aimed to instill soldierly virtues: strength, endurance, solidarity—survivors of the same schooling, Spartans called themselves *homoioi* (equals). The agoge also served to identify leaders, equally important to a polis that

FIG. 3   *Girl Runner*, bronze statuette, ca. 560 B.C.E. London, The British Museum, GR 1876.5-10.1

lived uncommonly close to ruin. (The Spartans were beset by enemies within—they controlled a large and self-conscious population of Greeks they had conquered in war—and driven by ambitions beyond their borders.) Here too the agoge might be an equalizer: son of a poor man, Lysander displayed his ability in the agoge, became eispnelas of the future king Agesilaus, and went on to command Spartan troops in the decisive victory of the Peloponnesian War. It is no wonder, however, that Pericles could imagine Spartan youth as akin to having no childhood at all.[67]

However much Spartan boys were cheated of their childhoods in Athenian eyes, those of Spartan girls were prolonged past the Greek norm. They married late by Greek standards, at eighteen or even twenty—the age when boys became fully fledged warriors.[68] Similarly, while boys may have seemed underfed, Spartan girls got richer rations than others.[69] So boys and girls were treated more alike at Sparta than elsewhere. Was there also a parallel upbringing for girls? Not, perhaps, as formally and finely structured as the boys' agoge. Nor is it probable that homosexual couples of older and younger girls were as common or as crucial (despite a tantalizing remark by Plutarch).[70] But that there was some system of public education, and that it involved all girls, is likely enough. Physical training (again) was at its core. Competitive races for unmarried girls are attested throughout the Greek world; those for Hera in the stadium at Olympia, where three age groups ran in tunics that left their knees and right shoulders bare, are the best known.[71] Spartan girls, however, contested in an expanded program: not just running (fig. 3) but "tests of strength," *bibasis* (an exercise in which the heels were brought up to the buttocks as many as one thousand times), perhaps wrestling, and even more.[72] This may be explained by Sparta's special concern for the safe birthing of healthy babies—future soldiers and mothers of soldiers. We get a glimpse of how Spartan girls were ideologically prepared for this role in a fragmentary poem they sang in chorus at a local festival.[73] Surviving portions praise the beauty of the chorus's leaders and its members and recount a struggle between mythical mortals and Sparta's model youths, Castor and Pollux, over the daughters of Leucippus. Castor and Pollux slay their rivals and win: Spartan girls are prizes worth fighting for, even for the sons of a king and a god. There must have been more to their education than physical training and trials, however. Spartan girls were renowned for their outspoken intelligence as well; for example, Gorgo, Cleomenes' insightful daughter, figures in a number of vignettes of ready repartee. Spartan boys are said to have observed and commented on the behavior of their elders at their own mini-messes and (as usual) had their performance judged.[74] Perhaps girls exercised their wits in a similarly competitive context.

CHANGE OVER TIME

The scarcity of evidence, its tendency to bunch within certain periods, the variety of its forms, each with its own conventions influencing the inclusion of subjects and the ways they are treated—all combine to make identifying change over time in Archaic and Classical Greek childhood a challenge.[75] Some scholars have been willing to tackle it, of course: culture abhors a vacuum. For instance, an imaginative discussion of Sparta's fourth-century decline identifies as one cause a change in childrearing practices. Women, now more engaged in managing their extensive property holdings, delegated much of their mothering to nurses. Neither Spartans nor consistent in their attitudes or actions, these nurses undermined the cohesion fundamental to the success of the agoge.[76] Even when shifts are (seemingly) more secure they may prove difficult to explain. The small choes with their many scenes of children, connected to the Anthesteria, came into use about 430 B.C.E.; more than 90 percent of those that survive were painted within the next thirty years. This may be artistic fashion, no more. However, it is tempting to link their popularity with the outbreak of the Peloponnesian War and the catastrophic mortality from plague and battle it intro-

duced. But just how? Should we see these choes as adult nostalgia for carefree childhood days now gone for good, or—like the young Athenians who got them as gifts—as indicators that life could still bloom amidst the ruins?[77] And, in either case, how are they related to the increasing naturalism in the depiction of babies—larger heads, chubby limbs, more lifelike poses—some have spotted in this same period? Finally, given the gaps in our evidence, it is easier to discover new developments than to tell whether they represent real and long-lasting shifts in ideas or behaviors or simply the constant play of variation from which no society, however stable and monolithic it may appear, is free. Nevertheless, we can (cautiously) note three areas in which changes reflected new ideas about children at Athens or affected their lives.[78]

Personal Names
Athenians (like other Greeks) bore only one personal name. They were distinguished from their fellow citizens, when necessary, by the use of a patronymic, a form of the father's name, and a demotic, an indication of the civic deme to which they belonged. There was a tendency for names to run in families; children might bear their father's name or (much more often) names that incorporated a common semantic element. So Androcles of Acharnae named his sons Androsthenes and Androteles; Hegesias of Sounium chose Hegias, Hegesandrus, and Hegesippus. The frequency of such linked names increased significantly over time, reaching approximately one-third of known father-son pairs in the fourth century.[79] Their incidence rose sharply at the ends of the sixth and fifth centuries. Each, as it happens, was a period in which parents may have felt the need to assert family unity in the face of a challenge (Cleisthenes' reforms) or a crisis (the Peloponnesian War again). The pattern holds for both the Athenian elite and those less prosperous and prominent (though, as usual, our evidence underreports the poor majority of the population). But gender and local variation come into play. Girls' names were much more rarely linked with their fathers' at Athens; as they shared the family property (through dowry) but got less than their brothers, so also they were less likely to carry a family element in their names. Meanwhile, Spartan names reveal a similar upsurge in linkages at the end of the fifth century, but are less common at almost all periods. In this area too, it may be, the father's influence was weaker.

Nothoi
In 451/0, the assembly approved a measure ("Pericles' citizenship law") restricting citizenship to those whose parents

were both Athenian citizens and formally married to each other. Others henceforward joined the ranks of *nothoi* (bastards). The legal liabilities this status incurred are controversial but likely encompassed both private life (the capacity to inherit fully) and public.[80] No doubt there was a social stigma for children who were nothoi as well: one of Athens's gymnasia, Cynosarges, was the haunt of nothoi, and the injunction "Go to Cynosarges" was an insult.[81] Sometime in the aftermath of the Peloponnesian War, one Theozotides proposed that adopted sons and nothoi be denied the support provided to children of those who had died fighting for the democracy.[82] Given Athens's straitened circumstances, Theozotides' motive may simply have been the expense.[83] His proposal, however, was probably made more palatable by the inclusion of nothoi—already marginalized—along with adopted sons.

Producers and Pederasty

In the fifth century, *choregoi*—citizens responsible for the training of choruses of boys for festival competitions—could be young; one such producer was not yet twenty.[84] Boy choristers might train not merely under a producer's supervision and at his expense but in his home. They would inevitably come into contact with him, perhaps under his influence. Some might enter sexual liaisons. Homoerotic relations between men (and youths) and boys became more problematic in the fourth century, judging at least from some admittedly weak indications: the parading in a political prosecution of laws that protected students from approaches by their teachers or other males; Plato's reference to "the passion for *paides*, both male and female . . . which has given rise to countless evils for individuals and for entire cities"; Aristotle's concern about the long-term effects of the passive role on the eromenos.[85] This unease may be linked to the raising of the minimum age for choregoi to forty, to match the officials in charge of ephebes.[86] Greeks (immune to or unaware of midlife crises) thought men grow more temperate and self-controlled as they age.

SENTIMENT AND STRATEGY

It is an odd irony of the historiography of childhood, of sentiment and emotion above all, that it has spent so much time in the shadow of mortality. Debates on the feelings of parents have concentrated on the frequency of their children's deaths, their responses (real or imagined) to them, and the conclusions to be reached as a result. In the 1960s and 1970s, the subject's infancy, leading scholars of early

modern Europe argued that parents did not love their children as often or as well because the elevated level of mortality made emotional investment too perilous for individuals and insupportable for their societies. We might call this the Mary Poppins approach, recalling her query toward the end of the famous film: "And what would happen to me, may I ask, if I loved all the children I said goodbye to?" More often, it is a failing people attribute to others: General William Westmoreland's account of his enemies in Vietnam—"They do not grieve the way we do"—is echoed by what an Israeli soldier told a visitor to a Palestinian family whose ten-year-old had been killed.[87] The Greeks themselves yielded to this impulse. Herodotus writes that Persian fathers see their sons only after they reach the age of five, to save themselves from sorrow if the child dies young.[88]

However, this theory of a calculus of grief, a kind of demographic determinism, has attracted many critics. Evidence from high-mortality populations of the past and present suggests that most parents in fact love their children, take every measure they can to keep them from harm—they know how much at risk they are—and grieve when they die. Individuals can bear up beyond expectation for a number of reasons. Since they have followed customary and socially sanctioned childrearing practices, parents' grief is not fueled by guilt. Child care itself is often shared with others; they too may carry the burden of loss. Of course, it is a burden they have in common with many others around them in high-mortality populations: as a result, many such societies have elaborate and well-recognized ritual behaviors and beliefs about the afterlife that help them cope. Finally—something too rarely realized—these rituals and the mourning that accompanies them are primarily the province of women. Institutions that are mainly men's responsibilities—government, warfare, foreign trade—carry on much as always.

There are certainly exceptions. In an award-winning study, Nancy Scheper-Hughes has described the responses of mothers in a shantytown community in northeast Brazil to the sickness and death of children they believe to be doomed.[89] She refers to an "old" reproductive strategy common to pretransitional populations (401–403) that makes child death "a predictable and relatively minor misfortune, one to be accepted with equanimity and resignation as an unalterable fact of human existence" (275). It is important to note, however, that the poverty and despair Scheper-Hughes portrays so powerfully—she is anything but a disinterested outsider—is a contemporary creation, the legacy of Brazil's military dictators, their death squads, and the free-market economic programs they put in place. Far from being exem-

CAT. 17 Medea Escaping in Her Chariot, Lucanian red-figure calyx-krater,
attributed to the Policoro Painter, ca. 400 B.C.E. The Cleveland Museum of Art,
Leonard C. Hanna, Jr., Fund

plars of preindustrial or Third World modes of thought, the poor Brazilians of the northeast are the victims of modern, developed nations' political priorities and of the ideologies developed within them.

This debate is of direct relevance to Archaic and Classical Greece, where mortality (though impossible to establish accurately) was probably high: 25 percent of newborns or even more may have died before their first birthdays. Generalizations are of limited use: parents probably did not care for their daughters just as they did for sons, fathers' and mothers' feelings probably differed, children of different ages were not treated the same, one's own children counted for more than others' did (as is true even in supposedly child-centered societies today). Nevertheless, there is ample evidence that parents loved the children they decided to rear.[90] The assumption that children are to be cherished pervades texts of every genre, from the historian Thucydides' judgment on the slaughter of the schoolchildren of Mycalessus—"a most complete, most sudden, most horrible disaster which struck the entire city"—to the words of Euripides' tragic Herakles ("both the best of mortals and those who are nobodies love children . . . the whole race is child-loving") and Aristotle's opinion that the most intelligent species, human beings and some quadrupeds, devote attention and care to their children for the longest time.[91] Even the stern Spartans could unbend enough to enjoy their children. Plutarch relates an anecdote about the warrior king Agesilaus playing horsey with his—though he asks a neighbor not to let anyone know.[92] Medical treatises advise of times of special danger (the fortieth day of infancy, the seventh month).[93] Popular prophylactics and remedies included plants, incantations, magical stones, rattles, amulets incorporating galactite or the eyes of a hyena, and the hide of an ass for babies to sleep on.[94]

Some of this anxiety was surely whetted by self-interest in communities that knew no pension plans. The double meaning of the word *tokos*, both "offspring" and "interest" (in the financial sense), suggests as much. But the gulf between sentiment and practicality is not always wide. Those who regard only their own interests are sociopaths, but to ignore them is also unhealthy—a mix or balance is best. Besides, the associations of tokos may be apt if we reflect that interest compounds over time. Not only may economic dependence intensify emotions, but care and contact often encourage commitment. In the end, it is impossible to guarantee what Archaic and Classical Greeks felt for their children. However, in the absence of compelling evidence to the contrary, it is best to accept their many expressions of concern and affection at face value.

CONFLICT AND CONTROL

If only parents and children were always in accord! But—to begin at the most fundamental level—not all children were reared.[95] Unpalatable as exposure may seem, however, it is crucial to recognize that the practice does not invalidate the conclusions I have just reached. Exposure—and even child sacrifice—are known to coexist with both community encouragement of reproduction and personal affection for children.[96] Abortion today is rather similar: Québec, the only Canadian province to pay mothers birth bonuses, also produced the juries who repeatedly refused to convict a doctor who performed illegal abortions—one on Mother's Day and broadcast on television. Furthermore, follow-up studies seem to show that women who terminate pregnancies generally care as do any other mothers for children they choose to birth. Greek parents too could endorse the slogan "Every child a wanted child." Once a child was accepted into the household, its death was tragic, its murder appalling. This is what feeds Medea's revenge and makes her successful escape (in a god's chariot, no less) such a shock (cat. 17).

Outside Sparta, this acceptance was a father's prerogative. As kyrios (so Aristotle says), he ruled his wife as one citizen does another (save that this household magistracy has no term), his slave like a tyrant, and his children *basilikos*, like a king.[97] This appears to mean that the father's authority is hedged around with something like divine sanction—like Spartan kings in Aristotle's time. It also implies that children who challenged or flouted that authority got more tender treatment than slaves. It has been plausibly argued that this was indeed so at Rome, where citizen fathers among the elite made a point of sparing sons the physical punishment they meted out to slaves.[98] *Pais*, however, sounds a lot like a form of *paio*, "I hit"—an overtone picked up on the comic stage: other evidence suggests that parental discipline in the Greek household could be harsh. It comes as no surprise, then, that the rod, the emblem of education on Attic vases, was a staple of Greek schooling. (The use of *typto*, "I beat," in verb paradigms in Hellenistic Greek classrooms may have served as a reminder to students.) Herakles' response—to kill his music teacher Linus—was probably unusual in its violence but not, perhaps, in its impulses (fig. 4). Soldiers who served under Clearchus, an especially severe commander, resented his harshness as boys do a schoolmaster's.[99]

Untroubled by the terrible twos and midlife crises, did the Greeks also escape the turmoil of the teenage years? They clearly recognized *hebe* (puberty), set at fourteen—twice the earlier critical age of seven and, like it, linked to number magic. The voice broke; hair grew on the skin, cheeks, arm-

FIG. 4   Herakles Attacks His Music Teacher, Attic red-figure kylix, attributed to
Douris, ca. 480 B.C.E. Munich, Staatliche Antikensammlungen und Glyptothek,
2646

pits, genitals; breasts developed; semen began to be produced.[100] How about tension and conflict with the other older
generation? As we have seen, the very existence of adolescence as a distinctive stage of life in antiquity is a subject of
debate. Some see teenagers as apprentice adults, modeling
themselves on their elders and joining with their world
without much fuss—ancient youth, as Marc Kleijwegt calls
them.[101] For others, the warmth of the blood fueled the
passionate irrationality of youth, and bodily strength made
it as dangerous as it was disruptive.[102] What is beyond doubt
is that Archaic and Classical Greek adolescence, defined as
the period between puberty and social maturity, was prolonged. Men married at around thirty, and full political rights
might take as long to attain or longer. (Both Athens and
Sparta reserved important political offices for those older
than thirty and established special responsibilities for the
elderly.) So though we do hear of disagreements and worse

involving fathers and sons, these normally (as far as we can
tell) concern older adolescents or young men in their late
teens and early twenties, feeling their strength and impatient,
perhaps, to exercise it like their elders (or, as they may believe,
better than them). Pheidippides in Aristophanes' *Clouds*, horse-
crazy and a fan of the Sophists, must already be an adult.
Plato's Athenian stranger hints at this truth: "A child in his
present helplessness loves and is loved by his parents, though
he is likely to be at odds with them at some future time."[103]

Gender and class figured in all of this. Though mothers
might (literally) lend a hand, corporal punishment (of older
children especially) was usually a paternal duty. Socrates
imagines truant boys fleeing their fathers, and a vase attributed to the Sandal Painter shows a boy beaten by a man who
runs toward a female figure, surely his mother (fig. 5).[104]
A father educates, a mother nurtures.[105] As for rich children,
they are said to be unused to submitting to authority, even in

school.[106] Tension and conflict over money ought to have been less prevalent among the elite; yet—given the nature of our sources—most grousing about the costs of raising children occurs in the context of lawsuits brought by well-off Athenians. Here ancient Greek attitudes both sound familiar—it is the wealthy who campaign for tax cuts today—and confound expectation. This and much more remain mysterious. In particular, we are left to wonder about the thoughts and feelings we miss most, those of the children of Archaic and Classical Greece.

NOTES

1 Aeschines, *Speeches* 3.77–3.78.

2 Plutarch, *Demosthenes* 22.3–22.7.

3 J. Killen, "Earliest Writers of Greek," in P. Easterling and C. Handley, eds., *Greek Scripts: An Illustrated Introduction* (London, 2001), 1–9, esp. 8; K. A. Kamp et al., "Discovering Childhood: Using Fingerprints to Find Children in the Archaeological Record," *American Antiquity* 64 (1999), 309–315. For the identification of children among prehistoric flint knappers, see N. Finlay, "Kid Knapping: The Missing Children in Lithic Analysis," in J. Moore and E. Scott, eds., *Invisible People and Processes: Writing Gender and Childhood into European Archaeology* (London, 1997), 203–212.

4 Golden 1995, 1.11–34.

5 D. R. Jordan, "A Personal Letter Found in the Athenian Agora," *Hesperia* 69 (2000), 91–103.

6 B. G. Robertson, "The Scrutiny of New Citizens at Athens," in V. Hunter and J. Edmondson, eds., *Law and Social Status in Classical Athens* (Oxford, 2000), 149–174, argues that the scrutiny did not depend on boys' chronological age. He accepts, however, that those not yet accepted into the deme were *paides*.

7 For a more extended account of the vocabulary and characteristics of ancient Greek childhood, see Golden 1990, 1–22.

8 Aeschines, *Speeches* 1.18, cf. 39, *Tragica Adespota*, R. Kannicht and B. Snell, eds. (Göttingen, 1981), 515a.

9 Aristotle, *Eudemian Ethics* 7.1240b33; Aristotle, *Nicomachean Ethics* 1.1100a3, 3.1111a26.

10 A. Motte, "Le thème des enfances divines dans le mythe grec," *LEC* 64 (1996), 109–125; C. Cusset, "L'enfance perdue d'Héraclès: L'Image du héros au service de l'autre," *BAGB* (1999), 191–210; R. A. Segal, "Adonis: A Greek Eternal Child," in D. C. Pozzi and J. M. Wickersham, eds., *Myth and the Polis* (Ithaca, N.Y., 1991), 64–85.

11 Aristotle, *Eudemian Ethics* 2.1219b5; cf. Aristotle, *Politics* 1.1260a14, 8.1339a30; Aristotle, *Problems* 10.46.896a19.

12 For example, Xenophon, *Symposium* 1.1; Plato, *Laws* 1.647D, 5.732D, 7.796D; Plato, *Politics* 288C; Plato, *Republic* 10.602B.

13 Diogenes Laertius, *Lives of Eminent Philosophers* 9.3.

14 Dolls: *Palatine Anthology* 6.280, reading *koras*; see, however, Reilly 1997, esp. 159.

15 Xenophon, *Cyropaedia* 1.3.7–4.4.

16 Plato, *Symposium* 217E; cf. Photius, s. v. *oinos aneu paideuton*.

17 Johnston 2001. For the link of children with the divine, cf. Mühlbauer and Miller 1988. Hellenistic child priests might be as young as eight (Segre, ED 215.8–215.9; Cos, cf. Pausanias, *Description of Greece* 10.34.8 [Phocis]).

18 Herodotus, *The History of Herodotus* 5.49–51.

19 Sophocles, *Oedipus the King* 180–181.

20 A. Carson, *The Autobiography of Red* (New York, 1998), 79.

21 Slater 1968, 37–66.

22 Sophocles, *Ajax* 558–559, 1409–1411; Euripides, *The Trojan Women* 749, 1182–1184; cf. M. Menu, "L'enfant chez Euripide: Affectivité et dramaturgie," *Pallas* 38 (1992), 239–258.

23 As an example of self-contradiction, Aristotle offers a gradualist view of children's biological development that is at odds with the sharp distinction he makes between children and adults as moral agents; A. Coles, "Animal and Childhood Cognition in Aristotle's Biology and the *scala naturae*," in W. Kullman and S. Föllinger, eds., *Aristotelische Biologie: Intentionen, Methoden, Ergebnisse: Akten des Symposions über Aristoteles' Biologie vom 24.–28. Juli 1995 in der Werner-Reimers-Stiftung in Bad Homburg* (Stuttgart, 1997), 287–323, esp. 315–317.

24 V. French, "Children in Antiquity," in J. A. Hawes and N. R. Hiner, eds., *Children in Historical and Comparative Perspective* (Westport, Conn., 1991), 13–29, esp. 16–18.

25 See most recently Ham 1999.

26 P. Ariès, *L'enfant et la vie familiale sous l'ancien régime*, 2d. ed. (Paris, 1973 [1960]), 1–22.

27 For a brief critique of Ariès, see H. Cunningham, *Children and Childhood in Western Society Since 1500* (London, 1995), 30–40.

28 An issue in modern scholarship and society as well: see the thoughtful discussion by A. Oakley, "Women and Children First and Last: Parallels and Differences between Children's and Women's Studies," in B. Mayall, ed., *Children's Childhoods: Observed and Experienced* (London, 1994), 13–32. Section epigraph is from K. Govier, *The Truth Teller* (Toronto, 2000), 266–267.

29 M. Golden, "Children's Rights, Children's Speech and *Agamemnon*," in R. Osborne and S. Hornblower, eds., *Ritual, Finance, Politics: Athenian Democratic Accounts Presented to David Lewis* (Oxford, 1994), 371–383; M. C. Miller, *Athens and Persia in the Fifth Century BC* (Cambridge, 1997), 249–250.

30 Hippocrates, *On the Articulations* 37.4.166.18 L., cf. 38.4.168.4 L.

31 SEG 9.3 = 5 R. Meiggs and D. Lewis, *A Selection of Greek Historical Inscriptions to the End of the Fifth Century B.C.* (Oxford, 1969).

32 Beaumont 1995 and 1998; Vollkommer 2000.

33 Hesychius, s. v. *stephanon ekpherein*.

34 The birth of a boy may have brought midwives special recognition: C. W. Müller, "Aristophanes Eccl. 549," *RhM* 131 (1998), 98.

35 R. Osborne, "Law, the Democratic Citizen and the Representation of Women in Classical Athens," *Past and Present* 155 (1997), 3–33, esp. 14.

36 *Homeric Hymn to Demeter* 241; *Homeric Hymn to Hermes* 17–19; Hesiod, *Theogony* 492–493; Sophocles, *Ichneutae* 277–278; *Homeric Hymn to Apollo* 123–125.

37 Xenophon, *The Constitution of the Lacedaeimonians* 1.3; cf. *Oeconomicus* 7.6; Aristotle, *The History of Animals* 9.608b15.

38 Xenophon, *Memorabilia* 1.5.2.

39 Euripides, *Iphigenia Among the Taurians* 823–826.

40 PCG, Fragment 69.

41 B. Robertson, "Personal Names as Evidence for Athenian Social and Political History about 507–300 B.C." (Ph.D. diss., University of Toronto, 1999), 103–105.

42 Thucydides, *The History of the Peloponnesian War* 6.56.1.

43 T. Vestergaard et al., "The Age-structure of Athenian Citizens Commemorated in Sepulchral Inscriptions," *C&M* 43 (1992), 5–21.

44 D. Pritchard, "Fool's Gold and Silver: Reflections on the Evidentiary Status of Finely Painted Attic Pottery," *Antichthon* 33 (1999), 1–27.

45 Plato, *Axiochus* 366C; Scholion on Plato, *Republic* 10.600C (p. 273 Greene), *Suda* π 2958 Adler; cf. Quintilian, *Institutio Oratoriae* 3.1.10.

46 Lysias, *Speeches* 20.11.

47 Plato, *Republic* 5.467a; cf. *Laws* 6.769B (painters), *Protagoras* 328A (artisans).

48 *PCG*, Sosipater fragment 1.7; Hippocrates, *The Law* 2, 3; Hippocrates, *The Oath* 13.

49 Plato, *Republic* 7.540E–7.541A.

50 Scholion on Aristophanes, *Lysistrata* 643; Eustathius, *On the Odyssey* 1885.15; cf. Hesychius, s. v., *Aletrides*.

51 D. Pritchard, "Dancing for Dionysos," *Classicum* 27, no. 2 (2001), 6–13.

52 N. B. Crowther, "Athlete and State: Qualifying for the Olympic Games in Ancient Greece," *Journal of Sport History* 21 (1996), 34–43.

53 D. C. Young, *The Olympic Myth of Greek Amateur Athletics* (Chicago, 1984), 158–162; N. Fisher, "Gymnasia and the Democratic Values of Leisure," in P. Cartledge, P. Millett, and S. van Reden, eds., *Kosmos: Essays in Order, Conflict, and Community in Classical Athens* (Cambridge, 1998), 84–104, esp. 86–94.

54 Demetrius of Phaleron, *FGrH* 228 F 5, Poll. 3.55, Scholion on Aristophanes, *Birds* 1551.

55 Demosthenes, *Speeches* 59.18–59.19.

56 Isocrates, *Speeches* 16.33.

57 J. Pouilloux, *Recherches sur l'histoire et les cultes de Thasos I* (Paris, 1954), 371, no. 141.

58 Xenophon, *Hellenica* 5.4.32, cf. *The Constitution of the Lacedaeimonians* 3.5; D.-A. Kurofka, "Die paidiskoi im System der spartanischen Altersklassen," *Philologus* 137 (1993), 197–205.

59 See here especially Kennell 1995.

60 More detail and nuance—though not uniformity—may be found in F. A. Beck, "Spartan Education Revised," *History of Education Review* 22 (1993), 16–31; Kennell 1995; E. Lévy, "Remarques préliminaires sur l'éducation spartiate," *Ktema* 22 (1997), 151–160; J. Ducat, "Perspectives on Spartan Education in the Classical Period," in S. Hodkinson and A. Powell, eds., *Sparta: New Perspectives* (London, 1999), 43–66; P. Cartledge, *Spartan Reflections* (London, 2001), 79–90.

61 Plutarch, *Lycurgus* 16.1.

62 Plutarch's sources are Archaic: D. Ogden, "Crooked Speech: The Genesis of the Spartan Rhetra," *JHS* 114 (1994), 85–102, esp. 91–93. Skeptical: M. Huys, "The Spartan Practice of Selective Infanticide and Its Parallels in Ancient Utopian Tradition," *AncSoc* 27 (1996), 47–74.

63 So, e.g., Pomeroy 1997, 49. Contra: Cartledge (supra n. 60), 113.

64 See S. Link, "Zur Aussetzung neugeborener Kinder in Sparta," *Tyche* 13 (1998), 153–164.

65 *Tes Hellados paideusin*, Thucydides, *A History of the Peloponnesian War* 2.41.1.

66 S. Link, "Der geliebte Bürger: *Paideia* und *paidika* in Sparta und auf Kreta," *Philologus* 143 (1999), 3–25; Cartledge (supra n. 60), 91–105.

67 Thucydides, *A History of the Peloponnesian War* 2.39.1.

68 Plutarch, *Lycurgus* 15.3; Cartledge (supra n. 60), 115–116.

69 Xenophon, *The Constitution of the Lacedaeimonians* 1.3.

70 "This sort of love was so accepted among them that good and noble women took even unmarried girls as sexual partners": Plutarch, *Lycurgus* 18.9; H. Parker, "Sappho Schoolmistress," *TAPA* 123 (1993), 309–351, esp. 325–331.

71 Pausanias, *Description of Greece* 5.16.2–4; T. Scanlon, *Eros and Greek Athletics* (Oxford, 2002), 98–120.

72 Xenophon, *The Constitution of the Lacedaeimonians* 1.4; Scanlon (supra n. 71), 121–138.

73 Alcman, fr. 1.

74 Plutarch, *Lycurgus* 18.2–3.

75 M. Golden, "Continuity, Change and the Study of Ancient Childhood," *EMC* 36 (1992), 7–18; Golden 1997.

76 V. French, "The Spartan Family and the Spartan Decline: Changes in Child-rearing Practices and Failure to Reform," in C. D. Hamilton and P. Krentz, eds., *Polis and Polemos: Essays in Politics, War, and History in Ancient Greece in Honor of Donald Kagan* (Claremont, Calif., 1997), 241–269.

77 G. Raepsaet and C. Decocq, "Deux regards sur l'enfance athénienne à l'époque classique," *LEC* 55 (1987), 3–15, esp. 14–15; Ham 1999, 209–213.

78 I leave aside some changes at childhood's end, such as the (possible) shift of responsibility for the scrutiny of those presented to the demes from panels of jurors to the Council of 500 (F. Montana, *L'Athenaion Politeia di Aristotele negli Scholia Vetera ad Aristofane* ([Pisa, 1996], 226–233), and the introduction or at least the reorganization of the *ephebate*, the two years of military service that followed it for successful candidates.

79 M. Golden, "Names and Naming at Athens: Three Studies," *EMC* 30 (1986), 245–269, esp. 257–269.

80 For Pericles' law and Athenian *nothoi* in general, see D. Ogden, *Greek Bastardy in the Classical and Hellenistic Periods* (Oxford, 1996), 32–212.

81 E.g., Scholion on Plato, *Axiochus* 364A (p. 409 Greene); J. Bremmer, "es Kunosarges," *Mnemosyne* 30 (1977), 369–374.

82 Lysias, *Speeches* fr. 6.

83 N. W. Slater, "Theozotides on Adopted Sons (Lysias fr. 6)," *Scholia* 2 (1993), 81–85.

84 Lysias, *Speeches* 21.1–5.

85 Aeschines, *Speeches* 1.9–12; Plato, *Laws* 8.836A; Aristotle, *Nicomachean Ethics* 7.1149a15; D. Cohen, *Law, Sexuality, and Society: The Enforcement of Morals in Classical Athens* (Cambridge, 1991), 171–202 (useful but erratic). Whatever the roots of this anxiety, they are unlikely to be the medical theories of Democritus (despite E. C. Keuls, "The Greek Medical Texts and the Sexual Ethos of Ancient Athens," in P. J. van der Eijk et al., eds., *Ancient Medicine and Its Socio-Cultural Context* [Amsterdam, 1995], 261–274).

86 Aeschines, *Speeches* 1.11; [Aristotle], *Constitution of the Athenians* 56.3; cf. Plato, *Laws* 6.764E; [Aristotle], *Constitution of the Athenians* 42.2.

87 Westmoreland is quoted in N. Scheper-Hughes, *Death Without Weeping: The Violence of Everyday Life in Brazil* (Berkeley, Calif., 1992), 400; "But Arabs don't even notice when a child dies," quoted by G. Svirsky, "Women's Peace Work in Israel," *Outlook* (Vancouver, B.C.) 35, no. 1 (January–February 1997), 10.

88 Herodotus, *The History of Herodotus* 1.136.

89 Scheper-Hughes (supra n. 87).

90 For some distinctions, see M. Golden, "Did the Ancients Care When Their Children Died?" *G&R* 35 (1988), 152–163; Golden 1990, 94–99.

91 Thucydides, *A History of the Peloponnesian War* 7.29; Euripides, *Hercules Furens* 634–636; Aristotle, *Generation of Animals* 3.753a7–15.

92 Plutarch, *Agesilaus* 25.5. Was such levity unseemly for a king?

93 C. Hummel, *Das Kind und seine Krankheiten in der griechischen Medizin* (Frankfurt, 1999).

94 S. I. Johnston, "Defining the Dreadful: Remarks on the Greek Child-killing Demon," in M. Meyer and P. Mirecki, eds., *Ancient Magic and Ritual Power* (Leiden, 1995), 361–397, esp. 381–387.

95 For speculation about conflict at an even earlier stage, between fetus and mother, see E. Morgan, *The Descent of the Child: Human Evolution from a New Perspective* (London, 1994).

96 Golden 1990, 87–88; Scott 1999, 88–89.

97 Aristotle, *Politics* 1.1259a38–b18.

98 R. P. Saller, *Patriarchy, Property, and Death in the Roman Family* (Cambridge, 1994), 133–153.

99 Xenophon, *Anabasis* 2.6.12.

100 Aristotle, *The History of Animals* 5.544b20, 7.581a9.

101 M. Kleijwegt, *Ancient Youth: The Ambiguity of Youth and the Absence of Adolescence in Greco-Roman Society* (Amsterdam, 1991).

102 E. Eyben, *Restless Youth in Ancient Rome* (London, 1993).

103 Plato, *Laws* 6.754E.

104 Plato, *Republic* 8.548B; lekythos, attributed to the Sandal Painter, ca. 550, Bologna, The Archaeological Museum of Bologna, PU 204, ABV 70.7, Para 28. Comedy offers a less forbidding picture of fathers: see V. French, "Aristophanes' Doting Dads: Adult Male Knowledge of Young Children," in R. Mellor and L. Tritle, eds., *Text and Tradition: Studies in Greek History and Historiography in Honor of Mortimer Chambers* (Claremont, Calif., 1999), 163–181.

105 [Aristotle], *Oeconomica* 1.1344a6.

106 Aristotle, *Politics* 4.1295b15.

Jeremy Rutter

CHILDREN IN AEGEAN PREHISTORY

EVIDENCE FOR the appearance, activities, and social roles of children in the prehistoric Aegean has come down to us in a number of different forms: pictorial art depicting babies, juveniles, and adolescents; objects that are likely to have belonged to them or served their needs; surviving traces of their presence, such as fingerprints; and their actual physical remains, most commonly found in graves.[1] A few texts written in the syllabic script known as Linear B, used principally by palatial administrators from the fifteenth to the thirteenth centuries B.C.E., mention children, but these hardly go beyond quantifying nameless groups of children by sex. Arguably more important than any of the preceding items taken in isolation are their places of discovery. For it is chiefly through the networks of associations established by particular find contexts that we can infer the temporal, social, psychological, religious, or other possible significances of such discoveries.[2]

The various regions within and around the Aegean Sea were inhabited in prehistoric times by both Greek-speaking and non-Greek-speaking populations.[3] The linguistic affiliations of the non-Greek-speakers, who included the residents of Crete (whom we refer to as Minoans, after the island's mythical ruler, Minos), are hotly debated. So, too, is the date of the initial appearance of the first Greek-speakers on the Greek mainland.[4] During the Late Bronze Age, the mainlanders, by this time certainly Greek-speaking but ordinarily

Table 1: Chronological Chart of the Prehistoric Aegean	PERIOD (APPROXIMATE CALENDAR DATES)	REGION WITHIN AEGEAN (ARCHAEOLOGICAL TERM FOR PERIOD)	SITES MENTIONED IN TEXT OR FINDSPOTS OF ILLUSTRATED ARTWORKS	STAGES OF SOCIAL COMPLEXITY	SCRIPTS
	Middle Stone Age (ca. 8000–6500 B.C.E.)	Greek mainland (Mesolithic)	Franchthi Cave	Nomadic hunting and gathering	—
	New Stone Age (ca. 6500–3000 B.C.E.)	Greek mainland, Crete, Aegean islands, western Turkey (Neolithic)	Franchthi Cave, Sesklo, Platia Magoula Zarkou	Settled village farming	—
	Early Bronze Age (ca. 3000–2050 B.C.E.)	Greek mainland (Early Helladic); Crete (Early Minoan); Central Aegean islands (Early Cycladic); western Turkey (Western Anatolian Early Bronze)	Troy, Paros	Settled village farming with emerging social stratification and settlement hierarchies	—
	Middle Bronze Age (ca. 2050–1700/1600 B.C.E.)	Greek mainland (Middle Helladic); Crete (Middle Minoan); Central Aegean islands (Middle Cycladic); western Turkey (Western Anatolian Middle Bronze)	Phaistos, Mallia, Knossos, Anemospilia	No significant change except on Crete, where literate administrations centered in palatial complexes appear ca. 1900 and flourish until destroyed by earthquake ca. 1750/1650 B.C.E. (Protopalatial era); immediate rebuilding of some of these complexes in Middle Minoan III inaugurates Neopalatial era	Hieroglyphic and Linear A (Crete) B.C.E.
	Late Bronze Age (ca. 1700/1600–1050 B.C.E.)	Greek mainland (Late Helladic = Mycenaean); Crete (Late Minoan); Central Aegean islands (Late Cycladic); western Turkey (Western Anatolian Late Bronze)	Knossos, Palaikastro, Kamilari, Ayia Triadha, Mochos, Akrotiri (Thera), Aphaia (Aigina), Mycenae, Tiryns, Tanagra, Palaioboukouvina	Neopalatial administrative complexes flourish until all but that at Knossos are destroyed ca. 1490/1450 B.C.E.; for most of a century (until ca. 1375 B.C.E.) Knossos alone boasts a palace (Monopalatial era); after Knossos is destroyed by fire, palatial establishments spring up on the mainland at several locations, launching the Mycenaean palatial era (ca. 1375–1200 B.C.E.); all palatial centers throughout the Aegean are destroyed in the later thirteenth century B.C.E., inaugurating the Postpalatial era (CA. 1200–1050 B.C.E.)	Linear A (until ca. 1450 B.C.E.); Linear B (from ca. 1450 to 1200 B.C.E.)

termed Mycenaeans after the capital (Mycenae) of the legendary king Agamemnon (celebrated by Homer as the leader of the Greek forces in the *Iliad*), spread throughout the Aegean basin. Both the earlier Minoan culture of Crete and the related but distinct Cycladic culture of the central Aegean islands were modified and in the case of the smaller islands altogether swamped by Mycenaean forms, practices, and cultural preferences. By the mid-fourteenth century B.C.E., Mycenaean material culture was at home as far north as the coasts of Macedonia and Epirus and as far east as the western coast of Turkey. Crete managed to hang onto a distinct cultural identity, albeit no longer a purely Minoan one, down to the end of the Bronze Age. The following review canvasses the available evidence from the first appearance of children in the Aegean archaeological record a little more than ten thousand years ago to the beginning of the Greek Iron Age, shortly before 1000 B.C.E.[5]

The Greek mainland has thus far provided the earliest surviving physical remains of Aegean children as part of the first attested mortuary ritual in the region, and also the earliest preserved images of them. The physical remains from Franchthi Cave (northeastern Peloponnese) feature the intact flexed inhumation burial of a young man between twenty-five and thirty lying at the top of a small cluster of earlier burials, all of Lower Mesolithic date (second half of the eighth millennium B.C.E.). The burials included both inhumed and cremated remains representing adults and an infant, with scattered bones in the vicinity from another infant, a child, and an adolescent.[6] A Middle Neolithic inhumation (mid-sixth millennium) of a newborn baby from the same site was remarkable for being accompanied by an intact marble vessel together with a half-preserved clay vase, the latter having been perhaps ritually broken prior to its deposition.[7] These discoveries, though humble in comparison to the far more complex works of art and resulting chains of associations of later eras, are nevertheless of profound importance for their periods. For example, they show that the earliest Aegean society to have furnished evidence for purposeful burial made no detectable distinctions in terms of placement or nature of burial between adults and children. They likewise suggest that burials may have been clustered spatially according to kinship groupings: that is, the Mesolithic cluster at Franchthi Cave may represent a family.

Two discoveries of the Late Neolithic period from sites farther to the north are additional important firsts in the long story of prehistoric Greek children. The terracotta figurine from Sesklo (southeastern Thessaly) of an adult female seated on a stool and holding an infant in the crook of her left arm is the earliest known occurrence in the Aegean of the so-called *kourotrophos* (child-nourisher) figural type, the most common combination of adult and child in subsequent prehistoric or, for that matter, Western art (fig. 1).[8] Although the head of the child was modeled as part of this almost completely preserved group composition, the missing head of the adult female was separately shaped or carved and attached by means of a cylindrical mortise between the figure's shoulders. Unfortunately found in a disturbed surface level and thus lacking a meaningful context, this well-known piece is securely datable to the late fifth or early fourth millennium by its elaborately but abstractly rendered, dark-on-light painted ornament.

A terracotta building model from Platia Magoula Zarkou (northeastern Thessaly), complete with eight movable

FIG. 1 Kourotrophos, terracotta figurine from Sesklo, Late Neolithic. Athens, National Archaeological Museum, 5937

human occupants, belongs to an earlier phase of the Late Neolithic (fig. 2).[9] It was found in a shallow pit directly below the floor of an only partially excavated but otherwise unremarkable house. This group of individually rather unimpressive miniature clay objects communicates an enormous amount of information about Greek family life by virtue of its circumstances of discovery: it has been plausibly identified as a "foundation deposit" interred beneath the floor of a family dwelling in order to secure simple good luck or perhaps even divine protection. The collection consists of a roofless structure on whose roughly rectangular floor the eight human figures, differently sized and shaped so as to allow both sex and age to be inferred, appear to be arranged in significant clusters. The groups of figures are separated by built-in furnishings such as a raised platform (for sleeping?) in one corner and a domed oven farther along the same long wall, almost directly opposite the structure's single, axially positioned doorway. On the platform lie the two largest figures, a female on her back and a male on his side, both decorated with incised ornament that may have been intended to represent clothing.[10] In the diagonally opposite corner lie the two next-largest figures, similar to the first two in shape and positioning but somewhat more simply decorated and with the male resting on his face rather than on his side. In the corner closest to the oven lie three differently sized but consistently smaller figures, all on their sides, of which only the largest bears any incised decor and can be identified by sex (female) thanks to her modeled breasts. And finally, a fourth juvenile human figure, the smallest of the entire series, lies directly adjacent to the smaller of the two adult females. Two other loose, hence movable, objects inside the structure are probably supposed to be inanimate; neither one is positively identifiable, although a boat or tool

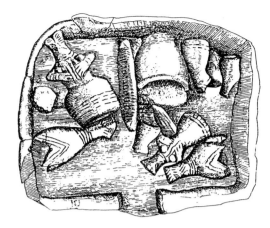

FIG. 2 House Model, terracotta from Platia Magoula Zarkou, Late Neolithic. Larissa, Archaeological Museum, ML.PMZ.619

of some sort has been suggested for the larger, a loaf of bread or a baby for the smaller. The architectural context, the pairing of the larger females and males, the rendering of the smallest figures at three or four different scales, the variable amount of incised decoration, and the spatial segregation of the eight human figures into three distinct clumps all work in combination to suggest a single-family dwelling housing three generations' worth of occupants, each with its own designated space. The fact that all the figures were found in horizontal or recumbent rather than vertical or standing positions further suggests that those who buried this figurine assemblage might have been marking the spaces as sleeping areas, although the identification of the adult males as figures seated on four-legged stools makes such an interpretation problematic. Whatever the assemblage's full set of meanings may have been, it seems undeniable that only the peculiarities of the undisturbed and careful arrangement of this group of terracottas make it possible for us to recognize adults and children, much less multiple generations of a single family.

One consequence of the disturbed or secondary contexts in which the vast majority of prehistoric figurines are found, certainly in the Neolithic era and even later on in the Bronze Age, is that very few can be recognized as representations of juveniles. Only if the degree of naturalism in their rendering is exceptional can a persuasive case in favor of such an identification be made with regard to single figures. Since virtually all Neolithic figurines and most Bronze Age ones are schematically modeled, especially when produced in readily available materials such as clay, bone, or local stones, the apparent dearth of prehistoric Greek figurines of children is hardly surprising. Many may, in fact, exist, but they cannot be positively identified, whether among the hundreds of known Neolithic anthropomorphic images or the even more numer-

ous figurines in an expanded range of materials dating from the Early Bronze Age.[11] Three-dimensional groups of two or more human figures during the almost five millennia between the beginning of the Neolithic era and the end of the Middle Bronze Age in the Aegean are exceedingly rare. Aside from the one or two Neolithic kourotrophoi in terracotta already cited, the only surviving specimens are four marble types from the Cycladic islands dating to around the middle of the third millennium or a little later (ca. 2500–2300 B.C.E.). Since the multiple figures in two of these types are rendered at the same scale and the females ordinarily have distinctly modeled breasts, there is no reason to consider any of these figures as a juvenile.[12] The third combination features a diminutive female figure standing on the head of a larger female, both rendered in the typical folded-arm position (fig. 3).[13] The difference in scale between the figures may reflect an attempt on the artist's part to depict a child, but if so the breasts clearly indicated on at least some of the smaller figures reveal a discrepancy between an adolescent's or older child's anatomy and a young child's scale.[14] The fourth combination consists of just one fragment of a small figure, seemingly a juvenile female, clasped in the outstretched hands of a larger figure of which only the hands and lowermost forearms survive (fig. 4).[15] Despite the substantial number of anthropomorphic images found in all four culture areas of the Aegean during the third millennium, only the last of these Early Cycladic group compositions appears to depict a child unambiguously. This is all the more surprising when one considers that juvenile animals are portrayed more than once in mainland Greek art of this period.[16]

PHYSICAL REMAINS FROM BURIALS AND OTHER LOCALES

This dearth of pictorial evidence would render children all but invisible were it not for the evidence to be gleaned from their surviving physical remains and associated funerary rituals. Unfortunately, human bone assemblages continue to be woefully understudied in the Aegean area, despite the large quantities of surviving material and the fact that the contemporary attitudes of the Greek and Turkish inhabitants of this region do not prevent such remains from being exhumed and subjected to detailed, long-term study. Thus analyses of children's nutrition levels and mortality rates, inferred distinctions according to gender, age, or class in their access to resources along the lines of studies applied to large prehistoric burial populations elsewhere, and determination of the ages at which and stages by which the engendering of children may have occurred have yet to be

FIG. 3 Double Figurine, marble from Paros (?), Early Cycladic II. Karlsruhe, Badisches Landesmuseum, B839

FIG. 4 Kourotrophos fragment, marble, Early Cycladic II. Athens, The N. P. Goulandris Foundation—Museum of Cycladic Art, 968

undertaken.[17] But it is quite clear from the different forms and settings of infant and even older children's burials that the kind of egalitarian treatment accorded the dead at seemingly all stages of life at Franchthi Cave in the Mesolithic era was no longer common practice in the Aegean by 3000 B.C.E. For example, the evidence from a very early phase in the long Bronze Age occupational sequence at Troy shows that newborns and infants were buried in or immediately around the house, while the remains of older children and adults were deposited somewhere outside of the settlement area.[18] A similar distinction between the very young and other members of the family group appears to have prevailed on the Greek mainland during the Middle Bronze Age and throughout much of the subsequent Mycenaean era.[19] The exact age at which a child was no longer given a spatially and sometimes formally discrete kind of burial, and how this age may have varied through space and time throughout Aegean prehistory, are questions that cannot yet be answered but that are certainly capable of being resolved.

So, too, is the issue of what kinds of burial goods may have been considered particularly appropriate for children at various ages, to what extent such goods were gendered and hence when gender was officially recognized by Aegean societies, and also perhaps how status was marked among children as opposed to the world of adults. A major impediment to progress on such issues has always been that communal rather than single burial was the rule for many prehistoric Aegean populations, with the result that establishing which burial goods are to be associated with which set of human remains is all too often impossible. Further complicating the effort to establish what grave goods juveniles may have been buried with are the long periods of use of many Bronze Age tombs and the routine disturbance of earlier burials by later ones.[20] A preliminary study devoted to Mycenaean children's burials focused on a relatively small sample of a half-dozen tombs, almost all richly furnished and of relatively early date (Late Helladic I–IIIA1, ca. 1675/1575–1400), in order to draw attention to the frequency with which pottery and jewelry accompany the remains of juveniles.[21] Since these particular burials can hardly be considered typical of the Late Bronze Age mainland, even for the two centuries they span, the prominence given to items of jewelry in this study, particularly necklaces, was somewhat misleading. A second, considerably more detailed survey of the evidence for Mycenaean children's burial, relying on a much larger and thus more representative sample, has put more emphasis on the wide range of tomb types, tomb locations, and burial assemblages connected with Mycenaean children.[22] Both studies draw

FIG. 5 Feeding Bottle, terracotta, Late Helladic III. Lamia, Archaeological Museum, K2542

attention to certain recurring items among these complexes of grave goods: "feeding bottles" in the form of either wheel-made, basket-handled, and tubular-spouted jars with necks (fig. 5; cat. 30) or smaller handmade containers resembling miniature bedpans with round or oval mouths (fig. 6); small painted figurines of terracotta produced in a relatively re-stricted range of schematic types, mostly anthropomorphic females (cat. 21; see p.30), animals, including birds, items of furniture, and occasional model chariots and boats; beads of various materials; and sea shells.[23] Regrettably, the lack of published information on the ages of individual children continues to make it impossible to connect particular cate-gories of grave goods, raw material, or specific type of object with particular age ranges.

While the bones of buried individuals so far have attracted insufficient scholarly attention, the same can hardly be said for concentrations of human bone, whether articu-lated or not, found in settlement contexts. The body of a young man around eighteen years of age found lying slightly above the floor of the southwesternmost chamber of an isolated building at Anemospilia, on the northern slope of Crete's Mount Iuktas, has been identified by its excavators as the remains of a human sacrifice of late Protopalatial date (ca. 1750/1650), buried in the collapsed building debris resulting from a massive earthquake.[24]

Hundreds of children's bones found in an unarticulated heap within a late Neopalatial burnt stratum (Late Minoan IB, ca. 1490/1450) in a basement room of the so-called North House at nearby Knossos present a more complex interpre-tive problem for archaeologists. More than a fifth of these bones exhibited knife marks of precisely the same kind as are often found on butchered animal bones. Hughes in his thorough and evenhanded review of the evidence has noted that the condition of the Knossian children's bones could have resulted from an extended process of burial (or reburial) of individuals who had been dead for up to several years. A more controversial interpretation by Wall, Musgrave, and Warren posits that the bones with cut marks suggest ritual-istic sacrifice.[25] Representing at least four juveniles, the ages of two of whom could be quite precisely gauged at eight and twelve, these bones belonged to individuals of undetermin-able sex who appear to have been in good health at the time of their deaths. Some sheep vertebrae found mixed among the bulk of the children's bones suggested that the dismem-berment of the children may have been accompanied by a sheep sacrifice, an indication that all of the remains in ques-tion may have been connected with a religious ceremony conducted during the troubled times when Minoan palatial culture was coming to its violent end.[26]

PROTOPALATIAL AND NEOPALATIAL ERAS ON CRETE

During the more than three centuries that constitute the Middle Bronze Age in the Aegean (ca. 2050–1700/1600), the only subregion in which representational art was at all common is the island of Crete. No children can be positively identified among the hundreds of terracotta figurines found at peak sanctuaries, however, nor among the considerably rarer human figures executed in media such as vase painting

FIG. 6 Askoid Feeding Bottle, terracotta from Korakou, Late Helladic IIB. Corinth, Archaeological Museum, CP206.

or metallic relief. The only image in Minoan Protopalatial (ca. 1900–1750/1650) art that has universally been considered a child is the bust of a probable boy preserved as a sharply defined impression on a sealing from the so-called Hieroglyphic Deposit at Knossos (fig. 7), romantically identified by Sir Arthur Evans as an infant prince whose image was sometimes paired with that of his wavy-haired father in twin impressions on a single sealing.[27] What the connection between these two heads may be, and whether they are even to be accepted as portraits, must remain pure speculation at present, but there seems no reason to doubt that the carver of the signet responsible for the impression intended to create a child's face. The remarkable success of this eighteenth-century seal cutter in rendering a recognizably juvenile head in profile at such a small scale tellingly foreshadows the amazing achievements of later Minoan artists of the seventeenth through fifteenth centuries. The explosion of pictorialism that characterizes the art of the Neopalatial era (ca. 1750/1650–1490/1450) on Crete is nonetheless surprising in its range and in the relative suddenness of its appearance. It seems to have inspired a comparably exponential rise in pictorialism in the Cyclades, along with a desire on the part of the Greek mainlanders to acquire such art even if they were able actually to produce only limited quantities of it themselves. Whatever its ultimate cause may have been, this rapid and dramatic increase in the quantity of representational art produced within the southern Aegean has provided us with a host of juvenile and adolescent human figures, in a variety of age stages within both sexes. This wealth of Minoan images has furnished the bulk of the iconographic evidence for previous reviews of children in prehistoric Aegean art.[28] Such a

rich body of material is best surveyed according to medium and form, with commentary on the material, scale, and possible functions of the art in question as appropriate.

For the first time in the Aegean, Minoan Neopalatial artists produced individual three-dimensional figures that are immediately recognizable as children, even in the absence of accompanying adult images. In anticipating some of the achievements of Classical and Hellenistic Greek sculptors by more than a millennium, they showed themselves to be keen observers not only of children's physiognomies but also of their activities and favorite postures. Thus a bronze figurine of a crawling infant from the Psychro Cave (cat. 38), though less than two inches long, nevertheless reproduces the visual essence of the human infant in its pudgy torso and limbs, its oversized head, its crawling pose, and above all the upward tilt of its head, which successfully captures and communicates the ceaseless curiosity of children at this stage of life.[29] A somewhat older but still arguably infant child carved from ivory, found in Block S of the town at Palaikastro, once again communicates its extreme youth by a combination of bodily proportions (for example, the large head), the nature of its pose (seated supply on the ground and leaning forward with both legs bent at different angles and with both arms extended toward the object on which its attention is riveted), and the treatment of its hair (shaved off to no more than stubble length; fig. 8).[30] A second ivory figurine from the same block at Palaikastro, though much simpler in its symmetrical standing pose with arms held at the sides, is still recognizable as a child from its relatively large, shaven head, soft body musculature, and rather broad waistline, albeit the oldest child of the trio just surveyed (fig. 9).[31] The two ivory figures are shown by their exposed genitalia to be male, all three are depicted nude and with either shaved or

hairless heads, and all are produced from expensive materials (bronze, ivory) at a small scale. There are no comparable figures in terracotta or stone nor any additional comparanda in metal. Unfortunately, not one of these three figures comes from a meaningful context, so their function and even precise date within the Neopalatial era remain obscure. On the other hand, a fair number of ivory comparanda include several fragmentary male acrobats from Knossos, a number of heads and limbs from Archanes (including a stippled head designed to be mortised into a separately carved body that is virtually certain to have represented another boy), and the magnificent chryselephantine youthful male from Palaikastro Building 5 interpreted by its discoverers as a divine cult image (fig. 10).[32] This last, identified as an adolescent chiefly on the basis of his exquisitely executed and wonderfully preserved hairstyle, is the only Minoan Neopalatial ivory figure whose painstakingly analyzed context of discovery allows its original function as a cult image to be surmised.[33] It is also the only such figure to have preserved portions of all the additional materials that originally embellished at least some of these ivory figures: gold leaf, rock crystal, serpentine, wood, and Egyptian blue.[34] The acrobats from Knossos probably represented somewhat older but perhaps still not fully adult males; unfortunately, only traces of their separately attached, gilded

bronze locks of hair have survived, so the details of their hairstyles cannot be used to supply them with a precise age.[35]

Figurines in high-value materials were thus clearly exploited as an artistic form by Minoan artists during the Neopalatial era to represent a number of distinct developmental stages of male youth. Most of the effort devoted to unraveling how many different stages of male development the Minoans recognized and to what age ranges these may have corresponded has so far concentrated principally on hairstyle and stature as age markers.[36] Surprisingly, bodily proportions have so far not been part of the broader debate, despite substantial disagreements among authorities over the ages of some of the figures in question and the investment of considerable energy in attempts to identify Minoan schemes of human proportions.[37]

Among the surviving single ivory figures whose authenticity is unquestioned, female figures are decidedly scarce. Yet the best preserved of all prehistoric Aegean figural groups in this material, found at Mycenae but almost universally considered to be of Minoan Neopalatial workmanship, consists of three females, the smallest of whom is undoubtedly a young child (fig. 11).[38] Often identified in the past as a divine triad consisting of two adult females and a male child, this magnificent composition too unfortunately lacks a

FIG. 8 Figurine of a Small Boy, ivory from Palaikastro, Late Minoan I. Herakleion, Archaeological Museum, 142

FIG. 9 Figurine of a Boy, ivory from Palaikastro, Late Minoan I. Herakleion, Archaeological Museum, 143

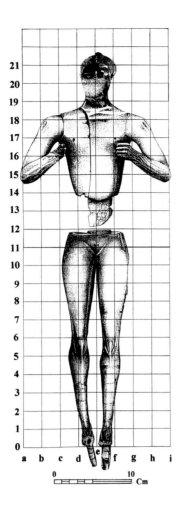

FIG. 10 Kouros, chryselephantine from Palaikastro, Late Minoan IB. Siteia, Archaeological Museum

context that can provide any aid in its interpretation even in its Mycenaean place of discovery, much less in the Minoan cultural setting for which the work was originally intended. The superb quality of this miniature sculptural group, as evidenced by its composition, the rendering of detail, the successful communication of the protective, collegial warmth of the mature women, and the capturing of the characteristically childlike pose and proportions of the young girl, has been commented on by many observers, even when the girl has been mistaken for a boy. The importance of this juvenile figure, despite her small size, has also been conveyed by the artist through the ready visibility of her profile from multiple angles. Like many of the more impressive Neopalatial single ivory figures, this group would originally have been embellished by inlays in other materials, of which sadly nothing but the disfiguring cuttings for their attachment survive.

A series of terracotta groups found in two annex rooms attached to the Middle Minoan tholos tomb at Kamilari have not heretofore been recognized as including representations of children, although a number of features of several figures in no fewer than three of these complex compositions suggest that children were intended subjects. The best known depicts two small standing human figures serving what may be food

FIG. 11 Female Triad, ivory from Mycenae, Late Minoan I. Athens, National Archaeological Museum, 7711

a

b

FIG. 12 Group Model of Food Offering, terracotta from Kamilari Tholos, Late Minoan IA Final. Herakleion, Archaeological Museum, 15074

FIG. 13 Group Model of Grain Grinding, terracotta from Kamilari Tholos, Late Minoan IA Final. Herakleion, Archaeological Museum, 15072

or drink to four much larger seated figures, each of whom extends his or her right forearm to the front toward his or her own hourglass-shaped table or altar (fig. 12).[39] The four seated figures are not obviously gendered, although at least one is noticeably smaller than the remaining three. The two much smaller standing figures extend both arms forward, the fully preserved one holding what appears to be a bowl. These diminutive figures are unmistakably male, the fully preserved one certainly and the second possibly intended to be perceived as nude.[40] Because only male children are depicted nude in Minoan art, the combination of small stature and nudity in this Kamilari offerant suggests that he is a child.[41] The scene as a whole takes place in a structure fronted by two columns and backed by a high wall pierced near its top by two rectangular windows flanking a central square one. This model structure is likely to represent a real building that was roofed, perhaps a small freestanding stoa-like affair within which the offering ceremony depicted in the model took place. Interpreted by the excavator and subsequent authorities as "a shrine with votaries pouring libations or setting offerings on altars before a pair of couples, who may be gods or goddesses, or perhaps the dead regarded as divine," both structure and ceremony represented by the model clearly merit rethinking if the smaller figures in it are acknowledged to be depictions of children.[42]

A second model from Kamilari also shows human figures at two markedly different scales, once again raising the possibility that the smaller is to be viewed as a juvenile (fig. 13).[43] This model is conventionally interpreted as an indoor tableau showing a woman grinding wheat or kneading dough at a table, in conversation with a seated adult female (?) companion. The two are being watched by a third, diminutive figure standing in the doorway that leads into the roughly circular space defined by the model's floor.[44] In the absence of any evidence of either clothing or genitalia on the childlike figure in the doorway, it is possible that this is intended to represent a little girl, although the figure's sex may just as well have been irrelevant to the artist who produced such schematically rendered figures.

A third model from Kamilari depicts four male figures dancing with linked hands in a circle (fig. 14).[45] Similar in stature, these four figures might all be nude. More significant, perhaps, is the peculiar character of the hairstyle on three of them, featuring what appears to be a single backward-curving lock of hair in the middle of what may be an otherwise shaved head, a form of male coiffure that is ordinarily identified as peculiar to younger boys.[46] The physiognomy of the head of the fourth figure is notably different, being almost flat on top and thus suggesting that the artist who modeled this group was genuinely interested in render-

FIG. 14   Group Model of Males Dancing, terracotta from Kamilari Tholos, Late Minoan IA Final. Herakleion, Archaeological Museum, 15073

FIG. 15   Relief-Decorated Chalice, steatite, from Ayia Triadha, Late Minoan I. Herakleion, Archaeological Museum, 341

ing another category of male image. Religious significance has been attributed to each of these terracotta groups from Kamilari on the grounds of the "horns of consecration" that form part of all three compositions. Yet the activities depicted in all three could well be characterized as genre scenes, especially in the case of the dough-kneading group and particularly if children play a significant role in each and every one. The models' context of discovery should also figure importantly in any interpretation of their significance. The fact that they were all found in rooms attached to but outside of the central burial chamber in a monumental communal tomb implies that they have some connection with funerary behavior or ideology. The additional fact that in three out of four instances they were placed close to doorways leading from the main route from the complex's exterior to the burial chamber at its core supports Daniela Lefèvre-Novaro's view that the models depict significant rituals associated with rites of passage involving the dead.[47]

The complex imagery carved in low relief on numerous Neopalatial vessels of serpentine or steatite, some of them originally covered in gold foil, includes scenes in which differently aged males participate in initiatory rituals.[48] The most fully preserved and persuasively interpreted of these is that decorating a chalice, conventionally known as the "Chieftain Cup," found at Ayia Triadha (fig. 15).[49] The scene in question illustrates the presentation of weaponry and bulls' hides by an older youth to a younger youth, a ceremony

that has been argued to have brought an end to a coming-of-age ritual for the latter. The differences in age between the two principals in this scene are conveyed by distinctions in stature and hairstyle; differences in their clothing and the quantity of jewelry the two wear are more likely to reflect differences in status. Only the heads of the subsidiary male figures who carry the bulls' hides in this scene are visible, thus focusing the viewer's attention on the uniformity of their hairstyles as an indicator of age or status at the same time as these figures are stripped of any further narrative interest.[50] Other vessels of this class that are decorated with multiple male figures and consist of more than single small fragments also feature males seemingly differentiated by age (the Harvester Vase) or younger males engaged in activities such as boxing and bull-jumping that have been argued to be initiatory rituals (the Boxer Vase).[51] The absence of female figures from the iconography peculiar to these relief-decorated stone vases has often been commented on; the comparable absence of younger, and especially nude, male figures has not. Thus not only are chalices like the Chieftain Cup, whether produced in stone or in terracotta, likely to be peculiar as a vessel form to activities involving males in their mid-to late teens, but relief-carved vessels in general, when they bear human rather than marine or some other iconography, may be peculiar to adolescent males.

At the other end of the gender spectrum, Neopalatial seals and signet rings with unambiguous depictions of chil-

FIG. 16 Lentoid Seal with Goddess and Two Girl Attendants, steatite from Mochos, Crete, Minoan Neopalatial. Herakleion, Archaeological Museum, 148

FIG. 17 Lentoid Seal with Goddess and Two Girl Attendants, agate from Mycenae, Minoan Neopalatial (?). Athens, National Archaeological Museum, 6235

a

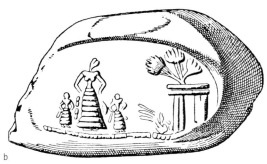

b

FIG. 18 Sealing with Goddess and Two Girl Attendants, clay from Ayia Triadha, Late Minoan IB. Herakleion, Archaeological Museum, sealings 505–506

dren, as opposed to the tiny figures floating in the background of glyptic scenes that are usually interpreted as divine epiphanies, show girls rather than boys. Two lentoid seals (figs. 16, 17) and a sealing made by a metal ring (fig. 18) all show a pair of identical, diminutive females flanking a much larger woman.[52] All three are dressed and posed in a similar fashion, but the large figure has far more accentuated breasts and probably a different hairstyle as well.[53] In view of the virtually certain religious nature of the scene depicted on the sealing from Ayia Triadha and the likelihood that all three scenes show this trio of females dancing, Hilde Rühfel may

well be correct in seeing in the two smaller figures a pair of young acolytes loosely comparable to the *arrephoroi* of Classical Athens.[54]

The far more complex scene illustrated on a large signet ring found at Mycenae depicts at least five females, three of them lined up in a procession bringing flowers to a fourth seated under a tree, while the fifth and smallest seems to be trying to pick blossoms or grab hold of some foliage on the other side of the tree (fig. 19).[55] Despite the small scale mandated by the ring's size, the five figures are individualized by differences in size, details of dress, hairstyle, breast development, and pose; the three largest are clearly adult, the two smallest just as obviously juvenile. A sixth figure, floating high in the background behind a figure-of-eight shield and brandishing a spear in one hand, is not obviously gendered. A large, double-bladed, and elaborately decorated double axe floating in the approximate center of the ring's elliptical field suggests a cult context for the scene as a whole, as may the six disembodied animal heads (of lions?) framing the scene behind the last woman in the procession, and also the combination of solar disc and lunar crescent in an exergue demarcated by a double wavy line at the top of the composition. At least three, and possibly as many as five, stages in the lives of womankind are represented in this scene. Like the ivory triad also found at Mycenae, this striking signet ring, though found in a mainland Greek context, is undoubtedly a Minoan Neopalatial creation.[56] In its combination of compositional complexity, lavishness of detail, high material value, and focus on feminine experience, it is an instructive counterpart to the ivory triad, even if its iconographic message is in many ways just as obscure.

Much less precious as objects, but unfortunately at least as full of unsolved questions owing to their sadly fragmentary state, are Minoan wall paintings depicting children and adolescents. The most famous of these are undoubtedly those that illustrate the peculiarly Knossian (at least within Crete) sport of bull-jumping.[57] Almost as well known are two of several attempts by Knossian fresco artists to picture large crowds in both indoor and outdoor settings, the miniature-style wall paintings often termed the "Grandstand" and "Sacred Grove and Dance" frescoes.[58] Although there has been some debate in recent years as to whether the white skins together with the boyish figures of some bull-jumpers necessarily identify these figures as young females, this remains the majority opinion.[59] And if the female bull-jumpers were girls of the age of contemporary world-class gymnasts, their male colleagues and apparent teammates in this dangerous activity are likely to have been of roughly the same age or only slightly older. Thus bull-jumpers as a class

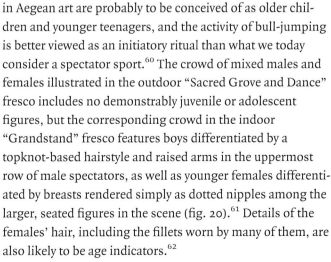

FIG. 19 Signet Ring, gold from Mycenae, Minoan Neopalatial. Athens, National Archaeological Museum, 992

FIG. 20 "Grandstand" fresco from Knossos, Minoan Neopalatial. Herakleion, Archaeological Museum

in Aegean art are probably to be conceived of as older children and younger teenagers, and the activity of bull-jumping is better viewed as an initiatory ritual than what we today consider a spectator sport.[60] The crowd of mixed males and females illustrated in the outdoor "Sacred Grove and Dance" fresco includes no demonstrably juvenile or adolescent figures, but the corresponding crowd in the indoor "Grandstand" fresco features boys differentiated by a topknot-based hairstyle and raised arms in the uppermost row of male spectators, as well as younger females differentiated by breasts rendered simply as dotted nipples among the larger, seated figures in the scene (fig. 20).[61] Details of the females' hair, including the fillets worn by many of them, are also likely to be age indicators.[62]

A small fragment of a miniature fresco from Knossos depicts a lively group of naked males, hence boys, seemingly playing a game on a paved surface of some kind (fig. 21).[63]

Although its highly fragmentary state necessarily makes interpretation of the youths' individual poses somewhat speculative, there can be little doubt that these are unusual. The central figure, viewed in profile facing to the viewer's right, appears to be resting his weight on his extended right hand and on the knee of his flexed left leg, while his right leg is fully extended downward and is closest to the viewer, as though he were positioned on a slope or perhaps a set of steps. The figure in front of him, further to the viewer's right, seems to be depicted almost frontally in a crouching position, his buttocks hovering just above the surface on which his feet rest on either side. Both postures are ones that one would be strongly tempted, even in the absence of the figures' telltale nudity, to attribute to children rather than adults. As in the case of the Psychro bronze, a Minoan artist has succeeded in choosing a bodily position that in and by itself communicates extreme youth.

FIG. 21 Fragment of Boys Playing a Game, fresco from Knossos, Minoan Neopalatial. Herakleion, Archaeological Museum, Tray P X

FIG. 22 Theran Girls of Various Ages in Frescoes from Akrotiri: Crocus Gatherer from Xeste 3 (a); Young Priestess from the West House (b); Girl from the Lustral Basin from Xeste 3 (c); Crocus Gatherer from Xeste 3 (d); and Maiden with the Necklace from the Lustral Basin from Xeste 3 (e), Late Cycladic I

AKROTIRI ON THERA

The conclusions about children's roles and activities that can be gleaned from the badly battered and often burned bits of surviving Minoan frescoes are necessarily limited. The remarkable preservation of numerous contemporary wall paintings from the houses so far excavated in the large Late Cycladic I town of Akrotiri on the island of Thera (modern Santorini), just 110 kilometers north of Knossos, shows how complex and sophisticated such mural decoration can be. Preliminary publication of the findings in just six of these buildings, buried suddenly by masses of debris in one of the largest volcanic explosions to have occurred in the world during the past five millennia, has brought about a virtual revolution in prehistoric Aegean iconographic studies. For the first time, whole programs of mural decoration can be reconstructed in detail—multiple compositions covering all four walls of rooms at both the ground and second-story levels. Thanks to several lavishly illustrated volumes in which these magnificent paintings have been extensively reproduced in both color and black-and-white, the scholarship devoted to them over the past two decades has been prolific.[64] Since one of the principal subjects of these paintings has turned out to be age-based initiatory rituals, the amount of new information they have provided concerning Cycladic children and adolescents at the beginning of the Late Bronze Age has been enormous and can be only briefly summarized here.[65]

CHILDHOOD I

YOUTH II

ADULTHOOD III

FIG. 23 Sequence of Minoan and Theran Male Hairstyles by Age Grade: Figurine of Child, ivory from Palaikastro (a); Yellow Boy, fresco from Akrotiri, Xeste 3 (b); Boxing Boy, fresco from Akrotiri, Building B (c); Fishing Boy, fresco from Akrotiri, West House (d); Shorter Male, low relief on stone vase, Chieftain Cup (e); Taller Male, low relief on stone vase, Chieftain Cup (f); Seated Male, fresco from Akrotiri, Xeste 3 (g); Seal of "Chanting Priest" from Knossos (h); Seal of "Priest's Head" (i)

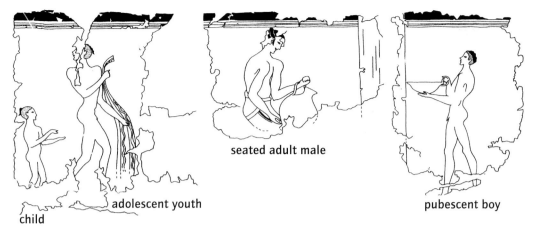

seated adult male

adolescent youth

child

pubescent boy

FIG. 24 Scene with Male Children and Youths of Different Ages, fresco from Akrotiri Xeste 3, Room 3b, Late Cycladic I. Thera, Archaeological Museum

Building upon the groundbreaking work of Ellen Davis and Christos Doumas on female stages of development and of Robert Koehl on the similar but not absolutely parallel male stages, various authorities now recognize up to five stages of female development and as many as nine for males.[66] Age for females is signified, as on Crete, principally through hairstyle, breast development and degree of exposure, and stature (fig. 22). For males, hairstyle and stature are the chief indicators of age, although nudity regularly marks the younger stages preceding the transition to manhood (fig. 23).[67] Markings in blue and red on the interior of the eye are occasional indicators of relative age but do not appear to be utilized consistently, while double chins may be a stylistic trait of selected artists rather than a widely employed signifier of age, as may also be true of a pudgy stomach on males.[68] Unfortunately, since infants and extremely young children so far have not appeared in Theran fresco art, it is uncertain at precisely what age nudity in and by itself becomes a gender signifier, but to date no example of a fully nude female exists, nor can any particular item of female clothing, as opposed to jewelry, be associated with a particular age grade.[69] On the other hand, the youngest thus far identifiable males in Theran wall paintings exhibit a chromatic difference in the form of a yellow ocher rather than red or white skin color. In Xeste 3 this color covers the entire body of the smallest of four male figures depicted in Room 3b, while in the case of the Boxing Boys from Room B1 this distinctive color is limited to just the head of the more richly accoutered, left-hand figure (figs. 24, 25).[70] What do Theran children actually do in the paintings? Boys may box (fig. 25), or else carry strings of fish, metal vessels, or garments (fig. 24).[71] Girls may carry metal vessels and also items of jewelry, or else after picking crocuses they may carry them in baskets as offerings to a goddess, or they may sit in pain after injuring a foot

FIG. 25 Boxing Boys, fresco from Akrotiri Room B1, Late Cycladic I. Thera, Archaeological Museum

necklace swinger   wounded woman   veiled girl

FIG. 26 Lustral Basin Scene with "Wounded Woman," fresco from Akrotiri
Xeste 3, Room 3a, Late Cycladic I. Thera, Archaeological Museum

(fig. 26). In scenes where girls of more than one age grade
are shown working together, as in crocus-gathering, the age
grades are differentiated from each other not only in terms
of physical appearance but also by the nature of the physical
activities being undertaken (picking crocuses in dangerous
locales, as opposed to coordinating the collection of the
picked crocuses).[72] Unlike some Cretan depictions of children, however, none of these Theran youthful figures strikes
a pose that we today can recognize as inherently childlike,
even if upon occasion their bodies are unmistakably those of
children for reasons other than a distinctive hairstyle,
diminutive size, immature breast size, or nudity.[73]

MYCENAEAN CHILDREN

In contrast to the wealth of Minoan and Cycladic representations of children in the earlier Late Bronze Age (seventeenth
to fifteenth centuries), the surviving pictorial and textual
evidence for children in Mycenaean palatial culture of the
fourteenth to thirteenth centuries comes across as impoverished in its range, though it is distinctive in character.[74]
Despite the abundance of wall paintings in Mycenaean palatial contexts, for example, no unambiguous depictions of
infants, juveniles, or adolescents can be identified in them. In
three-dimensional art, however, one of the most frequently
occurring varieties of Mycenaean terracotta figurine is the
kourotrophos, or adult female holding an infant child (see cat.
21, p. 30). Over the more than two centuries during which the
eighty or so surviving examples of this sculptural theme were

produced, a fair number of typological variants flourished.
Thus the body type of the adult female may take the form of
the Greek letters Φ, Ψ, and T, the earliest Φ's being more
naturalistic, and some "transitional" forms also being
attested.[75] Two examples of seated Φ's exist, as do at least
two examples of a "transitional" type that is supplied with
two infants rather than one, in addition to a parasol to shield
one of the babies from the sun.[76] A fragment from the later
sanctuary of the goddess Aphaia on Aigina features such a
parasol for a figure holding just one child.[77] There are even
three examples of groups featuring a pair of Φ-shaped adult
females with a single Ψ-shaped child either hanging on to
their shoulders behind them or else sitting on top of their
shoulders, an arrangement that has been compared both to
an Early Cycladic marble threesome and to the Mycenae ivory
triad already described, parallels that have prompted an identification of the terracotta trios as divine triads, the adults
being nurses rather than mothers.[78]

Found at sixteen different mainland Greek sites in
the Argolid, Attica, Boiotia, and Corinthia, as well as
commonly on the island of Aigina but only singly on the
islands of Kythera and Cyprus and just once at the inland
Syro-Palestinian site of Hazor, this form of group figurine has
been variously interpreted as a children's toy, occasionally
deposited with them as a grave offering if they died young,
or else as a votive offering when found in locales that have a
claim to being Mycenaean sanctuaries, such as the Aphaia
sanctuary on Aigina. In a child's grave, such a figurine might
have been viewed as a nourishing or protective talisman; in a

sanctuary, it might have expressed a wish for motherhood, or alternatively, thanks for having achieved this goal; and it could well be, of course, that this figurine type served both purposes.[79] The formal parallels between the much earlier marble and ivory triads and the rare three-bodied clay kourotrophoi are not particularly close. Because the former are both products of cultural milieus (the Cycladic islands and Crete, respectively) in which the terracotta kourotrophos was never adopted as a form, neither the marble nor the ivory merits invocation as a source for the interpretation of the terracottas.[80] The concentration of kourotrophoi of all types at the later sanctuary of the local Aiginetan goddess Aphaia does suggest that they may have served a votive purpose in a sacred context, but Olsen is probably correct to suggest, on the basis of the wide range of different contexts in which they have been found, that, like the later Archaic marble statues of nude youths known as *kouroi*, these smaller and much more cheaply produced statuettes could serve multiple purposes. The earliest and one of the most naturalistic examples known on the Greek mainland was found in a Late Helladic II context in a tomb at Aidonia. More or less contemporary is the single example of a child-holding terracotta female from Crete that wears a wheelmade, bell-shaped skirt, from a Late Minoan II context in the Mavrospelio cemetery at Knossos (fig. 27).[81] Olsen's interpretation of this last item, which in both form and context is so atypical for Minoan culture, as the product of a Minoan artist commissioned by a Mycenaean mourner, or more generally as an unusual Minoan-Mycenaean hybrid, is surely on the right track.[82] Her view receives additional support from the highly naturalistic, and thus for its time equally atypical, rendering of another kourotrophos, in this case of Late Helladic IIIA2 date (mid-fourteenth century), found at a second interface between Minoan and Mycenaean culture, namely the island of Kythera.[83] Thus, as Olsen has emphasized, these kourotrophos figures are not only far and

away the most common representations of children in Mycenaean pictorial art, but they are also to all intents and purposes peculiar to the Mycenaean mainland. Despite the extreme schematization that effectively robs these miniature sculptures of any real human interest, they nevertheless serve to highlight the fact that such "madonna-and-child" compositions are strikingly absent from the Minoan artistic repertoire. Notwithstanding the regular placement of the infant's head on the left-hand side of its mother's (surely!) upper torso, so that the child's head would be closer to the reassuring sound of the maternal heartbeat at the same time as the mother's right hand and arm would remain free, these figurines were so hastily produced that they serve as little more than symbols of maternalism.[84]

In a broadly comparable fashion, the only mentions of children in the Linear B administrative documents recovered from the Mycenaean palace at Pylos and from its earlier functional equivalent at Knossos stress the childrearing function of women in nameless groups rather than putting any emphasis on the individual identities of either children or mothers.[85] Olsen has usefully summarized the documentary evidence for Mycenaean children as follows:

> Approximately 200 tablets from these two centres record children in the so-called personnel series tablets; approximately 90 tablets at Knossos with an additional 110 at Pylos. Children appear primarily in three contexts: as components of family units, as recipients of rations, and accompanying workgroups of specialized labourers. About a dozen or so tablets record what appear to be households, listing numbers of men, women, girls, and boys, respectively; the remainder record children accompanying workgroups of women. At Pylos, in the personnel series that record the working strength of women's workgroups, the census and rations tablets consistently count boys and girls with their mothers.

a　　　　　　　　　　　　　　　　　　　b

FIG. 27　Kourotrophos, terracotta from Knossos, Mavrospelio Cemetery, Late Minoan II. Herakleion, Archaeological Museum, HM 8345

At Knossos the process is further elaborated since the children are differentiated not only by sex, but also by age, with two separate age grades for "older" and "younger" children. We see, accompanying the women of working groups, children differentiated by sex and by age grades: younger girls, older girls, younger boys, and older boys. It is interesting to note that the persons designated older boys continue to be grouped with their mothers rather than their fathers. There is unfortunately no way of knowing just what is meant by "older" and "younger." . . . In the few tablets where boys are recorded as accompanying men, the texts are explicit that these sons are older boys and accompany their fathers for the purpose of instruction in their trade: these are not young children requiring care. Men are never listed with children unless those children are older boys specifically undergoing training in a trade, in contrast to women, who tend children of both sexes until the age when boys leave for professional training. In short, child care in both the Mycenaean mainland and Mycenaean Crete is clearly a role assigned to women and receives fairly equal treatment in the tablets of each centre.[86]

This characterization of children in Mycenaean texts as components of family units on the one hand and as young apprentices detailed to learn the trades of their fathers on the other is supported by the only other significant category of evidence for Mycenaean children at our disposal. On LH IIIB *larnakes* (terracotta chests used as coffins) from Tanagra in Boiotia and on a recently published LH IIIC krater from Ayia Triadha Palaioboukouvina in Elis, images of children figure prominently in a traditionally family-oriented ritual, the mourning over and laying to rest of the dead. On two larnakes from Tanagra, dead children are shown being deposited in such terracotta coffins by two adults, presumably the parents in each case of the child, although it is possible that both of the adult figures are in fact female (fig. 28).[87] On the krater, a helmeted warrior is being mourned by a second male warrior, two adult females, and, judging by her dress, a young girl (fig. 29). As in Attic Late Geometric *prothesis* scenes almost four centuries later, the child stands closest to the bier of the deceased, at the head end.[88] Occasional diminutive figures occur in earlier Mycenaean pictorial vase painting, but rarely can they be securely identified as images of children.[89]

Finally, detailed analysis of the palmprints impressed on the Linear B tablets from Knossos has resulted in the discovery that a good number of them belong to children. This evidence is perhaps best interpreted as showing that young boys prepared unbaked clay tablets for use by older male scribes, in some cases perhaps the boys' fathers.[90]

The preceding review of six millennia's worth of evidence for the activities, appearance, and social roles of Aegean prehistoric children has made clear how spotty that evidence is and how unevenly distributed it is through space and time. Its discovery has often been entirely serendipitous, at times occurring in altogether unexpected places and at surprisingly early dates. As always in archaeology, the recovery of such information in context dramatically enhances its value, even when the state of preservation is less than ideal and the artistic medium relatively humble. The details of its context are what make the Neolithic house model from Platia Magoula Zarkou such an extraordinary find, whereas the lack of a helpful context of discovery mutes the importance of such complex works of art as the ivory triad or large gold signet ring from Mycenae.[91] Yet even fabulous states of preservation and context cannot make up for what is now lost

FIG. 28 Larnax, terracotta from Tanagra Chamber Tomb 22, Late Helladic IIIB. Thebes, Archaeological Museum

FIG. 29 Krater, terracotta from Palaioboukouvina [Elis] Chamber Tomb 5, Late Helladic IIIC

to us simply as a result of the passage of time and the destructive actions of both nature and man: the Theran wall paintings, no matter how many of them have been found and still remain to be discovered, cannot compensate for the loss of the paintings that once decorated the palace at Knossos. Such discoveries as the cluster of Lower Mesolithic burials at Franchthi Cave should remind us not to underestimate even our more distant ancestors, and also to attach as much value to efforts in the laboratory as to the primary fieldwork of excavation. Perhaps most important, we need to recognize that what we know about a key dimension of human experience in the past—the lives of children, for example—can be dramatically altered overnight by a chance new discovery. This simple fact is what makes archaeology so exciting on the one hand, and yet so humbling and downright frustrating on the other. How can we be sure that we actually *do* know what we think we do?

As far as prehistoric Aegean children are concerned, a significant distinction has emerged between the attitudes of the mainland Greeks on the one hand and the southern Aegean islanders, in particular the Minoans of Crete, on the other, certainly during the Late Bronze Age and possibly as far back as the Neolithic era. The mainlanders view children

first and foremost as junior family members, with the result that they are routinely accompanied by one or more parents, and perhaps occasionally even by grandparents, wherever they appear. The Minoans, on the other hand, are far more intent on tracking the experience of their young through various stages of life as either individuals or members of peer groups rather than as components of a nuclear family.[92] One other regional difference is worth remarking on. While virtually all of the artifactual evidence for mainland Greek children takes the form of a relatively narrow range of clay objects, usually painted or incised, and most of the evidence for Cycladic children so far known consists of either painted wall plaster or marble statuettes, the enormous variety of artifactual types, materials, and scales through which the Minoans expressed themselves on the subject of children is by contrast truly striking. The Minoans may have come relatively late to the exploration of their children's lives in their art, but when they finally did so, they made a real splash. Despite the lamentable state of preservation of so much Bronze Age Minoan art, it is fair to say that Neopalatial Cretan artists rivaled the achievements of Classical and Hellenistic artists working more than a millennium later in the sensitivity of their renderings of the juvenile human form.

Notes

1. For bibliographical assistance and helpful comments on earlier versions of this text, I am very grateful to Paul Christensen, Tracey Cullen, Jack Davis, Karen Johnson, Robert Koehl, Merle Langdon, Daniela Lefèvre-Novaro, Jenifer Neils, Marie-Louise Nosch, John Oakley, Thomas Palaima, Paul Rehak, Curtis Runnels, Maria Shaw, Aleydis Van de Moortel, James Wright, and John Younger. For permission to cite as yet unpublished information, I am particularly beholden to Tracey Cullen. I also owe a special debt of gratitude to Anne Wadlow and Katherine Hart for their efforts in securing permission to use the illustrations reproduced here as figs. 1–29.

2. The absolute chronology of the Aegean Bronze Age, and especially the dating of the end of the Middle Bronze Age and the earlier stages of the Late Bronze Age, has been the subject of fierce debate for the past fifteen years. For a sampling of views on this subject, see P. Warren and V. Hankey, *Aegean Bronze Age Chronology* (Bristol, England, 1989); S. W. Manning, *The Absolute Chronology of the Aegean Early Bronze Age: Archaeology, History, and Radiocarbon* (Sheffield, England, 1995); P. Warren, "Aegean Late Bronze 1–2 Absolute Chronology: Some New Contributions," in M. S. Balmuth and R. H. Tykot, eds., *Sardinian and Aegean Chronology: Towards the Resolution of Relative and Absolute Dating in the Mediterranean* (Oxford, 1998), 323–331; Rehak and Younger (infra n. 38), pl. XXV; S. W. Manning, *A Test of Time: The Volcano of Thera and the Chronology and History of the Aegean and East Mediterranean in the Mid-Second Millennium B.C.E.* (Oxford, 1999). The transition from the Middle to the Late Bronze Age is therefore placed at ca. 1700 (high chronology) / 1600 (low chronology) in table 1, a two-track dating scheme that is also alluded to by slashed datings at several points in the text.

3. For the cultural geography of the Aegean during the Bronze Age, see S. Hood, *The Arts in Prehistoric Greece* (Warminster, England, 1978), 15 (chronological chart), 17–26; D. Preziosi and L. A. Hitchcock, *Aegean Art and Architecture* (Oxford, 1999), 1–20.

4. For the current state of the debate over the arrival of the Greeks, some idea of the range of different opinions can be gleaned from J. T. Hooker, "The Coming of the Greeks," *Historia* 15 (1976), 129–145; R. Drews, *The Coming of the Greeks: Indo-European Conquests in the Aegean and the Near East* (Princeton, 1988); J. P. Mallory, *In Search of the Indo-Europeans: Language, Archaeology, and Myth* (London, 1989); C. Renfrew, "'Ever in Process of Becoming': The Autochthony of the Greeks," in J. A. Koumoulides, ed., *The Good Idea: Democracy in Ancient Greece* (New Rochelle, N.Y., 1995), 7–28; M. B. Cosmopoulos, "From Artefacts to Peoples: Pelasgoi, Indo-Europeans and the Arrival of the Greeks," in R. Blench and M. Spriggs, eds., *Archaeology and Language*, vol. 3, *Artefacts, Languages, and Texts* (London, 1999), 249–256; J. E. Coleman, "An Archaeological Scenario for the 'Coming of the Greeks' ca. 3200 B.C.E.," *JIES* 28 (2000), 101–153.

5. For a previous cross-cultural review of prehistoric Aegean children, see Rühfel 1984a, 13–30. A forthcoming dissertation by M. Pomadère at the University of Paris I, with the title "L'enfant dans le monde égéen, de la préhistoire aus périodes historiques," was announced in *Nestor* 29, no. 1 (January 2002), 3506.

6. T. Cullen, "Mesolithic Mortuary Ritual at Franchthi Cave, Greece," *Antiquity* 69 (1995), 270–289, esp. 274–279, 284–286, table 1; C. Runnels, "Review of Aegean Prehistory IV: The Stone Age of Greece from the Palaeolithic to the Advent of the Neolithic," in T. Cullen, ed., *Aegean Prehistory: A Review* (Boston, 2001), 225–258, esp. 247–248. Scattered human bones from Mesolithic levels elsewhere in the cave include copious additional evidence for infants, juveniles, adolescents, and adults of various ages as well (Cullen, 278–280, table 2, fig. 5). Even earlier in date are six small human fragments from Final Palaeolithic levels (ninth millennium) that include two shed milk teeth and a piece of an infant's rib. A tooth from another infant (eighteen to twenty months old) may date as early as the fifteenth millennium (Upper Palaeolithic) but is more likely to represent yet another Final Palaeolithic individual (T. Cullen, personal communication).

7. T. W. Jacobsen, "17,000 Years of Greek Prehistory," *Scientific American* 234, no. 6 (1976), 76–87, esp. 84–85; T. W. Jacobsen and T. Cullen, "A Consideration of Mortuary Practices in Neolithic Greece: Burials from Franchthi Cave," in S. C. Humphreys and H. King, eds., *Mortality and Immortality: The Anthropology and Archaeology of Death* (London, 1981), 79–101. The notion that the valuable grave goods accompanying the Middle Neolithic baby show that status could already be inherited in this society rather than having to be acquired, while certainly a possibility, seems a rather dubious inference in view of how poorly furnished the vast majority of child burials are throughout the Aegean during the Neolithic era (T. Cullen, personal communication). For the dating of this burial to the early sixth millennium (Franchthi Ceramic Phase 2.2, early Middle Neolithic), see K. D. Vitelli, *Franchthi Neolithic Pottery*, vol. 1, *Classification and Ceramic Phases 1 and 2* (Bloomington, Ind., 1993), 66, 67 n. 13.

8. Athens, National Archaeological Museum, 5937: C. Marangou, EIDOLIA: *Figurines et miniatures du Néolithique Récent et du Bronze Ancien en Grèce*, BAR-IS 576 (Oxford, 1992), 38, 266 NR479, fig. 74a; D. R. Theocharis, *Neolithic Greece* (Athens, 1973), pl. 56; G. Papathanassopoulos, *Ethniko Archaiologiko Mouseio: Neolithika kai Kykladika* (Athens, 1981), 92–95, nos. 36–40; G. A. Papathanassopoulos, ed., *Neolithic Culture in Greece* (Athens, 1996), 307, no. 221. A possible second kourotrophos figure comes from Corinth: Marangou, 46–47, 165, 270 NR637 = W. W. Phelps, "Prehistoric Figurines from Corinth," *Hesperia* 56 (1987), 233–253, esp. 248 no. 29, pl. 38.

9. Larissa, Archaeological Museum of Larissa, ML.PMZ.619: K. J. Gallis, "A Late Neolithic Foundation Offering from Thessaly," *Antiquity* 59 (1985), 20–24; Marangou (supra n. 8), 36–37, 265 NR427–434, 268 NR571–573, fig. 24f; Papathanassopoulos 1996 (supra n. 8), 328–329 no. 266.

10. The male figurines from Platia Magoula Zarkou feature armless torsos from whose bottoms spring four tapering, pointed legs on which the figures, when positioned erect, would have stood. Marangou (supra n. 8: 36) interprets these compositions as males seated on four-legged stools. The females, by contrast, are rendered standing, with arms extended toward the side and

sharply flexed at the elbow, so that the hands rest just below their modeled breasts. It is not immediately clear why the males should have been rendered in recurring "seated" poses, so obviously different from the identical standing poses of the females.

11 During the Neolithic era, virtually all of these images are three-dimensional, most of them modeled in terracotta, although some are carved from stone. For recent surveys, Marangou (supra n. 8), 12–61, 138–146, 162–166, 173–185, 202–209, 218–230; L. E. Talalay, *Deities, Dolls, and Devices: Neolithic Figurines from Franchthi Cave, Greece* (Bloomington, Ind., 1993), esp. 53–79; G. Ch. Chourmouziadis, *Ta Neolithika eidolia* (Thessaloniki, 1994); D. Kokkinidou and M. Nikolaidou, "Body Imagery in the Aegean Neolithic: Ideological Implications of Anthropomorphic Figurines," in J. Moore and E. Scott, eds., *Invisible People and Processes: Writing Gender and Childhood into European Archaeology* (London, 1997), 88–112. Early Bronze Age: Marangou (supra n. 8), 62–137, 146–161, 166–172, 185–201, 209–217, 230–253; P. Getz-Preziosi, *Sculptors of the Cyclades: Individual and Tradition in the Third Millennium B.C.E.* (Ann Arbor, Mich., 1987), esp. 9–23; P. Getz-Gentle, *Personal Styles in Early Cycladic Sculpture* (Madison, Wis., 2001); C. Marangou, "Anthropomorphic and Zoomorphic Figurines of the Early Bronze Age in the North Aegean," in C. G. Doumas and V. La Rosa, eds., *E Poliochne kai e Proïme Epoche tou Chalkou sto Boreio Aigaio* (Athens, 1997), 649–665; E. Sapouna-Sakellaraki, "To eidolio tou Sampa kai ta amorpha lithina eidolia tes Proïmes Epoches tou Chalkou sten Krete," *ArchEph* (1983), 44–74; Hemingway (infra n. 30), 113–115, fig. 9.1.

12 Three-figure groups, two standing males supporting a slightly smaller seated female on their shoulders: Getz-Preziosi (supra n. 11), 21–22, 46–47, fig. 24, pl. 1C; Marangou (supra n. 8), 193; Getz-Gentle (supra n. 11), 27 table 1, 34 fig. 16b, 38. Two-figure groups in which two standing females each have one arm draped over the shoulders or behind the back of their companions, while their second arm is bent at the elbow and held tightly across the middle of the torso as in the standard folded-arm pose for Cycladic female figures of marble during this period: Getz-Preziosi (supra n. 11), 23, 145–146

n. 13, fig. 12b–c; Marangou (supra n. 8), 192–193; Getz-Gentle (supra n. 11), 27 table 1, 33, 34 fig. 16e, 38, 73 fig. 34, 136 n. 63, pl. 26d. The latter type is prefigured by a Neolithic version in terracotta from Domeniko in Thessaly: Papathanassopoulos 1996 (supra n. 8), 314 no. 234.

13 Getz-Preziosi (supra n. 11), 23, figs. 12a, 19, pl. 1A-B; Marangou (supra n. 8), 193; Getz-Gentle (supra n. 11), 25–26, 27 table 1, 36–37, 137 nn. 70–73, pls. 19, 26a–b.

14 Notwithstanding this problem, Getz-Gentle (supra n. 11: 36) confidently identifies the personnel in this last two-figure type as mother and daughter and claims that this odd composition would have made the group easier for its creator to carve and simpler for its audience to understand.

15 Athens, the Nicholas P. Goulandris Foundation Museum of Cycladic Art, 968; Getz-Gentle (supra n. 11), 36–37, fig. 18, pl. 26c.

16 M. Kostoula, "Die frühhelladischen Tonplomben mit Siegelabdrücken aus Petri bei Nemea," in W. Müller, ed., *Minoisch-mykenische Glyptik: Stil, Ikonographie, Funktion, CMS Beiheft 6* (Berlin, 2000), 135–148, esp. 145–146, figs. 6a–b; J. B. Rutter, "Review of Aegean Prehistory II: The Prepalatial Bronze Age of the Southern and Central Greek Mainland," in Cullen 2001 (supra n. 6), 95–155, esp. 118 and n. 98, fig. 10. Similar scenes of young animals, both real and imagined, being fed by their parents also become oddly popular in Postpalatial (Late Helladic IIIC = twelfth century) ceramic art on the Greek mainland; see J. B. Rutter, "Cultural Novelties in the Post-Palatial Aegean World: Indices of Vitality or Decline?" in W. A. Ward and M. S. Joukowsky, eds., *The Crisis Years: The 12th Century B.C.* (Dubuque, Iowa, 1992), 61–78, esp. 65 and n. 13; K. Demakopoulou, ed., *The Mycenaean World: Five Centuries of Early Greek Culture, 1600–1100 B.C.* (Athens, 1988), 128 no. 68; they were also popular in Minoan Neopalatial art (Olsen [infra n. 74], 388), although in neither later instance are such nurturing scenes ever anthropomorphic in character. A recently published bell-krater from Tiryns may show a nursing "infant sphinx," possibly to be dated as early as LH IIIB2 (late thirteenth century); see *AA* (1983), 308 fig. 35; W. Güntner, *Tiryns*, vol.

12, *Figürlich bemalte Mykenische Keramik aus Tiryns* (Mainz, 2000), 20–21, 181 no. 180, 194, pl. 4: 1a–b (where the figure identified here as a baby sphinx is instead taken to be a diminutive human being grasped in the talons of a hybrid monster). The disparity in size between the two sphinxes on a LH IIIC Middle krater fragment from Lefkandi is surely intended to communicate parent (mother?) and child, here certainly in a nursing scene: E. T. Vermeule and V. Karageorghis, *Mycenaean Pictorial Vase Painting* (Cambridge, Mass., 1981), 144, 223 XI.65. Fresco painters who depict adult birds together with their young in some of the wall paintings at Late Cycladic I Akrotiri on Thera choose altogether unrealistic coloration for the juvenile birds: A. Vlachopoulos, "The Reed Motif in the Thera Wall Paintings and Its Association with Aegean Pictorial Art," in Sherratt (infra n. 37), vol. 2, 631–655 (esp. 641).

17 Examples of this kind of study in other regions of Europe include M. C. Lillie, "Women and Children in Prehistory: Resource Sharing and Social Stratification at the Mesolithic-Neolithic Transition in Ukraine," in Moore and Scott (supra n. 11), 213–228; E. Rega, "Age, Gender, and Biological Reality in the Early Bronze Age Cemetery at Mokrin," in Moore and Scott (supra n. 11), 229–247. Note also the observations of A. T. Chamberlain, "Commentary: Missing Stages of Life: Towards the Perception of Children in Archaeology," in Moore and Scott (supra n. 11), 248–250. The only significant amount of published work of this kind on skeletal remains from the Aegean Bronze Age is that by P. J. P. McGeorge on Late Minoan and Mycenaean populations: "Health and Diet in Minoan Times," in R. E. Jones and H. W. Catling, eds., *New Aspects of Archaeological Science in Greece* (Athens, 1988), 47–54; "A Comparative Study of the Mean Life Expectation of the Minoans," in *Pepragmena tou ST' Diethnous Archaiologikou Synedriou* (Chania, Greece, 1990), A1, 419–428; "The Anthropological Approach to the Pylona Tombs: The Skeletal Remains," in E. Karantzali, *The Mycenaean Cemetery at Pylona on Rhodes, BAR-IS 988* (Oxford, 2001), 82–104.

18 House 102 of Blegen's Troy Ib: C. W. Blegen, J. L. Caskey, M. Rawson, and J. Sperling, *Troy: Excavations Conducted by the University of Cincinnati, 1932–1938*, vol. 1, *General Introduction; The First and Second Settlements* (Princeton, 1950), 89–97 (esp. 94–95). No significant numbers of adult, adolescent, or even child burials dating to the Early or Middle Bronze Ages have ever been found at Troy, notwithstanding more than a century of excavation at the site in no fewer than four major series of campaigns (led respectively by H. Schliemann, W. Dörpfeld, C. W. Blegen, and M. Korfmann). It is conceivable that children's and adults' bodies were disposed of in some way that left behind no readily recoverable physical evidence. The important point here is simply that the bodies of newborns and young infants were treated in a different way.

19 W. G. Cavanagh and C. Mee, *A Private Place: Death in Prehistoric Greece*, SIMA 125 (Jonsered, Sweden, 1998), 111.

20 The problems in recovering data on individuals that are posed for archaeologists by communal burial practices are particularly acute for the Early and Middle Bronze Ages on Crete and for the Early Helladic II and Mycenaean periods on the Greek mainland.

21 C. Gates, "Art for Children in Mycenaean Greece," in R. Laffineur and J. L. Crowley, eds., EIKON: *Aegean Bronze Age Iconography: Shaping a Methodology*, Aegaeum 8 (Liège, 1992), 161–171, esp. 163–166.

22 N. Polychronakou-Sgouritsa, "Paidikes taphes ste mykenaïke Ellada," *ArchDelt* 42A [1987] (1994), 8–29.

23 Gates (supra n. 21), 166–171; Polychronakou-Sgouritsa (supra n. 22), 22–26. On the miniature vessels that are often found with later Mycenaean child burials, see U. Damm, "Die spätbronzezeitlichen Miniaturgefässe und Hohlgeformten Stiere von Tiryns: Eine Analyse der Form und Funktion" (Ph.D. diss., Rheinische Friedrich-Wilhelms-Universität zu Bonn, 1997), esp. 165–169.

24 Y. Sakellarakis and E. Sapouna-Sakellaraki, "Drama of Death in a Minoan Temple," *National Geographic* 159, no. 2 (1981), 205–222; D. D. Hughes, *Human Sacrifice in Ancient Greece* (London, 1991), 13–17; on possible depictions of human sacrifice in Aegean prehistoric art, see also R. Jung, "Menschenopferdarstellungen? Zur Analyse minoischer und mykenischer Siegelbilder," *PZ* 72 (1997), 133–194.

25 S. M. Wall, J. H. Musgrave, and P. M. Warren, "Human Bones from a Late Minoan Ib House at Knossos," *BSA* 81 (1986), 333–388; Hughes (supra n. 24), 18–24. Wall, Musgrave, and Warren catalogue 327 bones from the so-called Room of the Children's Bones, a further 50 bones from LM IB destruction contexts in four other locales within and around the North House, and 10 bones (including a number belonging to adults) from less reliably dated contexts in the immediate vicinity (345–346, 349). Hughes's figure of "371 bones and bone fragments found in the room" represents the total number of human fragments recovered in the Room of the Children's Bones, reduced to 327 by joins and considered to represent a minimum number of 199 different bones in the opinion of Wall, Musgrave, and Warren (supra n. 25, 333 n. 2, 374 table 2). The percentage of bones exhibiting cut marks ranges between 22 and 36, depending on what figures are used for both total bones and bones bearing marks (total fragments recovered? total non-joining fragments? minimum number of bones represented?). These cut marks, some of which were even found on the inside surface of skull and rib fragments, lead Wall, Musgrave, and Warren to conclude that the cutting was followed by the ritual consumption of flesh. For further discussion of the interpretation of these bones, see "Site of Western Extension to Stratigraphical Museum at Knossos" in lesson 15 of the website entitled "The Prehistoric Archaeology of the Aegean" at <http://projects.dartmouth.edu/history/bronze_age/lessons/les/15.html#21>.

26 J. Driessen and C. F. Macdonald, *The Troubled Island: Minoan Crete Before and After the Santorini Eruption*, Aegaeum 17 (Liège 1997), 105–115, 160–161.

27 For Middle Minoan terracotta figurines, see A. Pilali-Papasteriou, *Minoïka pelina anthropomorpha eidolia tes Sylloges Metaxa: Symbole ste melete tes mesominoïkes peloplastikes* (Thessaloniki, 1992); B. Rutkowski, *Petsophas: A Cretan Peak Sanctuary* (Warsaw, 1991). For bronze figurines of this period, see Verlinden (infra n. 29) and Sapouna-Sakellaraki (infra n. 29). I have not seen H. Wingerath, *Studien zur Darstellung des Menschen in der minoischen Kunst der älteren und jüngeren Palastzeit* (Marburg, Germany, 1995). For painted female images on a set of cult equipment from Phaistos, some identified as "maidens" on the basis of questionable parallels in later Cycladic art, see most recently W. Schiering, "Goddesses, Dancing, and Flower-gathering Maidens in Middle Minoan Vase Painting," in P. P. Betancourt et al., eds., MELETEMATA: *Studies in Aegean Archaeology Presented to Malcolm H. Wiener as He Enters His 65th Year*, Aegaeum 20 (Liège, 1999), vol. 3, 747–750, pl. CLXV (with references to earlier literature on these same objects). For the acrobat rendered in relief on a gold sword pommel from Mallia, often claimed to be a youth as well as a tumbler, see O. Pelon, "L'acrobat de Malia et l'art de l'époque protopalatiale en Crète," in P. Darcque and J.-C. Poursat, eds., *L'iconographie minoenne*, BCH Supplément 11 (Paris, 1985), 35–39; O. Pelon, "L'épée à l'acrobate et la chronologie maliote I-II," *BCH* 106 (1982), 165–190; 107 (1983), 679–703. For the seal impression of the "prince" from Knossos (Crete, Archaeological Museum of Herakleion, 180), A. Evans, *The Palace of Minos at Knossos*, vol. 1 (London, 1921), 8–9 fig. 2b, 271–272 fig. 201b; Hood (supra n. 3), 218 fig. 217, 272 n. 64; Rühfel 1984a, 17 fig. 4, 20, 313 n. 18.

28 Rühfel 1984a, 13–24.

29 Oxford, Ashmolean Museum, 1938.1162: Rühfel 1984a, 312 nn. 5–6, fig. 1; Hood (supra n. 3), 112 fig. 98; C. Verlinden, *Les statuettes anthropomorphes crétoises en bronze et en plomb, du IIIe millénaire au VIIe siècle av. J.-C.*, Archaeologia Transatlantica 4 (Providence, 1984), 83, 191 no. 38, pl. 19; E. Sapouna-Sakellaraki, *Die bronzenen Menschenfiguren auf Kreta und in der Ägäis*, Prähistorische Bronzefunde I/5 (Stuttgart, 1995), 33–34 no. 49, pl. 12; L. V. Watrous, *The Cave Sanctuary of Zeus at Psychro: A Study of Extra-Urban Sanctuaries in Minoan and Early Iron Age Crete*, Aegaeum 15 (Liège, 1996), esp. 88, 94.

30 Crete, Archaeological Museum of Herakleion, 142: R. C. Bosanquet and R. M. Dawkins, *The Unpublished Objects from the Palaikastro Excavations, 1902–1906, Part I* [BSA Supplementary Paper 1] (London, 1923), 125–127, fig. 107, pl. XXVII; A. Evans, *The Palace of Minos at Knossos*, vol. 3 (London, 1930), 445–446, fig. 310a, pl. XXXVIIB; Hood (supra n. 3), 120, fig. 108; Rühfel 1984a, 16–17, 312 n. 7, fig. 3; S. Hemingway, "The Place of the Palaikastro Kouros in Minoan Bone and Ivory Sculpture," in J. A. MacGillivray, J. M. Driessen, and L. H. Sackett, eds., *The Palaikastro Kouros: A Minoan Chryselephantine Statuette and Its Aegean Bronze Age Context*, BSA Studies 6 (London, 2000), 113–122, esp. 119, fig. 9.3: d; K. D. S. Lapatin, *Chryselephantine Statuary in the Ancient Mediterranean World* (Oxford, 2001), 32–33.

31 Crete, Archaeological Museum of Herakleion, 143: Bosanquet and Dawkins (supra n. 30), 125–127, fig. 107, pl. XXVII; Evans (supra n. 30), 445–446, fig. 310b, pl. XXXVIIB; Rühfel 1984a, 16–17, 312 nn. 7–8, fig. 2; Hemingway (supra n. 30), 119, fig. 9.3: c. Lapatin (supra n. 30) helpfully draws attention to Egyptian predecessors in ivory for the Palaikastro boys but surely goes too far in intimating that the latter may not be Minoan products.

32 For recent overviews of Minoan Neopalatial anthropomorphic ivories, see Rehak and Younger (infra n. 38), 239–241; Hemingway (supra n. 30), 115–122, figs. 9.2–3, pls. 29–31; Lapatin (supra n. 30), 22–37. For the Palaikastro youth, see MacGillivray, Driessen, and Sackett (supra n. 30); Lapatin (supra n. 30), 28–32, esp. 29–30 for a critique of the term *kouros* as applied to this figure.

33 For the youth's hair, see M. Moak, "The Palaikastro Kouros," in MacGillivray, Driessen, and Sackett (supra n. 30), 64–83, esp. 73–74, pls. 16–17; Lapatin (supra n. 30), fig. 40. For the significance of this hairstyle as an indicator of the youth's age, see R. Koehl, "Ritual Context," in Mac-Gillivray, Driessen, and Sackett (supra n. 30), 131–143, esp. 134–137, fig. 11.1. For the recovery of the Palaikastro youth, found over three field seasons in an extremely fragmented condition, see H. Sackett and A. MacGillivray, "The Excavation," in MacGillivray, Driessen, and Sackett (supra

n. 30), 21–34. For the architectural context and original display of this remarkable work of art, see J. Driessen, "The Architectural Environment" and "A Late Minoan IB Town Shrine at Palaikastro," in MacGillivray, Driessen, and Sackett (supra n. 30), 35–50, 87–96, fig. 6.1, pls. K, N.

34 Moak (supra n. 33), 65.

35 Hemingway (supra n. 30), 118; Lapatin (supra n. 30), 22–24.

36 R. Koehl, "The Chieftain Cup and a Minoan Rite of Passage," JHS 106 (1986), 99–110, esp. 100–103; Koehl (supra n. 33), 134–138. Considerations of stomach and shoulder musculature, nudity, and skin coloring have been adduced as age markers in discussions of painted figures in which two-dimensional renderings, the exploitation of color, and the portrayal of figures at substantially larger scales significantly alter the problems confronted by an artist in depicting age (see further infra nn. 66–67).

37 Rühfel 1984a, 312 n. 8, considers the standing boy from Palaikastro (Crete, Archaeological Museum of Herakleion, 143) to be about two years old, as opposed to Evans's estimate of four or five years (supra n. 30: 446). She considers the Psychro bronze to depict a roughly one-year-old infant (Rühfel 1984a, 16), while Verlinden thinks this child is only about half that age (supra n. 29: 83). J. Weingarten, "Measure for Measure: What the Palaikastro Kouros Can Tell Us About Minoan Society," in R. Laffineur and W.-D. Niemeier, eds., *POLITEIA: State and Society in the Aegean Bronze Age*, Aegaeum 12 (Liège, 1995), 249–264; J. Weingarten, "Proportions and the Palaikastro Kouros: A Minoan Adaptation of the First Egyptian Canon of Proportions," in J. Phillips, ed., *Ancient Egypt, the Aegean, and the Near East: Studies in Honour of Martha Bell* (San Antonio, 1997), 471–481; J. Weingarten, "Male and Female S/he Created Them: Further Studies in Aegean Proportions," in Betancourt et al. (supra n. 27), vol. 3, 921–930; J. Weingarten, "Reading the Minoan Body: Proportions and the Palai-kastro Kouros," in MacGillivray, Driessen, and Sackett (supra n. 30), 103–111; E. Guralnick, "Proportions of Painted Figures from Thera," in S. Sherratt, ed., *The Wall Paintings of Thera* (Piraeus, 2000), vol. 1, 173–190.

38 Athens, National Archaeological Museum, 7711: H. Wace, *Ivories from Mycenae I, 1939: The Ivory Trio* (Athens, n.d.), 1–14; Hood (supra n. 3), 124–126, fig. 114; Rühfel 1984a, 24–26, 314 n. 44, fig. 7 (facing p. 64); P. Rehak and J. G. Younger, "International Styles in Ivory Carving in the Bronze Age," in E. H. Cline and D. Harris-Cline, eds., *The Aegean and the Orient in the Second Millennium*, Aegaeum 18 (Liège, 1998), 229–254, esp. 240; Lapatin (supra n. 30), 34–35. The clothing worn by the smallest of the three figures marks her unambiguously as female. For the rarity of individual Minoan female figures of ivory in the round, see also Lapatin (supra n. 30), 28.

39 Crete, Archaeological Museum of Herak-leion, 15074 (Festos Inv. No. 2632): D. Levi, "La tomba a tholos di Kamilari presso à Festos," *Annuario* 39–40 (1961–1962), 7–148, esp. 123–139, figs. 170a–f; Hood (supra n. 3), 105 fig. 88; G. Rethemiotakis, *Anthropomorphike peloplastike sten Krete apo te Neoanaktorike eos ten Ypominoïke periodo*, Bibliotheke tes en Athenais Archaiologikes Etaireias 174 (Athens, 1998), 36 no. 120, 144–145; D. Lefèvre-Novaro, "Un nouvel examen des modèles réduits trouvés dans la grande tombe de Kamilari," in Laffineur and Hägg (infra n. 46), 89–98, esp. 95–96, pl. XXVId. The date of the context in which these models were found has now been established as early LM IB: D. Novaro, "I modellini fittili dalla tomba di Kamilari: Il problema cronologico," in V. La Rosa, D. Palermo, and L. Vagnetti, eds., *Epi ponton plazomenoi: Simposio italiano di Studi Egei dedicato a Luigi Bernabò Brea e Giovanni Pugliese Carratelli* (Rome, 1999), 151–160; Rethemiotakis, op. cit., 59. For comparanda from the immediate area of Phaistos for the hourglass-shaped altars or tables, see V. La Rosa, "Preghiere fatte in casa? Altari mobili da un edificio di H. Triada," and L. A. Hitchcock, "Of Bar Stools and Beehives: An Interpretive Dialog About a Minoan Store Room," in A. Karetsou, ed., *Pepragmena H' Diethnous Kretologikou Synedriou* (Herakleion, 2000), A2, 137–153 and A1, 593–606, respectively.

40 The exposure of the genitalia, hence the nudity, of one if not both of the smaller males is clearly visible in the views illus-trated by Levi (supra n. 39), figs. 170c–d, f.

41 Exclusivity of depictions of male nude children: P. Rehak, "The Construction of Gender in Late Bronze Age Aegean Art: A Prolegomenon," in M. Casey et al., eds., *Redefining Archaeology: Feminist Perspectives* (Sydney, 1999), 191–198, esp. 192–193; L. Morgan, "Form and Meaning in Figurative Painting," in Sherratt (supra n. 37), vol. 2, 925–944, esp. 934, 937–940.

42 Quotation: Hood (supra n. 3), 105. An alternative interpretation is the serving of food to adult males in a Minoan *andreion* by young male attendants (*parastathentes*), as proposed by R. B. Koehl ("The Villas at Ayia Triada and Nirou Chani and the Origin of the Cretan *andreion*," in R. Hägg, ed., *The Function of the "Minoan Villa"* [Stockholm, 1997], 137–147), to whom I am grateful for this suggestion.

43 Crete, Archaeological Museum of Herakleion, 15072 (Festos Inv. No. 2633): Levi (supra n. 39), 145–147, figs. 177a-c; Rethemiotakis (supra n. 39), 36 no. 118, 145–146; Lefèvre-Novaro (supra n. 39), 92–95, pl. XXVIc. In Mycenaean cult depictions—for example, the wall painting from the so-called Room with the Fresco at Mycenae depicting large-scale female divinities rendered in outline and miniature, seemingly male worshipers portrayed in silhouette (S. A. Immerwahr, *Aegean Painting in the Bronze Age* [University Park, Pa., 1990], 191 My No. 6, pls. 59–61; R. Rehak, "Tradition and Innovation in the Fresco from Room 31 in the 'Cult Center' at Mycenae," in Laffineur and Crowley [supra n. 21], 39–62; Rehak [supra n. 41], 195)—differences in scale distinguish divine from mortal figures. But this distinction, though often assumed, cannot be so readily applied to Minoan art. The larger scale of the "Mistress of Animals" relative to the young girl in the crocus-gathering scene on the north wall of Xeste 3's upper floor (C. Doumas, *The Wall Paintings of Thera* [Athens 1992], fig. 122) could be due entirely to the age distinction between a fully adult female and a "pubescent girl" (Doumas [infra n. 53], 973).

44 Hood (supra n. 3), 105: "the second [model from Kamilari] represents a woman squatting on the ground and kneading dough."

According to Lefèvre-Novaro (supra n. 39: 93; personal communication), the figure at the table exhibits male as well as female sexual attributes. The feature that she interprets as a penis, however, is so enormously exaggerated, to judge from Levi's illustrations (supra n. 39, fig. 177b, to left of figure's left leg; fig. 177c, to right of figure's right leg), that one wonders whether something else altogether may not have been intended by the artist. For example, might this feature be meant as a duplicate of the object that the figure appears to hold in her left hand? Note also that the original model in Novaro's view featured a fourth human figure, of which only traces of one hand and one foot survive in a second doorway located behind the large "bisexual" figure who dominates the surviving composition.

45 Crete, Archaeological Museum of Herakleion, 15073 (Festos Inv. No. 2634): Levi (supra n. 39), 139–145, figs. 174a–b; Hood (supra n. 3), 105; Rethemiotakis (supra n. 39), 36 no. 119, 147; Lefèvre-Novaro (supra n. 39), 90–92, pl. XXVIb.

46 Koehl (supra n. 33), 135; R. Koehl, "The 'Sacred Marriage' in Minoan Religion and Ritual," in R. Laffineur and R. Hägg, eds., *POTNIA: Deities and Religion in the Aegean Bronze Age*, Aegaeum 22 (Liège, 2001), 237–243, pls. LXXVII: b–d.

47 For a thorough reevaluation of the Kamilari figurines, see D. Novaro, "I modellini fittili dalla grande tomba circolare di Kamilari (Creta)" (thesis, Scuola Archeologica di Atene, 1996), a study that I have unfortunately not been able to consult. I am extremely grateful to Daniela Lefèvre-Novaro for taking the time to discuss these models with me in some detail on several different occasions during 2001–2002. My identification of certain figures in these models as children or adolescents does not seem to me to be incompatible with her interpretation of the scenes as depictions of rituals associated with rites of passage involving the dead. For the findspots of the models within the Kamilari burial complex, see Lefèvre-Novaro (supra n. 39), pl. XXVb.

48 P. M. Warren, *Minoan Stone Vases* (Cambridge, 1969), 174–181; Hood (supra n. 3), 143–147; P. Rehak, "The Ritual Destruction of Minoan Art?" *Archaeological*

News 19 (1994), 1–6; Koehl (supra n. 33), 137: "all sixty-two of the human figures preserved on the vases and fragments [of this class of object] are male."

49 Crete, Archaeological Museum of Herakleion, 341: Hood (supra n. 3), 143–145, fig. 137; Rühfel 1984a, 20–21, 313 n. 20, figs. 5a–b; Koehl (supra n. 36); Koehl (supra n. 33), 137–138.

50 Koehl (supra n. 33), 103, fig. 1F.

51 Harvester Vase: Hood (supra n. 3), 145–146, fig. 138; Rehak (supra n. 41), 194, fig. 4. Boxer Vase: Hood (supra n. 3), 146, fig. 139; Koehl (supra n. 33), 142.

52 *CMS* II, 3: 218 (Crete, Archaeological Museum of Herakleion, 148: steatite lentoid said to be from Mochos) = A. Evans, *The Palace of Minos*, vol. 2, part 1 (London, 1928), 341 fig. 194b; Rühfel 1984a, 26–28, 314 n. 56. *CMS* I: 159 (Athens, National Archaeological Museum, 6235: agate lentoid from Mycenae) = Evans, op. cit., 341 fig. 194c; Rühfel 1984a, 26–28, 314 n. 56. *CMS* II, 6: 1 (Crete, Archaeological Museum of Herakleion, sealings 505–506 from Ayia Triadha, impressed by an elliptical metal bezel) = Evans, op. cit., 341 fig. 194a; Rühfel 1984a, 26–28 fig. 9, 314 n. 55. The second lentoid, though found at Mycenae, may well be an originally Minoan rather than Mycenaean product.

53 For breast size and hairstyle in addition to stature as the principal vehicles for communicating age differentiation among females in both Late Cycladic I and Minoan Neopalatial art, see E. Davis, "Youth and Age in the Thera Frescoes," *AJA* 90 (1986), 399–406; Rehak (supra n. 41), 192–194; Morgan (supra n. 41), 937–938; C. Doumas, "Age and Gender in the Theran Wall Paintings," in Sherratt (supra n. 37), vol. 2, 971–980, esp. 972–973.

54 Rühfel 1984a, 28.

55 Athens, National Archaeological Museum, 992: *CMS* I: 17; Evans (supra n. 52), 341 fig. 194e; Hood (supra n. 3), 225–227, fig. 228d; Rühfel 1984a, 26–28 fig. 8, 314 n. 51; K. Demakopoulou, ed., *The Aidonia Treasure: Seals and Jewellery of the Aegean Late Bronze Age* (Athens, 1996), 93 no. 15.

56 According to Hood, however, "the maker . . . may have been a native of the mainland rather than a Cretan: the heavy style of the engraving, and the lack of feeling for composition, while not typical of Cretan signets, are reminiscent of the clumsy designs of the shaft grave gold." (supra n. 3: 227).

57 The best-known depictions of bull-jumping are the panels of the so-called Taureador fresco: Evans (supra n. 30), 209–218; A. Evans, M. Cameron, and S. Hood, *Knossos Fresco Atlas* (Farnborough, England, 1967), pls. A, figs. 1–2; IX–X; M. A. S. Cameron, "The 'Palatial' Thematic System in the Knossos Murals: Last Notes on Knossos Frescoes," in R. Hägg and N. Marinatos, eds., *The Function of the Minoan Palaces* (Stockholm, 1987), 321–327, esp. fig. 12; Immerwahr (supra n. 43), 90–92, 175 Kn No. 23. Actually of Monopalatial (i.e., Late Minoan II–IIIA1, ca. 1450–1380 B.C.E.) rather than Neopalatial date, this particular painting had numerous thematic antecedents of Neopalatial date that have simply not survived. On artistic depictions of bull-jumping, see J. G. Younger, "Bronze Age Representations of Aegean Bull-leaping," *AJA* 80 (1976), 125–137; J. G. Younger, "A New Look at Aegean Bull-leaping," *Muse* 17 (1983), 72–80; J. G. Younger, "Bronze Age Representations of Aegean Bull-Games, III," in Laffineur and Niemeier (supra n. 37), 507–545; Marinatos 1989, 1994 (infra n. 59); Morgan (infra n. 59); M. C. Shaw, "Bull Leaping Frescoes at Knossos and Their Influence on the El Dab'a Murals," *Ägypten und Levante* 5 (1995), 91–120; M. C. Shaw, "The Bull-Leaping Fresco from Below the Ramp House at Mycenae: A Study in Iconography and Artistic Transmission," *BSA* 91 (1996), 167–190. On bull-leaping as particularly Knossian, see also B. P. and E. Hallager, "The Knossian Bull: Political Propaganda in Neopalatial Crete?" in Laffineur and Niemeier (supra n. 37), 547–556.

58 Evans (supra n. 30), 29–37, 46–88; Evans, Cameron, and Hood (supra n. 57), pl. B, figs. 1a–b; pls. II, IIA, IV, figs. 1–3; E. N. Davis, "The Knossos Miniature Frescoes and the Function of the Central Courts," in Hägg and Marinatos (supra n. 57), 157–161; Immerwahr (supra n. 43), 63–66, 173–174 Kn Nos. 15–18.

59 For color conventions in the rendering of gender in Aegean painting, see most recently Rehak (supra n. 41), 192, and Morgan (supra n. 41), 939–940 and n. 14. The principal skeptics about the rigid interpretation of white as an indicator of female gender have been S. Damiani Indelicato ("Were Cretan Girls Playing at Bull-leaping?" *Cretan Studies* 1 [1988], 40–47), N. Marinatos ("The Bull as Adversary: Some Observations on Bull-Hunting and Bull-Leaping," in *Aphieroma ston Styliano Alexiou*, Ariadne 5 [Herakleion, 1989], 23–32; "The Export Significance of Minoan Bull Hunting and Bull Leaping Scenes," *Ägypten und Levante* 4 [1994], 89–93), and L. Morgan ("Minoan Painting and Egypt: The Case of Tell el-Dab'a," in W. V. Davies and L. Schofield, eds., *Egypt, the Aegean, and the Levant: Interconnections in the Second Millennium B.C.* [London, 1995], 29–53, esp. 42–43; [supra n. 41], 940–941).

60 W. G. Arnott, "Bull-leaping as Initiation," *Liverpool Classical Monthly* 18, no. 8 (1993), 114–116; W. Decker, *Sport in der griechischen Antike: Vom minoischen Wettkampf bis zu den olympischen Spielen* (Munich, 1995); see also the titles cited supra n. 57.

61 Several different developmental stages of female breast appear to be indicated in this fresco (all references are to Evans [supra n. 30]): simple dots: 51 fig. 29: A2–4, pl. XVIIA; 52 fig. 30: B4, pl. XVIIB; 57 fig. 34: E3; small pendent arcs: 53 fig. 31: C9, pl. XVIIC; 55 fig. 32: D1,5; small circles: 53 fig. 31: C6, pl. XVIIC; large pendent arcs with distinct pendent nipples: 52 fig. 30: B2, pl. XVIIB.

62 Davis (supra n. 58), 160.

63 Evans (supra n. 30), 396, pl. XXVa; Evans, Cameron, and Hood (supra n. 57), pl. A, fig. 4; Immerwahr (supra n. 43), 174 Kn No. 19.

64 For color images, see especially Doumas (supra n. 43). For detailed iconographic analyses of the complex series of paintings from the West House, see L. Morgan, *The Miniature Wall Paintings of Thera: A Study in Aegean Culture and Iconography* (Cambridge, 1988), and C. A. Televantou, *Akroteri Theras: Oi toichographies tes dytikes Oikias*, Bibliotheke tes en Athenais Archaiologikes Etaireias 143 (Athens, 1994). For the three-volume proceedings of the most recent major conference devoted to these Theran paintings, see Sherratt (supra n. 37).

65 Studies published within the past few years based principally or exclusively on the Thera frescoes and focusing on topics involving children, adolescents, and the social dynamics of maturation include Doumas (supra n. 53); I. Papageorgiou, "On the Rites de Passage in Late Cycladic Akrotiri, Thera: A Reconsideration of the Frescoes of the 'Priestess' and the 'Fishermen' of the West House," in Sherratt (supra n. 37), vol. 2, 958–969; R. Laffineur, "Dress, Hairstyle, and Jewellery in the Thera Wall Paintings," in Sherratt, op. cit., vol. 2, 890–906; Morgan (supra n. 41); P. Rehak, "The Aegean Landscape and the Body: A New Interpretation of the Thera Frescoes," in N. L. Wicker and B. Arnold, eds., *From the Ground Up: Beyond Gender Theory in Archaeology*, BAR-IS 812 (Oxford, 1999), 11–22; A. P. Chapin, "Maidenhood and Marriage: The Reproductive Lives of the Girls and Women from Xeste 3, Thera," *Aegean Archaeology* 4 (1997–2000), 7–25; Koehl (supra n. 33); P. Rehak, "Imag(in)ing a Woman's World in Bronze Age Greece: The Frescoes from Xeste 3 at Akrotiri, Thera," in N. S. Rabinowitz and L. Auanger, eds., *Among Women: From the Homosocial to the Homoerotic in the Ancient World* (Austin, 2002), 34–59.

66 Davis (supra n. 53); C. Doumas, "E xeste 3 kai oi kyanokephaloi sten techne tes Theras," in L. Kastrinaki, G. Orphanou, and N. Giannadakis, eds., *EILAPINE: Tomos timetikos yia ton Kathegete Nikolao Platona* (Herakleion, 1987), 151–159; Koehl (supra n. 36); J. Younger, "Bronze Age Representations of Aegean Jewelry," in Laffineur and Crowley (supra n. 21), 257–293, esp. 288–289; Morgan (supra n. 41), 937–940; Doumas (supra n. 53), esp. 977 table 1; Koehl (supra n. 46), 238–239, pl. LXXVII; Rehak 1999 (supra n. 65), 12.

67 Doumas (supra n. 53), 974.

68 Eye markings and double chins: Davis (supra n. 53); Morgan (supra n. 41), 938–939. Male stomach musculature: Doumas (supra n. 53), 972; Morgan (supra n. 41), 938. Rehak (supra n. 65 [1999: 13; 2002: 49–50]) interprets the blue eye markings, as well as the yellow ocher skin color

of some juvenile males (infra n. 70), as the result of a diet rich in vitamins A and B and carotenes, all derived from saffron consumption. The red streaking of some eyes, on the other hand, might indicate a vitamin A or riboflavin deficiency.

69 Doumas (supra n. 53), 974–975.

70 Doumas (supra n. 43), figs. 109, 112 (Xeste 3, Room 3b), 78, 80 (Room B1). For the view that this yellow ocher color is a "variation on the convention for indicating immaturity" and can hence be interpreted as signifying a status intermediate between either feminine and masculine or between pre- and post-initiatory male stages, see Morgan (supra n. 41), 939–940. See also supra n. 68.

71 Whether some of the running figures at the top of the miniature style frieze decorating the south wall of Room 5 in the West House are juveniles or adolescents is difficult to determine; the unambiguous boy standing behind his waving or saluting mother (?) on the roof of a house in Town 5 on the same wall does not appear to be doing anything in particular (Doumas [supra n. 43], fig. 38). Boxing boys: ibid., figs. 79–81. Boys carrying fish: ibid., figs. 18–23; Papageorgiou (supra n. 65), 964–966. Boys carrying metal vessels and garment: Doumas (supra n. 43), figs. 109, 111–113, 115.

72 Girl carrying metal brazier: Doumas (supra n. 43), figs. 24–25; Papageorgiou (supra n. 65), 959–964. Nubile young woman carrying necklace: Doumas (supra n. 43), figs. 100–102. Crocus-pickers of various ages: ibid., figs. 116–124, 129–130. Seated "wounded girl": ibid., figs. 100, 105–106. Exactly what the young girl to the right of the "wounded girl" is doing, aside from looking away from the nubile young woman in pain and so toward the bloody "horns of consecration" on the adjacent wall, is uncertain: ibid., figs. 100, 107–108; for suggestions as to how this scene should be interpreted, see Rehak (supra n. 65) and Koehl (supra n. 46). For the assignment of specific age grades to particular tasks, see A. Sarpaki, "Plants Chosen to Be Depicted on Theran Wall Paintings: Tentative Interpretations," in Sherratt (supra n. 37), vol. 2, 657–680, esp. 661–662.

73 The boxing boys from Room B1 are shown to be young by their swaybacked torsos and protruding bellies (supra n. 70). The youngest boy from Room 3b in Xeste 3 likewise has a protruding belly that contrasts markedly with the flatter stomach profiles of the two older boys in the paintings from this room (Doumas [supra n. 43], figs. 109, 112 vs. 111, 113, 115).

74 By far the most extensive survey of the evidence for Mycenaean children to date is B. A. Olsen, "Women, Children, and the Family in the Late Aegean Bronze Age: Differences in Minoan and Mycenaean Constructions of Gender," World Archaeology 29 (1998), 380–392. Paul Rehak has kindly drawn my attention to two possible girls in Mycenaean fresco art: first, a white-skinned figure with a large red ear from Pylos (M. Lang, The Palace of Nestor at Pylos in Western Messenia, vol. 2, The Frescoes [Princeton, 1969], 76 33Hsw, pls. 24, C) who is in some ways reminiscent of the so-called Young Priestess from the West House at Akrotiri (here fig. 22c; L. Kontorli-Papadopoulou, Aegean Frescoes of Religious Character [Göteborg, 1996], 57 no. 57, color plate XVI); second, a small female figure dressed in a red-spotted yellow robe from Mycenae, who is held in a large white hand, perhaps that of a goddess (I. Kritseli-Providi, Toichographies tou threskeftikou kentrou ton Mykinon [Athens, 1982], 41–42, B-2, pl. 6a; Kontorli-Papadopoulou, op. cit., 62 no. 71, pl. 93). In Rehak's view, the backward tilt of the second figure's head suggests that it represents a live figure rather than simply a doll or statuette.

75 E. French, "The Development of Mycenaean Terracotta Figurines," BSA 66 (1971), 101–187, esp. 142–144; K. Pilafidis-Williams, The Sanctuary of Aphaia on Aigina in the Bronze Age (Munich, 1998), 30–35, 171–181; Olsen (supra n. 74), 384–388.

76 Seated Φ's: Pilafidis-Williams (supra n. 75), 175–176 no. 22, 179 no. 71; Olsen (supra n. 74), 387. Two-baby kourotrophoi: Pilafidis-Williams, op. cit., 173 nos. 10, 12; Olsen, op. cit., 386; French (supra n. 75), 143–144; Demakopoulou (supra n. 16), 190–191 no. 165.

77 Pilafidis-Williams (supra n. 75), 34 no. 168, pls. 2, 43. Olsen (supra n. 74: 386) appears to have mistaken this fragment as being supplied with two infants.

78 Early Cycladic marble threesome: supra n. 12. Mycenae ivory triad: N. Polychronakou-Sgouritsa, "Trimorpha mykenaïka eidola," AAA 19 (1986), 153–158; Pilafidis-Williams (supra n. 75), 35 no. 176, pls. 2, 43.

79 Pilafidis-Williams (supra n. 75), 135–137; Olsen (supra n. 74), 387–388.

80 The Early Cycladic marble group features two male figures supporting a female figure of roughly the same scale on their shoulders (supra n. 12). The poses of both child and adults in the ivory group differ altogether from those of the terracotta triads, thus leaving the two forms with only the three total figures and the female sex of the adults in common.

81 Aidonia "naturalistic" kourotrophos (Nemea, Archaeological Museum of Nemea, 489): Pilafidis-Williams (supra n. 75), 174 no. 16; Demakopoulou (supra n. 55), 45 no. 11; Olsen (supra n. 74), 386. Mavrospelio figurine (Crete, Archaeological Museum of Herakleion, 8345): E. J. Forsdyke, "The Mavro Spelio Cemetery at Knossos," BSA 28 (1926–1927), 243–298, esp. 290–291, pl. XXI; Rethemiotakis (supra n. 39), 27 no. 55, figs. 12, 97, pls. 14d, 15a–b.

82 Olsen (supra n. 74), 390.

83 J. N. Coldstream and G. L. Huxley, eds., Kythera: Excavations and Studies (London, 1972), 267 no. 3, pl. 86: 3; Olsen (supra n. 74), 386; French (supra n. 75), 143.

84 Positioning of baby's head on kourotrophoi: Pilafidis-Williams (supra n. 75), 30. A group of relatively small Φ-shaped figurines are sometimes claimed to represent children (ibid., 8–9, 12–13 nos. 44–46, pl. 32), but no compelling case for such an identification can be made without the discovery of one or more of these miniature Φ's in a telling context such as that provided by the Platia Magoula Zarkou Neolithic house model.

85 J. C. Billigmeier and J. A. Turner, "The Socio-Economic Roles of Women in Mycenaean Greece: A Brief Survey of Linear B Tablets," in H. Foley, ed., Reflections of Women in Antiquity (London, 1981), 1–18; J. C. Billigmeier, "Studies on the Family in the Aegean Bronze Age and in Homer," Trends in History 3 (1985), 9–18; S. Hiller, "Familienbeziehungen in den mykenischen Texten," in T. G. Palaima, C. W. Shelmerdine, and P. H. Ilievski, eds.,

Studia Mycenaea, Ziva Antika Monograph 7 (Skopje, Macedonia, 1989), 40–65; M.-L. B. Nosch, "Kinderarbeit in der mykenischen Palastzeit," in F. Blakolmer and H. D. Szemethy, eds., *Akten des 8. Österreichischen Archäologentages*, Wiener Forschungen zur Archäologie 4 (Vienna, 2001), 37–43.

86 Olsen (supra n. 74), 383–384. Hiller (supra n. 85: 40) draws attention to the fact that the Pylian boys to whom Olsen alludes are described either by the disyllabic sign group *ko-wo* or by the same sign group prefaced by the ideogram *VIR* (= MAN). These two ways of counting male subadults are usually interpreted as reflecting two different age grades. Whether these corresponded precisely to the two age grades recognized at Knossos with the adjectives *me-zo* (older) and *me-wi-jo* (younger) applied to both girls and boys is unknown.

87 Immerwahr (supra n. 43), 157–158 and n. 3, fig. 41e, pl. XXIII; K. Demakopoulou and D. Konsola, *Archaeological Museum of Thebes: Guide* (Athens, 1981), 83 nos. 1, 4, pl. 42, lower; W. Cavanagh and C. Mee, "Mourning Before and After the Dark Age," in C. Morris, ed., *KLADOS: Essays in Honour of J. N. Coldstream*, BICS Supplement 63 (London, 1995), 45–61, esp. figs. 4, 7. If both adults are female, they may represent the same pairing of women portrayed in the terracotta three-bodied kourotrophoi surveyed above. The small figure on a third larnax from Tanagra may depict a statuette serving as a divine image, or even the soul of the deceased, rather than a child: Cavanagh and Mee, op. cit., 46–47, fig. 10; Hiller (infra n. 89), 46 and n. 4, pl. 5: 2.

88 C. Schoinas, "Eikonistike parastase se ostraka kratera apo ten Ayia Triada Eleias," in E Periphereia tou Mykenaïkou Kosmou (Lamia, Greece, 1999), 257–262, esp. fig. 1. The krater, one of three found in the dromos of Chamber Tomb 5 (for a plan, see O. Vikatou, "To mykenaïko nekrotapheio tes Ayias Triadas, N. Eleias," in op. cit., 237–255, esp. fig. 3), has been interpreted by the excavators as part of the debris from a funeral meal celebrated at the time of the burial rather than as an element of the grave goods deposited in the tomb. Conceivably part of another funerary scene depicted on a LH IIIC krater is a fragment from Lefkandi

that preserves two pairs of legs rendered at quite different scales, the smaller possibly belonging to a male child: Vermeule and Karageorghis (supra n. 16), 137, 223 XI.66.

89 S. Hiller, "Kleine Leute-Grosse Tiere: Themen in der ägäischen Bildkunst der späten Bronze-und der frühen Eisenzeit," in Blakolmer and Szemethy (supra n. 85), 45–52, esp. 45–46. An amphoroid krater of LH IIIA2 date from Klavdhia on Cyprus (London, The British Museum, C342) illustrates the difficulties of identification clearly: on one side is a small, sexless figure held aloft in the arms of two large ones, a relatively unambiguous rendering of a young child being carried by its parents (ibid., pl. 5:1); on the other side, a diminutive human figure positioned between two chariot groups is unmistakably rendered as male, but does his small stature identify him as younger in age or just socially inferior (ibid., 46–47, pl. 5: 5; Vermeule and Karageorghis [supra n. 16], 30, 198 IV.18)?

90 K.-E. Sjöquist and P. Åström, *Knossos: Keepers and Kneaders*, SIMA Pocketbook 82 (Göteborg, 1991), 25–28, 30–33, fig. 30. I am grateful to T. G. Palaima for bringing this evidence to my attention.

91 Comparable in some respects to the find circumstances of the fifth-millennium B.C.E. model from Platia Magoula Zarkou is that of a building model, assorted figurines, and a collection of stone tools—fifty-seven objects in all—from a third-millennium (Chalcolithic) pit at Kissonerga on Cyprus: E. Peltenburg, ed., *Lemba Archaeological Project II, 2, A Ceremonial Area at Kissonerga*, SIMA 70, no. 3 (Göteborg, 1991). This complex assemblage has been persuasively interpreted as a "functional set of equipment used in connection with real childbirths": E. Beausang, "Childbirth in Prehistory: An Introduction," *EJA* 3, no. 1 (2000), 69–87, esp. 79–82. Other prehistoric Cypriot building models—for example, the well-known "sanctuary" from Vounous illustrated by Levi (supra n. 39), figs. 173a–b—also feature probable children in complex multi-figural compositions that may have been the ultimate inspirations for the Late Minoan I models from Kamilari.

92 This conclusion is also the thrust of the article on Mycenaean children by Olsen (supra n. 74).

Lesley A. Beaumont

The Changing Face of Childhood

"Pictures of children are at once the most common,
the most sacred, and the most controversial images of our
time." These words by Anne Higonnet reflect the special
place claimed by children and childhood in today's Western
society.[1] While, for example, advertising companies exploit
the positive and familiar image of the child in order to market
their clients' products, and while Christmas cards annually
depict Christ in appealing infant form, by contrast pictures
of child soldiers in the Third World have the power to shock
and disturb us. This is because in the modern Western mind
childhood is identified and idealized as, among other things,
a time of carefree and untarnished innocence: a period of
life with its own desirable qualities and characteristics and
its own special needs. And yet, as Higonnet points out, this
concept of "romantic childhood" can be traced back only as
far as the seventeenth century C.E., and its artistic representation only to the eighteenth.[2] Before that the child had been
perceived as a flawed and incomplete being and had been presented in art as a diminutive adult.

Such a fundamental change in the social and artistic
persona of the child over a recent and relatively short period
of historical time serves to illustrate the point that concepts of
childhood are culturally and temporally flexible. For while the
state of physical immaturity is undeniable and is biologically
determined, the notion of childhood itself is subjective and
culture specific and is determined rather by imposed social

59

established as a subject worthy of depiction in its own right. Ultimately the image of the child was imbued with emotional sentiment.

In this essay I shall trace these and other developments in the representation of the child in Greek art of the Archaic, Classical, and early Hellenistic periods. Governed as we are by the nature of the available archaeological evidence, we must rely heavily on Athenian artistic sources for the Archaic and Classical periods, while for the Hellenistic period much of our evidence is drawn from outside Athens. Furthermore, though limitations of space do not permit a full consideration of regional variation, it must be stressed that particularly for the earlier parts of the period under study our Athenocentric bias presents a misleadingly homogenous picture of the child. We must remember that other regions of the Greek world developed their own artistic peculiarities of expression for children and childhood.

With the exception of the modern science of photography, which has the singular distinction of precisely recording a moment in time, representational art is mediated by human perception of the subject depicted. Thus the changes that occurred over time in the presentation of the child in ancient Greek art can inform us not only about developments in artistic style and draftsmanship but also about shifts in the social status and perception of children and childhood. I attempt, therefore, to locate the iconographic changes within the wider sociological and historical framework of the periods under study in order to venture some explanation for the developing concept of childhood and its expression in art. Such an approach, however, mandates great care in the interpretation of the images. We must, for example, be aware of the filters of gender, social class, and ethnicity that affected both the perception and the experience of childhood in Classical antiquity (as indeed they still do today), and we must familiarize ourselves with any artistic conventions employed in the service of these cultural variables. One such convention, expressive not only of childhood age but also of inferior social class, was the diminution of the figure in question: not only children but also adult slaves or servants were often depicted as miniaturized adults in the sixth and fifth centuries B.C.E.[3] Adolescent males of citizen status—that is, youths between the age of puberty and their eighteenth year—can furthermore be particularly hard to identify in art, because this transitional life stage was characterized by the possession of contradictory juvenile and mature traits and seems to have been open to correspondingly ambiguous iconographic expression that wavered between the figure of the child and that of the man.[4]

and legal criteria. It is revealing to compare this change in the social perception and artistic representation of the child over the past three hundred years or so with that undergone in the ancient Greek world between the Archaic and Hellenistic periods—that is, between roughly the sixth and third centuries B.C.E. In a remarkably similar transformation, in a culture removed from our own by time and space, the art of the period allows us to trace the iconographic development of a naturalistic infant and child body type from its earlier presentation as a miniature adult. During these centuries, from being a rare commodity in art children also came to be more frequently represented, and artists came to recognize the existence of a number of developmental phases within childhood. Furthermore, the child, initially of no interest to the artist, or at best of secondary interest, was also gradually

FIG. 1 Departure of Warriors: Farewell Scene, Attic black-figure belly amphora attributed to Group E, ca. 540 B.C.E. Universität Würzburg, Martin von Wagner Museum, 247

CHILDREN IN ARCHAIC GREEK ART

It is indicative of the lowly social position accorded young children in the sixth century B.C.E. that the exhibition *Coming of Age in Ancient Greece* contains so little material of the Archaic period. During this epoch children, particularly infants, were infrequently depicted and when accorded artistic expression tend to appear in the minor and relatively inexpensive arts of painted plaques and vases or terracotta figurines. Rarely were they included in the subject matter chosen for the costly medium of carved stone. Many of the surviving terracotta figurines that incorporate the figure of the child fall into the category of *kourotrophos*—that is, the group of infant or young child in the care of an adult woman.[5] Such a group can be seen in cat. 23, dated to about 700, where a seated female cradles a baby in her arms. Often kourotrophos figures are found dedicated as votive gifts in sanctuaries, particularly those of such divinities as Artemis, who played an important role in the lives of women and children, or of Eileithyia, goddess of childbirth.[6] Elsewhere the kourotrophos figurines appear as grave goods, buried alongside women or the young. Fewer in number are the delightful terracotta groups depicting vignettes from everyday life, which sometimes include child figures. One such is the terracotta showing a young girl learning to cook from an older seated woman, perhaps her mother (cat. 61; see p. 112). The girl peers attentively into a cooking pot set over a fire, clutching the woman's arm as the ingredients are added and mixed. These everyday scenes in clay are found particularly in the central Greek region of Boiotia in the years between about 510 and 470. It has been suggested that one function they may have served

was as children's toys, beloved playthings that were buried with their owner when he or she died.[7]

Mortal children were an uncommon subject in the medium of Attic black-figured vase-painting of the Archaic period. When they were portrayed it was in such particular restricted contexts as the departure of the warrior to battle or ritual scenes and processions. A belly amphora of about 540 by Group E in Würzburg provides one such example (fig. 1).[8] Here two women and an old man take their farewell of three armed figures; the diminutive naked male, closely associated with the woman in the center, can probably be identified as the young son of one of the warriors. Ritual settings in which children may appear include marriage processions and funerary ceremonies. On a plaque attributed to the Sappho Painter, now in the Louvre and dated to the end of the sixth century, three children, presumably of differing ages, to judge

FIG. 2 Woolworking Scene (?), late Corinthian alabastron, second half of the sixth century B.C.E. Berlin, Staatliche Museen, Antikensammlung, Preussischer Kulturbesitz

FIG. 3 Head of a Dead Baby Cradled in Its Mother's Hand, fragmentary Attic funerary stele, ca. 530 B.C.E. Athens, National Archaeological Museum, 4472

by their relative heights, take part in the mourning of the deceased (see Oakley, fig. 3, p. 165).[9] The two girls, the smaller of whom is named by an inscription as the dead youth's sister, join with the adult women of the family in wailing and tearing their hair in a demonstrative outpouring of grief, while the smallest of the children, a boy, stands at the foot of the bier, positioned symbolically midway between the women's domain that he inhabits while an infant and the more controlled sphere of the men gathered behind him, into whose world he will gradually be incorporated on reaching puberty. In these scenes the children are secondary or supporting figures, woven into the pictorial fabric of characteristic episodes in the life of the aristocratic Athenian adult male or, alternatively, playing their part in the ritual life of the Athenian *polis* or city state. In all cases they appear as miniaturized adult figures, no particular iconographic type having as yet been developed for the nonadult proportions of the infant and young child. It is, therefore, hard to identify any recognition on the part of the artists of the different stages of childhood, other than variation in the relative heights of the miniaturized figures. Female children appear even less frequently than male, and then most commonly in ritual funerary scenes of mourning, as on the Sappho Painter's plaque. This Archaic reticence to treat the subject of mortal childhood was, furthermore, far from being an Athenian peculiarity: at

Corinth, too, black-figure vase painters rarely depicted the figure of the child. One of the few Corinthian scenes representing what may be a mortal infant is found on an *alabastron*, or perfumed oil bottle, where a small boy stands astride the knee of an adult female, probably his mother (fig. 2).[10] As O. Hirsch-Dyczek has pointed out, the infant here replicates in miniature the figure of the *kouros*, or young adult male, an observation that implies much about Archaic Corinthian society's perception of the childhood state.[11]

In contrast to their reticent treatment of mortal childhood, vase painters of the Archaic period did show some enthusiasm for the subject of mythological childhood. Most popular were scenes of the birth of the goddess Athena and the infancy and education of the great Greek hero Achilles at the hands of the wise centaur Chiron.[12] An Attic black-figure amphora of about 550 presents us with an excellent example of a birth of Athena scene (cat. 5; see p. 116). The product of a sexual liaison between Zeus and the Titan female Metis, Athena suffered a most uncanonical birth from Zeus's head, after the god had swallowed his partner following a prediction that the child to be born of Metis would prove to be greater than its father. By incorporating mother and fetus into his own body, Zeus was able to usurp for himself the female power of gestation and childbirth. But Athena, of course, was no ordinary child and, as can be seen on the vase, emerged from her father's head as a fully developed, if miniaturized, adult figure, armed and ready to do battle as warrior goddess with anyone who should dare stand in her way.[13]

While a study of the representation of mortal children in the relatively inexpensive products of the coroplast and the vase painter provides us with a general picture of the insignificant social status of the child in the Archaic period, we must be cautious not to confuse this with a lack of love and concern for the individual youngster on the part of family members. The dedication of terracotta kourotrophos figurines in the sanctuaries of deities protective toward children bears witness to this, as probably does also an extraordinary little black-figure plaque painted about 560 and offered as a votive on the Athenian Acropolis (see Foley, fig. 7, p. 119).[14] In an apparently domestic setting, a seated woman bends attentively to her task while a naked white-painted child, a rare early representation of a female infant, is seated on the ground behind her. On exceptional occasions this concern for individual family offspring translated into permanent funerary monuments, erected for all to see in the quasi-public space of the cemetery. A unique, though sadly fragmentary, relief-carved stele of about 530 from Anavysos in Attica retains part of a group of woman with child, depicted with the utmost tenderness (fig. 3).[15] The head of the infant boy is cradled gently in the woman's left hand as she holds him before her. Though the paint that would have originally enlivened the features of both figures has disappeared, it seems that the baby's bulbous eye is closed in death, particularly since it bears none of the characteristic sharply carved delineation of upper and lower eyelids so evident in the woman's features. As no inscription accompanies the fragmentary relief, we cannot be certain in whose memory the stele was erected, though it is highly unlikely to have been in the child's honor alone. Could it perhaps have been commissioned by a distraught husband and father whose wife and infant son had died in the act of childbirth? Even so, in the absence of any other comparable pieces and the lack of Archaic funerary markers commemorating not only children but also, for the most part, women, this is a remarkable monument.

Also unusual for its time is a well-preserved gravestone of similar date, again from Attica, that presents the relief-sculpted figures of a male youth and a small girl (see Oakley, fig. 19, p. 179).[16] A fragmentary inscription on the stele base is usually restored to identify the two figures as Me[gakles] and his sister Philo, and to attribute the erection of this costly memorial to their father and perhaps also to their mother. Since the commemoration of aristocratic male youths who died before attaining full maturity was, as we shall see,

FIG. 4 Courtship Scene Between an Adult Man and Adolescent Boy, Attic black-figure kantharos, ca. 525 B.C.E. Boston, Museum of Fine Arts, Gift of E. P. and Fiske Warren, 08.292

nothing unusual during the Archaic period, the figure of the adolescent Megakles should not surprise us here. More notable, however, is the presence of the small female figure who, if relative size is a reliable indicator, would appear to be considerably younger than her brother. Because this is our only example of the representation of a girl child on extant Archaic Athenian funerary monuments, we might be forgiven for suspecting that if Megakles had not joined his sister in death, no such costly memorial would have been erected for the young girl alone.

Contrasting with the infrequent appearance of the infant and young child in Greek art of the sixth century is the popularity of the older, particularly male, youth. Not only were adolescent boys commonly chosen as subject matter for the decoration of black-figure pots, but the young male, as we have seen or soon shall, was also commemorated in costly stone on relief-carved grave stelai and further in the even more lavish form of the freestanding sculpted *kouros*. But whether executed in a humble or an expensive medium, the image portrayed was that of the idealized aristocratic youth. In vase painting he appears absorbed in characteristic upper-class pursuits, such as horse-riding or athletics, or is the focus of homosexual courtship by an older aristocratic male. An example of a courtship scene, a subject popular in Attic black-figure in the second half of the sixth century, can be seen on an Athenian *kantharos* of about 525, where a bearded man fondles the genitals of an adolescent boy, who replies by affectionately stroking his admirer's beard (fig. 4).[17] Though such pederastic behavior seems abhorrent to us today, in the context of ancient Athens the age difference between the two lovers was of paramount importance, for their homoerotic

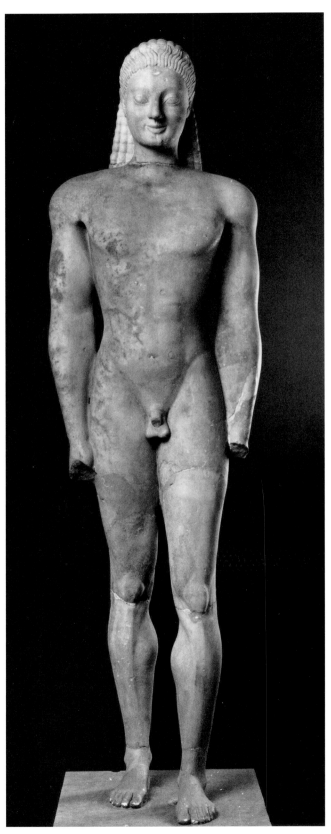

FIG. 5 Funerary kouros from Volomandra, Attic, ca. 560 B.C.E. Athens,
National Archaeological Museum, 1906

FIG. 6 Kore, votive offering from the Athenian Acropolis, ca. 535–530 B.C.E.
Athens, Acropolis Museum, 678

relationship was considered to provide not only pleasure for the adult male but also both a sexual initiation for the boy and, through the adult male lover, a role model for the aristocratic ideals and conduct to which the growing youth should aspire.

In the costly medium of freestanding stone sculpture the representation of the adolescent female of aristocratic lineage proved at Athens to be almost as popular in the Archaic period as that of the young male of noble descent. But while the statue of the *kouros*, or monumental stylized naked male depicted in all his youthful beauty, striding confidently forward into the world with left foot advanced, was both dedicated in the sanctuaries of the gods and used in the cemeteries to mark the graves of males, the sculpted figure of the *kore*, or demure, draped, and long-tressed maiden standing with her feet together, confined within her own space, was, while a frequent votive offering to the gods, rarely employed as a commemorative funerary marker (see figs. 5–6).[18] How then might we, in the sociohistorical context of sixth-century Athens, explain this gendered dichotomy in the artistic presentation of youth and, furthermore, account for the paucity of depictions of infancy and young childhood when contrasted with the penchant for representing adolescence in Greek art of the same period?[19]

During the Archaic period in Greece the wealthy, landowning aristocrats were preeminent in all things: political rule, state administration, religious control, and the commissioning of private artworks all lay within the hands of powerful noble families, which were represented in the public arena by the adult male family heads. Though the *oikos*, or family unit, was therefore of extreme importance to Archaic Greek society, the relative invisibility of young children in contemporary art can most likely be linked to this elite male sociopolitical power base, which encouraged little expression of its fiercely protected domestic affairs and which measured individual social significance against strict qualifications of gender, age, and class, thus temporarily relegating even its own immature male offspring to social irrelevance. Of fundamental importance was, of course, the continuation of the aristocratic bloodlines, down which the families' wealth and power passed, and indeed this seems to have found artistic expression in the figure of the adolescent youth about to assume a useful place in society. In the case of the male, the painted vases look to the future via their images of the grooming and education of the youth through appropriate aristocratic activities in preparation for his adult life in the public sphere, while the expensive funerary markers lament and commemorate the loss of a valuable son and, through him, honor his family. In the case of the pubescent

female of noble lineage, she was to be guarded within the safe and chaste confines of her paternal home and yet, if she was to honor her family with a desirable aristocratic alliance forged through marriage and was to fulfill her potential as a wife and mother, she must at the same time be given sufficient public "exposure" to attract a suitable husband. Whereas a lavish grave monument would therefore have been largely wasted in the event of her death before marriage, the dedication during her adolescence by her family of a magnificent stone kore statue in one of the major religious sanctuaries, which she herself would have been allowed to visit, probably sought to obtain the gods' favor in attaining the best marriage for her and, at least in part, served as a way of advertising her beauty and the promise of a rich dowry to other aristocratic families with unmarried sons.[20]

Children in Classical Greek Art

The Archaic period is considered by archaeologists and historians to have ended in 480 B.C.E. with the Persian invasion of Greece and the resulting destruction levels left behind, most notably on the Athenian Acropolis. This scholarly division of time into exact periods is, of course, an artificial one: though their world had been markedly changed by the Persian incursion into Greek territory, no Greek in 479 B.C.E. would have considered himself to be living in the new Classical period, as opposed to the old Archaic. It is not surprising, then, that there is no sharp change visible in the iconography of the child in 480. Rather, a gradual metamorphosis can be traced in the artistic presentation of children and childhood, beginning in the closing years of the sixth century and continuing into the first half of the fifth. In this period the image of the infant and young child becomes more familiar, children are represented both with greater frequency and in a wider range of pictorial contexts, artists begin to recognize the existence of a number of developmental stages within childhood, and, though by no means yet common, the child may be treated as a subject worthy of representation in its own right.

In Attic red-figure vase painting one of the new scene types that makes the child the focus of pictorial attention is the schoolroom scene. Developed in the first decade of the fifth century and popular until about 450, schoolroom scenes show boys attending the private educational establishments of the *grammatistes*, or letter teacher, and *kitharistes*, or music master.[21] A fine red-figure cup decorated by the painter Douris about 480 provides us with an excellent example of boys at their lessons (cat. 44). Here, boys sitting or standing before their teachers variously recite passages of poetry from an open scroll, have written work corrected, learn to play the

a

b

CAT. 44 School Scenes, Attic red-figure kylix, signed by Douris, ca. 490–480 B.C.E. Berlin, Staatliche Museen, Antikensammlung

lyre, or sing to the accompaniment of a double flute. On both sides of the cup, sitting a little apart from the lesson but watching attentively, is the mature bearded figure of the *pai-dagogos*, the family servant who chaperoned the young boy to school. Within the cup a further painted scene depicts an athlete loosing his sandal, symbolizing the third, physical, branch of traditional Athenian education.[22] These school scenes are not, of course, our first artistic reference to child-hood education; we have already noted earlier, black-figure representations of the boy Achilles in the care of his wise tutor, the centaur Chiron. However, the significance of the red-figure images lies both in their focus on the education of mortal children and in the emphasis they place on literacy as well as music, poetry, and athletics. By contrast, while Chiron versed his pupil in music, hunting, medicine, and moral discipline, no ancient literary or artistic reference is ever made to Achilles learning his letters from the centaur. Might we, then, shed some light on this apparent shift in the type of education and student witnessed by Athenian art in the opening years of the fifth century B.C.E. by casting a glance in the direction of contemporary sociopolitical change?

In 510 the old system of aristocratic tyrant rule collapsed at Athens with the exile of the governing Peisistratid family. Now in the closing years of the sixth century, Kleisthenes, a member of the rival noble Alkmaeonid family, came to pre-eminence. But instead of establishing himself at the head of a political chain of aristocratic power and privilege, he took the extraordinary step of setting Athens on the path to democ-racy by introducing measures that extended the right to citi-zenship across a greater section of the Athenian populace and that spread the power of government across the Athenian citizenry. All male citizens were enfranchised members of the decision-making *Ekklesia*, or citizen assembly, and all were eligible to serve on the *Boule*, or executive state council. The ability to read and write thus became of importance to a much wider cross-section of Athenian society than heretofore. It therefore seems likely that the artistic popularity of school-room scenes in the first half of the fifth century indicates that an increasing number of Athenian citizen families were investing in formal education for their sons. Since at this time no state education was provided, sending a child to a private grammatistes would have come at a cost, but one that was probably favorably weighed against the importance of literacy skills if the family's son, or sons, were to play their full part in the future civic and political life of Athens. Probably, too, the great number of images we have from the same period of boys being tutored by the kitharistes and the *paidotribes*, or athletics trainer, reflect the family's desire to give its son(s) the kind of education ideally suited to the model future citi-

FIG. 7 A Glimpse Inside the Athenian Household: A Private Moment Between Mother and Baby, Attic red-figure lekythos, attributed to the Manner of the Pistoxenos Painter, ca. 470 B.C.E. Oxford, The University of Oxford, Ashmolean Museum, V 320

FIGS. 8a, b (facing page)   Farewell Scene, Attic red-figure amphora of Panatheniac shape, attributed to the Boreas Painter, ca. 460–450 B.C.E. London, The British Museum, E282

zen: a strong body was not only aesthetically pleasing and the outward manifestation of a disciplined and ordered mind but would also be necessary to fulfill the state's requirement that the citizen serve as a *hoplite*, or foot soldier, in times of military need. Musical skills and familiarity with the works of the great poets, meanwhile, would equip the individual for participation in the adult social ritual of the *symposion*, or male dinner and drinking party.

Another of the new scene types that appears in Attic red-figure early in the second quarter of the fifth century presents us with the previously sparsely represented figure of the infant or young child, now depicted in a domestic context with its mother and sometimes a nurse. One such early example is found on a *lekythos*, or oil bottle, painted about 470 in the Manner of the Pistoxenos Painter (fig. 7).[23] The domestic setting is indicated by the cushioned stool and the mirror hanging on the wall, and the viewer is afforded a glimpse inside the world of the private Athenian household. The single iconographic focus on this vase, and others like it, is the group of the woman holding the naked infant in her arms. It is they who are the chosen subject matter and together reflect a newfound artistic and social significance. Even when they are included in traditional departure-of-warrior scenes, iconographic changes nonetheless indicate their newly enhanced status. Take, for example, the images that decorate a red-figure amphora of about 460–450 attributed to the Boreas Painter.[24] On one side stands the lone figure of the armed warrior, resplendent in his military finery (fig. 8a). On the other side is painted his wife and infant son, still a babe in arms, gesturing their farewells to husband and father (fig. 8b). In contrast to earlier black-figure departure-of-warrior scenes, where wife and child serve as secondary artistic and symbolic props underscoring the warrior's military duty and honor, the Boreas Painter's red-figure amphora accords mother and baby iconographic space and focus equal to that of the departing hoplite, balancing the prospect of military glory with the sadness of farewell and its emphasis on the family fractured by war. No longer treated in art simply as bit players in the life and concerns of the male citizen, wife and child have now begun to develop their own pictorial identity at the hands of Athenian artists. Can this change be traced back to the kinds of sociopolitical factors that we previously proposed in the context of the contemporary penchant for depicting older children in school scenes—namely, the emergence of Athenian democracy?

Under Kleisthenes' democratic reforms the criteria for claiming Athenian citizenship had been simplified. The old political system, which aimed to protect aristocratic privilege and power, had demanded that a citizen not only be able to demonstrate his legitimate membership in an identifiable oikos and an Athenian tribe but that he should also demonstrably belong to complex kinship groups. Because these kinship groups rested essentially on alliances between aristocratic oikoi, citizenship and associated political rights had remained confined largely to the noble classes. Kleisthenes was successful in undermining this exclusive aristocratic power base by extending the entitlement of citizenship to a wider cross-section of the Athenian male population. Citizenship was now determined by membership in an oikos, a tribe, and a *deme*, or local parish, registration in this geographical administrative district effectively replacing the old kinship criterion. Such a fundamental reform, as its political and social ramifications took effect, must have infused the oikos with a new meaning and status for much of the Athenian population and, by dispelling the tyranny of the kinship system, must have inspired a new pride in the family unit. Could this then help to explain the appearance of domestic scenes in Athenian vase painting? For women and children of citizen families, though without doubt still regarded as inferior to the adult male in all ways, nonetheless must now have gained newfound social status as representatives of the family unit underpinning the polis.

In tracing the development of the iconography of the child from the Archaic to the Classical periods, furthermore, it is important to note that while children, including infants, become generally more familiar figures in Greek art, the representation of childhood and adolescence is, by contrast, at least in the period between about 490 and 440, virtually absent from the expensive medium of carved stone. Once the series of costly sculpted funerary reliefs and freestanding funerary and votive kouroi and korai statues comes to an end in the opening years of the fifth century, the image of Athenian youth is transmitted to us largely through vase painting. This shift to a relatively cheap and easily obtainable medium appears to confirm that the commercial market for pictures of adolescence and childhood was now being generated by popular, rather than aristocratic, taste resulting from a socially wider based and economically less affluent clientele than heretofore.[25]

The first half of the fifth century thus saw significant changes in the artistic presentation and social status of the child at Athens. It was, moreover, a period in which the representation of mythological childhood achieved its greatest popularity.[26] Between about 490 and 440 Dionysos, Erichthonios, Herakles, Perseus, Astyanax, and Ganymede, among others, all appear as children in Athenian vase painting and, to a lesser degree, in monumental Greek sculpture.[27] A red-figure *hydria*, or water jar, decorated about 460–450 and attributed to the Nausicaa Painter, depicts the infant Herakles and his brother Iphikles in their bed (cat. 10). As the offspring of Zeus and the mortal woman Alkmene, Herakles became the subject of the enmity of Zeus's jealous wife, Hera,

who sent snakes to kill him while he was still a baby. The Nausicaa Painter shows Herakles doing battle with the serpents while his terrified brother, by contrast, holds out his arms to a fleeing woman, probably Alkmene. To the left Alkmene's husband, the mortal Amphitryon, runs up with drawn sword to rescue the children while Athena, Herakles' lifelong supporter, stands behind the bed lending divine assistance.

The theme of the endangered child is portrayed many times in Greek art and myth. Almost all divine infants and many of the child heroes are mortally threatened by danger, and it is their reaction to, or salvation from, this threat that reveals their special nature as "wonder children." In those cases, by contrast, where the imperiled mythological child meets with grievous physical violence and even death, we witness the Greek artist exploiting the helpless nature of the child as a means to arouse the pathos of his viewer.[28] This can be seen in those representations of the sack of Troy by the Greeks in which the shameful episode of the murder of the

CAT. 10 Herakles Strangling the Snakes, Attic red-figure kalpis, attributed to the Nausicaa Painter, ca. 460–450 B.C.E. New York, The Metropolitan Museum of Art, Fletcher Fund, 1925

FIG. 9 Death of Trojan Prince Astyanax,
Attic red-figure calyx-krater, attributed to the
Altamura Painter, ca. 465 B.C.E. Boston, Museum
of Fine Arts, William Francis Warden Fund,
59.178

defenseless youngest and oldest members of the Trojan household is depicted. On a red-figure calyx-krater decorated about 465 and attributed to the Altamura Painter, we see the Greek warrior Neoptolemos about to attack old King Priam, who has fled to an altar for refuge (fig. 9).[29] Not only does Neoptolemos show the old man no mercy, but he is about to brutally slaughter him by using the body of the king's grandson, Astyanax, as a human cudgel. The child, arms akimbo, hangs from the mighty warrior's raised right hand, suffering the last terrifying moments of his short life before he is smashed against the body of its grandfather. No ancient viewer could have looked at the image on this pot without pity or without remembering the dire consequences that the terrible and unholy nature of this action would engender for the Greeks as they sought to return home from Troy.

In comparing the figures of mortal, divine, and heroic children in Athenian vase painting, we note that while mortals and heroes may be represented either as babies or older children, divine offspring are almost always depicted as infants. This is probably not coincidental, for the ancient literary sources confirm that it was the gift of the gods, fed on nectar and ambrosia, to grow and develop at an abnormally rapid rate and pass quickly through childhood and its indignities.[30] Artistic experimentation with the representation of a wider range of infantile poses and behaviors in the third quarter of the fifth century, and subsequently with the development of a more naturalistic child figure type, corresponds to the decreasing frequency of mythological childhood scenes and an increase in the number of vases decorated with images of children in the context of everyday life. For while the depiction of suitably dignified conduct even in infancy, combined with the physical form of the miniaturized adult, had probably seemed appropriate for superhuman mythological progeny, the shift of subject emphasis to mortal children may well have inspired the artist more closely to observe the behavior and anatomy of youngsters around him. Not only cradled as babes in arms by mother or nurse, infants may, for example, start to crawl along the ground, as can be seen on a *pelike*, or storage jar, decorated in the Manner of the Washing Painter (cat. 37).[31] Often visible slung around the

CAT. 37 Baby Learning to Crawl or Walk, Attic red-figure pelike, attributed to the Manner of the Washing Painter, ca. 430–420 B.C.E. London, The British Museum

baby's torso is a string of protective amulets intended to ward off evil, a motif that appears in Athenian vase painting by at least the mid-fifth century and is common by the late fifth.

The representation of the infant or young child in a domestic context with its mother or nurse, first appearing in Attic red-figure early in the second quarter of the fifth century, became increasingly popular in the third quarter of the century. These images, such as that found on a hydria decorated by a follower of the vase painter Polygnotos about 440–430, sometimes also incorporate the male figure of husband and father (cat. 29, see p. 221). Here the mistress of the house, seated on a *klismos*, or high-backed chair, hands her naked infant son to a maidservant. Behind the seated woman stands her husband. His youthful appearance with newly sprouting beard and the wedding wreath hanging from the wall are probably meant to indicate that theirs is a new marriage and that the child is the first son of their union.[32] Indeed, because the hydria was associated with women's work, this vase may have been originally given as a wedding present. The loom positioned behind the maidservant, meanwhile, makes the household setting unmistakable. This

increase in the number of family scenes on painted vases can probably be linked with changes in the Athenian citizenship laws effected in 451/450. Seeking at this time to limit the growing number of Athenian citizens, Pericles successfully proposed that citizenship could be conferred only on those individuals born of two legally married Athenian citizen parents. Citizenship now thus rested not only on the civic status of the oikos as determined by the identity of the male family head but also on the wife and mother's own descent from a citizen oikos. A greater scrutiny was therefore brought to bear on female identity and on a child's inheritance of its "Athenian-ness" from mother as well as father. The painted image of mother and child must thus have assumed renewed significance, while the incorporation of the male in his roles of father and husband into the domestic arena of Athenian iconography served to underscore the bond that united mother, father, and child.

The second half of the fifth century also brought the emergence of the mortal infant and young child, as well as the revival of the adolescent mortal youth, in monumental Greek art of the sculpted and painted variety. They appear both in architectural sculpture, where their purpose would seem to be symbolic, and on relief-sculpted funerary stelai, where the images function on a far more personalized level to commemorate the death either of individual youngsters or of a close family relative. Though still the subject of much debate as to its correct interpretation, the Parthenon frieze, sculpted between 442 and 438, includes a number of children throughout its 160-meter length. Young boys, such as the seminaked boy positioned at the northwest corner of the frieze, assist in preparations for the procession, while the central section of the east frieze positioned above the entrance to the temple's cult chamber presents the viewer with three children of varying ages: the small figure of a semidraped boy and two apparently older clothed girls of varying heights (see Neils, fig. 24, p. 159).[33] Another architectural relief-sculpted frieze, though of a somewhat later date toward the end of the fifth century, from the Temple of Apollo Epikourios at Bassai in Arkadia, employs the figures of far younger children in an appeal to the viewer's emotional sensibilities in the dramatic setting of a raging battle between Greeks and fierce centaurs (fig. 10).[34] Here the children are no more than naked babes in arms, clinging in terror to their mothers, who are under vicious attack from the centaurs. The intense bond between mother and child is emphasized by the sculptor, who effectively conveys the absolute dependence of the infant on its mother and the mother's willingness to fight to the death to protect her offspring.

a

b

FIG. 10 Centaurs Attacking Lapith Women and Children, east frieze of the Temple of Apollo Epikourios at Bassai in Arkadia, end of the fifth century B.C.E. London, The British Museum.

One of the earliest surviving funerary stelai of the Classical period erected to commemorate a child's death comes not from Athens but from the Cycladic island of Paros. Dating to about 450 B.C.E., this poignant memorial depicts a little girl clasping her pet birds to her chest and gazing at them with mournfully downcast head (fig. 11).[35] Her long wavy hair falls over her shoulders, and she is clothed in a long *peplos* dress, which gapes a little at the side to reveal part of her buttock. At Athens children appear slightly later on grave stelai, about 435–430, and are subsequently represented with increasing frequency throughout the last quarter of the fifth century and into the fourth.[36] A great variety of childhood images can be found, in terms both of the child's age and of the pictorial composition, with the youngster variously presented alone as on the Paros stele or in the company of an adult female, usually identified as its mother, and perhaps a nurse or servant, and more unusually with an adult male, usually identified as its father. In the fourth century larger family groups incorporating children become more common. The funerary monuments thus either celebrate the child as an integral family member or, particularly in the case where one or more children appear without adults, commemorate the dead youngster as a significant being in its own right. Where funerary inscriptions survive, on most occasions only the child's name is given, with but a handful of memorials also identifying one or both parents. This suggests that by the late fifth and fourth centuries the status of the young child had risen sufficiently at Athens to justify the considerable outlay of expenditure on a memorial that apparently did little to overtly enhance the profile of the oikos to which the deceased belonged but that rather commemorated an individual who had as yet fulfilled no practical function within society. Instead the children's tombstones seem first and foremost to give expression to the very personal emotions of love and loss felt by those family members left behind.

Concurrent with the production of these expensive stone funerary markers at Athens in the second half of the fifth century, we find cheaper tomb offerings being manufactured in the form of the white-ground lekythos. This tall and slender ceramic vessel with high handle and elongated neck was placed either in or on top of the grave and, together with its contents of olive oil, served as a gift to the deceased. Many of the lekythoi are decorated with appropriate funerary iconography, and in the last thirty years of the fifth century children increasingly appear in these scenes. As on the stelai, the child's presence sometimes functions as an indicator of the familial context, but on other occasions the child itself is clearly identified as the dead individual. Such a scene, which places the dead child center stage, decorates a white-ground lekythos painted about 430–420 and attributed to the Painter of Munich 2335 (cat. 115, see pp. 162, 174). The setting is the banks of the Styx, the river that separates the world of the living from that of the dead. Charon the ferryman draws close in his boat and extends his hand to a naked toddler who turns to wave goodbye to his mother. With the other hand the little boy clutches his toy, a stick on wheels, used in antiquity as now to help an infant learn to walk.

In addition to the representation of childhood and youth in monumental sculpture of the second half of the fifth century, we learn from the ancient literary sources that by the late fifth or early fourth century mortal children had also become of interest to the great wall painters of the day. Though sadly none of these paintings, so famous in their time, has survived, Pliny tells us that the artist Parrhasios "painted a Thracian nurse with an infant in her arms . . . and two children in which the carefree simplicity of childhood is

FIG. 11 "Dove Stele," Young Girl with Pet Birds, Parian marble grave stele, ca. 450 B.C.E. New York, The Metropolitan Museum of Art, Fletcher Fund, 1927, 27.45

clearly displayed."[37] He also records that Zeuxis "painted a child carrying grapes, and when the birds flew to the fruit . . . he strode up to the picture in anger with it and said, 'I have painted the grapes better than the child, as if I had made a success of that as well, the birds would inevitably have been afraid of it.'"[38]

Given that children become a popular subject for representation at Athens in the late fifth century and not uncommonly demand attention as the central pictorial subject, both in the cheaper medium of ceramic iconography and in the costly medium of the carved stone grave stele, might we perhaps be able to locate some causative link in the sociopolitical circumstances of the period? In 431 the Peloponnesian War broke out between Athens and Sparta. Many Athenians who in times of peace had lived in the countryside, outside the safety of the walls of Athens, now crowded into the city. It is not, therefore, surprising in the resulting overpopulated, cramped, and unhealthy living conditions that a dreadful contagion developed and spread like wildfire through the Athenian populace. In 430/429, and again in 427/426, plague killed huge numbers of people, including the great leader Pericles. Though adult and child, rich and poor all fell victim to the fatal sickness, the plague perhaps most particularly affected the more vulnerable members of Athenian society, decimating the ranks of the very young and the very old and drastically increasing the already high infant mortality rate. Such sad and anguished times must have had a deep and long-lasting effect on the Athenian psyche, especially because even when the plague ultimately burned itself out, the ongoing war, which did not finally end until 404, would have meant that families continued to suffer a higher than usual rate of bereavement through the loss of fighting men. The death of a child, always a distinct possibility before the development of modern medicine and raised standards of hygiene, must therefore have taken on even greater poignancy than heretofore and prompted a search for ways in which to more tangibly express the profound private grief suffered by so many. It is hardly a coincidence, furthermore, that at this time we also witness the production of large numbers of *choes*, miniature clay jugs made specifically for children and decorated with images of chubby babies and toddlers crawling along the ground or playing with wheeled stick or toy cart.[39] A number of such choes are discussed in this volume (cats. 41, 54, 66, 75, 79, 86, 91, 92, 95–101). Given to children in their third year on the occasion of the Dionysiac spring festival of the Anthesteria, the choes contained a small amount of wine, providing the toddler with his first symbolic taste of the fermented fruit of the vine. Probably in part

providing the child with an early initiation into Athenian society, the choes ritual must also have served as a celebration of the fact that the infant had survived the earliest and most vulnerable stage of his life and now had a fighting chance of reaching adulthood. The clientele purchasing the little jugs would thus have comprised thankful yet fearful parents, seeking through participation in cult both to mark and offer gratitude to the divine for their offspring's survival and to solicit the gods' future protection for their children. Because many choes have been found in graves, however, it also seems that the chous could, like the white-ground lekythos, accompany the child to the underworld in the event of an early death.

It is particularly noticeable in the images on the choes that by the last quarter of the fifth century the representation of a distinct infant body type has become commonplace. This is also obvious in the forms of the babies pictured on the Bassai frieze (see fig. 10). No trace remains of the earlier miniaturized adult figure; rather, in marked contrast, the artists now effectively realize the nonadult proportions of the child's body, emphasizing the large head, short limbs, and chubby torso. This is not to say that earlier attempts had not occasionally been made, sometimes very successfully, to depict the child's anatomy in more naturalistic fashion. The grave stele from Paros that we have discussed, sculpted about 450 with the figure of a young girl, presents a very convincing childlike form, with the head size large in relation to the rest of the body and the wrists and hands chubby (see fig. 11).[40] Nonetheless, not until the late fifth century does artistic concession to a childlike body ideal become the norm. This, however, is preceded by the artists' recognition of the existence of a number of developmental phases within childhood.[41] Already from the second quarter of the fifth century four stages of childhood can be identified in Athenian vase painting. The first is infancy, which was probably considered to last until the child's third year (see figs. 7, 8; cats. 10, 20, 29, 37, 38); it is followed by a phase of young childhood that probably extended to the seventh year of life, when gender distinctions started to gain significance in the child's education and training. A good example of this young childhood stage is seen on a red-figure water jar decorated by an artist akin to the Clio Painter (fig. 12).[42] Here within the household setting, where the youngster of the wealthier Athenian citizen family would have spent most of his or her time, a little boy stands clutching hoop and stick. He gazes up at a finely dressed woman, probably a close relative such as grandmother or aunt, while a second seated woman, probably his mother, spins wool in front of a cloaked man with staff in hand, probably the husband and father. The young childhood

FIG. 12 Boy with Hoop and Stick in the Family Home, Attic red-figure kalpis, attributed to an artist close to the Clio Painter, third quarter of the fifth century B.C.E. Munich, Staatliche Antikensammlungen und Glyptothek, SL 476

stage was followed by a phase of older childhood lasting until the onset of puberty around the thirteenth year and commonly illustrated in the school scenes discussed earlier (cats. 44, 45; see pp. 66, 101–102).

The fourth and last stage of childhood was adolescence: for the male, the time between puberty and legal enfranchisement in his eighteenth year; for the female, the the time between puberty and marriage, which was usually around age fifteen and followed quickly by motherhood.[43] The adolescent girl may be shown in art as a little shorter in stature than her adult companions, clothed, with breasts indicated under her garments, and generally sporting long loose or braided hair rather than the adult female coiffure of bun or chignon.[44] The adolescent male proves more difficult to identify, since youths passing through this transitional life stage seem capable, in iconographical terms, of adopting the appearance of either a child or an adult male. Sometimes, however, we are helped in the recognition of male adolescence by the addition of downy "fluff" on the youth's face and the presence of pubic hair. The former can, for example, be seen on an Attic red-figure water jar decorated by the Kleophrades Painter, where four youths,

accompanied by their dogs, engage in animated conversation (fig. 13).[45]

This artistic observation of a number of developmental stages in childhood, together with the introduction of an iconographic body type for the infant and young child and of a wider range of infantile poses and behaviors, and also the focus on the child in art as a subject worthy of representation in its own right, all suggest a gradual shift in the social perception of children and childhood at Athens over the course of the fifth century. Childhood, it would seem, came to be regarded not only as being different from adulthood but also as possessing its own particular characteristics. Furthermore, though boys appear in both vase painting and sculpture with much greater frequency than girls, underscoring the social importance of male offspring for inheritance purposes and the continuity of the family line, young female children are by no means missing from fifth-century iconography, acquiring a much greater visibility than had previously been their lot in the Archaic period. While boys (cats. 122, 123; see pp. 181, 306) therefore are commemorated twice as many times as girls on grave stelai erected in honor of a single child, girls such as our little figure from Paros are nevertheless not an uncommon sight on late-fifth- and fourth-century tombstones (see fig. 11, cats. 124–126).[46] Likewise, though male infants outnumber female on the choes, girl children are not absent from the corpus.[47] Furthermore, from the sanctuaries of Artemis at Brauron and elsewhere comes a whole category of ceramic pots made specifically for young girls, some even decorated with their images.[48] Taking the shape of a small pedestaled bowl, these *krateriskoi* were dedicated to the goddess on the occasion of the Brauronia festival, which centered around girls between the ages of five and ten and which provided a prepuberty ritual. Usually hasty in manufacture and decoration in the black-figure technique (see Neils, fig. 11, p. 152), one larger krateriskos with finer red-figure work, though unprovenanced, almost certainly relates to the Brauronia.[49] On this vase, young girls, dressed in short tunics and supervised by adult women, can be seen participating in a ritual race within the sanctuary of Artemis, indicated by the presence of a palm tree and an altar. Though we do not know what proportion of Athenian girls took part in the Brauronia festival, it was clearly held to be an important event in the calendar of female childhood, foreshadowing the day when puberty would be reached and the girl would attain marriageable status.

CHILDREN IN LATE CLASSICAL AND HELLENISTIC GREEK ART

Once again, as with the transition from the Archaic to the Classical period, no sharp division exists between the Classical and Late Classical periods. Many of the changes and developments in the social perception and artistic representation of the child continue unbroken from the late fifth century into the fourth. However, the effects on Greek society and politics caused by the upheaval and turmoil of the protracted Peloponnesian War had profound ramifications for the Greek world, which in turn helped to shape the fourth-century view of childhood and its representation in art.[50] By 404 B.C.E. a whole generation of men knew little but war and fighting, and even after the Peloponnesian War had been concluded many of them continued in their role as warriors to earn their living as mercenaries, rejecting the old ideal of the citizen soldier fighting for the good of his own polis. This blow to the polis system was compounded by the social disruption, disorientation, and eventual disillusionment caused by the phenomenon of a long period of war, which undoubtedly contributed to the dilution of the rigid distinction between the male-populated public domain and the private female sphere of existence, which had hitherto circumscribed the

lives of women and children and had shaped social perceptions of these discrete groups. Now, by contrast, a growing emphasis came to rest on the individual within society. This, combined with an upsurge in the fourth century of prosperity among what we might call the "middle classes" of merchants, industrialists, and the like, led to an increased outlay of wealth on permanent monuments purchased by families in honor of their young offspring, both living and deceased.

While relief-sculpted grave stelai continued to be erected in memory of dead children, we now also witness the manufacture of costly freestanding stone statues of the infant and young child as votive offerings dedicated to the gods in their sanctuaries (see cat. 2).[51] As votives, these serve the same kind of function as the terracotta kourotrophos figurines that we noted already in the sixth and fifth centuries: gifts to the gods dedicated in their sanctuaries to secure divine protection for the child. In form, however, they differ markedly from the earlier clay kourotrophos groups: now not only rendered in expensive stone, the child is also depicted as a freestanding figure in its own right, no longer existing solely as an appendage to an adult female nurse. First appearing early in the fourth century, these statues are well established by about 330. Both male and female children are depicted, either as crawling or seated babies or as somewhat older standing figures, and while the boys are most commonly shown nude or seminude, the girls even at this tender age appear modestly draped in a high-belted long tunic. A good example of the type is illustrated in a marble statuette of a baby girl dating to about 340–330 (fig. 14).[52] Found in Athens, the figure, which measures some forty-one centimeters in height, realistically portrays the suppleness of the seated infant's body, with its legs characteristically disposed

FIG. 13 Four Adolescent Youths Engage in Animated Conversation, Attic red-figure kalpis, attributed to the Kleophrades Painter, first quarter of the fifth century B.C.E. Malibu, The J. Paul Getty Museum, 82.AE.7

in a fashion impossible for the adult anatomy. Her large
rounded face has chubby cheeks, and she is caught in the
moment when all her childish curiosity and attention is
captured by the little bird she holds in her right hand.
Although we cannot claim the sculpture to be a portrait likeness of an individual, specific child, it does, nevertheless, like
other fourth-century examples, express a significant degree
of feeling for the childhood condition and in this constitutes
a forerunner to the subsequent pathos-imbued Hellenistic
genre of child sculptures. The most notable single collection
of fourth-century stone votives of children comes from the
sanctuary of Artemis at Brauron, dedicated there to the
goddess who played a particularly important role in the
youngster's life from birth through adolescence.[53] Similar
statuettes have also been found in a number of other sanctuaries elsewhere across the Greek world, among which cults of
healing and medicine such as those of Asklepios and
Amphiaraos are represented. By about 330 the type was also
being produced in the cheaper medium of terracotta figurines

in the so-called Tanagra style, many of them dedicated in
sanctuaries where fertility cults were practiced.[54] Seated Girl
with Tambourine and Wreath (cat. 109) presents a fetching
example of this genre.

During the course of the fourth century the Greek city-
states came increasingly under the power and influence of the
Macedonian kings, first Philip II (ruled 359–336) and then
Alexander the Great (ruled 336–323). With the accession of
Alexander to the throne, furthermore, the Macedonian
empire was vastly extended, ultimately stretching as far east
as India. Though following Alexander's death this empire
fractured in the early third century into three (and later four)
major kingdoms, the Greek world had changed forever. The
effects of Greek culture now extended far beyond the borders
of the Greek city-states and, by the same token, foreign
cultural influence mingled in return with traditional Greek
tastes and style. The result provided fertile ground and inspiration for artists working in the early Hellenistic period of the
third century B.C.E. Though by no means turning their backs

on the Classical artistic heritage, they now incorporated it into a new exploration of and experimentation with areas such as portraiture and the representation of the minutiae of daily life.[55] Where the presentation of children in art is concerned, this departure produced several very important developments. On one hand, the image of children and childhood was now sentimentalized and idealized, both through the representation of cute childish behavior and physical attitudes and through the iconographic adoption of physically charming childish anatomy. These developments can, for example, be seen in the much copied group of a naked, chubby baby boy grappling playfully with a goose almost his own size (fig. 15).[56] On the other hand, realism also now enters Greek art and manifests itself in the child figure either through an increasing interest in portraiture, which can be seen in the extraordinarily fine head of a young boy (fig. 16), or through the near grotesque portrayal of the not always attractive state of infancy, well illustrated by the double-chinned baby holding his puppy (fig. 17).[57]

FIG. 16   Head of a Young Boy, Roman copy of a Hellenistic original of the third century B.C.E. Rome, Capitoline Museums

FIG. 15   Baby Boy Grapples with a Goose, Roman copy of a Hellenistic original of the late third century B.C.E. Munich, Staatliche Antikensammlungen und Glyptothek, 268

FIG. 17   Infant Boy with Puppy, Roman copy of an original Hellenistic sculpture group of the second century B.C.E. Rome, Capitoline Museums

FIG. 18 African Youth as Groom, Attic red-figure kylix, attributed to Onesimos, ca. 480 B.C.E. New York, The Metropolitan Museum of Art, Gift of Norbert Schimmel Trust, 1989, 1989.281.71

Servant and slave children, too, were now treated in monumental art with an eye both to portrait realism and to sympathetic expression of their lowly social status. Already identifiable in Archaic and Classical Greek vase painting as a social or ethnic type (fig. 18), and in late-fifth- and fourth-century funerary reliefs as adjuncts to the master or mistress for whom the gravestone had been erected, the individualism and pathos of the young servant or slave's social and ethnic status seem to be deliberately exploited by Hellenistic artists.[58] A good example is provided by a third-century limestone figure of a boy found in the necropolis of the Greek city of Taranto in southern Italy: sporting a short belted tunic

and the cropped hairstyle fitting to his lowly position, he possesses the flat nose and full lips suggestive of his foreign origins (fig. 19).[59] Probably originally part of a sculpture group erected in memory of his dead owner, he stands slightly stooped by his labors and inferior position and looks up toward his master in a gaze mournfully expressive of his total dependence on the beneficence and protection of a good proprietor.

The question of whether these changes in Hellenistic iconography were accompanied by a change in the social perception and status of the child, however, is far more difficult to answer.[60] Sentimentality, pathos, portraiture, realism,

FIG. 19 Boy Slave, limestone figure from the Taranto necropolis, third century B.C.E. Berlin, Staatliche Museen, Antikensammlung, Preussischer Kulturbesitz, SK 502

FIG. 20 Eros as a Sleeping Baby, Roman copy of a Hellenistic original of the third or second century B.C.E. New York, The Metropolitan Museum of Art, Rogers Fund, 1943, 43.11.4

and the grotesque are all confusingly contradictory character-istics of Hellenistic art in general, which had transformative effects on almost all categories of artistic subject matter. Divine Eros at this time, for example, undergoes a process of romanticization both conceptually and in terms of his presentation in art as a much younger and more playful boy figure than his Classical portrayal as a dangerous adolescent youth.[61] A bronze copy of an original Greek statue of the third or second century shows Eros as a harmless sleeping baby lying atop a rock (fig. 20).[62] The bow slung around his back reminds us, though, of the mischief that he can cause with his arrows when he is awake and prompts us to ask

whether Hellenistic society's view of children was perhaps similar to their view of Eros: angelic and mischievous, inno-cent and knowing, vulnerable and yet a potent bringer of joy and fulfillment, beings filled with contradictory qualities, attributes, capabilities, and weaknesses. There is probably no single answer to this musing, for so-called Hellenistic civilization covered a vast swath of geographical territory and a dizzying number of subcultures, each of which must have possessed its own view of children and childhood. We must perhaps then reconcile the many faces of childhood presented in Hellenistic art as an expression of this new multicultural milieu.

Notes

1   A. Higonnet, *Pictures of Innocence: The History and Crisis of Ideal Childhood* (London, 1998), 7. The author is grateful to Jenifer Neils for reading a draft of this essay and contributing many helpful comments and suggestions.

2   Higonnet (supra n. 1), 8–9. See also Ariès 1962.

3   Golden 1985, 91–104; N. Himmelmann, *Archäologisches zum Problem der griechischen Sklaverei* (Wiesbaden, Germany, 1971).

4   Beaumont 2000, 39–50.

5   T. H. Price, *Kourotrophos: Cults and Representations of the Greek Nursing Deities* (Leiden, 1978).

6   Pingiatoglou 1981.

7   Higgins 1986, 84–92.

8   Attic black-figure belly amphora by Group E, Würzburg University, Martin von Wagner Museum, 247, ABV 134.17, BAdd² 36.

9   Attic black-figure plaque attributed to the Sappho Painter, Paris, Musée du Louvre, MNB 905. Rühfel 1984a, fig. 8.

10 Late Corinthian alabastron, Berlin, Staatliche Museen, 4285. Hirsch-Dyczek 1983, fig. 3.

11 Hirsch-Dyczek 1983, 16.

12 On the iconography of the young Achilles brought to Chiron see Beck 1975, 9–12: *LIMC* I (1981), Achilleus I, 40–42; Rühfel 1984b, 59–74.

13 On the iconography of the birth of Athena see *LIMC* II (1984), Athena, 985–990. For a discussion of the absence of the representation of the Greek goddesses as true child figures in Archaic and Classical Greek art see Beaumont 1998, 71–95.

14 Attic black-figure plaque from the Athenian Acropolis, Athens National Archaeological Museum, B. Graef and E. Langlotz, *Die antiken Vasen von der Akropolis zu Athen* (1909), pl. 104, no. 2525.

15 Stele fragment, Athens, National Archaeological Museum, 4472, G. M. A. Richter, *The Archaic Gravestones of Attica* (London, 1961), no. 59, figs. 151–153.

16 Grave stele, New York, The Metropolitan Museum of Art, 11.185, and Berlin, Staatliche Museen, A7, C. W. Clairmont, *Gravestone and Epigram: Greek Memorials from the Archaic and Classical Period* (Mainz, 1970), 13–15, pl. 1.

17 Shapiro 1981. Attic black-figure kantharos, ca. 525 B.C.E., Boston, Museum of Fine Arts, 08.292, E. Vermeule, "Some Erotica in Boston," *AntK* 12 (1969), 10, no. 2, pl. 5.1–2 and text fig. 2.

18 Kouros from Volomandra, Attica, ca. 560 B.C.E., Athens, National Archaeological Museum, 1906, G. M. A. Richter, *Kouroi: A Study of the Greek Kouros from the Late Seventh to the Early Fifth Century BC*, 3d ed. (New York, 1988), 80–81, no. 63, figs. 208–216. Kore, Athens, Acropolis Museum, 678, ca. 535–530 B.C.E., G. M. A. Richter, *Korai: Archaic Greek Maidens* (London, 1968), no. 112 and figs. 345–348.

19 B. S. Ridgway has suggested that some at least of the votive korai statues from the Athenian Acropolis may represent the goddess Athena rather than mortal Athenian maidens. B. S. Ridgway, "Images of Athena on the Akropolis," in J. Neils, *Goddess and Polis: The Panathenaic Festival in Ancient Athens* (Hanover, N.H., 1992), 119–142; B. S. Ridgway, "Birds, Meniskoi, and Head Attributes in Archaic Greece," *AJA* 94 (1990), 583–612; B. S. Ridgway, "The Fashion of the Elgin Kore," *GettyMusJ* 12 (1984), 29–58; B. S. Ridgway, "The Peplos Kore, Akropolis 679," *JWalt* 36 (1977), 49–61.

20 I do not intend to suggest here that the kore statue presents an actual likeness of the girl on whose behalf it was dedicated, but rather that it served to contribute some tangible form of idealized identity to the aristocratic maiden, who most of the time would have been kept safely at home.

21 On schoolroom scenes, see Beck 1975, 14–28.

22 On scenes of physical education, see Beck 1975, 29–37.

23 Attic red-figure lekythos in the Manner of the Pistoxenos Painter, Oxford, Ashmolean Museum, 320, ARV² 864.13.

24 Attic red-figure amphora of Panathenaic shape, attributed to the Boreas Painter, London, The British Museum, E282, ARV² 538.39, BAdd² 255.

25 Although the disappearance of funerary kouroi and korai at Athens in the Late Archaic period can probably in large part be attributed to legislation that sought to curb expenditure on funerary monuments, this cannot completely account for the virtual disappearance of the adolescent youth from nonfunerary monumental sculpture. A few examples do survive from the Early Classical period, such as the relief-sculpted votive stele of the Sounion youth (Athens, National Archaeological Museum, 3344, A. Stewart, *Greek Sculpture: An Exploration* [New Haven, 1990], pl. 303), or the boy sitting on the ground in the east pediment of the Temple of Zeus at Olympia (figure E: ibid., pl. 268), but in the main the adolescent figure now finds expression in vase painting. A younger boy being abducted by a centaur is also depicted in the west pediment of the Temple of Zeus at Olympia (fig. F: B. Ashmole and N. Yalouris, *Olympia: The Sculptures of the Temple of Zeus* [London, 1967], pls. 124–126.)

26 Beaumont 1995.

27 Although enjoying their greatest artistic popularity between 490 and 440, the young Herakles and Ganymede had already appeared in Athenian art by the end of the sixth century B.C.E.: Beaumont 1995, 344 n. 31 and 346 n. 39. Representations of the little Astyanax are found in Attic black-figure vase painting from 560 onward, while an even earlier depiction of the child's death perhaps appears on a relief pithos of the seventh century from Mykonos: *LIMC* II (1984), Astyanax I, 931–935.

28 It is notable in Archaic and Classical Athenian art that it is only in scenes representing imperiled non-Attic mythological children that grievous violence against the child may be shown or that the child may be depicted as dead: Astyanax is Trojan and the murdered children Dryas and Itys are associated with Thrace (Beaumont 1995, 348 nn. 46, 47). The slaughter of a child thus seems to have been perceived by the Athenians as barbarian in character. The fact that Itys's mother, an Athenian herself, killed her son in reaction to her Thracian husband's infidelity may have been intended to serve as warning of the negative consequences of intermarriage with foreigners. Dryas was hacked to death by his Thracian father, Lykourgos. The slaughter of Astyanax seems to have been regarded by the Greeks as a shameful act, resulting from a barbaric lack of moderation in the behavior of the Greek warrior Neoptolemos.

29 Attic red-figure calyx-krater, attributed to the Altamura Painter, Boston, Museum of Fine Arts, 59.178, ARV^2 590.11, *Para* 394, $BAdd^2$ 264.

30 For Zeus, see Hesiod, *Theogony* 492–493. For Hermes, see *The Ichneutae of Sophocles*, trans. R. J. Walker (1919), 271–272. For Apollo, see *Homeric Hymn to Delian Apollo* 123–135.

31 Attic red-figure pelike, Manner of the Washing Painter, London, The British Museum, E396, ARV^2 1134.6.

32 Alternatively, as Jenifer Neils suggested to me in a personal communication, the wreath hanging from the wall could perhaps be the olive wreath that was hung on the Athenian house to celebrate the birth of a male child.

33 Boy at northwest corner: London, The British Museum, Parthenon frieze slab N XLII: F. Brommer, *Der Parthenonfries* (Mainz, 1977), pl. 108. Central section of east frieze: Despite the arguments of Boardman, Robertson, and Connelly, among others, that the small figure should be identified as female, I do not believe that a seminude female figure would have been acceptable on a temple frieze of this date. See M. Robertson and A. Frantz, *The Parthenon Frieze* (London, 1975), discussion under fig. 4, East slab V 31–35; C. Clairmont, "Girl or Boy?" *AA* 1989, 496–497; J. Boardman, "The Naked Truth," *OJA* 10, no. 1 (1991), 119–121; J. B. Connelly, "Parthenon and *Parthenoi*: A Mythological Interpretation of the Parthenon Frieze," *AJA* 100 (1996), 59–63 and n. 44 for further bibliography. Older girls: London, The British Museum, Parthenon frieze slab O V, Brommer, op. cit, pl. 174.

34 C. Hofkes-Brukker, *Der Bassai-Fries* (Munich, 1975), pls. H2-522 and H3-525.

35 Grave stele from Paros, New York, The Metropolitan Museum of Art, 53.111.160, Stewart (supra n. 25), pl. 304.

36 Due apparently to legislation that sought to curb expenditure on funerary monuments at Athens, there is a dearth of sculpted grave markers between the Late Archaic period and the third quarter of the fifth century. When figured funerary stelai reappear, children are represented on some of the earliest monuments. See *CAT* and Hirsch-Dyczek 1983.

37 Pliny, *Natural History*, Loeb vol. 9, trans. H. Rackham (Cambridge, Mass., 1968), xxxv.70.

38 Pliny (supra n. 37), xxxv.66.

39 G. van Hoorn, *Choes and Anthesteria* (Leiden, 1951), Green 1971, Bazant 1975, Stern 1978, Hamilton 1992 (with further bibliography for choes given on 64–70).

40 An even earlier, quite extraordinary, representation of the infant body ideal can be found inside a cup decorated by an artist related to the Sotades Painter: Brussels, Musées royaux d'art et d'histoire A890, ca. 460 B.C.E., ARV^2 771.1, $BAdd^2$ 287.

41 For a detailed analysis of the various stages and ages of childhood depicted in Attic red-figure vase painting see Beaumont 1994.

42 Attic red-figure kalpis in Munich, Staatliche Antikensammlungen, SL 476, ARV^2 1083.2, $BAdd^2$ 327.

43 Beaumont 2000.

44 The Athenian artistic presentation of female adolescence can be seen on slab East VIII of the Parthenon frieze, where a group of maidens following an older woman assists in the ritual procession by carrying sacrificial equipment. Brommer (supra n. 33), pl. 188.

45 Attic red-figure kalpis, Malibu, Calif., The J. Paul Getty Museum, 82.AE.7.

46 *CAT*, vol. 1, 132.

47 See, for example, Athens, National Archaeological Museum, 1739 and 14532, van Hoorn (supra n. 39), figs. 278–279.

48 Kahil 1965, Sourvinou-Inwood 1988, pls. 1–3.

49 Kahil 1977, 89–90, fig. A, pl. 18.

50 On the effects of the Peloponnesian War see S. Hornblower, *The Greek World, 479–323 BC*, rev. ed. (London, 1991), 153–180.

51 Vorster 1983.

52 Athens, National Archaeological Museum, 695, Vorster 1983, cat. no. 59.

53 Vorster 1983, cat. nos. 41, 91, 91a, 92, 93, 115, 137, 171, 172, 173, 174, 175, 176, 178, 179, 180.

54 M. Lonnqvist, "'Nulla signa sine argilla': Hellenistic Athens and the Message of the Tanagra Style," in J. Frosen, ed., *Early Hellenistic Athens: Symptoms of a Change* (Helsinki, 1997), 147–182.

55 On Hellenistic art see Pollitt 1986; B. H. Fowler, *The Hellenistic Aesthetic* (Madison, Wis., 1989); B. S. Ridgway, *Hellenistic Sculpture*, vol. 1, *The Styles of ca. 331–200 BC* (Madison, Wis., 1990); R. R. R. Smith, *Hellenistic Sculpture: A Handbook* (London, 1991).

56 Munich, Antikensammlung and Glyptothek, 268. Although the original seems to date to the late third century, this group, like so much Hellenistic sculpture, survives only in later Roman copies. This, of course, complicates our understanding of the exact nature of the representation of children in Hellenistic art.

57 Respectively, marble copy of Greek original of third century B.C.E.: Rome, Capitoline, Palazzo dei Conservatori, Rühfel 1984b, fig. 102; marble copy of Greek original of second century B.C.E.: Rome, Capitoline, Palazzo dei Conservatori, Pollitt 1986, fig. 134.

58 For the depiction of servant and slave children in Archaic and Classical Greek vase painting, see Himmelmann (supra n. 3); Rühfel 1984b, 61–76; J. Oakley, "Some 'Other' Members of the Athenian Household: Maids and their Mistresses in Fifth Century Athenian Art," in B. Cohen, ed., *Not the Classical Ideal: Athens and the Construction of the Other in Greek Art* (Leiden, 2000), 227–247. For the depiction of servant and slave children on late-fifth- and fourth-century funerary reliefs, see Hirsch-Dyczek 1983, 54–55. On Hellenistic representations of children of low social status, see Rühfel 1984b, 268–280.

59 Limestone statue from the Taranto necropolis, Berlin, Staatliche Museen, Sk 502, E. Rohde, *Griechische und römische Kunst in den Staatlichen Museen zu Berlin* (Berlin, 1968), 154 fig. 112.

60 Golden 1997.

61 A good example of the adolescent Eros can be found on an Attic red-figure amphora attributed to the Oionokles Painter, dating to the second quarter of the fifth century B.C.E.: here Eros, whip in hand, flies in pursuit of a fleeing youth. London, The British Museum, E297, ARV^2 647.13.

62 New York, The Metropolitan Museum of Art, 43.11.4, Stewart (supra n. 25), pl. 821.

H. A. Shapiro

Fathers and Sons, Men and Boys

T HE RELATIONSHIP of father and son has always been a complex and difficult one.[1] The Greeks knew this as well as anyone, for embedded in some of their earliest recorded myths of the gods are the motifs of a father's fear of an up-start son and of a son chafing under the control of his father. The poet Hesiod, writing around 700 B.C.E., is our earliest source for these stories, and his account of the early genera-tions of the gods, down to the reign of Zeus, is a cycle of violent overthrow of fathers by their sons.[2] A rare scene on a vase of the mid-fifth century (cat. 4) illustrates the most im-portant of these stories, Rhea deceiving her child-swallowing husband, Kronos, by offering him a stone wrapped in swad-dling clothes in place of the infant Zeus.

But violent rivalry is not the only model for the father-son relationship among the gods, nor among Greek heroes, who offer several different paradigms of family life. In the Archaic and Classical periods, when Athenian artists usually favored the great deeds of gods and heroes, they were quite selective in the imagery of contemporary family life and parent-child relationships that they chose to represent. The myth scenes that they do show may therefore give us some insight into how their own society thought about the family relationships expressed in these mythological paradigms.

The God-Father

Myths of both gods and heroes are full of instances of what we might call the "absent father syndrome." In these families,

CAT. 45 Courting Scene (tondo), Attic red-figure kylix, signed by Douris, attributed to Python as potter, ca. 480 B.C.E. Malibu, The J. Paul Getty Museum

CAT. 4 Kronos and Rhea, Attic red-figure pelike, attributed to the Nausicaa Painter, ca. 460–450 B.C.E. New York, The Metropolitan Museum of Art, Rogers Fund, 1906

FIG. 1 Zeus Carrying the Baby Dionysos in a Procession of Gods (detail), Attic red-figure kylix, attributed to Makron, ca. 490 B.C.E. Athens, National Archaeological Museum, Acropolis Collection 325

fathers are unable or unwilling to take care of their young sons, and often the biological mother is out of the picture entirely, so that the boy must be entrusted to a surrogate parent. A classic case is that of Zeus and Dionysos. When the child's mortal mother, Semele, died while still pregnant (incinerated by the sight of the naked Zeus in full majesty), the god rescued the fetus and brought it to term in his own thigh.[3] As with his daughter Athena, Zeus plays the role of both mother and father. But once Dionysos was born, his father, unable to care for the baby, gave him over to the nymphs of Mount Nysa in Asia Minor to be brought up. On a red-figure *hydria* of about 480 B.C.E., we see Zeus handing the baby to one of the nymphs in an architectural setting that suggests the god's palace on Mount Olympos.[4] But on a contemporary vase, a remarkably elaborate drinking cup that was once a dedication on the Athenian Acropolis, Zeus joins a procession of gods that includes Athena, Poseidon, and Hermes, whose goal is evidently to deliver the baby Dionysos to the nymphs (fig. 1).[5] The proud but somewhat awkward father does not cradle the child in his arms, as mothers do, but holds him stiffly out in front of him like a trophy. Dionysos, dressed in a long *himation* like his elders, wears the ivy wreath associated with him and displays a vine heavy with bunches of grapes. While on the Paris hydria the nymph has come to Olympos, here Olympos has come to the mountain, indicated by leafy trees in rocky terrain on the far side of an altar where the nymphs prepare offerings to welcome the young god into their keeping.

By the mid-fifth century, however, the story has been altered so that Zeus is no longer directly involved at all but has delegated the task of giving away his son, usually to his trusty messenger Hermes.[6] But Zeus's genuine affection for his son is also illustrated in a small series of vases that show the boy-god standing in his father's lap just after his birth, steadied by Zeus's hand. Once they are even accompanied by Hera, who was not usually well disposed toward those children fathered by her consort on hapless mortals.[7]

Other absent fathers among the gods include Apollo, whose son Ion resulted from the rape of the Athenian princess Kreousa in a cave on the slope of the Acropolis. As so often happens in myth, the mother was left to raise the child while keeping secret her shame and the true nature of his paternity. But as fate would have it, the boy became a temple servant at Delphi, serving his divine father, a story best known from (and perhaps partially invented by) Euripides in his play *Ion*. Surprisingly, Euripides does little to excuse Apollo's cavalier attitude toward the mother of his child.[8] In the climactic moments, after mother and son have survived

FIG. 2a Delian Triad (Apollo, Artemis, and Leto) with Hermes and Ion, Attic red-figure pelike, ca. 460 B.C.E. Vatican Museums

FIG. 2b Nike

some narrow escapes and been happily reunited, when we would expect Apollo to make a conciliatory appearance, he absents himself once again, leaving Athena to make his excuses and explain to the audience the importance of the boy as eponym and ancestor of the Ionian race, hence of the Athenian people (1587–1588).

Though Euripides may have deliberately cast Apollo in an unflattering light, it is unlikely that the average Athenian male shared the eccentric views of the "protofeminist" playwright.[9] For many Athenians, what mattered most was the glory of claiming Apollo as an ancestor of their race. Ever since the tyrant Peisistratos fostered the cult of Apollo in Athens in the mid-sixth century, the triad consisting of the god, his twin sister, Artemis, and their mother, Leto, had been a popular image of family devotion, with a special resonance for Athens.[10] In rare depictions of the mid-fifth century, they are joined by a young boy who must be none other than Ion (figs. 2a, b).[11] The religious aura, with a procession of divinities including Nike under the handle, proclaims the confidence of the Athenians as their empire in the Aegean, begun as the Delian League under the patronage of Apollo, continued to grow.[12] The addition of Ion alongside his father, Apollo, this child conceived at the very heart of Athens's ancient center, makes visible the city's claim to natural leadership of all the Ionian Greeks.

Another child hero who was essential to the Athenians' identity is Erichthonios, who, like Ion, was conceived on the Acropolis by a father who was present barely long enough to

be called absent (cat. 6).[13] The child was "planted" in the seed that Hephaistos spilled on the Acropolis soil as he tried vainly to consummate his lust for the virgin goddess Athena.[14] His true mother was Ge, Mother Earth, thus helping to justify the Athenians' claim to being autochthonous ("sprung from the very earth").[15] Yet once again, in popular belief as reflected on Attic red-figure vases, the parental roles are not those we would expect from the narrative of the myth (fig. 3).[16] They have rather been reshaped by the exigencies of religious and civic identity. Athena, instead of spurning the child nearly fathered on her against her will, lovingly receives the newborn Erichthonios from the arms of Ge to signal that both the child and the people over whom he will one day rule are under her special protection. Hephaistos, too, stands by, reasserting his paternity, though, like a real-life Athenian father, never in physical contact with the child. The god's momentary indiscretion on the Acropolis has been forgotten, and his many shared concerns with Athena, above all for the welfare of the Athenians, take precedence. It is little wonder that these two are cordially seated together on the East frieze of the Parthenon.[17]

Among the Olympian gods, there may be only one real exception to the absent-father syndrome, and that is the god who in every way stands apart from the others, Dionysos. I have elsewhere suggested that Dionysos's predominant image in Archaic Athens is as a family man, with his consort Ariadne and their children Oinopion and Staphylos.[18] Perhaps the finest image of father and son in Attic black-figure is on Exekias's neck-amphora, where the majestic, bearded Dionysos is served wine by his son Oinopion.[19] A similar image in red-figure decorates the tondo of a cup that we shall consider later in another context.[20] Instead of the nude Oinopion of Exekias, the boy is now dressed in a simple himation draped over one shoulder. This is still far from the luxurious costume of his father, with a long crinkly chiton underneath his mantle, but it does reflect the proper attire of Athenian boys as we see it consistently on vases and reliefs of the fifth century (see figs. 17a, 22).

Dionysos's affinity for even younger children is attested by a series of black-figure vases on which he joins a woman who holds either one or two boys in her arms.[21] Her identity is debated (Ariadne or Aphrodite?), but it seems certain that the boys belong to Dionysos, especially since the poetic tradition consistently gives him twin sons.[22] Though these boys are otherwise difficult to find in red-figure, the image of Dionysos as affectionate father figure continued to be explored. A charming example is the scene on a krater of the Group of Polygnotos, in which a small satyr boy approaches

FIG. 3 Birth of Erichthonios, Attic red-figure stamnos, attributed to Hermonax, ca. 460 B.C.E. Munich, Staatliche Antikensammlungen und Glyptothek, 2413

the seated god.[23] Dionysos gently tips his large kantharos to give the child a sip of wine. The image could be a mythical paradigm for the Anthesteria festival, when little boys had their first taste of wine at their fathers' knees (see cats. 95–101).

MY SON THE HERO

Though the Olympian gods may have established certain patterns of family life that were universally applicable, it was also understood that gods were often not subject to the constraints that govern human behavior. It was rather to their heroes that the Greeks looked for paradigms of family relationships, some to be emulated and others to be avoided. One hero whose early childhood especially interested Athenian artists was Achilles, once again the son of an absent father. Two Olympians, Zeus and Poseidon, had vied for the affections of the beautiful sea goddess Thetis, until they learned that she was destined to give birth to a son more powerful than his father.[24] The motif of fathers fearing their sons is familiar, as we have seen, from Hesiod. To "neutralize" the prophecy's threat, the two gods agreed that Thetis should be given to a mortal, the hero Peleus (himself a grandson of Zeus). After a stormy courtship (recorded on hundreds of Greek vases), Peleus and Thetis had a glittering wedding attended by all the gods and, in due course, produced their famous offspring, Achilles.[25] But Thetis soon returned to her

CAT. 14 Chiron and the Baby Achilles, Attic black-figure amphora, attributed to the Group of Würzburg 199, Circle of the Antimenes Painter, ca. 520–510 B.C.E. Baltimore, The Walters Art Museum

family home with her sister Nereids beneath the sea and essentially abdicated responsibility for her child's upbringing: a rare instance of an absent mother. (She later took a keen interest in the grown-up Achilles, once he got to Troy, a relationship vividly rendered in the *Iliad*.) As a single parent, Peleus felt unable to care for his precocious child and entrusted him to the wise centaur Chiron. Here in the wild the boy hero developed the swift-footedness for which he was later renowned, as well as the skill in hunting that the Greeks considered ideal training for warfare.

Peleus bringing his son to Chiron is recorded on a series of Attic vases between about 520 and 470 B.C.E. (cat. 14). These reveal a range of emotional reactions, from the tiny baby impassive in his father's arms, to the small boy unwilling to let go, to the self-assured child standing quietly by as the two adult males seal the agreement with a handshake.[26] Our sources imply that Peleus placed his son with Chiron not only to learn the manly pastimes of running and hunting but also for the female presence that he would lack in Peleus's motherless household. For Chiron was himself a solid family man, with a devoted wife, Chariklo, his mother, Philyra, a daughter, Okyroe, and a son, Karystos, and perhaps other children as well. A few scenes of Peleus delivering the baby Achilles include the women of Chiron's family and a woman who has been called Thetis, though we would not have expected her here.[27] Among the finest depictions in black-figure is one that stands apart from the rest (fig. 4).[28] Achilles, though small, is muscular and well-developed, like an Archaic kouros. The gesture of Chiron's left hand seems to me to indicate that the moment shown here is not Achilles being brought to Chiron but rather being returned to his father at the end of his training.[29] He brings with him a pet fawn, a souvenir of his time in the wild. Peleus stares in wonder at the transformation of his son, whom he had left as a baby, into a powerful and self-possessed youth.

Perhaps the best example of a family torn apart by war, greed, and distrust is that of Amphiaraos, the Argive hero who became one of the "Seven Against Thebes": heroes who, led by Oedipus's son Polyneices, stormed the city to try to retake the throne from his brother Eteocles. Amphiaraos's story is especially poignant because, as a seer, he knew he was fated to die if he joined the expedition but could not refuse his wife, Eriphyle. She had been bribed by Polyneices, with the offer of a marvelous necklace, to persuade her husband to join against his better judgment. But the real victim was their young son, Alkmaion, who not only lost his father but, in obedience to his father's last wish, eventually murdered the mother who had betrayed them.

FIG. 4   *Chiron Returning the Boy Achilles to His Father, Peleus,* Attic white-ground lekythos, ca. 500 B.C.E. Athens, National Archaeological Museum, 550

This dramatic story is captured in a single moment in a series of remarkable black-figure vase paintings.[30] Amphiaraos, mounting his chariot to depart, turns to glare at his traitorous wife, who calmly clutches the fateful necklace. The boy Alkmaion reaches out pitiably to his father.[31] This iconographic formula may have provided the model for a larger series of black-figure scenes showing the departure for battle of an anonymous warrior with various members of his family present to see him off.[32] Though not filled with the intrigue and dark foreboding of the Amphiaraos myth, these scenes do explore the various emotions evoked by such a momentous occasion, including its impact on young children. A superb example by the great master Exekias shows two variants on the departure scene on either side of a big amphora (figs. 5a, b).[33] The departing warrior on the front, standing beside his chariot, is a towering figure who dwarfs the attendants and members of his family who have gathered around

FIG. 5a, b Departure of a Warrior, Attic black-figure amphora, attributed to
Exekias, ca. 540 B.C.E. Orvieto, Museo Claudio Faina, 120

him. The scene on the other side is fragmentary but preserves
the extraordinary pair of an old white-haired man bending
down to comfort a young boy. They are no doubt the father
and son of the departing warrior, and it is hard to tell who
derives the greater comfort from this tender moment.

   Herakles was always the hero who was larger than life,
the one whose domestic problems were as outsized as his
heroic deeds. As the son of two fathers, one mortal (Amphitryon), one divine (Zeus), his status was always ambiguous,
from his earliest deed, strangling the snakes sent by Hera to
destroy him (see cat. 10, p. 70). In young adulthood, his first
family came to a horrific end when Hera, his implacable foe,
sent the mad frenzy that caused him to slaughter his wife
Megara and their children. But Herakles expiated that awful
crime through his twelve labors and was rewarded with a
happy second family—for a while. Archaic Greek art shows
no interest in the story of Megara, and its interest in the
second wife, Deianeira, is largely limited to the one heroic
episode in which Herakles saves his bride from being violated
by the evil centaur Nessos.[34] But early in the fifth century, red-
figure vase painters suddenly started to explore the quieter,
domestic side of Herakles, when he becomes, unexpectedly,

the model of the loving husband and father.[35] A fine example
is the *pelike* attributed to the Siren Painter on which Herakles
and Deianeira share a tender moment with their son Hyllos
(fig. 6).[36] Herakles has put on the good Athenian citizen's
himation to indicate that he is "off duty" but has neglected to
remove his lion skin, creating an oddly incongruous look. He
has also held onto his bow and his club. The child is clearly
fascinated by these heroic accoutrements and in his curiosity
tries to wriggle free of his mother's grasp. At the right, a
bearded man with a long knotty staff gestures with upraised
hand as he admires his grandson. This is Oineus, king of
Kalydon in Aitolia, and father of Deianeira. The symmetrical
composition is completed by Athena, who also seems quite
taken with the little boy who is the center of attention.
Though Athena is often present to lend moral support as
Herakles performs his labors, her presence here implies that
she is equally concerned for the hero's family life. It may be
that she is here to call him away from domestic bliss, as she
does with another of her favorite heroes, Theseus.[37] That, at
least, seems to be the message of another version of the
same scene, this on a column krater of roughly the same date,
about 480 (figs. 7a, b).[38] Here, husband and wife are at

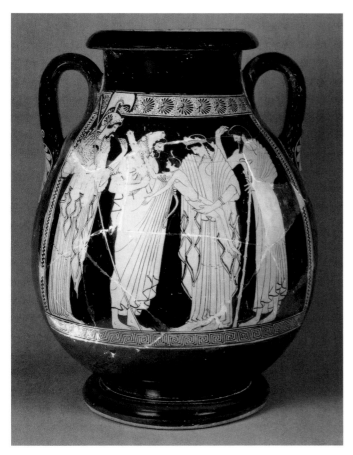

FIG. 6 Herakles and His Family with Athena, Attic red-figure pelike, attributed to the Siren Painter, ca. 480 B.C.E. Paris, Musée du Louvre, G 229

opposite ends of the scene, and the boy Hyllos reaches longingly for his father. Herakles' handshake with his father-in-law suggests that this is a leave-taking, the hero, with club already hefted to his shoulder, set to depart for another adventure. It was on one such adventure, in Oechalia, that he met the princess Iole and conceived the infatuation that was to put an end to his happy home.

There is a handful of other vases in this period showing either the wedding of Herakles and Deianeira or the couple in a quiet moment with or without the child.[39] A few more come later in the century, but not until a full century after the vases in Paris and Padula do we find another example of the whole family group (fig. 8). In this unusual image, a heroically nude Herakles receives his son from the seated Deianeira as her father looks on from the left.[40] A woman not easily identified holds the implements of libation—phiale and oinochoe—and a youth at the far left could be Herakles' cousin and constant companion, Iolaos. The setting is out of doors, as indicated by a herm at left, a tree at right, two columns of a distant shrine, and a window perhaps opening into the sanctuary. The columns recall those on other vases of this period that depict schematically a rectangular shrine of Herakles, probably a well-known cult place near the center of Athens.[41] The intimacy of father and son that we see here is unparalleled in the art of the Classical period.

FIGS. 7a, b Herakles and His Family, Attic column-krater, attributed to the Tyszkiewicz Painter, ca. 480 B.C.E. Padula, Museo, T.xliii

FIG. 8 Herakles and His Family, Attic red-figure bell-krater, attributed to the Pourtalès Painter, ca. 380 B.C.E. Munich, Staatliche Antikensammlungen und Glyptothek, 2398

But the hero with whom the Athenians identified most closely was surely Theseus, whose family history includes several of the motifs we have already seen.[42] Another son of an absent father, he was the result of a one-night stand at Troizen, where his father, Aegeus, had stopped briefly on the way home from Delphi to Athens. Theseus did not meet his father until he was an adolescent and made his way to Athens, surviving many tests of wit and endurance en route, all richly documented in vase painting and sculpture.[43] Yet growing up in Troizen he seems to have had no fewer than two surrogate fathers. One is his maternal grandfather, Pittheus (who had engineered the union of Aegeus and his daughter Aithra in the first place), a kindly old king who can be recognized by his white hair in a number of scenes of Theseus's departure for Athens.[44] The close relationship of grandfather and grandson, while the father is absent from the home, must reflect the reality of many Athenian families, especially in the fifth century, when the city was almost continually at war somewhere in the Aegean. The other father figure was Konnidas, Theseus's tutor or, in Greek terms, his *paidagogos*. The role of this figure must have been unusually important to the young Theseus, for we are told that Konnidas was later commemorated in a hero-cult in Athens, and it is for this reason that I have tried to recognize depictions of him in Attic vase iconography.[45]

Though ancient writers paint a vivid picture of Theseus's eventual reunion with his father, Aegeus—the attempt by his wicked stepmother Medea to poison him, the timely recognition of the tokens, sandals and sword, that Aegeus had left for the boy—it has proved surprisingly difficult to associate vase depictions with this dramatic moment with any

confidence. I believe the best candidate is a pelike of about 460 in Hamburg (fig. 9).[46] Theseus has entered from the left and approaches his father, whose ambivalent pose and refusal to extend a hand to meet the one proffered by Theseus suggest that he is still uncertain of the stranger's identity. Medea lurks at the right, while Athena, at the left, watches over her protégé.

Back in Troizen, the story was given out that Theseus's true father was the god Poseidon, in part to spare Aithra the embarrassment of having given birth to the child of a stranger. At another level, Theseus's divine paternity was necessary to place him on a par with his heroic role model, Herakles, who also had both a mortal and a divine father. By the early fifth century the family link of Poseidon and Theseus was well established in Athens, canonized both in one of Bacchylides' most beautiful odes and in a series of vase paintings that begins even earlier than the poem.[47] In these scenes, Poseidon acknowledges Theseus as his son by receiving him into his undersea palace when the young hero, challenged by Minos on the journey to Crete, jumps overboard to retrieve a golden ring. Eventually the vases reduce the message to a simple visual formula, a handshake shared by father and son.[48] Unlike the average Athenian, Theseus has a plethora of fathers and father figures, each enhancing his heroic

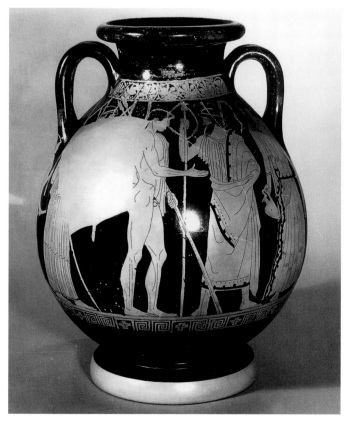

FIG. 9 Theseus and Aegeus, Attic red-figure pelike, ca. 460 B.C.E. Hamburg, Museum für Kunst und Gewerbe, 1980.174

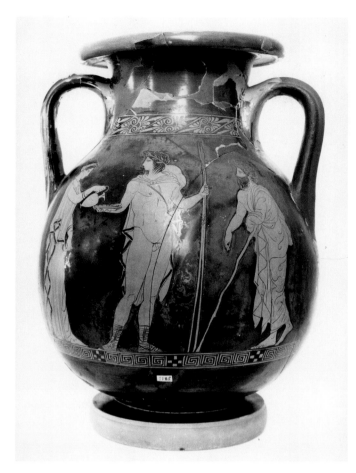

FIG. 10 Theseus and His Parents, Attic red-figure pelike, attributed to Aison, ca. 430 B.C.E. Athens, National Archaeological Museum, A1185

stature in a different way. Even though he inadvertently causes the death of his mortal father (forgetting to change the sails from black to white on his successful return from Crete), that too is a necessary step in his evolution toward adulthood and the assumption of power in Athens.

Taken all together, these stories suggest a rather chaotic upbringing for the future Athenian national hero. But the painters show once again that ideological needs could outweigh a literal rendering of the traditional story. Thus when

an image was needed of family unity in wartime, it was natural to show Theseus as a powerful, spear-carrying ephebe flanked by both his parents, Aithra and Aegeus (all three labeled by inscription; fig. 10).[49] There is no logical time or place, according to the myth, when these three could have come together as a family unit. The vase was made during the Peloponnesian War and probably used to hold the ashes of a brave young man who fell in battle, an Athenian close in age to the Theseus pictured here.[50] As Pericles reminded his audience in the Funeral Oration, the Athenian state counted on its citizen families to provide the sons who would one day defend it from its enemies.[51]

When the boy with many fathers grew to manhood, what kind of father did Theseus make? As with his rival, Herakles, the record is rather mixed. Euripides' play *Hippolytos* presents a disturbing story of a father and son utterly at odds and of a disastrous misunderstanding that results in the son's early death. By this point Theseus was near the end of his own life, having fathered Hippolytos on the Amazon Antiope, even as he saved Athens from the invasion of her sister Amazons.[52] But as a father figure to the Athenians, Theseus had to have more sons as well. His two by Ariadne, Akamas and Demophon, became exemplars of *pietas* by rescuing their grandmother Aithra from the ruins of Troy and found their reward in Classical Athens as eponymns of two of the ten tribes.[53] Another tradition, perhaps reworked in the fifth century, made Theseus the father by Ariadne of the two boys usually thought to be Dionysos's—Oinopion and Staphylos. This seems to be the story behind the two scenes on an enigmatic *skyphos* of the mid-fifth century (figs. 11a, b).[54] On the front, Theseus takes leave of Athena, perhaps returning to Athens after his dalliance with Ariadne.[55] On the reverse, the two boys are turned over to Ariadne by a nymph who had perhaps been caring for them.[56]

FIG. 11a Theseus and Athena, Attic red-figure skyphos, attributed to the Lewis Painter, ca. 450 B.C.E. Vienna, Kunsthistorisches Museum, 1773

FIG. 11b Ariadne Receiving Theseus's Sons from a Nymph

The mythological tradition thus provided the Greeks with a number of different models for the father-son relationship. Turning to the real-life families of Classical Athens, for which we have substantial visual as well as textual evidence, we find that certain motifs, like the absent father, still apply, even though the stability of the *oikos* remains the preeminent goal. In keeping with the theme of the exhibition, we will concentrate here on images of a father with his young son who has not yet reached the age of an ephebe. Scenes of a father with his adult son—for example, the warrior's departure on vases or grave stelai for sons who did not return from battle—are more plentiful but beyond the scope of this inquiry.

It is worth asking, first, what kinds of activities brought a father and his young son together. The visual evidence suggests that it was more likely to be a religious occasion than the regular intercourse of daily life, or at least that the former was more likely to be commemorated by painters and sculptors. Good cases in point are the marble votive reliefs to various gods and heroes.[57] From the Late Archaic period, but with greater frequency in the Late Classical and Hellenistic periods, these often show the dedicator and his family, always on a much smaller scale, approaching the god or gods or hero whose favor they sought. Such reliefs are plentiful at sanctuaries all around Attica and beyond, and in some cases the family depicted may be quite extensive: father and mother, three or four children, and one or two servants to carry the offerings.[58] Of particular interest for us are a few examples on which only a father and his young son are shown, and these seem to carry a specific meaning.

At the end of the fifth century, an Athenian named Sosippos dedicated a relief to Theseus (fig. 12). The original location is unfortunately lost, for the relief was purchased in Athens and in 1845 entered the collections of the Louvre.[59] Sosippos had himself depicted approaching the hero, with his hand raised in greeting and followed by his son. Theseus is nude but for the conical traveler's cap known as a *pilos*. The boy is tightly wrapped in his cloak, an indicator of a modest and well-behaved child, so that only the right hand emerges in a kind of shy greeting.[60] The boy's name is not given, though the father identifies himself in big letters—Sosippos son of Nauarchides—as well as the hero. Even though he remains anonymous, the boy occasions this relief. His father "presents" him to Theseus, in the hope that he will grow up to emulate the hero.

We cannot know the specific reason for setting up the votive, but as the boy looks to be about the age of puberty, this

FIG. 12   Votive relief to Theseus, marble, ca. 400 B.C.E. Paris, Musée du Louvre, MA 743

FIG. 13   Votive relief to Herakles, marble, ca. 375 B.C.E. Athens, National Archaeological Museum, 2723

transition is probably being commemorated. We might think of the festival called Oschophoria, in which Theseus played a key role. Though the festival was in honor of Dionysos and took its name from the god's vine laden with grapes (as shown in fig. 1), the story of its origins is set in the context of Theseus's triumphant return from Crete and procession in honor of the god.[61] This was led by the two boys dressed as girls whom Theseus had substituted for two of the Athenian girls. This curiosity was commemorated in the festival in historical times by having two boys in drag lead the procession.[62] The festival, like others of Dionysos, marked a coming of age for boys of the age of Sosippos's son on our relief.

The other hero who served as a role model for boys as they came of age was, of course, Herakles. His cult was often associated with *gymnasia*, where boys went to exercise.[63] There are many votive reliefs to Herakles dating to the late fifth and fourth centuries, but one is particularly interesting in our context (fig. 13).[64] The hero, as often in this period, is youthful and nude, carrying his two principal attributes, the club and lion skin. The four-columned structure he stands before must reflect a real shrine, for it is consistently depicted on both vases and reliefs beginning in the late fifth century.[65] On this example, Herakles is approached by two votaries, father and son, but this time the son is in the lead while his father makes a characteristic gesture of outstretched hand (sometimes with raised index finger) expressing the reverence of the worshiper before a god or hero.[66] In contrast to the son of Sosippos, this boy is nearly nude, a short mantle draped casually over one shoulder. It might be Herakles' association with the gymnasium that explains the boy's exceptional depiction as a young athlete, his contrapposto pose similar to Herakles', only turned toward profile. The boy and the hero seem to reach out to one another, but the surface is unfortunately too damaged to make out what object either might have held.[67] Both this relief and that of Sosippos to Theseus suggest that the father is in some sense "consecrating" his son to the hero as he enters adolescence.

A fragmentary relief dedicated on the Athenian Acropolis shows a father and his very young son before the goddess Athena (fig. 14).[68] We can recognize the goddess, even though only part of her outstretched arm is preserved, by the little owl perched on her wrist. The father is reverently enveloped in his himation, only the one hand emerging, but the boy is nude. Here the nudity is not that of the athlete but of the toddler. This relief may be seen as a much later echo of one of the earliest and best-known votive reliefs to Athena on the Acropolis, with a family bringing sacrificial animals to the goddess, and the later version provides confirmation for the thesis that both are connected to the festival of the Apa-

FIG. 14 Votive relief to Athena, marble, ca. 350 B.C.E. Athens, Acropolis Museum, 3030

touria.[69] The festival marked the registration of boys into the *phratry* of their father, and one of the several deities involved was Athena Phratria.[70]

We may consider one last votive relief, more enigmatic than the others because it is far from obvious who the recipient was (fig. 15). The relief shows a pair of votaries, father and son, approaching a much larger couple, a woman pouring a libation for a departing warrior who stands frontal.[71] The relief is broken off at the top right, leaving nothing of his head, which probably wore a helmet. He wears a bronze cuirass and part of his round shield can be seen, held in his lowered left hand. There are no inscriptions to identify the figures, and we have no idea where in Greece it was made or found, because it was brought to Sicily and is now in Palermo. It is unlikely, however, that it was made in Sicily, for this type of votive was not made in western Greece. Even the date is far from obvious: the relief has been dated to the period of the

FIG. 15 Votive relief to a hero, marble, ca. 400 B.C.E. (?) Palermo, Museo Archeologico, 768

FIG. 16 Hero and Woman at an Altar, Attic black-figure neck-amphora, ca. 510 B.C.E. Rome, Villa Giulia

Parthenon but could be up to a century later.[72] But the relief's basic meaning is clear from the iconography. The hero to whom it was set up was known principally as a warrior and is shown preparing to depart for battle. A heroine (his wife or consort?) pours the libation that carries prayers for his safe return, a motif that we find not infrequently in vase painting (fig. 16).[73] A small winged Nike holds out a wreath toward the hero, symbolizing the victory it is hoped he will bring back.[74] The bearded father and his young son observe and make gestures of reverence but do not interact with the hero as in other reliefs. But who is this hero? There were literally hundreds of minor local heroes in the demes of Attica (let alone elsewhere in Greece) to whom such offerings were made.[75] We might think, for example, of Kodros, an early king of Athens, who sacrificed himself to save his city by plunging into a battle with the Peloponnesians, knowing he was fated to die.[76] The little visual imagery we have for Kodros shows

him as a bearded, armed warrior, to recall the principal story told of him.[77] In cult he was associated with an even more obscure heroine, Basile, who could have played the role of the woman on our relief.[78]

BOYZ II MEN: THE ATHENIAN EXPERIENCE

If we turn to vase painting to look for evidence of what activities Athenian fathers shared with their young sons, the picture is meager indeed. The ancient equivalent of tossing a football in the backyard seems not to exist, or if so it may be rather less wholesome. An unusual scene of about 480 has been plausibly interpreted as a father taking his shy son for his first visit to a house of prostitution (cat. 62).[79] A woman, either the madam or one of her staff, sits on the porch awaiting customers. She is attended by a little boy who could well be her own son. If so, there is a curious asymmetry

CAT. 62 Visit to a Brothel (?), Attic red-figure hydria, attributed to the Harrow Painter, ca. 460 B.C.E. Tampa, Tampa Museum of Art, Joseph Veach Noble Collection, purchased in part with funds donated by Mr. and Mrs. James L. Ferman, Jr.

between the two sets of parent and child. The bearded man approaches and stands casually before her, as if familiar with the place and the woman. But the adolescent boy hangs back, stiffly wrapped in his garment, not unlike the well-behaved boys we have seen on the votives (see fig. 12).

If this is the correct reading of the scene, it will not have shocked anyone in Athens, for prostitution was a fact of everyday life and a subject that the vase painters loved to explore from every possible angle.[80] Mutatis mutandis, the reaction of the viewer was probably the same as to the charming scene of a father watching as his son is fitted for his first pair of grown-up sandals (cat. 43). At least in these outings the boy is in his father's care and not left to fend for himself. At the same age, barely entering his teens, an Athenian boy would be propositioned by older youths and adult men whom he would encounter at the *palaistra*, another subject the painters do not shy away from, especially in the

Archaic period.[81] The youth of these boys is underlined by the fact that their favorite gifts from older admirers are pet animals, like the rabbits that two of the boys receive on the cup by Douris in Malibu (cat. 45).

The boy's admirers might include men who had young sons of their own, a situation that prompted the comic playwright Aristophanes to imagine the following tongue-in-cheek fantasy of a place that was too good to be true: "a place where the father of some pretty young boy would come up to me and complain, 'O Stilbonides, that's no way to treat my son, he told me that you bumped into him outside the gym and you never tried to give him a little kiss or a cuddle, and what's more you didn't even bounce his balls! And you call yourself a friend of the family!'"[82]

Outside of comedy, we do not know what fathers thought about the emerging sexuality of their sons, but we do know that there were certain limits to this apparently laissez-

Boy at Shoemaker's, Attic black-figure pelike, attributed to the
Eucharides Painter, ca. 500 B.C.E. Oxford, The University of Oxford, Ashmolean
Museum

a

b

CAT. 45 Courting Scenes (exterior), Attic red-figure kylix, signed by Douris,
attributed to Python as potter, ca. 480 B.C.E. Malibu, The J. Paul Getty Museum

faire attitude. There were, furthermore, harsh punishments for a boy of the citizen class who was found to have prostituted himself, and when we see scenes of a man offering a money purse to a boy, we can imagine that there was a fine line between accepting token gifts from an admirer and risking one's reputation and legal standing (see fig. 17a).[83] Like the Aristophanes and Xenophon passages cited above, the tone and the nuances of many of the encounters on vases are difficult to gauge.

On one particularly fine cup, the painter Douris has given us a whole series of subtly observed vignettes of mature bearded men interacting with adolescent boys (figs. 17a–c).[84] In the tondo, a standing man and seated boy converse, the hand gestures implying nothing more than a friendly chat. Some have seen the purse in the man's left hand as signaling an offer, an attempt to buy the boy's favors, but it need not be read that way.[85] The purse, like the knotty walking stick that the man has laid aside to free his hand, is simply a token of the adult citizen male.[86] That it is so conspicuously displayed on many vases of this period has both practical and symbolic reasons. Because the himation had no pockets, the only way to carry money securely was to keep a firm grip on it at all times. At the same time, the purse symbolized something else (as it always has): the economic power and hence freedom and independence of the bearer. In the Greek household, it was the husband and father, and he alone, who literally held the purse strings at all times. The popularity of this motif in Late Archaic art may also reflect the novelty of coinage, which had not been the medium of exchange in Athenian daily life for long.[87] As the boy on our cup looks up and notices the man's purse, he may be thinking of the adult freedoms to which he can look forward.

The exterior of the cup is filled with encounters that are not always easy to interpret. Most straightforward, perhaps,

is the youth holding a tortoise-shell lyre conversing animatedly with a draped man (fig. 17b). More puzzling is the boy who, alone of all the figures, is naked (fig. 17c). As he lunges toward something that the man with him seems to hold or point to with his outstretched hand, the latter tries to take advantage of the momentary distraction to grope the boy. It appears to be a kind of sympotic joke to amuse the drinker and his companions, a visual counterpart to the Old Comedy topos of fondling a boy's genitals.[88] A third motif, repeated in variations on both sides of the cup, is of a boy with his garment pulled up over his head like a veil (compare the boy in the tondo of a second cup by Douris, cat. 45, see p. 84). Because this is primarily a female gesture, it casts these boys into a role similar to that of a shy and modest girl, and this is especially striking on side A, where the boy mimics exactly the look of a typical bride: walking slowly with head down, led by one man who looks back at him lovingly (like a groom) and followed by another who fusses over him (like a bridesmaid; fig. 17b).[89] One cannot help feeling that this little bit of gender-bending playacting is also meant as a visual joke.

The number of Athenian vases that can confidently be said to depict a father with his young son is extremely small, but each example is telling. We might expect a significant number to reflect festivals and religious occasions, because we are well informed about the crucial role of rituals in marking the incorporation of a young child into both his own extended family and the larger community.[90] The most important festival in this regard was the Apatouria, as we

CAT. 45 (detail)

FIG. 17b, c Men and Boys, exterior of fig. 17a

have seen in the contexts of votive reliefs to Athena (see fig. 14). An ingenious recent suggestion is that the unusual pairs of men and boys in a zone around the image of Dionysos and his son are the Athenian fathers presenting their sons at puberty to the phratry.[91] If so, this cup is a unique instance of a ritual that is not otherwise depicted.

In looking for ritual scenes, we are on firmer ground with the choes, whose distinctive shape immediately connects them with the Anthesteria (see cats. 95–101, pp. 285–287). This is the festival of Dionysos at which boys in their third year symbolically marked the transition into the world of men by tasting the new wine from special miniature versions of this globular vessel. One of the finest of all choes presents the

unique and touching scene of a father gently lifting his son into a swing as his two older sons look on (figs. 18a, b).[92] That the motif of swinging was a part of this festival may be inferred from the various etiological myths of Dionysos and the heroine Erigone that feature a swing.[93] The Eretria Painter's chous is unparalleled both for the carefully observed distinction of three different ages of the boys and for the tender intimacy of father and son. No wonder one scholar wanted to see here a self-portrait of the painter with his own children.[94]

The interaction of father and son depicted here, so natural to a modern viewer, points up the paucity of such intimate moments of physical contact elsewhere in Athenian

FIGS. 18a, b Father and His Three Sons at the Anthesteria, Attic red-figure
chous, attributed to the Eretria Painter, ca. 425 B.C.E. Athens, National
Archaeological Museum, Vlasto Collection

art. Scenes of mothers holding their babies or small children are, not surprisingly, relatively common on Attic vases, even more so from the middle of the fifth century, but equivalent scenes involving a father are virtually nonexistent. Even on those rare occasions when a father is seen in the presence of his child in a domestic setting, he is very much a marginal and detached figure, an observer of his own family rather than a participant.[95] Typically, he stands off to one side as his wife and sometimes a female servant attend to the child. The charming scene of a father watching his little son learning to walk (cat. 37, p. 72) is rather rare. In his first few years of life, the baby boy essentially lived in the women's quarters of the house and had little contact with his father. At age three the boy acquired male companionship in the form of a *paidagogos* and gradually moved closer to the sphere of his father.[96] On the relatively few vases that show a father in the *gynaikeion* (women's quarters), the boy is generally still a baby, as in the example in the exhibition (see cat. 29, p. 221).

EXCURSUS: THE UN-ATHENIAN SATYR FAMILY

The distancing of Athenian fathers from their young sons is thrown into high relief when we compare the very different model of family life offered by satyrs in Classical red-figure.

The usual image that comes to mind when we think of satyrs is the bestial, uninhibited, intoxicated followers of Dionysos, easily recognized by their state of constant sexual arousal.[97] That this desire is only rarely consummated, with often recalcitrant maenads and occasionally with other satyrs, only heightens the sense that this is the satyr's only preoccupation. This image is fairly consistent throughout black-figure and the red-figure of the late sixth and first few decades of the fifth centuries. Then a remarkable transformation starts to take place in the Early Classical period, a kind of domestication of the satyr into a mildly comical facsimile of the bourgeois Athenian citizen.[98] Previously always naked, satyrs now sometimes dress like Athenian men, and, like Athenian men, they have wives and satyr sons. Because satyrs are by definition male, there are no satyr daughters, and the wives are none other than those very maenads who had earlier resolutely rejected the satyrs' advances. In fact the maenads are undergoing their own analogous transformation, now less frequently the snake-wielding, ecstatic creatures possessed by the god.[99]

There is one subtle difference that sets the satyr family apart from the "normal" Athenian one: the affectionate relationship of father and son. While the Athenian father is a distanced observer of his own offspring, the satyr father likes

FIGS. 19a, b Satyr Family and Acrobatic Satyrs, Attic red-figure calyx-krater, attributed to the Niobid Painter, ca. 450 B.C.E. London, The British Museum, E 476

to pick up and hold his young son, to play games with him, and, when the boy has misbehaved, to discipline him.[100] Unlike their human counterparts, satyr families go out for a Sunday outing in the country. In one charming example, three generations are under way, with grandpa leading the way and playing the pipes, followed by his grandson and the boy's mother and father.[101] On another, a satyr family out for a stroll has encountered a jolly group of four young adults and joins them in a ballgame (figs. 19a, b).[102] Junior has brought along a hoop, the toy favored by that archetype of the beautiful and carefree boy, Ganymede.

As we might expect, satyrs, both adults and children, are often shown on the choes that celebrate their god, Dionysos, though not usually together. A fine exception is a chous of about 460 in Athens with a satyr father offering treats—a sweet roll and a drinking horn (*rhyton*) with wine—to his young son (fig. 20).[103] The boy perches on a large rock that has been draped with a spotted animal hide, turning him into a kind of miniature symposiast. Father and son share the baldness that, in the human world, is reserved for very old men. The satyr family thus presents a kind of antithesis, or alternate model, to the respectable Athenian family, one which, ironically, comes closer to modern notions of healthy family dynamics than do the Athenian families that they travesty.

SONS BURY FATHERS, AND FATHERS SONS

Croesus, king of Lydia, famously remarked that in peacetime, sons bury their fathers, while in wartime, fathers bury their sons.[104] Because the death of a son while his father was still alive was perceived as something out of the ordinary, a violation of the natural order, it often called for special commemoration. Hence the large number of Classical gravestones that show a mature man taking leave of his adult son who has presumably fallen in battle. A remarkable black-figure funerary plaque of about 500 B.C.E. is our most informative

source (thanks to its many inscriptions) for the roles played by various family members at the funeral (see Oakley, fig. 3, p. 165).[105] The deceased is a young man whose parents are both still living. His mother cradles his head as he lies stretched out on his bier, while his little sister, standing alongside, mimics the standard female mourning gesture of lifting a hand to her head to tear the hair. The other mourning women are mostly the aunts of the deceased. The young man's father, standing at the foot of the bier, greets the other male mourners as all exchange solemn gestures of a raised, outstretched hand. At the far left is an older man who could well be the grandfather. Alongside the father is his youngest child, a small son, who joins his more stoic elders but makes a spontaneous gesture of longing toward his older brother.

The death of a father whose children are still young has its own special poignancy, even if more "natural" for the Greeks. Only a small handful from among the thousands of

FIG. 20 Satyr Father and Son, Attic red-figure chous, ca. 460 B.C.E. Athens, The N. P. Goulandris Foundation—Museum of Cycladic Art, 751

FIG. 21 Father and Son, Attic marble grave stele, ca. 400 B.C.E. Athens, National Archaeological Museum, 3947

FIG. 22 Father and Son, Attic marble grave stele, ca. 400 B.C.E. Paris, Musée du Louvre, MS 773

extant Attic grave stelai show a father taking leave of his young children. In one instance we can be certain of the relationship, since both names are inscribed (fig. 21).[106] Following the usual Athenian custom of alternating between two names over the generations, the father is called Philokles son of Dikaios and the son, Dikaios son of Philokles. Here and on a similar relief in the Louvre, the son, though no more than about ten years old, is dressed just like his father, in a long himation draped over one shoulder, leaving the other shoulder and much of the chest bare (fig. 22). He lacks only the walking stick on which his father leans.[107] It is the outfit of the young citizen-to-be that distinguishes these boys from the small male slaves and attendants who often appear on the gravestones, but always nude. On the Louvre stele, the son has an *aryballos* hanging from his left wrist, a token of the athlete-in-training, while the pinched fingers of his outstretched right hand suggest that he held a (painted) flower. This gesture was equally common for boys and for girls.

As he says farewell to his son, Philokles hands him a bird, a favorite pet of children of both sexes and often depicted on the gravestones (see fig. 21). Likewise, on another stele, a father named Euempolos, shown with his young son and daughter, holds out a pet bird toward them in one hand and, with the other, playfully extends his index finger to the boy (fig. 23).[108] The man who in life was the distanced patriarch of the household is remembered in death as a tender and affectionate father.

Another father and son, of about the same ages as Philokles and Dikaios, say their farewell with the traditional

gesture of a handshake (fig. 24).[109] This gesture is found on hundreds of gravestones, shared by pairs of adults—husband and wife, father and grown son, two brothers—and has been thought to symbolize the spiritual unity that will continue to exist across the great divide of life and death.[110] Our example is remarkable in showing that a young child may also participate in the same sentiment.[111] Like the boy's citizen dress, the "grown-up" gesture of the handshake suggests that the Athenian boy was treated less as the child that he is at this moment than as the man he will grow up to be. That sentiment is especially relevant here, for with his father's early death, the boy assumes the legal responsibilities as head of the household.

ATHENS AND BEYOND

The discussion of historical Greek fathers and sons in the second half of this essay has been limited to the city of Athens, for the simple reason that almost all the relevant evidence is Athenian. Thus, for example, while the painted pottery of several other cities (Corinth, Sparta, Greek colonies in southern Italy) is rich in mythological scenes and in certain types of genre scenes—warfare, hunting, symposium— nowhere outside Athens did vase painters leave a record of the typical household and the relationships among its various members. Similarly, while carved gravestones and votive reliefs were made in all parts of the Greek world, only those from Athens document so fully the interaction of members of the same household, including multiple generations.

The one city for which we have enough textual evidence to make comparisons with Athens is Sparta, which not only was Athens's great enemy through much of the Classical period but also, in its social and cultural life, consistently played the role of "other" from the Athenian perspective.[112] With this in mind, we might have expected that the Spartan father would present an alternative to the absent and aloof Athenian father. But in fact just the opposite is true, for in Spartan society the bond between father and son was, if anything, even more radically severed than in Athens. According to the Spartan constitution laid down by Lycurgus in the Early Archaic period (but apparently still in force in the Classical), a man could choose to father children on another man's wife (with the husband's permission), in the interest of producing especially strong and healthy offspring. In such cases, the father probably had little or no role in the rearing of his own son. Furthermore, a Spartan father had little say in his son's education, because this was regulated by a public official, the *paidonomos*. Men took their meals together outside the home, at a public mess, or *syssition*, and from the age of seven, boys also spent most of their time in military and athletic training, living and eating apart from both parents.[113] The boy belonged, effectively, not to his own family but to the state, and the goal was to produce a strong and efficient military machine whose men were loyal only to each other and to Sparta.

FIG. 24 Father and Son, Attic marble grave stele, ca. 380 B.C.E. Piraeus, Archaeological Museum, 46

The contrast with Sparta may cause us to rethink the Athenian household, where father and son did at least live under the same roof and, after the boy's first few years in the women's quarters, probably had regular and close contact. In place of the Spartan syssition, Athenian men gathered at private symposia at home, and their sons were no doubt initiated into this form of social bonding with their elders from an early age.[114] Because the son continued to live at home until he married, which in Athens was not until about age thirty, many young men would have lived with their parents well beyond the norm in some modern Western societies. No wonder the theme of domestic tensions and the generation gap between fathers and their young adult sons offered such promising comic material for Aristophanes' portrayal of such characters as Strepsiades and his wastrel son Pheidippides in *Clouds* or Bdelycleon and his lawcourt-addicted father, Philocleon, in *Wasps*. These situations must have been painfully recognizable to a large segment of the Athenian audience if they were to have the desired comic effect.

Writing about Greek family relationships, and especially that of father and son, Sarah Pomeroy recently lamented that modern scholars "have not yet found an appropriate methodology for the recovery of private, personal feelings."[115] Certainly the travesties of Aristophanes can at best hold up a distorting mirror to a private life that often eludes us. But the images created by Greek painters and sculptors, speaking to us directly and unmediated across two and a half millennia, have the greatest potential to express those personal relationships that, for all their exotic otherness, are at some level universal.

FIG. 23 Father and Daughter and Son, Attic marble grave stele, ca. 420–400 B.C.E. Athens, National Archaeological Museum, 778

Notes

1 The theme of friction between father and son is a commonplace in the literature of Classical Athens, the one place and time in Greek history for which we have by far the most evidence for family relationships. See the extended study Strauss 1993; also Golden 1990, 105–111; Cox 1998, 84–88. These studies, based to a large extent on court cases, deal mainly with tensions that arose between father and son over such issues as inheritance and filial obligations once the latter had reached adulthood. The present essay focuses on fathers and their young sons of up to the age of *ephebe* (about eighteen).

2 Hesiod, *Theogony* 549 ff. See M. L. West, ed., *Hesiod: Theogony* (Oxford, 1966), 290–292, on the "Succession Myth" and its Near Eastern parallels.

3 *LIMC* III (1986), 417, s.v. Dionysos. For scenes of the birth of Dionysos from Zeus's thigh on Attic and southern Italian vases see cat. 7 and *LIMC* III (1986), 478–479, s.v. Dionysos.

4 Paris, Cabinet des Médailles 440; *ARV*² 252,51; A. B. Cook, *Zeus: A Study in Ancient Religion*, vol. 1 (Cambridge, 1914), 708, fig. 524.

5 Athens National Museum 325; *ARV*² 460,20; N. Kunisch, *Makron* (Mainz, 1997), 207, cat. 437; pl. 149.

6 Most famously illustrated on the great white-ground krater, Vatican 16586; *ARV*² 1017,54; J. H. Oakley, *The Phiale Painter* (Mainz, 1990), 75–76, cat. 54; pl. 38.

7 *LIMC* III (1986), 481–482, s.v. Dionysos, nos. 701–705. Among the best-known is the black-figure neck amphora, Cabinet des Médailles 219; *ABV* 509,120 (name vase of the Diosphos Painter); *CVA* (2) pl. 76. The inscription ΔΙΟΣ ΦΩΣ can be translated "light of Zeus" or "man [i.e. son] of Zeus." The finest depiction in red-figure of the newborn Dionysos on his father's lap is on the bell-krater Ferrara 2738; *ARV*² 593,41; T. H. Carpenter, *Dionysian Imagery in Fifth-Century Athens* (Oxford, 1997), pl. 19B.

8 On Apollo in the *Ion* see F. I. Zeitlin, "Mysteries of Identity and Designs of the Self in Euripides' *Ion*," in *Playing the Other* (Chicago, 1996), 285–338, esp. 335–336.

9 On Euripides as feminist or misogynist, see N. S. Rabinowitz, *Anxiety Veiled* (Ithaca, N.Y., 1993), 12–14.

10 H. A. Shapiro, *Art and Cult Under the Tyrants in Athens* (Mainz, 1989), 56–58.

11 Pelike, Vatican, no inv. no.; *ARV*² 580. Cf. the red-figure cylindroid vase, Cambridge, Fitzwilliam Museum, x 13; *ARV*² 623,73; *CVA* (Cambridge 1), pl. 38.

12 I have discussed Apollo's role as patron of the Delian League in "Athena, Apollo, and the Religious Propaganda of the Athenian Empire," in P. Hellström and B. Alroth, eds., *Religion and Power in the Ancient Greek World* (Uppsala, 1996), 101–113. See also M. A. Tiverios, "Attiki erythromorphi lekythos apo tin archaia Argilo," in *Archaia Makedonia* 4 (Thessaloniki, 1986), 600–602.

13 Euripides several times exploits the parallels between Ion and Erechtheus in the play (*Ion* 267–270; 1427–1429).

14 On the birth of Erichthonios see U. Kron, *Die zehn attischen Phylenheroen, Mitteilungen des Deutschen Archäologischen Instituts, Athenische Abteilung*: 5 (1976), 55–67; cat. 6.

15 V. Rosivach, "Autochthony and the Athenians," *CQ* 37 (1987), 294–305.

16 E.g., the stamnos Munich 2413; *ARV*² 495,1; A. Greifenhagen, *Griechische Eroten* (Berlin, 1957), 28–31.

17 J. Neils, "Reconfiguring the Gods on the Parthenon frieze," *Art Bulletin* 81 (1999), 9.

18 Shapiro (supra n. 10), 92–95.

19 London B 210; *ABV* 144,7; E. Simon and M. Hirmer, *Die griechischen Vasen* (Munich, 1981), pl. 75.

20 Paris, Musée du Louvre, G 138; *ARV*² 365,61; *AA* 1996, 222–223, figs. 1–2.

21 T. H. Carpenter, *Dionysian Imagery in Archaic Greek Art* (Oxford, 1986), 24; G. M. Hedreen, *Silens in Attic Black-Figure Vase-Painting* (Ann Arbor, Mich., 1992), 53–54, n. 37. Cf. Shapiro (supra n. 10), 94.

22 *LIMC* VIII (1997), 920–922, s.v. Oinopion.

23 Compiègne 1025; *ARV*² 1055,76; S. Moraw, *Die Mänaden in der attischen Vasenmalerei des 6. und 5. Jahrhunderts v. Chr.* (Mainz, 1998).

24 Pindar, *Isthmian*, 8.31–40.

25 Courtship: *LIMC* VII (1997), 255–261, s.v. Peleus.

26 *LIMC* I (1981), 45–47, s.v. Achilleus nos. 19–44. Handshake: no. 36 (black-figure lekythos on the Swiss market); Achilles unwilling: no. 20 (black-figure amphora, Baltimore, The Walters Art Museum, 48.18 = cat. 14); Achilles as a babe in arms: no. 27 (black-figure, white-ground oinochoe, London B 620); cf. Rühful 1984a, 67.

27 Siana cup, Würzburg L 452; *LIMC* I (1981), 46, s.v. Achilleus, no. 35.

28 White-ground lekythos, Athens, National Archaeological Museum, 550; *ABV* 476; Rühful 1984a, 71.

29 H. A. Shapiro, *Myth into Art* (London, 1994), 102–105.

30 K. Schefold, *Götter- und Heldensagen der Griechen in der früh- und hocharchaischen Kunst* (Munich, 1993), 280–285; *LIMC* I (1981), s.v. Amphiaraos, nos. 7–27.

31 The most famous example is on a Corinthian krater lost in World War II and now known only in a drawing: K. Schefold, *Frühgriechische Sagenbilder* (Munich, 1964), pl. 67a. For other examples see supra n. 30 and the recent comments of R. Vollkommer in Vollkommer 2000, 374–375. The scene is reimagined on a late red-figure krater, with Amphiaraos departing on foot, handing the sword of vengeance to an early adolescent Alkmaion as Eriphyle looks on impassively: Syracuse 18421; *ARV*² 1075,7; *CVA* (1) pl. 17. Cf. also the contemporary red-figure kalpis with Amphiaraos observing as Eriphyle suckles their baby Alkmaion (Berlin F 2395; *LIMC* I (1981), 697, s.v. Amphiaraos, no. 27), a mythologized version of family scenes in red-figure such as the Harvard kalpis (cat. 29).

32 A. B. Spiess, *Der Kriegerabschied auf attischen Vasen der archaischen Zeit* (Frankfurt, 1992), esp. 127–128 on the relative paucity of young children in these scenes.

33 Orvieto, Faina 120; *ABV* 144,10; M. R. Wójcik, *Museo Claudio Faina di Orvieto: Ceramica attica a figure nere* (Perugia, 1989), 69–71, no. 8.

34 The only depictions of the Megara story are on southern Italian vases and other media: *LIMC* IV (1988), 835–836, s.v. Herakles. Deianeira: *LIMC* VI (1992), 839–843, s.v. Nessos.

35 *LIMC* V (1990), 34, s.v. Herakles, nos. 1674–1679.

36 Paris, Musée du Louvre, G 229; *ARV*² 289,3; *CVA* (6) pl. 45, 5–7.

37 E.g., on the well-known lekythos attributed to the Pan Painter, Taranto, Archaeological National Museum, 4545; *ARV*² 560,5; F. Brommer, *Theseus* (Darmstadt, Germany, 1982), pl. 21, where Athena calls Theseus away from his marriage bed with Ariadne to return to Athens.

38 Padula T. xliii; *ARV*² 1642,5bis; *BAdd*² 210; *AJA* 64 (1960), pl. 104.

39 E.g., the red-figure lekythos Oxford 1890.26; *ARV*² 627,1; *LIMC* IV (1988), 834, s.v. Herakles, no. 1678.

40 Munich 2398; *ARV*² 1446,3; H. Metzger, *Recherches sur l'imagerie athénienne* (Paris, 1965), pl. 32 below. Metzger identifies the bearded man at left as Iolaos, but I rather think we should see him in the youth at right, whom Metzger neglects to mention.

41 *LIMC* IV (1988), 801–804, s.v. Herakles. On the shrine of Herakles in Melite see infra n. 65.

42 See Strauss 1993, ch. 4: "Conflict: The Sons of Theseus," 100–129.

43 J. Neils, *The Youthful Deeds of Theseus* (Rome, 1987).

44 *LIMC* VII (1994), 925, s.v. Theseus, no. 31: amphora, London E 264. Cf. the Nolan amphora, St. Petersburg B 1616; *ARV*² 1209,48; A. Lezzi-Hafter, *Der Schuwalow Maler* (Mainz, 1976), pl. 89c (identified as Theseus's arrival in Athens in *LIMC* I [1981], 362, s.v. Aigeus, no. 32, and *LIMC* VII [1994], 935, s.v. Theseus, no. 162, but I believe the white hair and beard characterize Pittheus rather than Aigeus).

45 Plutarch, *Theseus* 4; "Comings and Goings," *Métis* 5 (1990), 121, n. 35. E. Simon, *LIMC* VI (1992), 98–99, s.v. Konnidas, collects the sources on this figure but suggests only one certain depiction of him, on a black-figure

amphora in a very different guise as the armed charioteer of Theseus.

46 Hamburg 1980.174; *Jahrbuch der Hamburger Kunstsammlungen* 1 (1982), 104–109; *LIMC* VII (1994), 935, s.v. Theseus, no. 164.

47 On Bacchylides 17, see A. P. Burnett, *The Art of Bacchylides* (Cambridge, Mass., 1985), 22–39; for the vases, see P. Jacobsthal, *Theseus auf dem Meeresgrunde* (Leipzig, 1912); H. A. Shapiro, "Theseus: Aspects of the Hero in Archaic Greece," in D. Buitron-Oliver, ed., *New Perspectives in Early Greek Art* (Washington, 1991), 123–139, esp. 127–129.

48 E.g., the oinochoe New Haven 1913.143; *ARV*² 503,25; Neils (supra n. 43), fig. 56. For other examples see Neils, 110, fig. 55.

49 Red-figure pelike, Athens, National Archaeological Museum, 1185; *ARV*² 1176,26; *LIMC* I (1981), s.v. Aigeus, no. 37.

50 S. Karouzou, "Deux vases à figures rouges d'Aison au Musée National d'Athènes," in *Architecture et poésie dans le monde grec: Hommage à G. Roux* (Lyons, 1989), 285–292.

51 Thucydides, *The History of the Peloponnesian War*, 2.44.

52 W. B. Tyrrell, *Amazons: A Study in Athenian Mythmaking* (Baltimore, 1984), 84–85.

53 Kron (supra n. 14), 141–147.

54 Vienna 1772; *ARV*² 972 (Lewis Painter); *CVA* (1) pl. 39; *LIMC* I (1981), 436, s.v. Akamas et Demophon, no. 1.

55 Cf. the lekythos in Taranto (supra n. 37).

56 The scene is usually identified as Ariadne, at left, giving over the children to the woman (inscribed ΝΥΦΗΕ) at right (e.g. in *CVA* p. 32). But since the boys' gestures indicate that they are being reluctantly separated from the nymph, it seems that Ariadne is taking them back.

57 See in general U. Hausmann, *Griechische Weihreliefs* (Berlin, 1960); E. Mitropoulou, *Corpus I: Attic Votive Reliefs of the 6th and 5th Centuries B.C.* (Athens, 1977).

58 Sites in Attica that have yielded many votive reliefs include Brauron, Oropos, and the Athenian Acropolis. See Mitropoulou (supra n. 57), 268–269. For a good example from Brauron of a large family group, see Rühful 1984a, endpaper. Cf. M. Edelmann, *Menschen*

auf griechischen Weihreliefs (Munich, 1999), 209–211, who collects all examples with parents and children.

59 Paris, Musée du Louvre, 743; M. Hamiaux, *Musée du Louvre: Les sculptures grecques* (Paris, 1992), 142, "said to have been found in Athens in 1840."

60 For this style as a symbol of modesty (*aidos*) see G. Ferrari, "Figures of Speech: The Picture of Aidos," *Métis* 5 (1990), 185–200.

61 See L. Deubner, *Attische Feste* (Berlin, 1932), 77–79; C. Calame, *Thésée et l'imaginaire athénien* (Lausanne, 1990), 143–147.

62 Plutarch, *Theseus* 23.3.

63 Shapiro (supra n. 10), 158–160.

64 Athens, National Archaeological Museum, 2723; E. Tagalidou, *Weihreliefs an Herakles aus klassischer Zeit* (Jonsered, Sweden, 1993), cat. 21, pl. 12 (dated 380–370).

65 J. Travlos, *Pictorial Dictionary of Ancient Athens* (London, 1971), 274–277; S. Woodford, "Cults of Heracles in Attica," in D. G. Mitten, J. G. Pedley, and J. A. Scott, eds., *Studies Presented to George M. A. Hanfmann* (Mainz, 1971), 211–225; H. Froning, "Un Eracle attico in Sicilia," in F. Giudice, ed., *I vasi attici ed altre ceramiche coeve in Sicilia* (Catania, Italy, 1996), 107–119.

66 G. Neumann, *Gesten und Gebärden in der griechischen Kunst* (Berlin, 1965), 82.

67 Tagalidou (supra n. 64), 215, suggests that Herakles held a drinking cup.

68 Athens, Acropolis Museum, 3030; S. Casson, *Catalogue of the Acropolis Museum* (Cambridge, 1912), no. 3030; Rühfel 1984a, 215. The date is mid-fourth century.

69 Earlier votive relief: Athens, Acropolis Museum, 581; M. Brouskari, *The Acropolis Museum* (Athens, 1974), 52–53; fig. 94. Association with festival of the Apatouria: Palagia 1995, 493–501 (dated ca. 510). Cf. Mitropoulou (supra n. 57), 106, who had tentatively associated this relief with the Apatouria. She noted yet another votive relief, possibly of the late fifth century, that showed a father and son before Athena: Ince, Blundell Hall; B. Ashmole, *A Catalogue of the Ancient Sculptures at Ince Blundell Hall* (Oxford, 1929), pl. 42, no. 267. The relief

was subsequently chipped away and the stone reused on the other side, so the subject can barely be discerned. Still, there are clear traces of a snake coiling up at Athena's feet.

70 See the essay by J. Neils in this volume; S. Lambert, *The Phratries of Attica* (Ann Arbor, Mich., 1993), 162–166.

71 Palermo, Museo Archeologico, 768; Mitropoulou (supra n. 57), no. 47, fig. 71.

72 Mitropoulou's date is 442–438 (supra n. 57: 37). Olga Palagia has suggested to me a date in the late fourth century.

73 Attic black-figure neck-amphora, Villa Giulia. The bird would be a good omen of victory or safe return, like the hovering Nike on the Palermo relief. Mitropoulou (supra n. 57: 37) identifies the pair as Ares and Aphrodite, but there is no parallel on votive reliefs to support this idea.

74 Nikai on votive reliefs are rare. There are a few shown fluttering beside a four-horse chariot: see G. Waywell, "A Four-Horse Chariot Relief of the Fifth Century B.C.," *BSA* 62 (1967), 24.

75 See E. Kearns, *The Heroes of Attica* (London, 1989), 139–207, for a survey that includes every attested hero.

76 Because of the model of self-sacrifice on behalf of the city, his cult seems to have thrived during the Peloponnesian War, when a sanctuary in Athens is attested. See C. L. Lawton, *Attic Document Reliefs* (Oxford, 1995), 83–84; pl. 2, no. 4. Cf. Kearns (supra n. 75: 178) for the sources on Kodros.

77 E.g., the name vase of the Kodros Painter, Bologna, The Archaeological Museum of Bologna, PU 273; *ARV²* 1268, 1; Kron (supra n. 14), 222; pl. 15, 1.

78 Basile is mentioned in the document relief, supra n. 76. See H. A. Shapiro, "The Attic Deity Basile," *ZPE* 63 (1986), 134–136. Many votive reliefs of the fourth century, from different parts of Greece, feature the motif of a woman pouring a libation for the hero. A group of ten, on which the hero is a young horseman, has been collected by E. Voutiras, "Hephaistion heros," *Egnatia* 2 (1990), 142–145.

79 D. Williams, "Women on Athenian Vases: Problems of Interpretation," in A. Cameron and A. Kuhrt, eds., *Images of Women in Antiquity* (Detroit, 1983), 97–98.

80 See E. Keuls, *The Reign of the Phallus* (Berkeley, 1992); I. Peschel, *Die Hetäre bei Symposion und Komos* (Frankfurt, 1987); and, most recently, J. Neils, "Others Within the Other: An Intimate Look at Hetairai and Maenads," in B. Cohen, ed., *Not the Classical Ideal* (Leiden, 2000), 203–226. Keuls, though generally sensitive to depictions of prostitution on vases, offers an oddly "innocent" reading of the Tampa hydria as "a vignette of family life, perhaps a henpecked husband trying to appease his wife with money" (260). Cf. Neils, op. cit., 212, fig. 8.4: "Brothel and Customers."

81 Koch-Harnack 1983. On the successive phases of homoerotic relationship that the Athenian male passed through as he grew older, see M. Golden, "Slavery and Homosexuality at Athens," *Phoenix* 38 (1984), 308–324, esp. 318–319.

82 *Birds* 137–142, trans. P. Meineck. See Aristophanes, *Birds*, ed. N. Dunbar (Oxford, 1995), 177–179. The name Stilbonides, which is not the real name of the speaker and occurs only here, is probably meant to evoke aristocratic associations. The fantasy here is clearly an inversion of reality, but compare a scene in Xenophon's *Symposium* (8.42) where a young man and an adolescent boy are described as "cruising" each other in the presence of the boy's father, with no apparent censure.

83 K. J. Dover, *Greek Homosexuality* (London, 1978), 20–23; V. J. Hunter, *Policing Athens* (Princeton, 1994), 104–105, 222 n. 18.

84 New York 52.11.4; *ARV²* 437, 114; D. Buitron-Oliver, *Douris* (Mainz, 1995), 82, no. 152; pl. 88.

85 M. Meyer, "Männer mit Geld," *JdI* 103 (1988), 87–125, comes closest to my view. Cf. Keuls (supra n. 80), 260–266.

86 H. Hollein, *Bürgerbild und Bildwelt der attischen Demokratie auf den rotfigurigen Vasen des 6.–4. Jahrhunderts v. Chr.* (Frankfurt, 1988). Cf. other scenes with a man alone prominently displaying his purse—e.g., on the tondo of another cup by Douris, once in Dresden, Buitron-Oliver (supra n. 84), pl. 40. Note that on the exterior of this cup, bearded men court youths with animals and wreaths, but no money purse is shown.

87 See L. Kurke, *Coins, Bodies, Games, and Gold* (Princeton, 1999), 301–331, on the symbolic meanings of coinage in Athens.

88 As in the *Birds* passage cited above. Cf. *Wasps* 578, where the speaker claims one of the perks of serving on juries is being able to inspect the private parts of boys in disputed cases of registration in the demes.

89 See Oakley and Sinos 1993, 32–34; figs. 90–91.

90 See the essay by J. Neils in this volume.

91 Red-figure cup attributed to the Triptolemos Painter (supra n. 20); E. R. Knauer, "Two Cups by the Triptolemos Painter: New Light on Two Athenian Festivals," *AA* (1996), 221–246.

92 Athens, National Archaeological Museum, Vlasto Collection; *ARV²* 1249,14; A. Lezzi-Hafter, *Der Eretria Maler* (Mainz, 1988), pl. 136. Cf. a recently published chous by the same hand, with a scene that could be read as a father with his older and younger son at the Anthesteria: O. Tzachou-Alexandri, in J. H. Oakley, W. D. E. Coulson, and O. Palagia, eds., *Athenian Potters and Painters* (Oxford, 1997), 473–490.

93 H. W. Parke, *Festivals of the Athenians* (Ithaca, N.Y., 1977), 118.

94 Lezzi-Hafter (supra n. 92), 202. One undecorated chous is inscribed from a father to his son: *CVA* (Robinson Collection 3), 21, pl. 12, 3.

95 I am grateful to Robert Sutton for a copy of his paper "Men in the House: Domestic Space on Attic Pottery," presented at the conference of the Archaeological Istitute of America in 2001, which collects and discusses scenes such as cat. 29.

96 On paidagogoi see Harten 1999. On the boy's move from the sphere of the mother to that of the father, see Ham 1999, 207–208.

97 See, in general, Hedreen (supra n. 21); see Carpenter (supra n. 7) for the fifth century.

98 This is particularly comical when the satyr takes on the traditional roles of the Athenian aristocrat, such as wooing a boy with the gift of a hare: red-figure pelike, St. Petersburg B 1625; *ARV²* 531,33; A. A. Peredolskaya, *Krasnofigurnye Attischeskie Vazy* (Leningrad, 1967), pl. 68, 4. On "bourgeois" satyrs see F. Lissarraque, "Intrusions aux gynécée," in P. Veyne et al., *Les mystères du gynécée* (Paris, 1998), 181–197; R. Krumeich, in Krumeich, N. Pechstein, and B. Seidensticker, eds., *Das griechische Satyrspiel* (Darmstadt, Germany, 1999), 65–69.

99 See Moraw (supra n. 23), 149–155. For maenads as mothers of baby satyrs see J. M. Padgett, "An Attic Red-Figure Volute Krater," *The Minneapolis Institute of Arts Bulletin* 66 (1983–1986), 67–77.

100 For examples of the satyr father holding his son, see the chous Florence 22B324 + Leipzig T 727; Lezzi-Hafter (supra n. 92), pl. 142, no. 230; or the name-vase of the Flying Angel Painter, showing a satyr lifting his young son to give him a better view (at a festival): Boston 98.882; *ARV²* 279,7; L. D. Caskey and J. D. Beazley, *Attic Vase-Paintings in the Museum of Fine Arts, Boston* (Oxford, 1963), vol.3, pl. 82, 1–2. According to Beazley, this is the earliest representation of a satyr child. Game playing: the bell-krater Ancona 105; F. Brommer, *Satyrspiele*, 2d ed. (Berlin, 1959), 42, fig. 38 (a satyr balancing his small son on his outstretched foot). Satyr spanking his son: cup, Vatican H 569; Brommer op. cit., fig. 34.

101 Calyx-krater, Karsruhe 208 (B3); *ARV²* 618,3; *CVA* (1) pl. 19.

102 Calyx-krater, London E 467; *ARV²* 601,23; Brommer (supra n. 100), 41, figs. 36–37; cf. J. D. Beazley, *Hesperia* 24 (1955), 318.

103 Athens, The Nicholas P. Goulandris Foundation Museum of Cycladic Art, 751; L. I. Marangou, *Ancient Greek Art: N. P. Goulandris Collection* (Athens, 1996), 106, no. 147 [L. Palaiokrassa].

104 Herodotus, *The History of Herodotus*, 1.87.4.

105 Paris, Musée du Louvre, MNB 905; M. Denoyelle, *Chefs-d'oeuvre de la céramique grecque dans les collections du Louvre* (Paris, 1994), 112–113.

106 Athens, National Archaeological Museum, 3947; D. Woysch-Méautis, *Les représentations des animaux et des êtres fabuleux sur les monuments funeraires grecs* (Lausanne, 1982), pl. 20, no. 120.

107 Paris, Musée du Louvre, Ma 773, from the Piraeus; Hamiaux (supra n. 59), 145–146, dated 410–400. Only the name of the deceased is inscribed: Antiochos of Knidos.

108 Athens, National Archaeological Museum, 778, *CAT*, 1.690; Woysch-Méautis (supra n. 106), pl. 19.

109 Piraeus, Archaeology Museum of Piraeus, 46; *CAT*, 1.687.

110 See, among others, E. G. Pemberton, "The dexiosis on Attic Gravestones," *Meditarch* 2 (1989), 45–50.

111 *CAT*, 392, argues that the motif of dexiosis involving children is rare because one "cannot transmit emotion" between an adult and a child, but the examples cited here seem to belie that notion.

112 Pericles' *Funeral Oration*, contrasting the two societies (Thucydides, *The History of the Peloponnesian War*, 2.35–46), is surely the best-known locus classicus.

113 For discussion of the Spartan system, and of the reliability of our sources (primarily Xenophon's *Constitution of the Lacedaimonians* and Plutarch), see Patterson 1998, 73–79; Pomeroy 1997, 56–58.

114 The small boys serving wine and helping out in many symposium scenes on Attic vases are usually taken to be household slaves, but some could well be members of the host family. See J. N. Bremmer, "Adolescents, Symposion, and Pederasty," in O. Murray, ed., *Sympotica: A Symposium on the Symposion* (Oxford, 1990), 135–148.

115 Pomeroy 1997, 3.

Helene Foley

Mothers and Daughters

Recovering a picture of the relation between Greek mothers and daughters from the Archaic through Hellenistic periods is not easy. Words, images, dedications, and inscriptions made or written by women themselves are few. Greek art and literature by men had relatively little interest in the birth and parenting of young daughters, in part because these events were of greater concern to the private than to the public world, and perhaps also because when they came of age girls left their natal households to marry into another family. Although Greek mothers appear together with their daughters on gravestones, and inscriptions testify to the grief that they felt at losing each other, the details of family relationships during the childhood and early adolescence of these girls are with a few important exceptions shrouded in silence. Only in fragmentary poems by the female poets Sappho, Nossis, Anyte, and Erinna, in some inscriptions and dedications, and in papyrus letters from Egypt do we catch an occasional glimpse of Greek mothers and young daughters sharing ordinary family life.[1] We know somewhat more, however, about the mother's role in her daughter's life just before and during the marriage ritual and in later life. Marriage, the ultimate coming of age ritual for a girl, brought her at least to some extent into the public eye and involved a passage from a protected, family environment into the new and unfamiliar world of her husband's house. Both art and literature dwell in various ways on this exciting and potentially problematic period in the female life cycle.

CAT. 61 Woman Teaching Girl to Cook, Tanagra terracotta figurine, Boiotian, first quarter of the fifth century B.C.E. Boston, Museum of Fine Arts, Museum purchase by contribution

FIG. 1 Helen of Troy Born from the Egg of Nemesis (detail), Apulian red-figure bell-krater, second quarter of the fourth century B.C.E. Bari, Museo Archeologico, 3899

In this essay I explore daughters in relation to mothers from birth, childhood, and adolescence to the transition to marriage, their relationships in later years, and finally, the commemoration of their relationships in death on numerous grave stelai. Because Greek girls were given in marriage at an average age of fourteen to fifteen (the youngest marriage age was probably twelve, although in Sparta and at later periods, it could be as old as sixteen to eighteen), nearly all important aspects of a girl's coming of age, including her first child-birth, would ideally have taken place before she reached her late teens. Art and literature representing divine mothers and daughters can be similar. But Greek deities do not abide by mortal limitations, and sometimes their relationships reflect fantasies of escaping the separation or subordination experienced by their mortal counterparts.

BIRTH

While we know that many daughters were passionately loved by their parents, the birth of a daughter could pose serious economic problems for a Greek family. Providing a dowry for a girl, and especially for more than one daughter, could put a severe strain on a family's resources. Although a daughter's future husband and children could prove to be important sources of support, pleasure, and on occasion heirs to a girl's natal family, the necessity to give the daughter away to another family conditioned their relationship to her from birth. These factors may explain why the exposure of female children at birth was apparently practiced in a number of cities

throughout the Greek world. Indeed, in one first-century B.C.E. papyrus letter written from Alexandria, a man named Hilarion tells his pregnant wife, Alis, to raise a boy but cast out the child if it is a girl.[2] Furthermore, the birth of daughters rarely received public recognition even in Classical Athens, where from the mid-fifth century B.C.E. children were legitimate only if born from two citizen parents. Although both the birth and the coming of age of citizen boys in Athens were formally recognized by the father's tribe or *phratry*, the birth of a citizen girl was rarely if ever recorded, and her marriage was presented to the same group only irregularly. The only visual representation of the birth of a mortal (in this case, a half-mortal) female is that of the famous Helen of Troy from the egg of Nemesis (cat. 7). A comic version of this scene is represented on stage on an Apulian bell-krater from the second quarter of the fourth century (fig. 1).[3] On the left the mother, Leda, peeps from behind a door as an elderly comic figure (her husband, Tyndareus?) raises his axe to deliver a second blow to the egg cradled in a basket from which the lovely Helen emerges. The dark-haired comic servant on the right raises his right hand as if to stop the second blow.

In Greek representations of the divine world the birth of daughters attracted some attention, but, perhaps significantly, both goddesses whose birth is celebrated in art chose to remain virgins and thus never detached themselves from

FIG. 2 Leto Carrying the Infants Apollo and Artemis, Attic black-figure amphora, attributed to the Swing Painter, ca. 540–520 B.C.E. Paris, Musée du Louvre, F 226

CAT. 7   Birth of Helen, Apulian red-figure pelike attributed to the Painter of
Athens 1680, ca. 360–350 B.C.E. Kiel, Antikensammlung-Kunsthalle

CAT. 5 Birth of Athena, Attic black-figure amphora, attributed to Group E, ca. 550 B.C.E. New Haven, Yale University Art Gallery, Leonard C. Hanna, Jr., B.A. 1913 Fund

their parents. Indeed, Athena, whose birth from the head of her father Zeus was a popular subject in the visual arts (cat. 5), remains the sole example of a daughter who has no mother, because Zeus had swallowed the goddess Metis in order to prevent the birth of a son who would displace his father from power. Only in the case of the traumatic birth of Artemis and her twin brother, Apollo, to their mother, Leto, do both literature and the arts focus on celebrating the arrival of a female child to her mother. Leto, pregnant by Zeus and thus an object of hostility to his wife Hera, was forced to wander in great pain until the island of Delos risked giving her a spot where she could bring her children into the world. In some versions of the story Artemis was born first on the island of Ortygia before Apollo was born on Delos; in another version Artemis anticipated her later function as a goddess of child-

birth by precociously helping to deliver her brother immediately after her own birth.[4] An Attic black-figure amphora of about 540–520 shows Leto carrying her two infants between two columns topped by owls. The columns probably delineate a sacred space (fig. 2).[5]

Goddesses like Athena or Aphrodite are born as fully formed adults. Artemis is the only female deity who, like many male deities, can be depicted in both written and visual texts as an infant or a child. In the poet Callimachos's third-century *Hymn to Artemis*, for example, she sits on the knee of her father Zeus (4–5) and, at the age of three, demonstrates her extraordinary strength by tearing out hair from the chest of the Cyclops Brontes (72–79).[6]

This beleaguered birth and the eternally youthful status of the two deities may explain why Leto's divine children

FIG. 3. Zeus, Leto, and Their Children, Apollo and Artemis, marble votive relief, late fifth century B.C.E. Brauron, Archaeological Museum, 1180

FIG. 4. Artemis and Apollo Threaten Tityos as He Seizes Their Mother, Leto, Attic red-figure amphora, attributed to Phintias, from Vulci, ca. 520–510 B.C.E. Paris, Musée du Louvre, G42

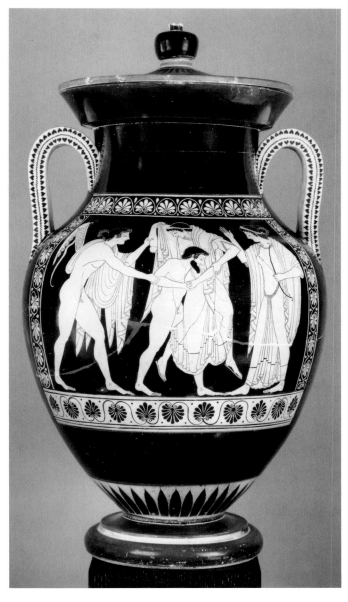

remained unusually close to their mother and protected her interests in later life. Artemis and Apollo were often depicted in art at their mother's side. On a late-fifth-century marble votive relief from Brauron, a sanctuary of Artemis on the east coast of Attica, for example, the father, Zeus, is seated with Leto, Apollo, and Artemis accompanied by a deer, largely lost but a frequent emblem of the goddess (fig. 3).[7] In Homer's *Iliad* 21, Leto picks up Artemis's bow and arrows after her daughter's defeat in the battle between the gods; at *Iliad* 5.447 Artemis and Leto help to heal the Trojan hero Aeneas after he has been wounded by Diomedes. The two children, or in one version Artemis alone (Pindar, *Pythian Ode* 4.90–92), prevent the monster Tityos from raping their mother. On an Attic red-figure amphora from Vulci of about 510 by Phintias, Tityos attempts to lift Leto from the ground while Apollo tries to

restrain him and Artemis holds her bow and arrow ready for action (fig. 4).[8] Apollo's bow and quiver are behind him. When the mortal woman Niobe made the mistake of boasting about her exceptional fertility in producing seven daughters and seven sons in contrast to Leto's two children, Artemis and her brother punished Niobe's children with death. Niobe was transformed into a rock over which the grieving mother's watery tears eternally dripped. A marble statue dating from the Hellenistic period depicts Niobe pathetically attempting to protect one of her daughters (fig. 5).[9] The famous name-vase of the Niobid Painter depicts the massacre of Niobe's children, as Artemis and Apollo pierce them with arrows (fig. 6).[10] The figures on various levels may reflect contemporary wall painting, and if so this indicates the importance of this subject in Classical Greece.

FIG. 5 Niobe Tries to Protect Her Daughter, marble, Roman copy of a Hellenistic original of the last quarter of the fourth century B.C.E. Florence, Uffizi, 294

CHILDHOOD

Female poets constitute one of our main sources for the relations between a girl child and her mother. Both the mother and the daughter of the seventh-century Lesbian poet Sappho were named Cleis. In one fragment Sappho refers to her beloved and beautiful Cleis, who looks like golden flowers; she apparently argues that she would not take all Lydia (or another place whose name is lost) in exchange for this child.[11] In another papyrus fragment Sappho regrets, perhaps due to a difficult political situation, that she is unable to provide a decorated headband for Cleis.[12] Probably mother and daughter were planning to go to one of the frequent religious events or festivals that women throughout Greece attended and to which literature explicitly refers. In the comic poet Aristophanes' *Lysistrata* (700–702), for example, an Athenian

mother mentions inviting the daughter of a neighbor to share in a celebration of the goddess Hecate. In a typical plot from the new comic poet Menander's *Samia*, a girl has become pregnant after being raped by her neighbor at an Adonis festival that her mother was celebrating in their house; respectable unmarried girls were normally so well protected that they would not have been sexually vulnerable to young men.[13] Her mother has made the rapist promise to marry the girl, and at the conclusion of the play he does.

Mothers all over the Greek world taught their daughters weaving, and on special occasions they might dedicate these weavings at a temple. On a sixth-century Athenian painted plaque, for example, an offering to Athena Ergane, the goddess of handicrafts, a woman, perhaps the girl's mother, weaves while a girl sits on the floor behind her (fig. 7).[14] Here the girl is not yet actively learning her craft, but we know that girls, again most likely trained by their mothers, entered carding contests. An inscription on an Attic black-figure vase of the fifth century, for example, records the victory of a girl named Melosa in a girls' wool-carding contest.[15] The lyric poet Nossis of Locri in southern Italy (first half of the third century) identifies herself as the daughter of Theophilis and granddaughter of Cleocha (matrilineal naming was a local

FIG. 6 The Massacre of Niobe's Children by Artemis and Apollo, Attic red-figure calyx-krater, attributed to the Niobid Painter, ca. 450 B.C.E. Paris, Musée du Louvre, G341

FIG. 7 Woman Weaves as a Girl Plays, Attic black-figure plaque, ca. 560 B.C.E. Athens, National Archaeological Museum, 2525

custom at Locri) as she dedicates to the goddess Hera a garment that she and her mother had woven together.

> Most reverend Hera, you who often descending from Heaven
> behold your Lacinian shrine fragrant with incense,
> receive the linen wrap that with her noble child Nossis
> Theophilis daughter of Cleocha wove for you.[16]

Mothers themselves frequently made dedications on behalf of their children, and epitaphs on grave monuments for them adopt the persona of the mother.[17] Some classical gravestones for daughters have only the mother's name.[18] Among the Hellenistic poet Anyte's four epigrams for girls and young women who died before marriage (dating to ca. 300), one speaks of her mother's erection of a grave monument:

> No bed-chamber and sacred rites of marriage for you.
> Instead, your mother put upon this marble tomb
> A likeness which has your girlish shape and beauty,
> Thersis; you can be addressed even though you are dead.[19]

The highly fragmentary poem "The Distaff" by Erinna of Teos (probably from the end of the fourth century) evokes domestic scenes from childhood: Erinna and her friend Baucis playing with dolls and engaging in childhood games. The mother-daughter relationship forms a leitmotif throughout the poem.[20] Erinna mentions her mother's supervision of the household's woolworkers and her use of the bogey-figure Mormo, who helped frighten children into obedience.

> Mormo brought fear,
> on [whose head are large] ears, and she comes and goes on feet
> four and from one [form to another] she changes her appearance.

Mormo herself was once a mother who ate her own children and thereafter attacked children and parturient mothers.[21] One of the games to which the poem refers involves a girl who is "it" playing a tortoise who crouches in the middle of a circle of other girls running around her chanting "Torty-tortoise, what are you doing in the middle?" The tortoise replies, "I weave wool and Milesian thread." The circling girls ask, "What was your son doing when he perished?" The tortoise replies, "From white horses into the sea he leapt." At the word leapt the tortoise jumps up and tries to tag another girl, who then becomes the tortoise.

> [Into the deep] wave
> from white horses [you leapt] with maddened feet
> "Aiai," I cried loudly; . . . tortoise
> [leap]ing [down] the enclosure of the great yard.

In "The Distaff," Erinna's recently married friend Baucis has died; the unhappy, unmarried Erinna is forbidden, probably by her mother, to attend the funeral. The poem links Baucis with the son who leapt to his death from white horses, whereas Erinna and her mother remain linked to the tortoise who stays confined safely at home working wool. The poem also tells us that Baucis forgot her own mother's advice:

> but when [you went] to the marriage bed [of a husband],
>   then you forgot all
> that . . . you heard from [your] mother,
> dear Baucis; forgetfulness . . . Aphrodite brought on.

According to Xenophon's fourth-century Oeconomicus, a treatise on household management, girls learned from their mothers woolworking and self-control in respect to their appetites (7.6). This same virtue is often attributed to good women on grave epitaphs. For example, on a mid-fourth-century epitaph from Attica, Peisicrateia "left her virtue and self-control to her children to exercise."[22] Indeed, the inculcation of values by mothers could even have long-term political implications. The historian Herodotus (1.146) tells us that when certain future Ionians from Athens came to colonize Miletus in Asia Minor, they brought no women with them. Instead, they murdered some Carians and made their daughters wives. These women bound their daughters by oath from one generation to the other never to share a meal with their husbands and never to call out to them by name. In "The Distaff," the young bride Baucis, under the influence of Aphrodite, the goddess of love, forgets the ideal female virtue of moderation or self-control. By contrast, the poem implies that Erinna seems to have obeyed her mother and, instead of going to mourn her friend, she laments her in a poem. This

interpretation fits with another epigram about Erinna that probably responds to "The Distaff": "She stood at her distaff, out of fear of her mother, or at her loom, a menial laborer occupied with the Muses."[23]

In Erinna's poem, the girls play, as they no doubt often did, while the mother works. But training in household tasks would have been a normal part of a girl's upbringing, as we see in the case of the more mature Erinna. Xenophon's *Oeconomicus*, which includes a discussion of a new Athenian wife's training and duties, suggests that the young bride arrived in an aristocratic household knowing nothing but how to make a cloak and how to distribute spinning to maids (7.6). This seems unlikely; an oration by Lysias, for example, praises a new wife for her excellent household management.[24] With the exception of Spartan women and girls, who had the subject population of Helots to perform household work for them, most Greek girls would have learned from their mothers a good deal about managing every aspect of the household's food production, the household's staff, illnesses in the family, and childcare. Because the household's men were often absent, women were also viewed as guardians of domestic goods. The wealthiest women had slaves to perform many tasks (cat. 63), but poorer girls would have learned from their mothers to do all of these things themselves, including agricultural work and the marketing of goods that the family produced. On an Archaic Boiotian terracotta of the late sixth century, for example, a woman, perhaps a mother, teaches a girl how to cook (cat. 61; see p. 112).

ADOLESCENCE

Literature suggests that relationships between Greek mothers and daughters were normally exceptionally close. The powerful bonds between the goddess Demeter and her daughter Persephone may have been paradigmatic in this respect. When a girl reached a marriageable age, her mother tried to keep an especially close eye on her. In Homer's *Odyssey*, both Queen Arete and her daughter Nausicaa of Phaeacia are concerned about Nausicaa's reputation. Nausicaa expresses these worries to Odysseus (6.273–288), whom she has found washed up and naked on a beach; she specifically refers to her parents' stake in maintaining her respectability (6.286–288). Later, Arete closely questions Odysseus about where he got the familiar-looking clothes that he is wearing (7.236–239).

Mothers and daughters in literature can have a virtually symbiotic relation. In Euripides' play *Hecuba*, the aged queen of Troy, Hecuba, and her daughter Polyxena have been enslaved by the Greeks after the fall of Troy. Hecuba learns from the chorus of women that the Greeks plan to sacrifice Polyxena to the ghost of Achilles, who has demanded this honor. Horrified, she desperately attempts to save her daughter, even to the point of substituting her own life for her daughter's; failing that, she is willing to die with her. She clings to her "like ivy to an oak" (398). She describes her daughter:

This one life
Redeems the rest. She is my comfort, my Troy.

My staff, my nurse; she guides me on my way.
She is all I have. (279–281)[25]

Polyxena's first thought when she learns of the sacrifice is concern for her mother (197–210). She regrets that she cannot share her mother's slavery and make it easier for her. Although she heroically accepts her sacrifice, she comes close to breaking down as she gives her grieving mother a final embrace, pillowing her head on the breasts that nurtured her (424). The violent sacrifice of Polyxena is depicted on the side of a newly discovered Ionic marble sarcophagus of about 520–500, now in the Çanakkale Museum (fig. 8).[26] On the right side stands the egg-shaped tomb of Achilles with a tripod placed in front of it. Next to the tomb, four men in short tunics hold the prone Polyxena, who wears a thin chiton and earrings. The man (Achilles' son Neoptolemus?) closest to the tomb grabs her hair with his left hand and plunges a dagger into her throat with his right. Polyxena's hands are bound, and the man at her left holds her legs at the ankles as he looks away toward an older man with chiton, himation, and staff (Nestor?). To this man's left are six mourning (Trojan?) women dressed in more or less the same fashion as Polyxena. One woman kneels and two tear their hair. The short side of the sarcophagus to the right of this scene consists of three mourning women. Here the veiled older woman may represent Hecuba herself. This version of Polyxena's death is similar to the sacrifice of Iphigeneia represented in Aeschylus's *Agamemnon*; in Euripides' novel version, by contrast, Polyxena heroically rips open her *peplos* and voluntarily offers her throat or breast to her sacrificers.

In Euripides' *Trojan Women*, Hecuba is equally concerned for her more problematic daughter, the seemingly

FIG. 8   The Sacrifice of Polyxena, Ionic marble sarcophagus, ca. 520–500 B.C.E. Çanakkale Museum

mad prophetess Cassandra. Hecuba tries to calm her when she makes an outrageous entrance waving wedding torches and calling on her mother and the Trojan women to dance at her ominous and fatal "wedding" with her new master Agamemnon (308–340). Similarly, the title character of Euripides' play *Helen*—a novel version of the story in which Helen's image went to Troy while the chaste heroine sat out the war in Egypt, where she had been carried by the god Hermes—shows her virtue by wishing to atone for the early death of her grieving, humiliated mother, Leda, and by her desire to return to her daughter Hermione, who remains unwed at Sparta due to her mother's bad reputation and her father's absence.[27] The Attic queen Praxithea of Euripides' *Erectheus* heroically agrees to sacrifice her daughter to save Athens, but the fourth-century orator Lycurgus, who quotes her famous patriotic speech in his oration *Against Leocrates*, makes clear that surrendering her daughter is the supreme sacrifice for a mother. "All women are by nature fond of children," he says, and if this woman could love her country more than her daughter, surely Leocrates should not have forsaken it (99–101). By contrast, in many versions of the story of the house of Atreus, the queen Clytemnestra kills her husband, Agamemnon, because he sacrificed their daughter Iphigeneia at Aulis in order to win favorable winds for the Greeks' voyage to Troy.[28]

Dramatic representations of Clytemnestra's relationship with her other daughter, Elektra, however, reveal powerful tensions between mothers and unmarried daughters that perhaps seem more familiar today. We should remember, however, that the situation in this case is anything but ordinary. Elektra, who is consistently represented as passionately attached to her father, cannot forgive her mother for killing him. In addition, Clytemnestra's fear that her son Orestes and Elektra will avenge their father sours her relation with Elektra (and, in Sophocles' *Elektra*, also with her sister Chrysothemis). In Euripides' *Elektra*, the heroine, after the return of Orestes, sends for her mother, pretending that she has just given birth to a child and needs her mother's help in performing the proper rituals for it. Elektra is furious that her mother has married her off to a virtuous but lower-status farmer in order to make sure that she will not produce noble sons to avenge Agamemnon. Clytemnestra had apparently done so in part to protect her daughter from her new husband, Aegisthus. When Clytemnestra arrives to help Elektra, she accepts her daughter's adolescent hostility and expresses some regret for her past actions. The confused, angry Elektra uses her guilty mother's sympathy to lure her to her death. It is Elektra, not Orestes, who passionately wants revenge on

FIG. 9 Orestes Stabs Aegisthus While Elektra Warns Him of Clytemnestra's Imminent Attack, Attic red-figure calyx-krater, attributed to the Dokimasia Painter, ca. 470 B.C.E. Boston, Museum of Fine Arts, William Francis Warden Fund, 63.1246

THE TRANSITION TO MARRIAGE

In the Archaic and Classical periods, Greek daughters were generally married off to men whom they did not know, and sometimes at a considerable distance from their families. Aristocratic marriages in the Archaic period often involved cementing military and personal alliances with men from other towns and cities. In Classical Athens from the mid-fifth century on, a man could produce a legitimate citizen only through marrying the daughter of another Athenian citizen. Even though many Athenian girls married relatives or family friends, they might still have to move at marriage to a house at a considerable distance from their parents. Mothers were probably rarely consulted in the process. By the Hellenistic period, however, a papyrus marriage contract of 311/310 indicates that both mothers and fathers could be involved in choosing a husband for a daughter and protecting her interests in the marriage—though indeed, the role of the mother in this contract is unique in our limited evidence. As the following excerpt indicates, the daughter's parents are concerned to protect her status as wife and after the marriage takes place will remain interested in where the couple shall live and how she and her husband will behave toward each other:

their mother, but both siblings become horrified at their own actions after the event (1183–1231).

Sophocles' Elektra is a more powerful, focused figure. Dressed in rags and obsessed with her father's death, she continually mourns him and attempts to keep his memory alive. Clytemnestra's consort Aegisthus is threatening to shut her up in permanent isolation. Clytemnestra, who enters to propitiate a bad dream that makes her fear for revenge, immediately gets into a royal battle with her daughter. Even as Elektra deflates her mother's claims to have killed Agamemnon justly, she is aware that their horrific family situation is making her more like her mother than she would have wished.[29] It is perhaps for this reason that her bloodthirstiness in this play too exceeds that of her brother. As Orestes kills Clytemnestra within the house, Elektra, standing outside the door, angrily calls on him to strike her once again (1414). In a variation on the myth, an Attic red-figure calyx-krater of ca. 470 shows Orestes stabbing a seated Aegisthus while Elektra, running in from the right with flowing hair, warns Orestes that Clytemnestra stands behind him to the left swinging an axe (fig. 9).[30] As in this case, vase painters can be inspired by tragedy, Archaic poetry, or earlier art, but they apparently also offer entirely new versions of famous scenes.

> Contract of marriage of Heraclides of Temnos and Demetria.
>
> Heraclides takes as his lawful wife Demetria of Cos from her father Leptines of Cos and her mother Philotis. He is free; she is free. She brings to her marriage clothing and ornaments valued at 1,000 drachmas. Heraclides shall supply to Demetria all that is suitable for a freeborn wife. We shall live together in whatever place seems best to Leptines and Heraclides, deciding together.
>
> If Demetria is caught in fraudulent machinations to the dishonor of her husband Heraclides, she shall forfeit all that she has brought with her. But Heraclides shall prove whatever he charges against Demetria before three men whom they both approve. It shall not be lawful for Heraclides to bring home another woman for himself in such a way as to inflict contumely on Demetria, nor to beget children by another woman, nor to indulge in fraudulent machinations against Demetria on any pretext. If Heraclides is caught doing any of these things, and Demetria proves it before three men whom they both approve, let Heraclides return to Demetria the dowry of 1,000 drachmas . . . and forfeit 1,000 drachmas of . . . silver coinage. Demetria and those representing Demetria shall have the right to exact payment from Heraclides and from his property on both land and sea, as if after a legal action.[31]

Even when a mother had no say in the marriage, she might discuss the choice with her husband out of concern for her daughter. Clytemnestra in Euripides' *Iphigeneia at Aulis*, for example, questions her husband about Achilles' heritage and moral character (695–712). Agamemnon had supposedly contracted a marriage between Iphigeneia and Achilles in an attempt to lure his daughter to Aulis in order to sacrifice her. In New Comedy, mothers might not only try to arrange marriage for a raped daughter but sympathize because they had been raped themselves. In Menander's *Heros* (see also his *Georgos*) a woman named Myrrhine had married a man named Laches, not realizing that he was the father of the two children she had borne after a rape and given to a shepherd to raise. Myrrhine's grown daughter Plangon is then raped by a young man named Pheidias. One of Laches' slaves, Daos, wants to marry Plangon and claims to have fathered her child, but eventually Plangon's true identity is discovered and she is free to marry the real father, Pheidias, who is someone of her own class. In this play Myrrhine actively tried to prevent the unsuitable marriage of her daughter Plangon to Daos.

Not surprisingly, literature indicates that the transition to marriage could be traumatic for both daughter and mother. In a fragment from Sophocles' play *Tereus*, for example, a female character recalls a childhood at home that is typically idyllic for girls in Greek literature and laments the loss of her blissful childhood at marriage:

> Now outside [my father's house] I am nothing. Yet I have often
> Observed women's nature in this regard,
> How we are nothing. When we are young in our father's house,
> I think we live the sweetest life of all humankind:
> For ignorance always brings children up delightfully.
> But when we have reached maturity and can understand,
> We are thrust out and sold
> Away from the gods of our fathers and our parents,
> Some to foreigners, some to barbarians,
> Some to joyless houses, some full of reproach.
> And finally, once a single night has united us,
> We have to praise our lot and pretend that all is well.[32]

The chorus of Sophocles' *Women of Trachis* describes the frightening courtship of the naive young Deianeira, who witnessed her two suitors, the River Acheloüs and the soon-to-be victorious Herakles, battling for her hand. The passage closes with a mention of her painful separation from her mother at marriage (503–530):

> But for our lady's hand
> Who were the two valiant contenders in courtship?
> Who were they who came out to struggle in bouts that were
> All blows and all dust?

> One was a strong river with the looks of a high-horned
> Four-footed bull,
> Acheloüs from Oeniadae; the other
> Came from Thebes of Bacchus,
> Shaking his back-sprung bow, his spears and club
> —the son of Zeus. They came
> Together in the middle, desiring
> Her bed. Alone, in the middle with them, their referee,
> Cypris, goddess of love's bed.
> Then there was thudding of fists and clang of bows
> And confusion of bulls' horns;
> And there was contorted grappling,
> And there were deadly blows from butting heads
> And groaning on both sides.
> But the tender girl with the lovely
> Eyes sat far from them on a hillside,
> Waiting for the one who would be her husband.
> So the struggle raged, as I have told it;
> But the bride over whom they fought
> Awaited the end pitiably.
> And then she was gone from her mother,
> Like a calf that is lost.[33]

Following this devastating courtship, the unfortunate Deianeira was nearly raped on her wedding journey by the centaur Nessos, who had offered to carry her on his back across the Evenus River. On the tondo of an Attic red-figure cup of about 400 B.C.E., a beardless Herakles swings his club at Nessos; the centaur brutally raises Deianeira off the ground as she appeals for her new spouse's help (fig. 10).[34]

FIG. 10　Herakles Threatens Nessos as He Tries to Rape Deianeira, Attic red-figure kylix, signed by Aristophanes, ca. 400 B.C.E. Boston, Museum of Fine Arts, Henry Lillie Pierce Fund, 00.345

Euripides' *Medea* complains about the difficulties a new (generally young and inexperienced) wife faced in a strange household with an unknown husband (*Medea* 230–251):

> *Of all things who breathe and have intelligence,*
> *We women are the most miserable creatures,*
> *First we have to buy a husband at a steep price,*
> *Then take a master for our bodies.*
> *The second evil is worse than the first, but*
> *The greatest contest turns on whether we get a bad husband*
> *Or a good one. Divorce is not respectable*
> *For a woman and she cannot deny her husband.*
> *Confronting new customs and rules,*
> *She needs to be a prophet, unless she has learned*
> *At home how best to manage her bedmate.*
> *If we work things out well and our husband*
> *Lives with us without resisting his yoke,*
> *Life is enviable. Otherwise it is better to die.*
> *A man when he is tired of being with those inside*
> *Goes out and relieves his heart of boredom,*
> *Or turns to some friend or contemporary.*
> *But we have to look to one person only.*
> *They say we have a life secure from danger*
> *Living at home, while they wield their spears in battle.*
> *They are mistaken! I would rather stand three*
> *Times beside a shield than give birth once.*

The seventh- to early-sixth-century Homeric Hymn to Demeter, however, explores in detail the reaction of a divine mother and daughter to the radical separation sometimes required by marriage.[35] The god Zeus agreed to the marriage between his daughter Persephone and Hades, the god of the underworld (also called Pluto), without her mother Demeter's consent. Hades abducts Persephone while she is picking flowers with her companions and carries her off crying for her mother. An Apulian red-figure hydria of the fourth century depicts Hades carrying off his bride in a chariot while Demeter, shown holding a torch on the lower left, raises her hands in distress (fig. 11).[36] A mid-fourth-century wall painting from the "Tomb of Persephone" at Vergina depicts Hades grasping the reins of his chariot with one hand and

FIG. 12   Hades Abducts Persephone as a Companion Watches, wall painting from the "Tomb of Persephone" at Vergina, mid-fourth century B.C.E.

FIG. 13   Persephone Rises from the Earth Greeted by Hermes, Hekate, and Demeter, Attic red-figure bell-krater, attributed to the Persephone Painter, ca. 440 B.C.E. New York, The Metropolitan Museum of Art, Fletcher Fund, 1928, 28.57.23

FIG. 14   Demeter and Persephone, Corinthian terracotta figurines, ca. 620–600 B.C.E. London, The British Museum, 897

clutching a distraught Persephone with the other (fig. 12). As the chariot lurches away, Persephone's playmate, cowering to the right, helplessly resists the abduction with her upraised hand.[37]

In the hymn, the distraught Demeter at once tears her veil and casts a dark cloak on her shoulders. As she searches for her daughter for nine days, holding torches in her hands, she neither eats nor drinks the divine foods nectar and ambrosia, nor bathes, as if she is a mortal mother in mourning, not a powerful goddess. Meanwhile, in Hades, Persephone reclines shyly on her spouse's couch, refusing to eat because she is "strongly reluctant through desire for her mother" (343). During her stay on earth, Demeter disguises herself as a mortal nurse engaged to the Eleusinian royal family but fails to immortalize their baby boy; she observes mortal girls and their mother who accept the traditional status of women at Eleusis. Both events begin to prepare the goddess for the inevitability of a partial loss of her daughter to marriage. Eventually Demeter, who is the goddess of grain, causes a famine on earth that forces Zeus to send for Persephone. The two goddesses share an ecstatic reunion on earth. An Attic red-figure bell-krater of ca. 440, the name-vase of the Persephone Painter, depicts Persephone rising from the earth in the presence of the messenger god Hermes, the goddess Hekate with torches, and on the far right the eager mother Demeter (fig. 13).[38]

Yet because Persephone ate a pomegranate seed in Hades, she must spend one-third of her life as queen of the world below and two-thirds in the world above with her mother. At the end of the hymn Demeter founds the famous annual rite known as the Eleusinian Mysteries on earth. Apparently pitying mortals after her own near experience of the loss of a loved one to the world of death, Demeter promises her initiates a better life in the world above and below. The exact details of the Mysteries remain a secret to this day, but we do know that mother and daughter presided over this famous cult together, which relied on Demeter's gift of grain to humanity and Persephone's influence in the world below. The myth of Demeter and Persephone was of particular importance to mothers and married daughters throughout the Greek world, since they celebrated it together in the all-female rituals based on the story, such as the Thesmophoria, even though they might see each other infrequently in their daily lives.[39]

Visual representations of Demeter and Persephone express the close identity between mother and daughter in their joint cult. A pair of linked Corinthian terracotta figurines of about 620–600 seated on a farm wagon depict an indistinguishable Demeter and Persephone wearing identical peploi, hairstyle, and poloi (conical hats; fig. 14).[40] The two

a   b

FIG. 15 Demeter and Persephone
Approached by Worshipers, Attic black-
figure clay stand from Eleusis, ca. 500
B.C.E. Athens, National Archaeological
Museum, 501

goddesses are often distinguished only by different positions (sitting or standing) or the different objects that they hold. An Attic clay stand from Eleusis of ca. 500 depicts the two similar goddesses wearing an identical polos. Demeter sits holding a wreath while her daughter grasps a branch; a procession of worshipers approaches them (fig. 15).[41] In a Tegean votive relief from the last quarter of the fourth century, Pluto is seated with a scepter and cornucopia, and Persephone, wearing a polos, has her hand, probably affectionately, on the shoulder of a veiled Demeter, who holds a torch and a *phiale* (shallow cup; fig. 16).[42] The symbiosis between the goddesses perhaps suggests both their close relationship and the similarity in social roles between mother and daughter from one generation of Greek women to the next.

Whatever difficulties the transition to marriage posed, Attic vases that depict weddings often romanticize the ceremony and especially the preparations for it. Both the goddess of love, Aphrodite, and her winged son Eros (or multiple winged Erotes) often preside over wedding preparations. On an Attic red-figure squat lekythos in the Manner of the Meidias Painter dating to around 410, what appear to be a bride and her mother prepare to make prenuptial offerings to a statue of Aphrodite, holding a phiale in each hand (fig. 17).[43] An Eros holds an incense burner on either side of the goddess. The woman on the far left with her hair tied back is probably the mother, while the one with the loosened hair must be the bride.[44] Although in reality the groom was likely to be a bearded man in his late twenties or early thirties, he is often depicted as youthful and beardless, making him a less threatening and perhaps more romantic figure to a teenaged bride. As we know from many sources, including Euripides'

Bacchae and the cult of the beautiful dead youth Adonis, beardless young men were thought to be particularly attractive to women. On an elaborate *lekanis* with relief decoration of about 360–350 attributed to the Eleusinian Painter, the bride sits on a stool while her *nympheutria*, or "bridesmaid," tends her hair (fig. 18).[45] Opposite the bride on the other side of the vase an older woman sits on a throne with her legs crossed as she holds a jewelry case. She is probably the bride's mother, while the young man to her right leaning on a staff is probably the youthful groom. At the center two women make sesame wedding cakes at a deer-legged tripod table. A young girl to their left apparently makes the dough, mixing in water from a hydria on the ground next to her. Two Erotes once again attend the process.[46]

FIG. 16 Pluto, Persephone, and Demeter, Tegean votive relief, last quarter of the fourth century B.C.E. Athens, National Archaeological Museum, 2.1422

a

b

c

FIG. 17 A Bride and Her Mother Make Prenuptial Offerings to Aphrodite, Attic red-figure squat lekythos, in the Manner of the Meidias Painter, ca. 410 B.C.E. Oxford, The University of Oxford, Ashmolean Museum, GR 1966.714

a

FIG. 18 Wedding Preparations Including Bride, Bridesmaid, Mother, and Groom, Attic red-figure lekanis with relief decoration, attributed to the Eleusinian Painter, ca. 360–350 B.C.E. St. Petersburg, Hermitage Museum, 1791

b

a   b   c

FIG. 19 Wedding Procession, Including the Couple and the Bride's Mother, Attic black-figure lekythos, attributed to the Amasis Painter, ca. 540 B.C.E. New York, The Metropolitan Museum of Art, Purchase, Walter C. Baker Gift, 1956, 56.11.1

Euripides' *Iphigeneia at Aulis* makes clear that a mother played a central role in her daughter's wedding. Agamemnon naturally wants Clytemnestra to depart from Aulis before the wedding in order to hide his plans for the sacrifice of Iphigeneia, but Clytemnestra insists on her maternal rights to plan and supervise the ceremony and the feast, to accompany her daughter, and above all to carry the wedding torches—normally in a procession from the bride's home to the groom's, where the bride was traditionally met by the groom's mother, who also carried a torch.[47] In Euripides' *Phoenician Women* the Theban queen and wife of Oedipus, Jocasta, also regrets that she could not light the torch at the wedding of her exiled son Polyneices (344–346). In another version of Iphigeneia's story, Clytemnestra even brings water for her daughter's nuptial bath to Aulis (Euripides, *Iphigeneia Among the Taurians*, 818–819). On a black-figure lekythos of about 540 attributed to the Amasis Painter, a wedding procession encircles the whole vase, starting and ending at a house under the handle (fig. 19).[48] The groom's mother stands in the doorway with a welcoming torch. The bride's mother, holding torches and walking beside two mules pulling the first cart, leads the procession. In the cart sit the bride holding her veil and the groom. Behind them is the groom's "best man," the *parochos*. The second cart holds four men seated back to back; other men and women walk alongside the carts. The vase apparently offers a complete depiction of an Athenian wedding

party of the mid-sixth century and confirms the important role of the mother at her daughter's wedding that we know of from literature.

Although written texts rarely draw attention to the relationships between the goddess Hera and her daughter Hebe (meaning youth) and Aphrodite and her daughter Harmonia (meaning concord), the visual arts occasionally represent these divine mother and daughter pairs, and sometimes in contexts relating to weddings. Jenifer Neils, for example, has argued that the red-figure column krater of about 470–460 attributed to the Cleveland Painter probably depicts the goddess Hera, shown with scepter, crown, and a phiale from which she pours a libation, in her role as goddess of marriage, sending off the youthful Hebe in a four-horse chariot to fetch her groom, the recently immortalized hero Herakles (fig. 20).[49] Apollo, with his laurel wreath and lyre, and Artemis, holding a flower and wearing a virginal hairstyle, stand behind the chariot to give the departure a musical accompaniment. If so, a divine bride can show considerably more independence than a mortal one (mortal women do not drive chariots or fetch their grooms), but the supporting role of the mother remains symbolically important in inaugurating the move to marriage. Hera's role here is particularly significant, because it is only after Herakles' death that she ceases to rage at this famous bastard son of her husband Zeus and accept him as her divine son-in-law.

MARRIED DAUGHTERS AND THEIR MOTHERS

Daughters could expect continued close relationships with their mothers after marriage unless they lived too far apart. Aside from the many religious events that might have reunited the two, every mother hoped to be present at the birth of her daughter's first child, which was the other most important coming-of-age experience for a young woman. In Euripides' *Alcestis*, the heroine, who is on the verge of dying heroically in place of her husband, bids a tender farewell to her little daughter. She fears that a stepmother might hinder her proper transition to adulthood, destroy her marriage prospects with false gossip, or fail to encourage her during childbirth, "where no one is more therapeutic than a mother" (313–319).

Demosthenes' fourth-century Oration 41 reveals extensive cooperation between a mother and her two daughters. The mother continues to make small loans throughout her life to her sons-in-law and to contribute goods to her daughters and their husbands. Both mother and daughters regularly witness economic transactions in the family. In another oration, the dowry of Demosthenes' mother, Cleoboule, which she received from her own mother, is embezzled by her second husband, Aphobus, guardian of Demosthenes' father's estate. When the younger Demosthenes sues Aphobus, his mother insists on including funds to be used for his unwed sister's dowry in the prospective compensation for the embezzlement (28.20–21). In Isaeus 6.40 a divorced mother collaborates with her daughters by her ex-husband to get some of his property on his death. Another mother looks to her daughter's husband to protect her sons from an abusive guardian (Lysias 32.9–10).[50] On a more amusing note the historian Herodotus tells us that the sixth-century Athenian aristocrat Peisistratus agreed to marry the daughter of another powerful aristocrat, Megakles, in order to become tyrant of Athens. Nevertheless, because he had adult sons by a previous marriage and Megakles' family, the Alcameonids, were under a curse, Peisistratus "did not have sex with her in the usual way." Eventually, however, the daughter told her mother, the secret was revealed, and Peisistratus had to get out of the country until he could reinstate himself in power.[51]

We also know of a number of curious circumstances in which adult daughters continued to live with or returned to live with their mothers. In Xenophon's fourth-century *Memorabilia*, for example, the philosopher Socrates goes to visit and talk with a high-class *hetaira* (courtesan) named Theodote. In this case, we hear in passing that the successful daughter is supporting her mother in style (3.11). Some fourth-century and later New Comedies turned on typical plots where

FIG. 20 The Goddess Hebe Departs in a Chariot for Her Wedding to Herakles (detail), Attic red-figure column-krater, attributed to the Cleveland Painter (name-vase), ca. 470–460 B.C.E. The Cleveland Museum of Art, Purchase from the J. H. Wade Fund, 1930.104

mothers or female guardians arranged liaisons for their daughters, either for profit or to provide them with a home.[52] Much later Greco-Roman literary treatments of courtesans indicate that mothers could induct their daughters into prostitution to support a family impoverished by a husband's death or to promote their careers.[53] In a more scandalous version of such a story described in the fourth-century court case *Against Neaira* (pseudo-Demosthenes 59), a Corinthian hetaira named Neaira moves to Athens after her freedom had been purchased by several lovers. Although she supposedly trained her daughter in the arts of the hetaira, she and her lover Stephanos twice attempt to pass her daughter off as his legitimate Athenian daughter in order to make a respectable marriage.[54] In each case the deceived husband eventually catches on to the truth and sends her home, but in one case not before she serves in an important civic or religious role reserved for chaste wives. In a still sadder story, Chrysilla, the perfectly educated wife of Ischomachus lauded in Xenophon's *Oeconomicus*, ends up after her husband's death disgraced and pregnant by Callias, the husband of her daughter (Andocides 1.124–126). After two years of living with her daughter, Callias makes Chrysilla his mistress and keeps both mother and daughter in his house. In Andocides' account, the daughter tries to hang herself, then runs away from home, driven out by her mother. Callias later tires of the mother and drives her

a   b

FIG. 21   Women and Girl Mourn the Dead
Myrrhine, phormiskos, end of the sixth century
B.C.E. Athens, Kerameikos Museum, 691

out in turn. At first he disowns the son she bore him, but later he reconciles with Chrysilla and tries to introduce the grown boy as his legitimate son. Similarly, the mother of the later Ptolemaic queen Berenice II had planned to marry her daughter to Demetrius, brother of King Antigonus, but ended by having a liaison with him herself. Her daughter later arranged her assassination.[55]

A fascinating archive in Hellenistic Egypt preserves documents in which a group of sisters ended up living with their mother and half-brother (the son of their father by a first marriage) on inherited property after their father's death and managing their own property themselves. In around 150 a woman named Apollonia married in Pathyris, fifty kilometers south of Thebes, and bore her husband Dryton five daughters. Dryton's various wills always favored his son, but the daughters got part of the estate. Two of the daughters married but apparently divorced and returned home to live with their unmarried sisters. Dryton not only left nothing to his wife, but stipulated that she could have income, wheat, and oil for a period of no more than four years if she stayed home to take care of her two youngest daughters, and then only if she was "irreproachable" in the eyes of his son and daughters.[56] Either the couple were very much at odds, or Dryton was counting on the independent income that we know Apollonia had.[57]

DEATH

Even as children, daughters learned from their mothers to mourn the dead, to begin a lifelong task of tending family graves, and to concern themselves with perpetuating the memory of their relationship after death on grave stelai. As is clear from both Homer and Greek tragedy, women played a major role in mourning the dead, both by preparing the body for burial and in offering lamentations at the wake (prothesis) and the funeral. At the funeral of the Trojan hero Hector in Iliad 24, his mother, Hecuba, his wife, Andromache, and his sister-in-law Helen all offer individual laments for the dead man, while the other Trojans join in group mourning. By the sixth and fifth centuries, women's lamentation was far less restrained than men's; women beat their breasts and tore their hair and cheeks for the dead, while men saluted the dead in a more formal manner and sang more restrained laments.[58] A funeral plaque of about 500 B.C.E. from the Musée du Louvre in Paris names all the relatives gathered to mourn a dead youth. (see Oakley, fig. 3, p. 165). Women with streaming hair, including a small girl in the foreground, gather close to the body and touch the corpse, whereas the men and boys stop at the end of the couch and salute each other with raised hands. On a phormiskos from the end of the sixth century, an unguent vase containing oil for anointing a corpse, female mourners, once again including a little girl in the foreground, join in lamenting a woman named Myrrhine (fig. 21).[59] In the sixth century, legislation throughout Greece began to restrict public female lamentation as socially disruptive. During the fifth century, lamentation continued to be performed in private houses or on the tragic stage, but mourning scenes in art became more restrained. The private tending of graves continued, however discreetly, and could include children. A small (child-sized?) white-ground lekythos from the second quarter of the fifth century depicts a young girl and a boy, probably siblings, flanking a tomb (cat. 113; see p. 168). On an Attic red-figure *skyphos* of about 440–430 the virginal Elektra, standing on the left, ties a wreath around her murdered father Agamemnon's tomb, while an attendant at the right holds more wreaths and offerings of fruit (fig. 22a). Part of Agamemnon's name is inscribed on his narrow stele. On the side of the skyphos, Elektra's brother Orestes and his friend Pylades, with travel gear (a cloak [*chlamys*] and broad-brimmed hat [*petasos*]) and spears, watch the girls unobserved (fig. 22b).[60] The scene corresponds closely to the opening of Aeschylus's *Libation Bearers*.

By far the greatest number of images left to us of the Greek mothers and daughters about whose lives we know so little appear on sculpted grave stelai, sometimes with accompanying inscriptions. This voluminous evidence presents many general problems of interpretation, however.[61] Virtuous Greek women generally have no history before their representation in death.[62] We often cannot tell what the exact relationship is between the people represented on the stele, or which one has died. The dead and the living may greet each other

with clasped hands or gaze at or past each other. Because slaves are often represented as smaller than their masters, we cannot be sure whether certain figures are slaves or children. Dead women—if not necessarily, from the fourth century on, surviving women—are usually presented with youthful beauty, so we cannot be sure of the age or status of many of them. When inscribed epitaphs accompany a relief, the written inscription does not necessarily correspond with the visual images on the grave relief, perhaps in some cases because the family purchased a prefabricated stele. Moreover, until the fourth century, women are rarely shown with more than two children, even if, as we can tell from the inscriptions, they had left more behind.

Women who died while of childbearing age appear to receive the most elaborate monuments. In the sixth and fifth centuries, women are known to have set up monuments for sons who died young, but only once for a daughter; although fathers left many epitaphs for sons, they set up only two that we know of for daughters.[63] Women who died young (in contrast to men) rarely received the poetic epitaphs they win in later centuries.[64] From the end of the fifth century funerary inscriptions inform us less about who sets up a monument and much more about emotions and the inner circle of mourners (with mothers prominent among them), as we see in this fourth-century epitaph for a twelve-year-old girl from Attica: "O wretched mother and siblings and Meidoteles, who begot you as a grief for himself, Kleoptoleme, who behold wailing, not your bridal chamber, since you have perished, and a dirge instead of a husband and a grave instead of marriage."[65]

a

b

FIG. 22 Elektra and Attendant Make Offerings at Agamemnon's Tomb While Orestes and Pylades Watch, Attic red-figure skyphos, attributed to the Penelope Painter, ca. 440–430 B.C.E. Copenhagen, National Museum, Department of Near Eastern and Classical Antiquities, 597

FIG. 23 Mynnia, Daughter of Euphrosyne, and Her Younger Sister, Attic marble grave stele, ca. 370 B.C.E. Malibu, The J. Paul Getty Museum, 71.AA.121

FIG. 24 Mother and Two Daughters, All Named Nausikrate, with Father and Baby Brother, Attic marble grave stele, ca. 400–375 B.C.E. Rhamnous, Apotheki

The death of a daughter before marriage was a matter of special sorrow to her family because she had not come of age and reached the goal of a girl's life. Literature often attempts to speak consolingly of a dead girl as "married to Hades." On gravestones, mothers mourn daughters more often than other family members.[66] In a fourth-century (after 350?) Attic inscription, a mother alone mourns her daughter: "Hymenaios, attendant of marriages, did not bless you in the house, Plangon, but wept for your perishing outside. Your mother dissolves at your misfortune, nor do the sad groans of lament ever leave her."[67] On another fourth-century (about 380–370) Attic inscription on the marble grave relief of Mynnia in the J. Paul Getty Museum, the mother's sorrow at losing her daughter is stressed: "Here lies Mynnia to the sorrow of her mother Euphrosyne" (fig. 23).[68] Later the names of her younger sister Artemisia and her father, Euteles, were added to the second line of the inscription. The adolescent figure on the right with the long braided hair of a maiden is Mynnia, while the full-breasted woman seated on a stool with a low cushion and wearing a *himation* over her head is the mother, Euphrosyne. The little girl at Euphrosyne's feet, most likely her sister, may have died after the stele was set up; by adding her name the family could commemorate both daughters. The mother, probably veiled out of grief, concentrates on her dead daughter and ignores the outstretched arm of her other child. Mynnia's downcast glance also underlines her own sorrow at early death.

A marble stele of about 400–375 from Rhamnous apparently depicts the loss of a young girl to her whole family (fig. 24).[69] On the left stands the mother, Nausikrate I, a mature woman in her prime, dressed in chiton and himation and wearing her hair in a roll around her head. She looks over her seated husband Arxias at her older daughter Nausikrate II, who shakes her father's hand. Nausikrate's brother Praximenes, a seminaked baby boy, squats beneath his father's chair. Nausikrate II holds the hand of her two- to three-year-old sister, Nausikrate III, who wears a sleeveless chiton and stands behind her to her right. Nausikrate II wears a sleeved chiton and mantle; a roll of hair encircles her head and ends in a long braid down her back. We cannot be certain of the identity of the deceased or the family relations, but apparently the family wished to pay tribute to their deceased older daughter while recording the presence of living siblings to soften their sorrow.

Equally pathetic is the loss of a young mother to death. On an Attic marble grave relief of about 420–410 a maidservant holds out a squirming baby girl dressed in a long transparent gown toward her mother, who is seated on a *klismos* (chair) with her feet on a footstool (fig. 25).[70] The mother, whose ear is pierced for an absent earring and whose garments reveal her youthful beauty, gazes eagerly at her child. The scene stresses the affection between mother and daughter. Although we cannot be certain, it is probably the mother rather than her daughter who is dead.

Unusually intense affection between mother and daughter also appears on a marble relief of about 420–400 in Rhodes (fig. 26).[71] The adolescent daughter Krito stands on the left with her head slightly bowed and wearing a thin

FIG. 25 Mother, Baby Daughter, and Maidservant, Attic marble grave stele, ca. 420–410 B.C.E. Leiden, Rijksmuseum, I 1903/2.1

FIG. 26 Timarista Embraces Her Daughter Krito, marble grave stele, ca. 420–400 B.C.E. Rhodes, Archaeological Museum, 13638

chiton and a mantle over her shoulder and back. Her arm rests on the shoulder of a woman in her prime called Timarista, who wears a belted chiton and a scarf on her head; her right hand embraces Krito's neck as she gazes at her daughter. Again, we cannot be sure which of the two is dead.

A marble stele of about 375–350 from Athens bears the verse inscription: "Here the earth has covered the noble and self-controlled Archestrate, most longed for by her husband" (fig. 27).[72] The relief, however, depicts three women. Archestrate sits to the right on a stool, wearing a chiton that has slipped from her right shoulder, a himation, and earrings now lost. A young girl with a braid around her head wearing a short garment and a himation leans against her thighs, holding a small bird in her right hand as she looks up at her. Presumably she is Archestrate's daughter. Perhaps she is not named because Archestrate left only a daughter rather than

the more desirable son. The identity of the young woman standing to the left with short, cropped hair, wearing a sleeved and sleeveless chiton and a himation, is unknown, but she is probably a servant, based upon her hairdo and attire.

Similarly, a stele of about 400–375 from Herakleion apparently shows a seated young mother contemplating her small daughter, who stands on her toes to hold out a pet bird and is seemingly unaware of her mother's death (fig. 28).[73] The sad young mother draws a mantle over a chiton that makes a curious snakelike pattern over her thighs.

The images on the mid-fourth-century Attic tomb of Myrtis are unusual in featuring the mother's loss of a married daughter: "Myrtis, daughter of Hieroclea and wife of Moschus lies here. In her ways she pleased both her husband and the children she bore very much." The stele shows the two women shaking hands in a parting gesture. We do not know why Myrtis's father is not mentioned, or why the image focuses on the two women despite the existence of a (presumably) living husband and children.[74]

FIG. 27 Archestrate and Her Young Daughter, Attic marble grave stele, ca. 375–350 B.C.E. Athens, National Archaeological Museum, 722

FIG. 28 Mother and Daughter with Pet Bird, marble grave stele, ca. 400–375 B.C.E. Herakleion, Archaeological Museum, 471

Similarly, an early-fourth-century marble Attic grave monument also includes the grief of the married Mnesarete's natal family, especially that of her mother (fig. 29):

> Mnesarete, daughter of Socrates.
> This woman left a husband and siblings [or brothers], and grief to
>   her mother,
> and a child and an ageless renown for great virtue [arete].
> Here the chamber of Persephone holds Mnesarete,
> who has arrived at the goal of all virtue [arete].

Mnesarete, whose name means "remembering virtue" (arete), has at least reached the goal of a woman's life, marriage and a child; she will be honored in the world below by Persephone. Mnesarete is seated to the right with her head bowed and her left arm wrapped in a mantle. On the left a young woman in a thin chiton (probably still living) may be either a slave or a sister contemplating Mnesarete's virtuous example.[75] A fourth-century (?) Chian epitaph features mother and husband as mourners of a married woman and names an even more specific set of typical female virtues: "Alas, Komallis, your wretched mother and your legitimate husband are grieved at your death, and the whole crowd of relatives loudly groans for you, tearing their hair in front of this tomb. For indeed you practiced clever work with your hands and chaste decorousness, and there was nothing blameworthy in you."[76]

Ampharete's stele of the late fifth century (see Intro-duction, fig. 1, p.3), found in the Athenian cemetery Kerameikos, unusually depicts ties between three generations. "I hold this dear child of my daughter, whom I held on my knees when we were alive, whom now dead, I dead hold."[77] The ideally youthful Ampharete gazes at a baby she holds in her left hand, enveloped by her cloak. (Of course, an Athenian grandmother could have been as young as thirty.) Because boys are often depicted as nude, this child could be a girl, who is diverted by a bird in her grandmother's right hand.

Our highly fragmentary evidence suggests that a girl's life in Archaic, Classical, and Hellenistic Greece was often sheltered and nurturing until she reached the age of marriage, around fourteen. Typically close to their mothers, as in many traditional societies, girls learned to be wives from female family members and from participation in religious rituals. The confinement of girls in the household or the immediate neighborhood undoubtedly reinforced these close relationships among female kin. The marriage ritual may at times have been romanticized, but the ceremony could not entirely soften this radical transition in a girl's life, where she moved into a strange household and soon faced the dangers of childbirth. If she lived close enough to her natal family, her continued relationship with her mother could soften this transition and be commemorated even in death. The relationships between divine mothers and daughters like Demeter and Persephone or Leto and Artemis, by contrast, often testified to the empowering and permanent aspects of their enduring bond.

FIG. 29 Mnesarete with a Young Woman, Attic marble grave stele, early fourth century B.C.E. Munich, Staatliche Antikensammlungen und Glyptothek

Jenifer Neils

CHILDREN AND GREEK RELIGION

THROUGHOUT history and throughout the world children have played important roles in religious rituals. Nearly every civilization has instituted ceremonial rites centered on children, from their entry into the world to their coming of age, the final stage of youth that represents their acceptance as adults into society. Children have also traditionally participated in adult rituals as acolytes, bearers of sacred objects, and even as victims of human sacrifice. Just as today we march little boys down the aisle at weddings as ringbearers, for instance, so in Greek antiquity a young boy "with both parents living" (pais amphithaleis) followed the bride to the abode of her new husband (cat. 110). In both instances the presence of a healthy male child at a wedding is intended to enhance the couple's fertility. More explicitly, in modern Greece young boys are often placed on the bride's knees or actually in the marriage bed. Rituals like baptism, circumcision, confirmation, the worship of child divinities, and even more social events like birthdays and debuts find ancient counterparts in Greek religious practice. In this essay I examine children as objects of worship, child-centered rituals, and children as assistants in religious ceremonies. I shall seek to explain how and why children were such a normal and essential aspect of classical Greek religion.

Before looking at children's roles specifically, a few general comments about Greek religious practice are in order. In Greek religion there are no sacred texts, so our only

CAT. 103   Girl with Box, Late Classical marble statue, ca. 340–330 B.C.E. Fort Worth, Kimbell Art Museum, Foundation Acquisition, 1972

a

b

evidence consists of inscriptions detailing cult activities, references in ancient authors and especially lexicographers who define otherwise obscure terminology, and archaeological artifacts and works of art. Given the conservative nature of Greek religion, procedures and rites were passed down from generation to generation without change, such that later generations often sought to explain some of the stranger rituals by means of an *ætion*, or foundation legend (what we would call a myth). Sometimes these myths help to elucidate the nature and purpose of particular rituals. First and foremost rituals were meant to be pleasing to the gods, but they could also serve to propitiate them in cases where their displeasure was manifested, as in plagues, or to expiate crimes against the gods. Because Greece was still largely agricultural, many religious rituals were designed to ensure fertility of the crops and livestock. In the case of children many rites are related to their maturation processes and highlight important stages in their physical growth and socialization. Performance played a large part in Greek ritual, and for this children were specially trained in dancing, singing, and

athletics—activities that may seem secular to us but were considered pleasing to the Greek gods. Although their voices are unfortunately silent, children's religious activities are eloquently represented in Greek art, especially Athenian vase paintings and votive reliefs.[1]

CHILDREN AS OBJECTS OF WORSHIP

In our time the Christ child may be the most conspicuous example of child worship. In contrast to a single god, the polytheistic Greeks stocked their pantheon with numerous divinities whose offspring occasionally became objects of worship in the guise of children.[2] The most ubiquitous example in Greek art is Eros, the god of love, who like Peter Pan seems never to grow up. He is usually depicted as a winged adolescent, and only in later Greek art does he become a pudgy baby with a bow, like our Cupid. In the earliest extant image, however, a fragmentary black-figure votive plaque from the Athenian Acropolis, he is shown wingless, seated on his mother Aphrodite's left arm while his twin,

Himeros (desire), sits on her right (fig. 1).[3] Because a century later a joint cult of Aphrodite and Eros was established on the north slope of the Acropolis, this fragment is often considered a harbinger of the worship of Eros in Athens. A later inscription from the north slope sanctuary reads: "This festival to Eros we establish on the fourth day of the month of Mounychion." We know nothing about this spring festival to the god of love, but it does indicate that he was worshiped here in his own right, independent of his mother, as he was elsewhere in Greece.[4]

More familiar is the image of Eros with his bow, and one of the best-known examples from antiquity is a statue preserved in numerous Roman copies, the original of which is often attributed to the famous fourth-century sculptor Lysippos (fig. 2). This Eros, with his arms outstretched to his right side, was probably shown in the act of testing the string of his bow and may have been a cult statue at the god's sanctuary in Thespiai in Boiotia. Quadrennial games with competitions for younger and older boys were held there in honor of Eros. If the interpretation of the statue as "testing the string" is correct, then it may serve as a metaphor for testing one's manhood, something these boy athletes did every four years. The special hairstyle seen on this statue, a braided lock running back from the center of the forehead, is one worn both by children and by the deities who protected them.[5] Given the importance of sexuality in Greek culture, it seems that they needed a male deity of love as well as a female one (Aphrodite): the female version is adult, voluptuous, and fertile; the male version is young, athletic, and protective.

FIG. 2 Eros Testing His Bowstring, Roman marble copy of Greek original of the fourth century B.C.E. Rome, Capitoline Museums, inv. 410

FIG. 1 Aphrodite Holding Her Children Himeros and Eros, Attic black-figure plaque from the Acropolis, ca. 560 B.C.E. Athens, National Archaeological Museum, Acro. 2526

In Greek legend children who died prematurely often became objects of worship. In more than one instance the death of a young royal child served as the pretext for establishing a hero cult. A case in point is the foundation myth of the famous Greek site of Nemea in the Peloponnese, where biennial games were held in honor of Zeus and victors were awarded wreaths of wild celery. According to the myth recorded in Euripides' partially lost play *Hypsipyle*, the king of Nemea and his wife, after years of infertility, bore a son whom they named Opheltes. To ensure the health and safety of their precious newborn they consulted the Delphic Oracle, who replied that the baby should not make contact with the ground until he had learned to walk (a challenge under the best of circumstances). The infant's caregiver, a slave woman named Hypsipyle (whose royal origins—former queen of Lemnos, captured by pirates and sold to the king of Nemea—were not uncommon in myth), one day set Opheltes down on

a bed of wild celery near a spring in order to fetch water for the "Seven," the doomed Greek warriors who were en route to attack Thebes. Predictably, a snake killed the baby, and so, to propitiate the gods, the Seven held funeral games in his honor. Thereafter the judges of the newly founded Nemean Games wore black as a sign of mourning, and the victors were awarded crowns of wild celery. This etiological myth helps to explain some of the peculiar aspects of these games (the black robes and celery wreaths), but it also highlights the importance of a child in Greek cult. The excavations at Nemea have uncovered small statuettes of babies who have naturally been identified as Opheltes (fig. 3), as well as a shrine surrounding the tomb of the heroized Opheltes mentioned by the second-century C.E. traveler Pausanias.[6]

Another expiation cult involves the slain children of Medea (see cat. 17, p. 23). Supposedly killed at the altar of Hera Akraia at Perachora (near Corinth), the two young boys were buried in the sanctuary along with the knife. The Corinthians, until they followed an oracle's advice and established an atonement ritual, suffered a plague of the deaths of newborns, apparently vengeance on the part of Medea's murdered sons. In the rite seven boys and seven girls chosen from aristocratic Corinthian families spent a year at the sanctuary, wearing black clothes and cutting their hair as signs of mourning. At the annual festival of the Akraia the knife was dug up and a black goat sacrificed with it. Thereafter the children returned home, replaced by another fourteen, and the knife was reburied for another year.[7] Such propitiatory rites conducted on behalf of a prematurely deceased child (or children) also were incorporated into other aspects of Greek cults, as we shall see.

While baby boys could become objects of worship upon their accidental deaths, young girls acquired heroine status in altogether different manners, namely through suicide, self-sacrifice, or as sacrificial victims. Often a virgin sacrifice was required in order to avert a plague or famine, or to obtain success in a forthcoming battle. In Greek mythology the most famous victim was Iphigeneia, the daughter of King Agamemnon, who was killed by her father at the altar of Artemis so that the stalled Greek fleet could set sail for Troy. Luring her to Aulis on the east coast of Boiotia with a promise of marriage to Achilles, Agamemnon thereby duped his daughter into being an unwilling sacrificial victim. Such an inauspicious event is rarely depicted in Greek art, but one beautiful white-ground *lekythos* shows the modest girl being led to an altar by a heavily armed Greek warrior holding ready his

FIG. 4 Sacrifice of Iphigeneia, Attic white-ground lekythos from Selinus, attributed to Douris, ca. 490 B.C.E. Palermo, Museo Archeologico, I.N. 1886

a

b

sword (fig. 4).[8] Her bridal gesture of holding her veil is in vain, for she will never be a bride. A cult of Iphigeneia (whose name means "strong in birth") was established at nearby Brauron in the sanctuary of Artemis, and the clothes of women who died in childbirth were dedicated here, according to the Athenian playwright Euripides (*Iphigeneia Among the Taurians*, 1464–1467). Other virgins went more willingly to their deaths, like the daughters of King Erechtheus of Athens, who died in order to save the city from military defeat. Whether voluntary or not, these legendary sacrifices of pure and innocent girls may have been the Greeks' way of atoning to the gods for the polluting but necessary slaughter of battle.[9]

Although child divinities are not common in Greek religion, the fact that they exist at all highlights the special importance that the Greeks accorded to childhood. Various gods or personifications depicted as youthful, like Eros (Love), Pothos (Longing), Hebe (Youth), Ploutos (Wealth), Paidia (Play), and Athanasia (Immortality), all represent positive qualities of central importance to Greek life. That negative qualities and unpopular divinities are never shown as young should provide a clue to the ancient Greeks' concept of childhood.

RITUALS FOR CHILDREN

From birth to the threshold of adulthood—which in ancient Greece was seventeen to eighteen for boys and thirteen to fifteen for girls—a variety of religious rites marked the coming of age of the Greek child. Evidence, mostly Athenian, for these rituals is derived from inscriptions, sparse references in ancient texts, and depictions on Greek vases and votive stelai. Beginning with birth these rites are often gender specific and reflect the future lifestyles of their participants: the girl clearly being prepared for a life in the household as a wife and mother, the boy for a more public existence as a warrior and statesman. For instance, a late-sixth-century C.E. literary source attests that in Athens it was customary to place a tuft of wool (symbolizing spinning) on the door of the house to mark the successful birth of a girl, and an olive wreath (prize for athletic victory at the Olympics) for that of a boy.[10] If the little owl bearing an olive wreath in its beak on the late-fifth-century B.C.E. Attic krater depicting the birth of the Athenian king Erichthonios (cat. 6; see also p. 88) alludes to this custom, then it can be documented much earlier. Although some of the rites for newborns seem to be the same for both sexes, they soon diverge and become gender specific.

Given the large number of women (10 to 20 percent) and babies who died in childbirth, it was essential for

CAT. 6   Birth of Erichthonios, Attic red-figure calyx-krater, attributed to the Nikias Painter, ca. 410 B.C.E. Richmond, Virginia Museum of Fine Arts, The Arthur and Margaret Glasgow Fund

mothers-to-be to seek the gods' goodwill beforehand. Even before the first birthing pangs, they made offerings to the foremost goddesses of childbirth, Eileithyiai and Artemis (see cat. 5, p. 116, where these goddesses assist Zeus giving birth to Athena), for a safe and quick delivery.[11] While divinities had a special goddess to assist them in childbirth, mortal women had a midwife, or *maia*, a woman who was required to be beyond the childbearing years. According to Socrates (Plato, *Theaitetos* 149c), Artemis, because she was a virgin and so childless, "assigned the privilege to women who were past childbearing years out of respect to their likeness to herself." Besides assisting in childbirth, the maia discharged such important religious functions as purging the women's quarters of pollution, uttering incantations to speed the delivery or alleviate labor pains, performing the solemn act of cutting the umbilical cord, and bathing the mother and newborn, preferably in water from a sacred spring, to wash away the pollution of childbirth. Just as in myth the hero Achilles was bathed in the River Styx to make his body (but not his heel) invulnerable, so newborns were occasionally bathed in supposedly protective liquids like wine or "the urine of an undefiled child."[12] The most common way of protecting the newborn from bad luck, illness, or the evil eye, then as also often today, was to provide it with amulets. These are frequently depicted in Greek art; rather like our charm bracelets, they consist of a cord with numerous pendants or beads

FIG. 5 Votive relief to Athena, Attic Pentelic marble, ca. 490 B.C.E. Athens, Acropolis Museum, 581

(*baskania*) that is slung across the child's chest from its shoulder to under its opposite arm (see cats. 75, 96–99). In fact, it is rare to see a newborn child in Greek art without these apotropaic devices.

Once the father decided that an infant would be reared rather than exposed, a celebration was held to signal its acceptance into the family. Called the Amphidromia (literally "running around"), it took place on or about the fifth day after birth and consisted of carrying the newborn at a run around the domestic hearth.[13] In a Greek home the hearth constituted the sacred center, and so this was the spot where newcomers (brides and slaves) were first presented to the family. Fire is also a form of purification, and so perhaps this strange rite also meant the end of pollution in the household. Less strange to us is the feasting associated with this ritual. According to a comic playwright, on this day the Greeks would "toast hunks of Chersonese cheese, boil cabbages gleaming in olive oil, bake fat breasts of lamb, pluck the feathers of doves and thrushes and finches all at the same time, nibble squid with cuttlefish, tenderize the tentacles of many octopuses, and drink many goblets of barely diluted wine."[14] A rather rich diet for a recent parturient!

At this point the newborn still did not have a name; this was conferred at a special name-giving ceremony conducted on the tenth day (*dekate*) after birth. Aristotle tells us that the reason for this delay in naming the baby is that the majority of infant deaths took place in the first week after birth. Only when the child's survival could be more or less assured was it given a proper name. Traditionally the firstborn male was named for his paternal grandfather, and the second after his maternal grandfather. Although the evidence is scant, it seems that the first daughter was named after her paternal grandmother.[15] Relatives and friends no doubt attended this ceremony and possibly brought birthday gifts (*genethlia*). According to a play by the fourth-century comedian Euboulos, women danced all night long in thanksgiving for the life of the child, and special prizes consisting of ribbons, apples, or kisses were offered.[16] However, neither this rite nor the Amphidromia seems to have been represented in Greek art. Because a Greek newborn had no legal identity, and these ceremonies, like the birth itself, were conducted within the context of a household polluted by childbirth, it is perhaps not surprising that they were not subjects of interest to artists or their patrons.

It is different with official ceremonies that took place outside the house. The first of these may have been the Apatouria, an annual autumn ceremony lasting three days in which all male citizens convened in their *phratries*, or brotherhoods, which were the age-old hereditary associations of all Ionian Greeks.[17] On this occasion children, boys and possibly girls, were officially introduced to their father's phratry—so, presumably, within one year of birth.[18] The new father presented an animal for sacrifice (and later feasting) and swore to the legitimacy of his child. Again when boys reached adolescence (age fourteen) they were registered in the phratry and made an offering of a lock of hair (koreion) to signify their attainment of manhood. In Athens the patron deities of the phratries to whom animal sacrifices were offered were Zeus Phratrios and Athena Phratria. There are no certain depictions of this ritual, but recently an Archaic votive relief from the Acropolis has been interpreted as a possible representation of an Athenian family celebrating the Apatouria (fig. 5). According to this reading Athena Phratria stands at the far left and is approached by two young boys (possibly twins since they are the same size) and their father leading a sow. Bringing up the rear are two women: the mother (possibly pregnant) and an older sister. As usual in Archaic art, the children are depicted an miniature adults, but it is unusual to find them so prominently represented on a relief of this early date—hence the suggestion that the relief alludes to the Apatouria.[19]

An exceptional votive relief, recently discovered at Echinos in northern Greece, shows what seems to be the presentation of a newborn child, probably a girl because of her clothes, to the goddess Artemis (fig. 6).[20] There is some debate about the identity of the mortal figures, but the larger-than-life goddess must be Artemis because of her attributes, torch and, just visible at the back of her neck, quiver. Also indicative of an Artemis sanctuary are the clothes hung up in the background. An ancient source, describing the habits of Greek women, states: "When they bear children, they dedicate clothing to Artemis."[21] Immediately in front of Artemis is an altar to which a male slave with a knife in hand is leading a sacrificial animal. In the exact center of the relief is the newborn baby, held forth in the arms of a young woman, possibly the mother but more likely a nurse. Behind her in lower relief is a servant carrying a tray of fruit and cakes on her head, and a jug in her lowered right hand. Last in this procession, and tallest, is a woman enveloped in her himation, raising her left hand in adoration while her right holds a small bowl, probably for incense. Given her size and elaborate dress, she is certainly the dedicant of this expensive relief—and so most likely the mother. She is giving thanks to Artemis for the successful birth of her child and presents it for the goddess's blessing in her sanctuary, along with the requisite animal sacrifice. The imagery is unique, but it expresses well the complex roles of Artemis as goddess of

FIG. 6 Mother Presenting Newborn to Artemis, marble relief from Echinos, fourth century B.C.E. Lamia, Archaeological Museum, inv. AE 1041

childbirth and later in life as kourotrophos, or protectress of young children, especially girls, as we shall see.

Another public ceremony involving Athenian children took place at the great spring festival of Dionysos, known as the Anthesteria. This important festival gave its name to the Ionian month Anthesterion and is derived etymologically from the Greek word for flower, anthos. On the first day the storage jars, or pithoi, containing the new wine were opened and tasted. On the second day of the festival, known as Choes, or the feast of the wine jugs, a drinking contest took place and children were given miniature versions of the adult drinking vessel. On the last day, which was dedicated to Hermes rather than Dionysos, the spirits of the dead roamed the earth and had to be appeased.[22] One scholar has summed up the festival as follows: "The Anthesteria was in large measure a festival that celebrated new growth and transformation: the juice of the vine into a potent drink, the bud to the blossom, and Athenian infants into the newest members of the community."[23]

With its single handle, trefoil mouth, and spherical body, the shape of this jug, called a chous, is distinctive, but its size can vary from a few centimeters to more than twenty centimeters in height (cats. 95, 101). Miniature versions of these jugs were apparently given at this time as presents to children between the ages of three and four, possibly for their first taste of wine. Today at least a thousand of these are extant, some having been retrieved from children's graves.[24] The scenes painted (see cats. 96, 97) on the smaller ones nearly all have to do with small children; the age of the child depicted is usually proportional to the size of the chous. The vase paintings are self-referencing in that they often show a small chous either resting on the ground (cat. 96) or being given a ride on a toy cart (see cat. 97, p. 285). Often this painted version of the chous is decked out with a wreath in

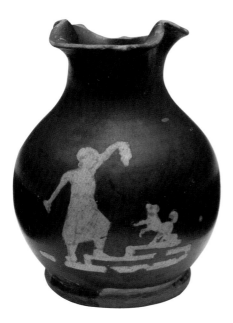

CAT. 95 Boy with Dog, Attic red-figure miniature chous, Six's technique, ca. 420 B.C.E. Cambridge, Harvard University Art Museums, Arthur M. Sackler Museum, Loan from Estate of Donald Upham and Mrs. R. U. Hunter

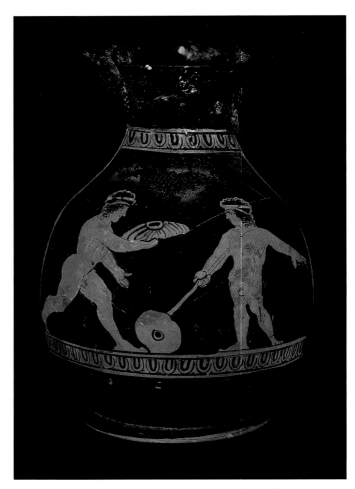

CAT. 101 Two Boys with Cake and Toy Roller, Attic red-figure chous ca. 420–410 B.C.E. Princeton, Princeton University Art Museum, Bequest of Professor George Rowley

reference to the festival (cat. 66), and later choes of ca. 400 bear an ivy vine around the neck as an allusion to Dionysos (cat. 99). Other elements that may refer to the festival are the cakes of various shapes and sizes held by the children; in the drinking contest whoever drained his chous first received a cake as his prize. The bunch of grapes (even though out of season) that can be found painted on many of these choes also no doubt alludes to the wine festival (see cat. 97). The children—primarily boys, but girls do appear (cat. 92, fig. 7)— usually themselves wear wreaths since it was the custom during this spring festival to crown them with flowers (*anthea*).[25] The importance of this festival as a special ritual for children, as well as adults, is attested by the fact that their age seems to have been reckoned in "choes." In Aristophanes' play *Thesmophoriazusae* (746–747), Mnesilochus asks a mother how old her child is by querying "Three Choes? Or four?" A late Attic grave stele of a boy holding a basket is inscribed "[He was] of an age for 'choic' things, but fate anticipated the Choes."[26]

These small vases are the best source of information regarding children's activities at specific ages in ancient Athens. From the crawling babies on the smallest choes (cat. 96) to the adolescent boys playing knucklebones on the larger ones (see cat. 86, p. 278) we find the entire range of childhood pastimes. Like the contemporary marble grave stelai (see cat. 124, p. xvi; see cats. 122–123 and 125–126, pp. 181, 306, 183, 190), they illustrate the types of toys (rollers, go-carts, balls, sticks) and variety of pets (birds, ducks, geese, hares, Maltese dogs, goats) that amused Greek children. Some special larger choes depart from such genre scenes and

CAT. 96 Crawling Baby, Attic red-figure chous, attributed to the Crawling Boy Workshop, ca. 420 B.C.E. Princeton, Princeton University Art Museum, Museum Purchase, Caroline G. Mather Fund

CAT. 99 Boy in Goat-Drawn Chariot, Attic red-figure chous with added color, ca. 400 B.C.E. New York, The Metropolitan Museum of Art, Rogers Fund, 1921

may provide glimpses into the ritual aspects of the Anthesteria, although not all scholars accept that the appearance of a religious scene on a chous signifies a relation to this festival of Dionysos.[27] For instance, the drunken, wreathed man on a large chous in Malibu could be interpreted as on his way home from the drinking contest that was the main activity of the middle day of the festival (cat. 66). The chous that he would have brought to the contest for guzzling the undiluted wine and that was later adorned with ivy rests on the ground at the far right. His slave is shouldering the provisions basket within which each contestant brought his own food and is holding forth another type of jug, into which the man is relieving himself after his surfeit of wine. This vase can easily be related to the activities of the Anthesteria, not only by its shape but by the wreathed chous depicted on it.

But what of other vases with more obscure imagery? A case in point is a famous chous attributed to the Eretria Painter, where we see what looks like a father placing his young son on a swing while his two older brothers look on (see Shapiro, fig. 18, p. 104).[28] All four wear laurel wreaths, and more hang from the supports of the swing. It is a charming family scene, and the other accouterments (upside-down footed bowl, *klismos* with drapery, *omphalos* cakes on a table) suggest that it represents some sort of ritual, but we do not know precisely what it is, or even whether it is related at all to the Anthesteria. The vase is one used at this festival, but as scholars have pointed out, it is the standard Athenian wine

CAT. 92 Girl with Toy Roller Chasing Bird, Attic red-figure chous, ca. 420 B.C.E. Worcester, Worcester Art Museum, Bequest of Sarah C. Garver

FIG. 7 Girl with Cake and Two Boys, Attic red-figure chous, ca. 400 B.C.E. Athens, Agora Museum, P7685

CAT. 66 Boy Serving a Reveler, Attic red-figure chous, attributed to the Oionokles Painter, ca. 470 B.C.E. Malibu, The J. Paul Getty Museum

FIG. 8 Girl on a Swing, Attic black-figure amphora, attributed to the Swing Painter, ca. 540 B.C.E. Boston, Museum of Fine Arts, Henry Lillie Pierce Fund, 98.918

jug and so was used in many contexts. Only the unusual element of the swing calls to mind a specific Athenian festival.

The swing is an unusual element in an all-male scene for, in the few other extant vase depictions, it is almost always shown holding a young girl. (Eros appears in the one exception.) So, for example, on a sixth-century amphora a girl suspended on a swing is flanked by four males, one of whom is of lesser stature and so presumably a boy (fig. 8).[29] This and the six other vases with similar scenes have not surprisingly been interpreted as representations of the ritual known as Aiora ("swinging").[30] The aetiological myth that explains this unusual rite in which girls swing centers around a girl named Erigone whose father Ikarios introduced viticulture to Attica. The resulting drunkenness caused the first wine drinkers to believe they had been poisoned, and so they murdered Ikarios. In sorrow for his death Erigone committed suicide by hanging, which in turn set off a rash of similar suicides on the part of young Athenian girls. In order to appease the ghost of Erigone, a festival was instituted wherein girls swing in a manner reminiscent of hanging, but without the dire consequences. This is clearly a cult of expiation on the part of the Athenians for the unfortunate death of an innocent victim. The third-century poet Callimachus mentions the annual rite of purification for Erigone in conjunction with events of the Anthesteria, and given her father's association with wine and Dionysos, scholars have placed it

within the context of this Dionysiac festival.[31] As such, it fits better with the third day of the Anthesteria, which was sacred to chthonic Hermes. A small lekythos of South Italian origin (see cat. 102, p. 6) may lend some support to this idea, for it shows a girl swinging over an altar beyond which stands the god Hermes. Because it involves viticulture and young girls, other scholars have interpreted this ritual as a fertility-enhancing rite, while still others see it as some sort of *rite de passage*. This underscores one of the problems with Greek ritual: with only an aetion and a few representations on vases, but no inscriptions or written description, one is left with numerous plausible meanings for an obscure ritual. Because these rites were essentially private, family affairs involving girls, they do not command the same attention from authors as the rites pertaining to boys and young men.

One famous choral ode in Aristophanes' *Lysistrata* (641–647) tells us the most we know from literary texts about the rites of passage experienced by Athenian girls: "Once I was seven I became an *arrephoros* [bearer of secret things]. Then at ten I became a grain-grinder [*aletris*] for the goddess. After that, wearing [?] a saffron robe, I was a bear [*arktos*] at Brauron. And, as a lovely young girl, I once served as a basket bearer [*kanephoros*], wearing a string of figs." Often this passage is taken at face value as representing the typical *cursus honorum* for a normal, albeit probably wealthy, Athenian girl. Since it appears in comedy it may be somewhat exaggerated

John H. Oakley

Death and the Child

In antiquity death intruded on the life of nearly every child. Because the infant mortality rate was so high—the survival rate is estimated at about one in three in the Classical period (480–323 B.C.E.), only half of whom reached adulthood—brothers and sisters dying within two years of their births was a commonplace in most children's lives. The life expectancy rate was much lower than today—45 years for males and 36.2 years for females in the Classical period—and because men normally married later in life than females (Aristotle suggests 37 and 18, respectively, as appropriate ages), it was not uncommon for a father to die before some of his children came of age. Mothers also died in childbirth much more commonly than today. This reality of the frequent experience of death in one's immediate family is reflected in Greek funerary art.[1]

Children at the Funeral and Grave

The funeral in ancient Greece was very much a family affair, as family members, rather than priests or undertakers, were responsible for all aspects of the ceremony.[2] Unlike in modern America, where a corpse might be picked up and sent to the funeral home so that the body can be embalmed and placed on view for visitors in a parlor, in antiquity the body was prepared and viewed in the deceased's home before being brought to the cemetery and buried.

FIG. 1 Mother Carrying Dead Son, Attic white-ground lekythos, ca. 460–450 B.C.E. Berlin, Staatliche Museen, Antikensammlung, F 2447

Shortly after death, the women of the house, particularly the older ones, prepared the corpse for burial. After closing the eyes, the women washed the body, anointed it with oil and perfume, and clothed it. It was then wrapped in a shroud (*endyma*) and placed upon the bier, usually a *kline* (couch or bed), and covered with a loose cloth (*epiblema*). The head was supported by pillows (*prokephalaiai*), and chin straps (*othonai*) sometimes held the jaw in place so that it did not gape. Branches were placed by the bier, and ribbons over the body and on the walls of the house. In Athens, *lekythoi* (oil or perfume vessels) were also set by the bier. Only one picture, that on an Attic white-ground lekythos in Berlin, can be associated with these preparations. It shows a woman carrying the stiff corpse of a wreathed boy in her arms (fig. 1).[3]

The preparations finished, the *prothesis* (lying-in-state) now took place. Close relatives came to view the corpse and pay their last respects. The women stood around the bier performing ritualized laments, while the men normally stood off to the side, performing the valediction—that is, a formal farewell salute by means of a raised and extended arm. Where the prothesis took place, inside the house or in the courtyard, is uncertain. There was probably some variety depending upon the season, weather, and size of the house. In Athens from the sixth century B.C.E. on, only close relatives were allowed to participate, so the audience was fairly small. For example, no woman under sixty was allowed to participate unless she was a child of a cousin (a first cousin once removed or second cousin) or closer relative.[4] Children, however, were present.[5]

Already in the eighth century on Attic Late Geometric vases we can observe children in several depictions. One of the best examples is the large grave marker in the form of a wine bowl or *krater* in the Metropolitan Museum of Art in New York (fig. 2).[6] In the middle of the upper register on the front side, the corpse of a dead man lies atop a bier flanked by rows of figures holding their hands to their heads in a traditional gesture of mourning. Atop the bier two small-scale figures, one smaller than the other, stand hand in hand at the corpse's feet in a pose common for children whose parents or older siblings lead them by the hand. Another child rests on the lap of an adult figure seated on a backed chair immediately to the left of the bier. The manner in which the child gesticulates with its arms raised reflects the behavior of a young child. The seated adult raises a twig branch in the direction of the bier, as does the figure immediately to the right of the bed. The smaller figure behind the latter may be an adolescent or an adult simply made smaller by the artist so that he could fit him into the space beneath the checkerboard epiblema. The size of a figure in Geometric vase painting is not always indicative of its age.[7] Note how the seated figure with the child on its lap is also proportionally small, because it is situated underneath the other side of the epiblema. Thus we cannot be certain whether the larger of the two small-scale figures standing on the bier is an adult or an adolescent.

Later Attic black-figure vase painting of the sixth and early fifth centuries gives us some of our fullest renditions of the prothesis. This scene is found frequently on *loutrophoroi* (tall, slender vessels used to carry bath water for weddings and to mark the tombs of the unmarried) from the second half of the sixth century to the beginning of the next, where children are often depicted among the participants. Scenes of the prothesis also occur on terracotta funerary plaques, probably meant to be attached to the sides of a grave monument.

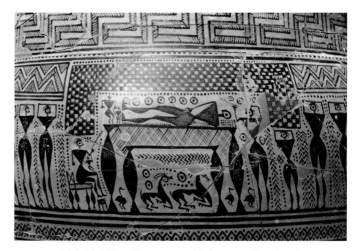

FIG. 2 Prothesis (detail), Attic Late Geometric krater, attributed to the Hirschfeld Workshop, ca. 740–730 B.C.E. New York, The Metropolitan Museum of Art, Rogers Fund, 1914, 14.130.14

FIG. 3 Prothesis, Attic black-figure plaque, attributed to the Sappho Painter, ca. 500–490 B.C.E. Paris, Musée du Louvre, MNB 905

One of the best examples is attributed to the Sappho Painter and shows a dead man lying on a bier in the center (fig. 3).[8] Mourning women surround the couch, many of whom are labeled, indicating their relationship to the deceased. These figures include his mother, who stands directly by his head, apparently touching it with her left hand, and at the head of the bed his grandmother, who cradles her own downcast head in her hands. Various aunts, including one labeled as being on the father's side, also mourn with both hands to their heads, or one to the head and the other held out. At the foot of the bed stands the father, who faces left and makes the gesture of valediction to a group of adult males. They appear to be just arriving and are also making the gesture of valediction. One of them is labeled as a brother of the deceased.

Three children also appear here. Between the mother and grandmother near the front of the bed stands a girl who mourns as the other women do. She is clearly labeled "sister," a fairly young one in this case. Typical of Archaic drawing, she is rendered as a miniature adult. This is also true of the older girl shown near the foot of the bed and the even younger boy behind her, who extends both hands out toward the bier, attempting to gain contact with his lost one. The female children perform similar roles to the women, but the boy is not able to control his emotions, as do the men. In this picture the emotional responses of the children, both male and female, are equated with those of adult females and differentiated from those of grown men, who are more restrained. Amplifying the emotional content of the scene are several inscriptions that are cries of grief—"oimoi" (woe is me).

Normally in scenes of the prothesis the deceased is an adult, but on several Classical white lekythoi attributed to the Sabouroff Painter, the deceased, as judged from the size of the corpse and proportions of the head, appears to be a teenage boy. A lekythos dating to 460–450 is a typical example (fig. 4).[9] Here, what looks to be a youth is about to have his head cradled by the left hand of a woman, most likely his mother, while a young man, possibly a brother, stands with hand to head mourning at the top of the bier. A second woman mourns at the couch's foot. Such scenes show that mourning rites for young males were as important in Greek society as those for adults.

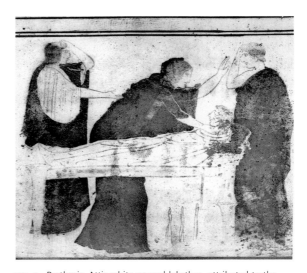

FIG. 4 Prothesis, Attic white-ground lekythos, attributed to the Sabouroff Painter, ca. 460–450 B.C.E. London, The British Museum

CAT. 113 Youth and Girl Visiting a Tomb, Attic white-ground lekythos, attributed to the Painter of Athens 1826, ca. 460 B.C.E. Malibu, The J. Paul Getty Museum

lekythos attributed to the Painter of Athens 1826 (cat. 113). She holds an alabastron in her left hand and a flower in the right. The *tymbos*, the mound of earth covering the grave, stands before a stele in the middle of the scene; a youth holding out a ribbon stands on the other side. The manner in which the Thanatos Painter shows a young girl moving toward a stele with a doll clasped before her in both hands indicates that she will leave it as an offering at the tomb (fig. 8).[14] Dolls (see cats. 72–74, pp. 267–268) are not infrequently found in graves and are also shown in girls' arms on gravestones (cat. 68).[15] A boy on a lekythos attributed to the Vouni Painter makes ready to offer a wreath, whose ends he prepares to tie before hanging it on the grave (fig. 9).[16] In front of the tymbos stand two stelai; they and their bases are decorated with offerings that include ribbons, wreaths, an *aryballos* (oil jar), *strigil* (scraper), and *halteres* (jumping weights). Joining the boy is a woman who stands on the left holding out a ribbon to decorate the tomb. Children, then, are shown leaving the types of objects that are found in tombs or that adults are depicted as offering.

Children, often girls, who are probably best interpreted as servants because of the manual labor they perform as well as (sometimes) their ethnicity, costume, and hairstyle, are shown carrying various objects to the tomb. Such a girl on a lekythos of 430–420 attributed to the Quadrate Painter labors

FIG. 8 Girl Bringing Doll to Tomb (detail), Attic white-ground lekythos, attributed to the Thanatos Painter, ca. 440 B.C.E. Private collection

FIG. 9 Visit to the Grave, Attic white-ground lekythos, attributed to the Vouni Painter, ca. 460 B.C.E. New York, The Metropolitan Museum of Art, Purchase, Alexander M. Bing Gift, 1935, 35.11.5

FIG. 10 Visit to the Grave, Attic white-ground lekythos, attributed to the Quadrate Painter, ca. 430–420 B.C.E. Athens, National Archaeological Museum, 1760

under the weight of a large *hydria* (vessel for transporting water) that she carries on her head, as she holds out an alabastron in her right hand (fig. 10).[17] Her mistress, who stands before the tomb with a funerary basket, looks down and back with a scowl upon her face toward the girl. Another woman sits upon a base *(trapeza)* before the tomb with her head turned downward in a sad, pensive pose. She may be the deceased, but here, as on many other lekythoi, this is not possible to say with certainty; to identify which, if any, figure is the deceased has long been a problem.[18]

Children are rare on South Italian vases, appearing mainly on Apulian red-figure. Sometimes they are servants, male and female, who are shown standing in the *naiskos* (nichelike structure) assisting an adult. At other times a child is shown with its mother. Most often, though, they are shown alone in the naiskos with toys and pets.[19]

Babies are also represented as visitors to the grave. Several lekythoi, such as one attributed to the Painter of Berlin 2451 from ca. 430–420, depict babies being held by a

FIG. 14 Charon with Boy in Boat, Attic white-ground lekythos, ca. 430–420 B.C.E. Athens, National Archaeological Museum, 16463

His mother looks down lovingly toward the child holding out both hands in vain to him—she wishes he were not leaving but knows that he cannot come back. The father stands behind her, and from what remains of his arm he seems to motion to the child also, but with less emotion than the mother. Greek fathers mourned the loss of children as did mothers, but not usually as openly. Charon, meanwhile, stands impatiently in his boat, his right hand on his hip, the other holding his pole upright. He seems less sympathetic than on the previous vase, more the laborer worried only about getting his job done. Indeed, there was naturally a variance in ideas about the nature of the afterlife, the exact form it took, and the personalities of the divinities connected with it.

Children in the Grave

We turn now from looking at children in the funeral and at the grave to the archaeological evidence for child burial in ancient Greece. In general, the burial of a child did not receive as much attention or care as that of an adult, although there are more than a few elaborate children's graves.[26] For example, a child was buried in the most famous of all Proto-Attic vases, the large neck-amphora from Eleusis of ca. 660–650 showing on the neck Odysseus with his companions putting out the eye of the Cyclops.[27] And, as we shall see, sculpted marble gravestones marked some children's tombs in Classical times. The grave of the ten- to fifteen-year-old Eupheros from 430, excavated in the Kerameikos, is one of the best known.[28] A finely carved stele showing a mantled

CAT. 115 Charon, Mother, and Baby Boy, Attic white-ground lekythos, attributed to the Painter of Munich 2335, ca. 430 B.C.E. New York, The Metropolitan Museum of Art, Rogers Fund, 1909

FIG. 15 Youth (Eupheros) with Strigil, Attic marble grave stele, ca. 430 B.C.E. Athens, Kerameikos Museum, inv. no. 797

youth with headband and sandals facing to the right and holding up a strigil in his left hand marked the interment (fig. 15). The boy was buried in a wooden sarcophagus that contained six white-ground lekythoi, several objects from the boy's earlier childhood—a small terracotta monkey, a *chous*, (type of oinochoe), a small black-gloss *kantharos* (high-handled drinking vase), and a black-gloss saltcellar—and other artifacts from his school days, including two small bronze strigils, a knucklebone, and the remains of a sheath with two bone styli inside, in addition to a bronze needle (fig. 16). In this instance the contents of the grave tell us much about the child, and there is a clear relation between them and the tombstone, for the strigils in the grave and the skeletal remains of the youth correspond in age with the youth shown holding a strigil on the stele.

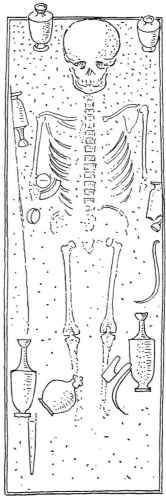

FIG. 16 Grave of Eupheros in the Kerameikos, ca. 430 B.C.E.

There was also a change in where children were buried. In the Late Geometric and Early Archaic periods child burials are most often located near adult male burials, while during the Classical period they are most often associated with adult female burials. This appears to reflect the change from the more male-oriented Archaic period to the democratic city-state of the fifth century, which promoted the role of women as mothers. The sudden increase in children's burials around 500, almost immediately after the institution of the democracy in 508/507, appears to reflect this change as well, suggesting that women were now more easily able to give proper burial to their dead children.[35] In addition, many more graves appear to have been placed in locations related to roads leading to the sanctuaries of such important female deities as Demeter and Artemis. This makes sense, considering the fact that women were primarily responsible for the burial of children. After 400, however, these traditions and preferred locations for burials cease, as Athens was at most times no longer a free state.

Perhaps this change reflects the loss of interest on women's parts in playing the role of the dutiful mothers of the democracy, due to a greater interest during the fourth century and Hellenistic period in luxury, leisure, and body care, as reflected in, among other things, the grave goods and monuments of the fourth century associated with adult graves. Thus Athenian burial practices provide an example of how children's graves can reflect political history. Likewise, these practices help to disprove the theory that there was not much interest in children's graves, despite literary evidence such as Plato's *Republic*, which has Socrates include in things "not worthy of record" those children who perish in earliest infancy.[36]

Having come to this conclusion, however, we need also to remember that infanticide was a widespread practice, as such ancient literary sources as Plato, Aristophanes, and Aristotle testify.[37] In many instances exposing a child was an economic necessity for a family. Female children in particular were prone to exposure, because of the economic pressure the provision of a proper dowry could place on a family. Sickly or deformed neonates were also often exposed. In Sparta, law required exposure of all malformed infants.[38] Those exposed, however, were newborns who had not yet been accepted into the family. To the Greek way of thinking, because nature killed them, the parents were not guilty or stained with pollution (*miasma*). Nor did one have the same attachment to a newborn as to a child who had spent some time with its family. This does not mean the parents had no feelings for the newborn but rather that they accepted what was a necessity.

Many Greek myths deal with the exposure of newborns, usually prompted by some prophecy that the infant will harm his parents in the future. The most famous mythological instance is that of the baby whose later name, Oedipus, derives from the swollen feet he received from having his ankles pierced and pinned for exposure. He is discovered by a Corinthian shepherd, who brings him from Mount Cithaeron near Thebes to King Polybus of Corinth. There he is raised, only to return later to Thebes, killing his father unknowingly along the way at the place where the three roads meet, after which he marries his mother and produces children with her. A unique scene on an Attic red-figure amphora with twisted handles by the Achilles Painter shows the young Oedipus resting his head on the shepherd's shoulder as he clings closely to him (fig. 17). The man is labeled Euphorbus (good nourisher or shepherd).[39] The light-haired, vulnerable child contrasts sharply with this straggly-haired, burly shepherd.

A unique scene of child exposure on a South Italian volute-krater attributed to the Underworld Painter of ca. 330 shows Aeolus and Boeotos, the twin sons of Poseidon and

Melanippe (fig. 18). They have been handed over to a shepherd who has been instructed to expose them.[40] The pair, packed tightly in swaddling clothes, with pointed bonnets on their heads, are held aloft in a skin by the shepherd. He places a staff through the skin's knot so that he will be able to carry the package over his shoulder. Among observers are the boys' mother, nurse, grandfather, and great-grandfather. A lost play of Euripides is the most likely source of inspiration for this picture.

Cronos set a divine precedent for this practice when he swallowed the children he had with Rhea because he had learned that one of them would overthrow him. Rhea decided to trick him by placing a stone in a cloth in lieu of the child Zeus and handing it over to Cronos to swallow. This moment is shown on a remarkable Attic red-figure pelike attributed to the Nausicaa Painter (cat. 4, see p. 86). She stands on the left, one foot propped atop a rock (ironically?) holding out the cloth-covered rock to Cronos on the right, who holds a scepter in his left hand while gesturing to her with his right. Exposure, then, is a subject in Greek art handled only in mythological scenes.

CHILDREN ON THE GRAVE

Sculpted gravestones often marked children's tombs in the Classical and Hellenistic periods and so provide a rich source for pictures of children.[41] The most common types include a thin, upright stone slab (stele) with a figure or figures carved in relief (see, for example, Beaumont, fig. 11, p. 74), painted, or engraved; a smaller version with a sunken rectangular

FIG. 19 The Youth Me[gakles] and His Sister Philo ("Brother and Sister Stele"), Attic marble grave stele, ca. 540–530 B.C.E. New York, The Metropolitan Museum of Art, Frederick C. Hewitt Fund, 1911, Rogers Fund, 1921, Anonymous Gift, 1951

FIG. 18 Aeolus and Boeotos (detail), Apulian red-figure volute-krater attributed to the Underworld Painter, ca. 330 B.C.E. Atlanta, Emory University, Michael C. Carlos Museum, Carlos Collection of Ancient Greek Art, 1994.1

picture field (Bildfeldstele; see cat. 123, p. 306); a naiskos, a small structure with an architectural frame, that can include antae, architraves, roof sima with antifixes, pediments, and acroteria (see Introduction, fig. 1, p. 3); stone lekythoi (for example, fig. 12); and stone loutrophoroi (for example, fig. 29). The markers were often inscribed with the name of the deceased, and sometimes with an epigram or other form of poetry. One of the most appropriate for our purposes was found on a third- or second-century child's stele from Kios in Bithynia: "Over Asklepiodotos who died before his time, Father Noetus piled up this well-enclosed mound, and before

FIG. 24 Mother (Asia) and Son, Attic marble grave stele, first quarter of the fourth century B.C.E. Athens, National Archaeological Museum, 767

covered the baby with part of her mantle, and the two stare intently at one another, the exchange underscored by the child's gesture with his raised right hand. Ampharete's right arm rests on the back of the chair, and in her right hand she holds a bird. The child's physiognomy is strikingly realistic, more so than is common at this time: round head, puffed cheeks, and small chin, nose, and eyes. Normally one would assume this is a mother with child, but the epigram carved on the architrave above tells us that it represents grandmother and grandchild, both of whom are dead:

> I hold this my daughter's dear child,
> whom I held on my lap, when we were alive
> and looked at the rays of the sun with our eyes,
> and now being dead, I hold it dead.

Again the identity of the figures is different from what one would guess, and this gravestone may also have been part of a standard stock.

Young children (three to six years old) are also often shown standing by the knees of a seated woman, presumably their mothers in most cases.[69] This is a time of life when children are particularly dependent on their mothers. The gravestone of Asia from the first quarter of the fourth century has a particularly touching picture: a young boy stands on tiptoes, reaching up with both hands to his mother—a universal gesture by which young children indicate that they want to be picked up (fig. 24).[70] The mother bends over slightly toward the child, her right hand touching underneath his left arm, her left arm embracing him around the back as they look at one another.

Fathers are also shown on occasion with their children. Xanthippos's stele of 430–420 is the most famous example (fig. 25).[71] The cobbler sits on a klismos facing left gazing at the cobbler's last (a wooden or metal model of a foot over which the shoemaker forms a shoe), which he holds up before him in his right hand. His left hand rests gingerly on the back of his youngest daughter, who raises both hands up. This is a rare representation in Greek art in which a father's affection for a female child is clearly shown. His older daughter stands before him by his knees. She stares up at him, holding a bird in her right hand while gesturing to him with the left. As often happens with parents today, his attention is divided between family and work.

FIG. 25 Cobbler (Xanthippos) and His Two Daughters, Attic marble grave stele, ca. 430–420 B.C.E. London, The British Museum, 1805.7-3.183

Multiple children occur on a substantial number of gravestones. In a few cases they may be twins. This appears to be the case on a stele of ca. 370 that may be either an Ionian work showing strong Attic influence or an Attic work (fig. 26).[72] A mature woman in chiton and mantle stands on the left holding a swaddled infant at her waist. On the right a young female servant in long chiton and *sakkos* (sack or bag used to cover the hair) stands and looks up at the woman while holding another swaddled infant who wears a bonnet, a frequent form of head protection for infants. The infants appear to be virtually the same age, so it is logical to identify them as twins.[73] It may be that the woman died in birthing the pair; then as now, giving birth to twins was much more dangerous than to a single child.

Many gravestones from the second half of the fourth century depict family groups, sometimes women only, sometimes males and females.[74] Children are often among their number and can provide an emotional accent to the picture.[75] Two children appear on another Attic stele (fig. 27).[76] A draped woman named Bako stands in three-quarter view on the left, grasping her mantle with her left hand while

FIG. 27   Mother, Grandmother, and Children (Bako, Socrates, and Aristonike), Attic marble grave stele, second half of the fourth century B.C.E. Paris, Musée du Louvre, MA 3113

FIG. 26   Woman and Servant Holding Twins, marble grave stele, second half of the fourth century B.C.E. Paris, Musée du Louvre, MA 2872

extending her right to perform the dexiosis with Aristonike, who is seated on a padded *diphros* on the right, her feet atop a footstool. Between them stands the small boy Socrates, who looks up, extending his right hand toward Bako, who may thus be his mother. In the background in lower relief between the two women stands a frontally posed maid in long chiton and sakkos, who grasps a small casket to her chest while reaching with her right hand toward her face, a gesture of mourning. Another maid stands behind Aristonike holding a swaddled infant. She also looks out toward the viewer, a common feature of the later gravestones, whose figures invite interaction with the viewer. The names of Bako, Socrates, and Aristonike are all inscribed on the architrave, but the style of lettering indicates that Aristonike's was added later than the other two. This suggests that Bako, having already successfully produced a son, Socrates, died during the birth of a second child, who is shown on the right. Her mother, Aristonike, died sometime later, at which point her name was added to the stele.

Most of the roughly eighty-five extant gravestones showing infants are thought by many scholars to have been used on graves of woman who died in childbirth, although the evidence suggests that they were more likely meant primarily to indicate one area of a woman's responsibilities.[77]

FIG. 28 Mother (Plangon) in Labor, Attic marble grave stele, second half of the fourth century B.C.E. Athens, National Archaeological Museum, 749

CAT. 19 Gravestone with Woman in Labor, Attic marble grave stele, ca. 330 B.C.E. Cambridge, Harvard University Art Museums, Arthur M. Sackler Museum, Gift of Edward W. Forbes

That the former was the case with a small group of gravestones, though, all from the second half of the fourth century, is certain from the depictions of women in labor on them.[78] The most explicit is the Boiotian Bildfeldstele of Plangon (fig. 28).[79] She is shown leaning back while partially seated upon a kline, her legs spread wide, her left foot resting on a platform. Her hair and garments are disheveled, and she is being aided by two women. The servant behind her places her right hand on Plangon's right shoulder; the other hand supports Plangon's left arm as she leans back. Another more elderly woman stands by Plangon on the platform extending her left hand toward her in a gesture of aid and concern while holding up Plangon's right arm with her left hand. On the far left a bearded, grieving man buries his head in his left hand. He is inscribed as Tolmides of Plataea, Plangon's father. The older woman, then, must be Plangon's mother. Both the pose

of Plangon and the nature of the other figure's activity indicate that Plangon is in labor, making it obvious that she died in childbirth.

Similarly posed women on chairs and aided by others are found on several other gravestones, including one in the Sackler Museum, which is the only one preserved in high relief (cat. 19). Here the woman leans back on a throne, supported from behind by a slave girl who holds the dying woman's left arm. An elderly man stands before her, his left hand raised palm up in a gesture of concern, while with his right he performs the dexiosis with her. Part of another woman remains behind him. The male figure, presumably the dying woman's husband, is rendered awkwardly because the figure was originally different. A sculptor, at some point after the original carving of the stele, reworked a female figure into that of the elderly male. Thus the composition of the scene was altered to the more common picture of a "seated woman at home." The dying woman's pose, her loose garments, her accentuated belly and upper body, and the presence of her husband all lend a tragic note to the scene, an ambiance not commonly found on Attic gravestones.[80]

Two children are shown on the lekythos of Lysistrate and Timophon (cat. 111). This is the most common number when more than one is depicted and may simply be a shorthand for two or more children, rather than an indication of exactly two.[81] A maid holding a swaddled infant with bonnet stands on the left behind Lysistrate, who performs the dexiosis with her husband, Timophon. Bearded and mantled, he leans over on his staff to the left while extending his right hand. She, likewise, extends her right while grasping her garment by the shoulder with the left. Between them stands a young girl, their daughter Kleippe. Is Timophon making ready to depart or is Lysistrate? The children are shown to give further poignancy to the family's loss.

In other cases there is no doubt that the man is departing, often to war. Departure in these scenes is a metaphor for death, that of the grave's inhabitant(s). A fragmentary marble loutrophoros-amphora in Athens shows Euthippos, from the deme of Cholleidai, standing before and shaking the hand of Persia, presumably his mother or wife (fig. 29).[82] He wears an *exomis*, and a *chlamys* is slung over his arms and around his back. Behind him stands a servant boy, who holds Euthippos's Corinthian helmet in his right hand and his shield on his left arm. Persia sits on a klismos whose seat is covered with a cloth. Against her knees leans a young girl, her left arm akimbo, the right resting on Persia's knees. She is either his

FIG. 29 (above) Departure, Attic marble loutrophoros-amphora of Euthippos and Persia, second quarter of the fourth century B.C.E. Athens, National Archaeological Museum, 953

CAT. 111 (left) Grave Memorial with Family Scene, Attic marble grave lekythos, Later Classical, ca. 400–375 B.C.E. The Cleveland Museum of Art, Gift of J. H. Wade

sical Attic tombstones depict children, as do about a quarter of all Thessalian gravestones—indeed, many of these tombstones show a single child.[90] And because the vases and gravestones were produced for various strata of society, not just the elite, we are undoubtedly correct to conclude that most Greeks had deep feelings for their children.[91]

The Greeks' cares and concerns for their children are also reflected by the way Greek artists and craftsmen were so observant of children, particularly in the Classical and Hellenistic periods. They carefully and accurately rendered the way children act, move, and interact differently at various ages, a fact we have observed several times in this essay, and something that is apparent to anybody who has reared a child. The tombstone of Apollonie is perhaps the single best example because of the realistic depiction of children at several different ages (see fig. 20).

Images of male children on funerary objects are more common than those of females, indicating the Greeks' preference for male children, but both the objects found in burials and several images indicate that the Greeks had love and affection for their daughters as well. The manner in which Xanthippos tenderly interacts with his daughters provides the best example (see fig. 25). And attention was often paid to detail when depicting girls, such as their hairstyle—tied up in a knot or a ponytail, for example—as well as their costumes, such as a girdled or cross-girt chiton and diadem.[92]

Although children of all ages are shown, perhaps not surprisingly infants received much less attention than older children, in respect to both their graves and their funerary art. When infants do appear in art, it is usually in the presence of their mothers, perhaps signifying in some instances that the latter had died in childbirth. In respect to graves, the number of gender-specific objects found in them increases as the age of the child buried increases, suggesting that infants were thought of as genderless and only over time began to take on a role as an important gendered member of the household. Exposure of newborns, particularly females, was a necessary fact of ancient life.

Depictions of children on funerary art often place them in their own world, not that of an adult. The classical gravestones, the artistic high point in depicting children in funerary art, in particular idealize them, and a considerable number of white lekythoi, more than has been previously recognized, harbor poignant images of children.[93] They are often shown with pets and toys. Birds, dogs, and balls are common to both sexes, while girls can have dolls or a mirror and boys toy-rollers and more rarely a lyre, hare, or cat. Scenes of happy, playing children must have given the parents who buried them a feeling that their children had had happy lives and despite their deaths remained happy—eternal play is not a bad thing. This sanitized view of childhood emphasizes the pleasant aspects, not the negative, such as crying and the soiling of clothes—just as modern advertising does.[94] One does need to remember, however, that the art reflects the parents' point of view, not the child's.

When children are shown in emotional situations, such as funerals, they act like women and old men and reveal their feelings. In funerary scenes children often seek to regain physical contact with the dead, in contrast to the restrained reactions of mature males. In this way children, like women and old men, play the "other" to the Athenian male citizen. And not all children were free, for child slaves, male and female, are shown performing their duties in funerary art, clear evidence of child labor. Boys assist at the palestra or help with the preparations to go off to war, for example, and females help with the house and the visit to the grave. This shows that, to the Greeks' way of thinking, happy, productive slaves had an important place in the well-functioning oikos.

Greek funerary art, then, provides insights into many aspects of Greek childhood, including, among others, family life, leisure, a child's relationship with siblings and parents, gender roles, and child labor. Children can be shown alone or as part of a household, where they supply a sense of more than one generation, and they are not normally rendered as potential adults but as individuals with their own rights, tasks, and fulfillments.[95] Just as important, however, is the sense these pictures give that children are the same today as they were back then. Who cannot feel an immediate connection with the image of a young boy on tiptoes extending his arms up to his mother so that she will pick him up (see fig. 24)? No other culture produced such touching funerary images of children on such a large scale for such a long time as did the Greeks'.

CAT. 126 Gravestone of the Girl Apollonia, Attic marble grave stele (with polychrome), ca. 100 B.C.E. Malibu, The J. Paul Getty Museum

57 *AAA* 6 (1973), 223, fig. 15; *ArchReports* (1973–1974), 25, fig. 46; Rühfel 1984a, 117, fig. 47b. Several others have been found at Sindos in Macedonia, see *Sindos: Catalogue of the Exhibition* (Athens, 1985), 139, 173, 185, and 273. For these carts, see J. H. Crouwel, *Chariots and Other Wheeled Vehicles in Ancient Greece* (Amsterdam, 1992), 77–88.

58 Athens, National Archaeological Museum, 3845: *CAT,* 1.610.

59 Clairmont (supra n. 44), 90, for the comparison with choes; Hirsch-Dyczek 1983, 18–21, for infants on the ground, the most common way of depicting them on fifth-century Attic tombstones.

60 *CAT,* introductory vol., 119–121; Bergemann (supra n. 21), 35–55; Himmelmann (supra n. 18), passim, especially 102–115.

61 *CAT,* introductory vol., 66–72.

62 Beaumont 1994, 83–84.

63 Stears (supra n. 21), 120–122.

64 Hirsch-Dyczek 1983, 54–55.

65 Chalkis, Museum, 11: *CAT,* 1.856.

66 E.g., Berlin, Staatliche Museen, Antikensammlung Inv. Sk 809: E. Pfuhl and H. Möbius, *Die ostgriechischen Grabreliefs* (Mainz, 1977), vol. 1, pl. 210, no. 1439. For boy servants, see Rühfel 1984a, 83–88.

67 A fragment of a stele from Anavysos preserves part of the head, chest, and left hand of a woman (probably seated) cradling the head of a child: Athens, National Archaeological Museum, 4472: Richter (supra n. 44), figs. 151–153; Rühfel 1984a, 80, fig. 32; Beaumont, fig. 3. For the composition, see also Rühfel 1984a, 142–151, and Vorster 1983, 2–6. Two Thessalian gravestones show a mother suckling a child, a subject not found on Attic tombstones: B. S. Ridgway, *Fourth-Century Styles in Greek Sculpture* (Madison, Wis., 1997), 171 and 190 n. 52.

68 Athens, Archaeological Museum of Kerameikos, P 695: *CAT,* 1.660.

69 Rühfel 1984a, 154–159.

70 Athens, National Archaeological Museum, 767: *CAT,* 1.700. Hirsch-Dyczek 1983, 40–44, for this subject.

71 London, The British Museum, 1805.7-3.183: *CAT,* 1.630. Hirsch-Dyczek 1983, 44–45, for stelai with man and child.

72 Paris, Musée du Louvre, Ma 2872: *CAT,* 2.810.

73 For twins, see V. Dasen, "Les jumeaux dans l'imaginaire funeraire grec," in G. Hoffmann, ed., *Les pierres de l'offrande* (Kilchberg, Switzerland, 2001), 72–89. Triplets are probably shown on a funerary base in London, The British Museum, 1816.6-10.324: *CAT,* 12.

74 Hirsch-Dyczek 1983, 51–53, for this type of scene.

75 Bergemann (supra n. 21), 86–95.

76 Paris, Musée du Louvre, Ma 3113: *CAT,* 4.910.

77 *CAT,* 91; Bergemann (supra n. 21), 64–65; Stears (supra n. 21), 125. A corpus of these has been assembled in an honors paper by my student M. Davis.

78 A. Stewart and C. Gray, "Confronting the Other: Childbirth, Aging, and Death on Attic Tombstones at Harvard," in Beth Cohen, ed., *Not the Classical Ideal: Athens and the Construction of the Other in Greek Art* (Leiden, 2000), passim and 257–258 n. 14, for a list of them; see also Bergemann (supra n. 21), 64–65, and Demand 1994, 122–128. A remarkable painted Hellenistic stele in Volos, that of Hediste, shows the dead mother on a couch with a woman in the background carrying a newborn, for Hediste had died in childbirth: J. Charbonneaux, R. Martin, and F. Villard, *Hellenistic Art* (New York, 1973), 130, fig. 127. For the inscription, see Peek, *Vers* (supra n. 42), 903, and Peek, *Grabgedichte* (supra n. 42), 142.

79 Athens, National Archaeological Museum, 749, *CAT,* 4.470.

80 Well-articulated by Stewart and Gray (supra n. 78).

81 Pomeroy 1997, 130.

82 Athens, National Archaeological Museum, 953, *CAT,* 2.855.

83 Athens, National Archaeological Museum, 869, *CAT,* 2.950.

84 For a good overview of Hellenistic grave reliefs, see B. Schmaltz, *Griechische Grabreliefs* (Darmstadt, Germany, 1983), 223–249. See also B. S. Ridgway, *Hellenistic Sculpture II: The Styles of ca. 200–100 B.C.* (Madison, Wis., 2000), 189–206; and S. Schmidt, *Hellenistische Grabreliefs: Typologische und chronologische Beobachtungen* (Cologne, 1991); for the few Hellenistic Attic grave reliefs, see J. B. Grossman, "Hellenistic Sculpted Funerary Monuments from the Athenian Agora," in O. Palagia and W. Coulsen, eds., *Regional Schools in Hellenistic Sculpture* (Oxford, 1998), 75–82.

85 Oxford, Ashmolean 1947.271: Pfuhl and Möbius (supra n. 66), vol. 1, 88, no. 149, pl. 33,149.

86 Delos: M.-T. Le Dinahet, "L'image de l'enfance à l'époque hellénistique: La valeur de l'exemple délian," in Hoffmann (supra n. 73), 90–106. For the Smyrnaean reliefs, see P. Zanker, "The Hellenistic Grave Stelai from Smyrna: Identity and Self-Image in the Polis," in A. W. Bulloch et al., eds., *Images and Ideologies: Self-Definition in the Hellenistic World* (Berkeley, 1993), 212–230; see 221 and fig. 16 for this relief and an interpretation of Archippos as an athletic victor; for him as a priest, see Schmidt (supra n. 84), 138 n. 5.

87 Grossman (supra n. 49), 69.

88 Golden 1990, 82–114; see also Charlier and Raepset (supra n. 5); M. Golden, "Did the Greeks Care When Their Children Died?" *Greece and Rome* 35 (1988), 152–163; and the essay by Golden in this volume.

89 Xenocleia: *IG* 22, 12335. See also Golden 1990, 89–92, and essay by Golden in this volume for other examples.

90 Rühfel 1984a, 92.

91 Pomeroy 1997, 117.

92 Stears (supra n. 21), 119.

93 For example, Garland 1985, 86, says they are rarely depicted on white lekythoi.

94 Scott 1999, 13.

95 These are the two ways children are normally viewed by other cultures: C. J. Sommerville's foreword in A. B. Kinney, ed., *Chinese Views of Childhood* (Honolulu, 1995), xi.

Catalogue

Jenifer Neils and John H. Oakley

Catalogue

The individual entries in this catalogue focus on what these objects tell us about Greek children and their lives; we do not attempt to discuss every aspect of each work of art. All measurements are in centimeters. The bibliography for each entry contains only the most recent major publications in which further bibliography can be found.

STATUES OF YOUNG CHILDREN

This statue of a young boy and a head of a girl (which was once attached to a full size sculpture), are just two examples from the hundreds that were sculpted in the later Classical and Hellenistic periods. In the 340s B.C.E. the famous Greek sculptor Lysippos created portraits of the child who was to become Alexander the Great (Pliny, *Natural History* 34.63), and this may have set a fashion for such images. At this time Athenian parents commissioned statues of their children to dedicate in sanctuaries of goddesses of fertility and childbirth, of which that of Artemis at Brauron is the best-known example. Here, and at the sanctuary of Eileithyia at Agrai, excavations have uncovered numerous marble statues of young children—standing, crawling, sitting—dating from the late fourth and beginning of the third centuries. Bronze statuettes of young boys were found at the sanctuary of Dione at Dodona, and dedicatory inscriptions for statues of *arrephoroi*, young girls in the service of Athena, are known from the Athenian Acropolis.

Inscriptions indicate that parents, mostly mothers, and even grandparents dedicated statues of young children in fulfillment of vows made before birth or to preserve their offspring from harm. This practice became increasingly widespread and may account for the large number of limestone "temple-boy" statues found on Cyprus. This type of seated toddler is known in a variety of media also in Etruria and the Near East; thirty marble statues of young boys were found in a votive pit of the fourth century at the healing shrine of Eshmun in Lebanon.

For sculptures of young children, see Thompson 1982; Vorster 1983; Raftopoulou 2001. For dedicatory inscriptions, see Geagan 1994. For the "temple-boys," see Beer 1987 and 1994. For the Eshmun sculptures, see C. Doumet-Serhal et al., *Stones and Creed: 100 Artefacts from Lebanon's Antiquity* (London, 1998), 56–57, nos. 29–38.

1
Young Boy

This young boy, perhaps three or four years old, stands looking pensively down to his left. He is draped in a voluminous *himation* (cloak), leaving only his right shoulder and arm bare. The heavy folds of the cloak do not conceal his childish physique, in particular his protruding abdomen. The sculptor has lavished attention on the boy's round face, with its high forehead, chubby cheeks, delicate nose, and fleshy lips. Especially distinctive is the boy's hairstyle: the head appears to be shaved except for a tuft of hair that is braided at the back. The preservation of one long lock of hair suggests that the child would dedicate it to one of the divinities who protect children, such as the Kourotrophoi, Asklepios, Demeter, or Artemis. The braid may be the attribute of a votary—that is, a child who has been dedicated to the service of some divinity for part of his childhood, such as the Egyptian goddess Isis.

The boy is dressed and posed, with his left arm enveloped in his cloak, like a Greek philosopher. His serious expression adds to the meditative aura of this statue. While clearly portrayed as a young child, he nevertheless foreshadows the elite adult male that his parents hope he will become.

> Pentelic marble statue, Late Hellenistic, ca. 100 B.C.E.–100 C.E.
> H. 87.6
> Richmond, Virginia Museum of Fine Arts
> The Adolph D. and Wilkins C. Williams Fund, 89.24 a/b

PUBLISHED: Virginia Museum of Fine Arts, *Annual Report 1989–90* (Richmond), cover; A. B. Barriault, *Selections: Virginia Museum of Fine Arts* (Richmond, 1997), 8; M. E. Mayo, *Ancient Art: Virginia Museum of Fine Arts* (Richmond, 1998), 62–63.

For a similarly posed and garbed boy, see E. M. Moormann, *Ancient Sculpture in the Allard Pierson Museum, Amsterdam* (Amsterdam, 2000), 210–212, no. 280, pl. 96. See also the small bronzes in Paris; J. Petit, *Bronzes antiques de la collection Dutoit* (Paris, 1980), 95–98, nos. 34–35. For the hairstyle, see V. von Gonzenbach, *Untersuchungen zur den Knabenweihen im Isiskult der römischen Kaiserzeit* (Bonn, 1957), esp. 27–29, 31; Harrison 1988, 247–254.

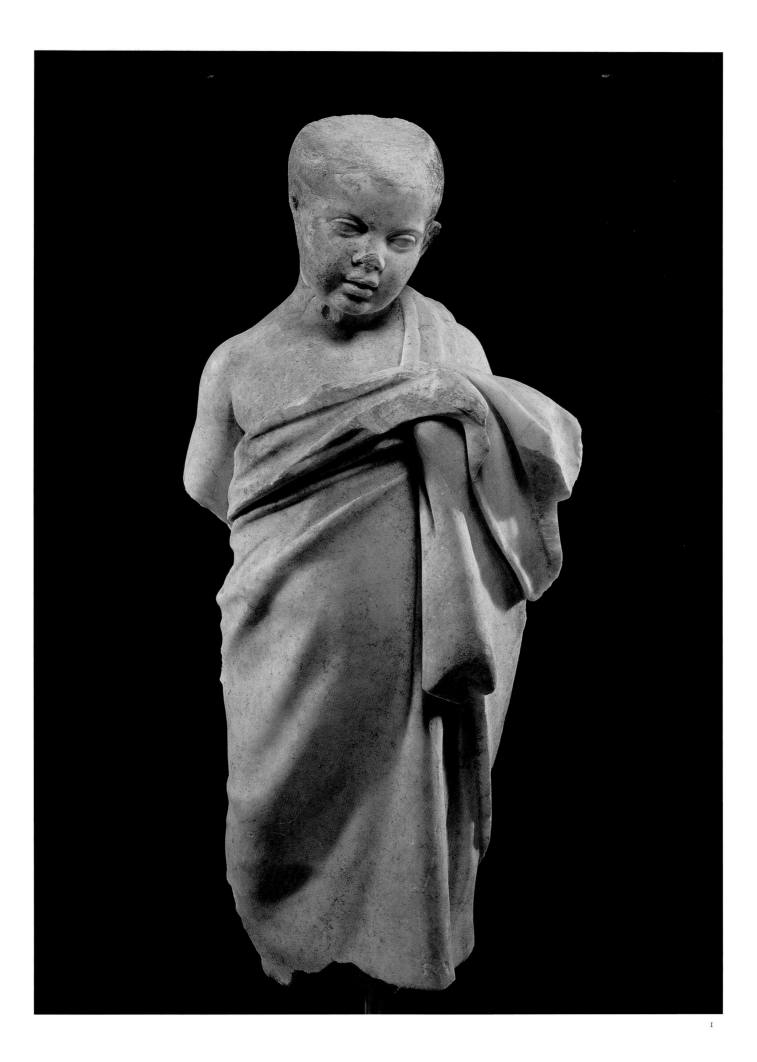

2

2
Girl with Melon Coiffure
(see also color front view p. 197)

Although most of the nose and part of the right ear are missing, this life-sized head of a young girl has lost none of its charm. Her eyelids are slightly lowered, as if she is modestly glancing down, and her full lips are carved in a faint smile. Her distinctive hairdo, known as a melon coiffure because of its division into lobes, consists of a double braid or twist encircling the back of her head and wavy sections at the front. The sculptor has gone to considerable effort to render the details of the hairdo and to model the soft features of the face.

The head almost certainly once belonged to a votive statue of a girl draped in a *chiton* and holding a small animal or bird. Such statues have been found in the sanctuary of Artemis at Brauron. Known as *arktoi* or "bears" because the bear played a role in the mythology of Artemis, the goddess of wild animals, these girls between the ages of five and ten served the goddess in her rural sanctuary, after which grateful parents dedicated statues of them. If this girl is not one of the "little bears," she could be the votary of another cult.

Hellenistic marble, probably Pentelic, head, ca. 300 B.C.E.
H. 19; W. 14.5; D. 16.2
Malibu, Calif., The J. Paul Getty Museum
Gift of Barbara and Lawrence Fleischman, 96.AA.106

PUBLISHED: M. True and K. Hamma, eds., *A Passion for Antiquities: Ancient Art from the Collection of Barbara and Lawrence Fleischman*, exhib. cat. (Malibu, Calif., 1994), 113, no. 50.

For votive statues of young girls, see Bieber 1961, 137–138, figs. 541, 544; Vorster 1983. A close parallel for this head is the statue in Munich (490); see Vorster 1983, 92–93, 339 no. 24, pls. 1,3 and 12,1.

9a   9b

9
Hermes with Infant Arkas

In Greek mythology, children who were the result of Zeus's illicit loves often became orphaned at birth on the death of their mothers, Dionysos and Semele being the best known examples. The child Arkas, who gave his name to the area of central Greece known as Arcadia, was the result of the union of Zeus with the mortal virgin Kallisto. Out of jealousy Hera, Zeus's wife, had Kallisto changed into a she-bear, thus leaving Arkas without a guardian.

On this beautiful coin the god Hermes is shown transporting the orphaned baby Arkas to his own mother, Maia, to bring up on Mount Kyllene. The god is wearing his traveler's cap, or petasos, and cradles the nude child on his left arm, over which is draped his chlamys. He is moving energetically to the left but looks back at the newborn, who raises his right hand toward the god. In his right hand Hermes holds his traditional attribute, the kerykeion.

In Greek art Hermes, the messenger god, is often shown as a *pedophoros*, ferrying a child from its birth parent to a caretaker. The most famous example in sculpture is the marble statue of Hermes with the infant Dionysos by Praxiteles found at ancient Olympia. He is carrying the child to the nymphs to be reared, as we see on numerous Athenian vase paintings (see Shapiro, fig. 1, p. 86). Hermes also is depicted transporting the young heroes Herakles and Achilles to the centaur Chiron for their education.

The coin is inscribed with the name of the town where it was minted, ΦΕΝΕΟΣ, which is in Arcadia, and next to the head of the baby his name, ΑΡΚΑΣ. The obverse of this coin shows the head of the goddess Demeter, identified by ears of grain in her hair. She also wears a pearl necklace and elaborate pendant earring.

> Silver stater of Pheneos, ca. 360–330 B.C.E.
> WT. 11.92g
> Providence, Rhode Island School of Design, Museum of Art
> Gift of Mrs. Gustav Radeke, 26.118

PUBLISHED: S. Schulz, "Die Staterprägung von Pheneus," *Schweizerische Numismatische Rundschau* 71 (1992), 53 no. 5, pl. 8, no. 6.5; R. R. Holloway, *Ancient Greek Coins: Catalogue of the Classical Collection, Museum of Art, Rhode Island School of Design*, Archaeologica Transatlantica 15 (Louvain, 1998), 13 and 76 no. 356.

On Hermes and Arkas, see LIMC 2 (1984), s.v. Arkas (A. D. Trendall). For Hermes as *pedophoros*, see LIMC 5 (1990), s.v. Hermes, nos. 363–401 (G. Siebert).

HERAKLES STRANGLING THE SNAKES

Herakles was the result of the adulterous union of Zeus with the mortal woman Alkmene, who simultaneously conceived a son by her husband, Amphitryon. While these twins were still babies in their bed, a jealous Hera sent two snakes to destroy the hero. The cries of the mortal Iphikles woke the parents, but by the time they arrived, Herakles had strangled the snakes with his bare hands. This story was recorded in an ode by the poet Pindar (*Nemean Ode* 1,

35–72) and painted by the famous Classical artist Zeuxis. The earliest extant images are those on Attic red-figure vases of the early fifth century, such as cat. 10. These include all the main characters in the drama: Herakles and his twin on the *kline* (bed), Alkmene dashing off in fright, Amphitryon rushing in with his sword raised overhead, and, in addition, Athena, the patron goddess of the hero, standing calmly beyond the bed. In later works of art the narrative details are eliminated and the image is reduced to a dramatic single figure: the frontal kneeling or sitting baby, his arms entwined with snakes. This was a popular device for coins from Thebes (the birthplace of Herakles) and southern Italy (Herakles was reputed to be the founder of Croton; see cat. 11). This emblematic image then became popular in Hellenistic sculpture.

As they do today, so in antiquity snakes represented a special danger to children, who are much more susceptible than adults to their venom. Greek mythology abounds with stories involving infants and snakes, either as protective as in the case of Erichthonios (see cat. 6) or as the cause of death, as in the legend of Opheltes and the foundation myth of the Nemean Games (see Neils, fig. 3, p. 142).

On the imagery of Herakles and the snakes, see E. R. Williams, "A Terracotta Herakles at the Johns Hopkins University," *Hesperia* 51 (1982), 357–364, pls. 86–88; S. Woodford, "The Iconography of the Infant Herakles Strangling Snakes," in F. Lissarrague and F. Telamon, eds., *Image et céramique grecque* (Rouen, 1983), 121–129; LIMC 4 (1988), s.v. Herakles and the snakes, nos. 1598–1664 (S. Woodford). For the image on coins, see S. Karwiese, "Lysander as Herakliskos Drakonopnigon," *Numismatic Chronicle* 140 (1980), 1–27, pls. 1–2.

16

16
Hermes and Youth Spinning Top

> To Hermes, Philokles here hangs up these toys of
>   his boyhood:
> his noiseless ball, this lively boxwood rattle, his
>   knuckle-bones
> he had such a mania for, and his spinning top.
>   (trans. W. R. Paton)

This third-century verse from the Palatine Anthology (VI, 309) describes the typical toys of a young boy and the god Hermes, to whom he dedicates them when he comes of age. Therefore it is not surprising to find a representation in Greek art of this god teaching a youth how to whip his top. In fact, it has been suggested that Hermes invented the spinning top, a toy used by both boys and girls (see cat. 77).

Shown as a bearded man in traveling garb (petasos; chlamys pinned at the shoulder), Hermes is leaning over to the right and braces his left hand on his left knee. His right arm is raised overhead and holds a short stick with three white strings attached to the end. With this he has just whipped the large cylindrical top that sits on the groundline. At the right a boy,

wrapped modestly in his mantle, leans forward expressing amazement with his outstretched right hand. Above are two ivy tendrils and along the border the inscription KALOS XH (beautiful).

Although Hermes does not have his traditional attribute, the kerykeion, in this scene, he does in two other Attic vase paintings with a similar scene, thus assuring his identification here. As the patron deity of the gymnasium, he had a close association with Greek boys and thus is the obvious recipient for the toys of their youth.

This *kylix* (stemmed drinking cup) is undecorated on the outside, and belongs to the late period of the prolific Late Archaic cup painter Douris. A top is depicted on one of his early cups, dropped by a youth along with the whip as he is pursued by Eros.

Attic red-figure kylix, attributed to Douris, ca. 480–470 B.C.E.
H. 9.5; DIAM. OF RIM 22.5; W. 29.8;
DIAM. OF FOOT 8.2
Baltimore, The Johns Hopkins University, Archaeological Collection, B9
Ex Collection Hartwig, Rome
From Chiusi

PUBLISHED: *ARV*[2] 444, 251; *BAdd*[2] 241; *CVA* Robinson 2 USA 6, pl. 12; K. Schefold, *Die Göttersage in der klassischen und hellenistischen Kunst* (Munich, 1981), 213, fig. 293; E. Reeder, *The Archaeological Collection of the Johns Hopkins University* (Baltimore, 1984), 175–176, no. 114; D. Buitron-Oliver, *Douris* (Mainz, 1995), 85, no. 239, pl. 111.

For tops, see cats. 77–78. For Hermes as inventor of the top, see J. D. Beazley, *JHS* 58 (1938), 267. For the two other vases with Hermes: Tübingen, University S./10 814; *CVA* Tübingen 5 Germany 54, pl. 41,3–8, with earlier bibliography, and Vanhove 1992, 164, no. 17. Florence, Museo Archeologico Etrusco, 80528; *ARV*[2] 377,113; *Para* 366; *CVA* Florence 4 Italy 38, pl. 124,2. The cup by Douris with Eros and a top is Berlin 3168 (*ARV*[2] 428,13; *BAdd*[2] 236; Buitron-Oliver [supra], pl. 16).

17

Medea's Children and Baby Orestes

(see also color illus. p. 23)

This large krater (bowl) from southern Italy is uniquely decorated with two scenes dealing with children, both deriving from plays of the Athenian tragedian Euripides. On the reverse we see a struggling baby being threatened at an altar, while on the obverse the inert bodies of two slain boys are draped over a longer altar. The baby is Orestes, who eventually grows up and commits matricide, while the two boys are the sons of the leader of the Argonauts, Jason, and his wife, the famous sorceress Medea. Both myths show innocent children manipulated by adults for their own ends.

The scene on the reverse may derive from the lost play *Telephos* by Euripides that was first performed in Athens at the Dionysia festival of 438. The wounded Telephos, his right thigh bandaged, is holding Orestes hostage at a bloodstained altar, threatening to kill him with the dagger raised in his right hand. The baby wears short boots and a band of protective amulets across his chest. He is reaching out with both arms toward his parents, King Agamemnon and Queen Clytemnestra, who rush in to rescue him. The mother's gesture mirrors that of her son, while the king is drawing his sword. In spite of the high drama, the weapons, and the blood-stained altar, the story ends happily when the cure for Telephos's wound is revealed.

The other side of the krater is dominated by a large white nimbus surrounding the snake-drawn chariot of Medea, who hovers in midair above the carnage below. She has killed her sons in vengeance against Jason, who has left her for another woman, the daughter of the king of Corinth. As Medea leaves Corinth to find sanctuary in Athens, Jason rails at her from the lower left. Neither parent is grieving for their dead sons, whose nude bodies are flung over a triglyph altar. Instead that role goes to two close intimates of the Greek household, the nurse and the *paidagogos*, or

17b

17a

tutor. The mourning nurse, identified as a nurse by her short white hair and as Thracian by her tattooed arms, is practically flinging herself onto the altar in her grief. The balding paidagogos is more restrained, with only one hand to his head. This image is generally faithful to Euripides' play *Medea*, first produced in 431, except that in the play Medea takes the bodies of her sons with her, thus denying Jason the right of burying them. Flanking this macabre scene are two winged Furies, whose role in Greek myth is to avenge blood guilt, especially in the family.

The Greeks of South Italy, where this vase was produced, had a passionate devotion to Athenian drama and often reproduced tragic and comic scenes on their vases. Scenes of Medea and Telephos are not uncommon, but this is not only the earliest vase depicting the flight of Medea but the only extant vase to pair these two scenes. It is likely that the vase painter deliberately chose to contrast the mother (Medea) who kills her sons with the son (Orestes) who grows up to kill his mother.

Lucanian red-figure calyx-krater, attributed to near the Policoro Painter, ca. 400 B.C.E.
H. 50.5; DIAM. OF MOUTH 49.9;
DIAM. OF FOOT 22
The Cleveland Museum of Art
Leonard C. Hanna, Jr., Fund, 1991.1
Ex Collection Nelson Bunker Hunt, Dallas

PUBLISHED: *CVA* Cleveland 2 USA 35, pls. 89–91; T. H. Carpenter, *Art and Myth in Ancient Greece* (London, 1991), fig. 283; H. A. Shapiro, *Myth into Art: Poet and Painter in Classical Greece* (London, 1994), 178, and 180 fig. 127; Schulze 1998, pls. 34,1–2; N. M. M. Hardwick, "A Triglyph Altar of Corinthian Type in a Scene of Medea on a Lucanian Calyx-Krater in Cleveland," *Numismatica e antichità classiche* 28 (1999), 179–201; Harten 1999, 64–65, 380 no. VLk 1, pls. 5a–b; Hrdy 1999, 528, fig. 23.3.

For representations of Greek plays on vases, see A. D. Trendall and T. B. L. Webster, *Illustrations of Greek Drama* (London, 1971); O. Taplin, *Comic Angels and Other Approaches to Greek Drama Through Vase-Painting* (Oxford, 1993). For images of Medea and her children, see *LIMC* 6 (1992), s.v. Medeia, nos. 7–49 (M. Schmidt). For recent discussion of Medea, see J. J. Clauss and S. I. Johnston, eds., *Medea: Essays on Medea in Myth, Literature, Philosophy, and Art* (Princeton, 1997). For images of Telephos and Orestes, see *LIMC* 7 (1994), s.v. Telephos, nos. 51–79 (M. Strauss).

18a

18
Theseus Slaying the Minotaur

One of the most popular myths of ancient Greece was the slaying of the Cretan Minotaur by the Athenian hero Theseus. According to ancient sources, the Athenians were forced annually to send seven youths and seven maidens to Crete to be fed to the Minotaur, a half-human, half-bull monster who dwelt in the labyrinth at Knossos. Theseus, the son of King Aegeus, volunteered to go, and with the help of the Cretan princess Ariadne succeeded in killing the monster and finding his way out of the maze, thus saving the lives of the Athenian youths. This heroic legend was represented as early as the seventh century and reached its height of popularity in the sixth century in Attic black-figure vase painting. In the fifth century artists began to represent different aspects of the myth, such as the dead Minotaur, rather than the

slaying per se. The Copenhagen Painter's *stamnos* is unique in its juxtaposition of two dimensions of this heroic feat.

On the obverse is the slaying proper taking place in the Cretan labyrinth, as indicated by two elaborate Ionic columns supporting a triglyph-and-metope architrave. In characteristic pose and dress (short chiton), Theseus is about to plunge his sword into the nude monster's exposed flank. With his left hand the hero grasps the kneeling Minotaur by the muzzle while it pleads for mercy with its outstretched right arm. The combat is flanked by two standing figures: Ariadne at left within the labyrinth and King Minos at right outside, holding his scepter.

In contrast to the lively action on the front of the vase, the reverse is static and solemn. Here three boys of different ages stand paired with their mothers; all have

downcast heads and are enveloped in their drapery. The central woman even has her hand to her eyes in a gesture of despair, rare in Greek art. These anxious and mournful figures are surely the Athenian relatives, mothers and brothers, left at home to await the outcome of the overseas voyage. What makes this vase extraordinary is this compelling combination of the Cretan adventure with its repercussions in Athens. The artist has shown unusual sensitivity to the effects of such tragic situations on the mental health and well-being of the family. Such psychological insights were more common in the domain of Greek tragedy, where family relationships were a central focus.

Attic red-figure stamnos, attributed to the Copenhagen Painter, ca. 470 B.C.E.
H. 36.4; DIAM. OF MOUTH 21.4;
DIAM. OF FOOT 15.2
Malcolm H. Wiener
Ex Collections Athos Moretti, Bellinzona;
Pino Donati, Lugano

PUBLISHED: *ARV*[2] 257, 11 and 1640; *BAdd*[2] 204; B. Philippaki, *The Attic Stamnos* (Oxford, 1967), 63 no. 5 and 65, pl. 33; H. Bloesch, *Das Tier in der Antike: 400 Werke ägyptischer, griechischer, etruskischer und römischer Kunst aus privatem und öffentlichem Besitz* (Zurich, 1974), no. 245, pl. 41; C. Isler-Kerényi, *Stamnoi* (Lugano, Switzerland, 1977), 65–69; The J. Paul Getty Museum, *Stamnoi* (Malibu, Calif., 1980), no. 18; Münzen und Medaillen, *Kunstwerke der Antike 70* (1986), no. 206, pl. 43; H. A. Shapiro, "Theseus in Kimonian Athens: The Iconography of Empire," *Mediterranean Historical Review* 7 (1992), 40–42, figs. 4–5; *LIMC* 6 (1992), s.v. Minos I, no. 19; Christie's (New York), 8 June 2001, 22–23, lot no. 10.

For Theseus and the Minotaur, see F. Brommer, *Theseus: Die Taten des griechischen Helden in der antiken Kunst und Literatur* (Darmstadt, Germany, 1982), 35–64; *LIMC* 7 (1994), s.v. Theseus and Minotauros, nos. 228–260 (S. Woodford). For the dead Minotaur, see H. A. Shapiro et al., *Greek Vases in the San Antonio Museum of Art* (San Antonio, 1995), 148–149, no. 74.

Young women, in my opinion, have the sweetest existence known to mortals in their father's homes, for their innocence always keeps children safe and happy. But when we [young women] reach puberty and can understand, we are thrust out and sold away.

Sophocles, *Tereus* frag. 583

The pillar of the house [*oikos*] is the male children.

Euripides, *Iphigeneia Among the Taurians* 57

T HE ancient Greeks had no word for family; they used *oikos*, which means house. The members of the household normally included parents, children, living paternal grandparents, and slaves. Women and children stayed at home, whereas adult men spent much of their time outside the house involved in business, agriculture, and public life. Therefore, girls and boys up to the age of about seven were mainly under the influence of women and slaves. For families who could afford it, the two most important slaves in the household were the nurse (*trophos*) and the tutor of the male children (*paidagogos*).

The Greek house had quarters for women and children separate from those areas like the dining room (*andron*), which, as its name implies, was used exclusively by men. The hearth was the symbolic center of the house, and it was here that newcomers (brides, slaves, and newborns) were introduced to the family. In houses with upper stories, the women and children seem to have slept upstairs. Greek houses usually had central courtyards where many of the domestic activities like cooking and weaving took place. Above all the household was an economic unit, where raw materials like wool were processed into marketable products. Children no doubt assisted in these domestic activities from a fairly young age.

Depictions of home life are rare in Greek art, and it is even more unusual to see men interacting with women and children. Representations of the oikos most often show women (mothers and female slaves) with male infants and toddlers, highlighting the greater importance of male offspring. Furnishings are surprisingly spare in the Classical period in Athens, and decorations like wall paintings were frowned upon as too luxurious. Elite women are shown seated in curved-back chairs known as *klismoi* (see cats. 29 and 35), their wool baskets often at their sides. Infants may have been placed in a shallow basket known as the *liknon*, for the baby Hermes is occasionally depicted in one of these baskets used for winnowing grain. Very young children are shown in "high chairs" that may also have served as potty seats (see cats. 41 and 42). Probably made of ceramic or wood, they represent the only piece of extant furniture specifically manufactured for children. Simple wooden stools were the most common piece of household furniture, and toddlers are often depicted leaning on them for support (see cat. 91).

For discussion of the Greek house, see L. C. Nevett, *House and Society in the Ancient Greek World* (Cambridge, 1999); G. P. R. Metraux, "Ancient Housing: *Oikos* and *Domus* in Greece and Rome," *Journal of the Society of Architectural Historians* 58, no. 3 (1999), 392–405. On the oikos as an economic unit, see Cox 1998.

19

19
Gravestone with Woman in Labor
(see also color illus. p. 186)

One of a small number of gravestones that show a woman in labor, this memorial indicates that childbirth was the cause of her death. All such gravestones are nearly contemporary and depict the deceased in a similar awkward pose reclining back onto a chair or bed. On this stele she rests upon a well-cushioned throne and is supported from behind by a woman with short hair wearing the *chiton cheirodotos* who must be a maid or servant. This servant holds the dying woman's limply hanging left arm with her left hand. The dying woman's mantle is pulled down beneath her waist, to show a clinging chiton that reveals her swollen state, suggesting pregnancy. Her sandaled feet rest upon a footstool. Before her stands an old man in chiton and mantle with a wrinkled face who gestures to her with his left hand, palm up. With his right he grasps her right hand in the *dexiosis*. The remains of another female figure standing behind him mark the left border.

The scene is set in a partially preserved *naiskos*. The *anta* on the right and part of the roof and architrave across the top remain. On the latter is part of an inscription

OVERLEAF

CAT. 29 Household Family Scene, Attic red-figure hydria, attributed to the Circle of Polygnotos, ca. 440–430 B.C.E. Cambridge, Harvard University Art Museums, Arthur M. Sackler Museum, Bequest of David Moore Robinson

which reads [ΘΥ]ΓΑΤΗΡ (daughter). The lost section undoubtedly gave the dead woman's name and her father's name, and possibly the father's demotic as well.

The stele has been reworked in several places at least twice. The most substantive change is to the figure of the old man. He originally was an old nurse who supported the dying woman's right arm with her right hand. The alteration of this figure changed the composition of the scene to the much more popular one of "a woman seated at home." The identity of the old man remains uncertain. His age suggests that he is her father, but because the figure has been reworked, one cannot be sure that the features defining his age were not simply inherited from the original figure—the sculptor not being able to remove them without totally maiming the new figure. Thus he may represent her husband. This touching memorial reminds us of just how precarious childbirth was in antiquity.

To assure more rapid and easy deliveries, pregnant women wore birthing amulets (*okytokia*) tied around their thighs, or they applied a mixture of wild cucumber onto red wool and fastened it around the loins. In spite of these magical gems and recipes, Hippokrates (*Nature of the Child* 30) states, "if the baby's thrust is in the direction of the head, the woman bears her child easily. But if its side is proceeding, or it moves toward the feet, . . . the woman gives birth with difficulty. Already many of these women have perished, or their babies, or both."

Attic marble grave stele, ca. 330 B.C.E.
H. 83.8; W. 55.9
Cambridge, Harvard University Art Museums, Arthur M. Sackler Museum
Gift of Edward W. Forbes, 1905.8
Ex Collection Nanni, Venice

PUBLISHED: CAT 4.425; SEG 39, no. 391; U. Vedder, "Frauentod-Kriegertod im Spiegel der attischen Grabkunst des 4. Jhs. v. Chr.," AM 103 (1988), 166–167; U. Vedder, "'Szenenwechsel,' Beobachtungen an zwei Grabstelen in Cambridge und Athen," in H.-U. Cain, H. Gabelmann, and D. Salzmann, eds., *Festschrift für*

20

Nikolaus Himmelmann: Beiträge zur Ikonographie und Hermeneutik (Mainz, 1989), 169, fig. 30,4; C. C. Vermeule and A. Brauer, *Stone Sculptures: The Greek, Roman, and Etruscan Collections of the Harvard University Art Museums* (Cambridge, Mass., 1990), 41, no. 25; Demand 1994, 124, no. 4 and pl. 5; O. Cavalier, *Silence et fureur: La femme et le mariage en Grèce: Les antiquités grecques du Musée Calvet* (Avignon, 1996), 62 and 76, fig. 29; J. Bergemann, *Demos und Thanatos: Untersuchungen zum Wertsystem der Polis im Spiegel der attischen Grabreliefs des 4. Jahrhunderts v. Chr. und zur Funktion der gleichzeitigen Grabbauten* (Munich, 1997), 37 n. 21, 38 n. 32, 42 n. 79, and 169 n. 449; A. Stewart and C. Grey, "Confronting the Other: Childbirth, Old Age, and Death on an Attic Tombstone at Harvard," in B. Cohen, ed., *Not the Classical Ideal: Athens and the Construction of the Other in Greek Art* (Leiden, 2000), 248–274.

For birthing amulets, see A. E. Hanson, "Uterine Amulets and Greek Uterine Medicine," *Medicina nei secoli* 7, no. 2 (1995), 281–299.

20
Gravestone with Women and Infant

Swaddled infants occur on a small number of gravestones. On this one a seated woman and one standing across from her holding a wrapped infant in her left arm occupy a naiskos formed by an anta on each side, crowned with a pediment atop a narrow architrave. The lower half of the stele is lost, but based on comparisons to other stelai, a second, older child may have rested against the knees of the seated woman, possibly raising its arms up to her. The infant appears to be a newborn, suggesting that the seated woman was its mother and had died in childbirth. The ear, nose, mouth, and eyes of the baby are carefully rendered. The shape and proportions of the head, however, are more like that of a miniature adult than of a newborn. Hair may have been painted on its now bald head.

The seated woman wears a *chiton* and a mantle that is pulled up over the back of her head, the other a *peplos* and possibly a mantle. Both women look downward rather than at the infant, which further suggests that another child was present. Their reflective poses, enhanced by the gesture of the hand to the face, underscore the sad separation of mother and family caused by death. The status of the standing woman is not clear. She may be a younger family member or possibly a servant, based on her short hair.

Restrictive swaddling, such as the cloth wrapped tightly around this child, was normal, and Greek children could remain swaddled for more than a year (Plato, *Laws* 789E). Although swaddling has been said to be highly unsanitary, the reverse of a swaddled infant figurine from the sanctuary of Artemis at Mounychion shows that the buttocks were left bare, thus allowing the feces to escape. In addition, newborns are often shown on gravestones with pointed, conical bonnets (see cat. 111 and Oakley, fig. 26, p. 185).

> Attic marble grave stele, ca. 375–350 B.C.E.
> H. 44.5; W. 50.8, D. 9.5
> Houston, The Museum of Fine Arts
> Gift of Miss Annette Finnigan, 37.25
> From Athens

PUBLISHED: H. Hoffmann, *Ten Centuries That Shaped the West: Greek and Roman Art in Texas Collections* (Mainz, 1970), 22–23, no. 6; C. C. Vermeule, *Greek and Roman Sculpture in America: Masterpieces in Public Collections in the United States and Canada* (Malibu, Calif., 1981), 108, no. 78; E. Keuls, *The Reign of the Phallus: Sexual Politics in Ancient Athens* (New York, 1985), 139–140, fig. 120; CAT 2.795; Reeder 1995, 337–338, no. 105; J. Bergemann, *Demos und Thanatos: Untersuchungen zum Wertsystem der Polis im Spiegel der attischen Grabreliefs des 4. Jahrhunderts v. Chr. und zur Funktion der gleichzeitigen Grabbauten* (Munich, 1997), 53, 163 no. 195, and pl. 114,3.

For children on grave stelai, see Vorster 1983 and the essay by Oakley in this volume. For examples of tombstones with a child leaning on its seated mother's knees with upraised arms, see Athens, National Archaeological Museum, 3289 (CAT 2.846b), and Paris, Musée du Louvre, Ma 808 (CAT 2.858). On swaddling, see Garland 1990, 81–83. For the terracotta figurine, see L. Palaiokrassa, *To hiero tes Artemidos Mounichias* (Thessaloníki, 1983), pl. 16, no. E 86.

KOUROTROPHOI

The image of mother and child is ubiquitous in Western art, from the Egyptian representations of Isis with her son Horus to the Christian icon of the Madonna with the Christ child, but nowhere has this theme been explored more extensively than in the art of Greece. It begins in the Neolithic period and lasts until Roman times, a span of more than three thousand years. In Greek religion and art the type is called *kourotrophos*, a term that means "nursing mother of boys." It is an epithet of a number of female deities—Ge, the earth goddess; Demeter, the goddess of agriculture; even Athena, the patron goddess of heroes and by extension young men—all concerned with nursing and upbringing. Although the appearance and nomenclature of the Greek kourotrophos varies from region to region and changes over time, the basic sculptural type retains its essentials: a draped woman, standing or seated, holding an infant or child usually cradled in her left arm. Thousands of these exist, primarily in terracotta, covering the entire expanse of Greek art from the Bronze Age to the end of the Hellenistic period. They were dedicated in sanctuaries throughout the Greek world (especially in southern Italy and Sicily), where they may reflect parents' dedication of their children to a god or goddess. They were also placed in graves, and here the kourotrophic deity may represent maternal protection in the world beyond.

For the kourotrophos in Greek art, see Hadzisteliou-Price 1978.

21

21
Mycenaean Kourotrophos
(see also color illus. p. 30)

Small, abstract terracotta figurines of women were very common in Greece and beyond during the late Bronze Age. Made of a light-colored clay and decorated with wavy black lines, these figurines stand on a tall pedestal base and often wear crowns, or *poloi*. Their noses are beaklike, and the eyes are small black dots. More unusual are the figurines of women cradling infants in their left arms. These normally take the form of the Greek letter phi. Many figurines of the phi type have been found in children's graves, and some scholars believe they represent divine nurses in whose care the children were placed.

> Mycenaean terracotta phi-type figurine,
> Late Helladic IIIA-B, ca. 1400–1200 B.C.E.
> H. 13.3; W. 6.3; D. 2.9
> Raleigh, North Carolina Museum of Art
> Gift of Mr. and Mrs. Gordon Hanes,
> G.74.19.2

PUBLISHED: *North Carolina Museum of Art Bulletin* 13:1–2 (1975–1976), 36, no. 101.

For Mycenaean figurines, see E. B. French, "The Development of Mycenaean Terracotta Figurines," *BSA* 66 (1971), 101–187, esp. 142–144.

22
Sub-Mycenaean/Proto-Geometric Kourotrophos

This unique statuette is difficult to place in terms of style, iconography, and function. It represents a mother with child on her left hip. While reduced to its essentials, the three incised lines at the neck, a close-fitting necklace, also the way the toddler—unusual in size in proportion to the adult—is carried, are typically feminine. There is indication of neither breasts nor male sex.

There is no tradition of a male carrying a child at such an early date. A detail such as the delineation of the fingers on the mother's left hand and her three-dimensional appearance indicate an evolution, though she probably still belongs to a Mycenaean tradition (see cat. 21). Thus, she can be dated to the period between the end of the Mycenaean and beginning of the Proto-Geometric.

As for function, the lower part of her head is pierced from side to side, obviously for suspension. Pendants became common in the Geometric period. She could have been worn as an amulet for protection and/or offered as a votive in gratitude for a healthy child.

Bronze pendant or amulet, solid-cast
1150–1000 B.C.E.
H. 6.4
George Ortiz Collection
Allegedly from the Cyclades

23

22

PUBLISHED: Fogg Art Museum, *Ancient Art in American Private Collections*, exhib. cat. with contributions by G. Ortiz (Cambridge, Mass., 1954), 25, no. 128, pl. 33; K. Schefold, *Meisterwerke griechischer Kunst*, with contributions by G. Ortiz (Basel, 1960), 112–113, no. I 10; G. Ortiz, *In Pursuit of the Absolute: Art of the Ancient World: The George Ortiz Collection*, rev. hardcover ed. (Bern, 1996), no. 64.

(Entry composed by George Ortiz with Jenifer Neils.)

23
Geometric/Proto-Archaic Kourotrophos
(see also color illus. p. 60)

The enthroned kourotrophos type dates back to Mycenaean times. This example is seated on a high cylindrical throne decorated with rectilinear designs (meander and step-ornament). The upper body of the woman and the infant, which she cradles in her left arm, were made separately from the throne and projecting ledge on which her feet rest. Though certain of her features are not rendered to conform to reality, they express her presence and spirit. Noteworthy are her ecstatic expression, with her big almond eyes staring upward, and her prominent jutting chin and large hands, deeply incised to delineate the fingers, which are accentuated with paint. Globular earrings (or ears) are fastened on at the sides.

The elaborate throne and ecstatic expression of her face suggest that she is meant to be a mother goddess. Her excellent state of preservation points to her having come from a grave, where her protective powers would have served the spirit of the deceased.

> Terracotta statuette, ca. 700 B.C.E.
> H. 20.8
> George Ortiz Collection
> Boeotia or northern Attica

PUBLISHED: K. Schefold, *Meisterwerke griechischer Kunst*, with contributions by G. Ortiz (Basel, 1960), 136, no. II 84, 139 (illus.); P. Kranz, "Ein Meisterwerke frühattischer Koroplastik," *AA* (1978), 317–329; H. F. Mussche, ed., *Hommes et dieux de la Grèce antique*, with contributions by G. Ortiz (Brussels, 1982), 52–53, no. 15; G. Ortiz, *In Pursuit of the Absolute: Art of the Ancient World: The George Ortiz Collection*, rev. hardcover ed. (Bern, 1996), no. 84.

For a similar (wheel-made base) but somewhat later seventh-century Daedalic terracotta kourotrophos from Taranto (Trieste, Museo Civico di Storia ed Arte inv. 2393), see G. Pugliese Carratelli, ed., *The Western Greeks* (Venice, 1996), 383 and 668 no. 37.

(Entry composed by George Ortiz with Jenifer Neils.)

24
Early Classical Kourotrophos

This standing *peplophoros* represents the Early Classical version of the kourotrophos type. The nude young boy is resting lightly in the palm of the mother's left hand. She looks at him calmly while holding an attribute (now lost) in her raised right hand. The woman wears an elaborate diadem (once gilded), which may indicate her status as a goddess. Because the cult of Demeter and her daughter Persephone was so strong in southern Italy, this figurine from Lokroi is sometimes identified as Demeter with the grain god, Triptolemos, who is often depicted as a child. The monumental quality of this relatively large statuette suggests that it may copy a lifesize cult statue.

> South Italian terracotta statuette,
> ca. 470–460 B.C.E.
> H. 27.3; W. 12.7; D. 6.6
> Urbana, University of Illinois, Urbana-Champaign, The Spurlock Museum,
> 1928.01.0006
> From Lokroi

PUBLISHED: H. N. Couch, "An Archaic Goddess and Child from Lokroi," *AJA* 34 (1930), 344–352; Hadzisteliou-Price 1978, 54, no. 585, 222, fig. 49.

25
Hellenistic Kourotrophos

Although less popular in the Hellenistic period, the kourotrophos type continues to be made in terracotta until the period ends, as this piece illustrates. This baby is comfortably nestled in his mother's lap, his head leaning against her left arm as he sucks contentedly. As babies often do in this situation, he places his free arm to rest on the inside of her breast. She sits erectly on a *diphros* (backless stool) decorated with saltire squares, her right leg extended slightly farther than her left. With her right hand she seeks to protect the child should he stir. She wears earrings, shoes, and a

24

broached chiton, the left side of which is down to expose her shoulder and breast.

Myrina terracotta figurine, first century B.C.E./C.E.

H. 20.1

Boston, Museum of Fine Arts
Museum Purchase by Contribution, 01.7747
Ex Collection Metaxas

PUBLISHED: D. Burr, *Terra-Cottas from Myrina in the Museum of Fine Arts, Boston* (Vienna, 1934), 10 and 31, no. 5 and pl. 2; D. B. Thompson, *Troy: The Terracotta Figurines of the Hellenistic Period*, supplementary monograph 3 (Princeton, 1963), 137, under no. 278; Hadzisteliou-Price 1978, 54.

25

26
Standing Old Nurse with Baby

An unswaddled, squirming baby is carried by a bent-over old woman, who undoubtedly is his nurse. Held tight into the woman's torso by her large hands and arms, he has grabbed hold of the neckline of her chiton and pulls it down, while twisting his head to his left. This allows the viewer to contrast his smiling baby face with the nurse's, which is heavily wrinkled, with loose, hanging skin and double chin, deeply set eyes, and large nose. Childhood and old age are effectively contrasted here. The nurse's loose-fitting garment and short hair suggest that she is a slave, and she wears a large conical cap (*sakkos*) and slippers. Some of the red coloring for his hair remains.

Figurines of both seated and standing nurses with babies became popular in the fourth century. This specific type, of which many good examples still remain today, is a later one and reflects the interest in realism in the Early Hellenistic period. Its invention was probably due to the influence of New Comedy, in which the child-holding nurse was a common character. The same type was produced elsewhere in the Greek world and remained in use until the second century.

Tanagra terracotta figurine, Attic, last quarter of fourth century B.C.E.

H. 13.7

New York, The Metropolitan Museum of Art
Rogers Fund, 1910, 10.210.38
Possibly from Athens

PUBLISHED: Uhlenbrock 1990, 123, no. 16.
For this type, see D. B. Thompson, "The Origin of Tanagras," *AJA* 70 (1966), 56–58; Pinney and Ridgway 1979, 256–257, no. 125; Rühfel 1984a, 193–197; S. Pfisterer-Haas, *Darstellungen alter Frauen in der griechischen Kunst* (Frankfurt, 1989), 40–43, 96–97, 108, and figs. 52–53.

26

27
Seated Old Nurse Holding Baby

A nude, placid baby with limbs and body conforming to the lap, torso, and arms of an old nurse seated on a padded diphros looks up attentively at his caretaker. She stares straight ahead in a rigid pose, her sandaled feet propped atop a footstool. A mantle is pulled up over the back of her head and runs down her back over a girded, sleeveless chiton. Striking are the masculine features of her face, which suggest the influence of comic masks— sharply protruding eyebrows, a grimacing smile, and a full, heavy jaw.

This type, one of the earliest developed in the fourth century, has its roots in the tradition of kourotrophoi (see cats. 21–25). There is great variety in the facial features of the nurses on different examples, but the children are normally shown as docile appendages, as here. What is unusual and distinguishes this type from most other kourotrophoi is the fact that the child's head is at the woman's right side rather than the nearly universal left. Might this indicate some ill fate for the child, or a mythological character like Demeter, who changed herself into an old nurse to care for the Eleusinian prince Demophon?

27

Tanagra terracotta figurine, 350–325 B.C.E.
H. 23.5
Fine Arts Museums of San Francisco
Gift of Mrs. M. C. Sloss, 43.13.3
Possibly from Attica

PUBLISHED: Uhlenbrock 1990, 122, no. 15; Schulze 1998, 52 and pl. 20,4.

For this type, see D. B. Thompson, "The Origin of Tanagras," *AJA* 70 (1966), 56–58; S. Pfisterer-Haas, *Darstellungen alter Frauen in der griechischen Kunst* (Frankfurt, 1989), 37–40; Schulze 1998, 52.

28
Standing Old Nurse with Boy and Girl

A potbellied and large-breasted old nurse struggles along with two children. The boy does not want to go forward, yet she pulls him firmly by the hand, the result being that she has yanked his blue mantle away from his lower body. In her left arm she carries a girl in white chiton and pink mantle who supports herself with her left hand above the nurse's left breast. The girl is happy to be carried, in contrast to her struggling brother. The nurse has cropped hair, which indicates that she is a slave, and a fat oval face. She also wears a white chiton and a pink mantle that is wrapped around her body so as to emphasize her belly.

This figurine type appears to be of South Italian manufacture, in which the number and sex of the children varies. Any modern-day parent viewing this group would be immediately reminded of the chore of going shopping with uncoopera-tive small children.

South Italian terracotta figurine, first quarter of the third century B.C.E.
H. 14.3
Mr. and Mrs. John J. Herrmann, Jr.
Ex French Collection

UNPUBLISHED: For this type, see S. Pfisterer-Haas, *Darstellungen alter Frauen in der griechischen Kunst* (Frankfurt, 1989), 43–44, 97–100, and fig. 63; Schulze 1998, 52.

28

29

Household Family Scene

(see also color illus. p. 221)

Family scenes are rare on Attic vases, and this is perhaps the finest extant. The loom on the left indicates that the location is the women's quarters (*gynaikeion*), while the wreath hanging in the background may allude to the fact that the couple were recently married. The wife and proud new mother of a baby boy sits on a klismos in the center, her feet atop a flat platform. Wearing chiton, mantle, and sakkos, she hands over the child to a maid standing across from her. The thigh-length sleeved garment that the maid wears over a chiton, probably the chiton cheirodotos, indicates her servile status. She bends over to take the child, her left hand already grasping his chest. The child wears a string of amulets across his torso and reaches out with both hands toward the maid. Wet nurses were common in ancient houses, and this may be the reason why the child is eager to be picked up by the maid. Slaves also were often responsible for child care.

Behind the mistress on the right is a young man who stands cross-legged, leaning on the staff he holds in his left hand. His right hand is tucked beneath his garment at his waist. At first glance he might seem too young to be the husband, because we know that men married late in life, but grooms are often idealized and shown in wedding scenes as young men, which is probably the case here.

The picture is best interpreted as showing a recently married elite couple who are proud new parents of a baby boy, looking on with a sense of self-satisfaction as the maid takes over the care of the child. Boy babies were the ultimate goal of marriage in ancient Greece, because they represented the continuation of the oikos, the core family unit of Greek society. This vase provides a rare, intimate glimpse into the women's quarters in the Greek house.

> Attic red-figure hydria, attributed to the Circle of Polygnotos, ca. 440–430 B.C.E.
> H. 34.6; DIAM. 24.6
> Cambridge, Harvard University Art Museums, Arthur M. Sackler Museum Bequest of David Moore Robinson, 1960.342
> From Vari

PUBLISHED: *CVA* Baltimore, Robinson 2 USA 6, 31–32 and pl. 43,1; A. Cameron and A. Kuhrt, eds., *Images of Women in Antiquity* (London, 1983), 93, fig. 7,2; Bazant 1985, 2, pl. 26,44; E. Keuls, *The Reign of the Phallus: Sexual Politics in Ancient Athens* (New York, 1985), 73–74, fig. 58; *Antike Welt* 19 (1988), 4 and 45, fig. 3; *ArchDelt* 47–48 (1992–1993), 1, pl. 46; Reeder 1995, 218–219, no. 51; Massar 1995, 34–35, fig. 6; B. A. Sparkes, *The Red and the Black: Studies in Greek Pottery* (London, 1996), 138, fig. V.14; M. C. Miller, *Athens and Persia in the Fifth Century B.C.: A Study in Cultural Receptivity* (Cambridge, Mass., 1997), pl. 66; Schulze 1998, pl. 3,2; S. Blundell, *Women in Classical Athens* (London, 1998), 41–42, fig. 16; P. Cartledge, ed., *The Cambridge Illustrated History of Ancient Greece* (Cambridge, 1998), 136; Sutton 2003.

For family scenes in Attic red-figure, see Massar 1995 and Sutton 2003.

INFANT FEEDING

> Good Athenodora, wife of Thaumasius . . . bore children and nursed them when they were infants. Earth took this young mother and keeps her, though the children need her milk.
>
>   Greek epigram (Kaibel 176)

Although rarely represented on Greek vases, which provide so much other information about daily life, infant feeding practices are known from evidence including extant medical texts, artifacts like feeding bottles, epitaphs for nurses, and nursing contracts. Already in Homer, nursing mothers (Hecuba, Thetis, and Penelope) are mentioned, as well as slave women who performed the service of wet nurse (Eurykleia for Odysseus). In myth, exposed children are often suckled by animals, as in the case of Zeus, who was fed by the goat Amaltheia, or Telephos, the son of Herakles, who was suckled by a deer.

Children were probably weaned at two to three years of age, but artificial feeding may have begun earlier as a supplement to breast milk. The so-called feeding bottle or cup (*bombylios*), a small closed pot with an opening for filling and a tubular spout for sucking, was ubiquitous in Greece from prehistoric times to the Roman era. Because many of these vessels have been found in children's graves, they are traditionally identified as baby feeders, although other interpretations (for example, lamp fillers) have been suggested. However, a unique terracotta statuette (Geneva HM 2218) shows a woman with one of these vases in her right hand while in her left she cradles an infant who leans forward to suck from the spout. Some larger feeders are inscribed, one with the word *mamo* (breast), another with the expression "Drink, don't drop."

Because Greek mothers nursed their infants or handed them over to wet nurses, these feeders probably did not always contain milk or formula like our modern baby bottles. Rather, they may have sometimes held a mixture of honey and wine. Recent analysis of the contents of a Mycenaean feeder from Bronze Age Midea indicates that it once contained honey and a fermented product, such as wine, barley beer, or mead. Clearly these were used not only as feeders but as medicine dispensers to calm colicky infants. Hippokrates mentions that a painful condition known as "bladder stone" occurred in children, more often in boys than girls. He blamed it on faulty water and milk, but it is more likely a result of giving babies barley gruel when the mother's or nurse's milk was inadequate. The subsequent protein deficiency and mineral deposition would cause stones to form in the baby's urinary tract.

Contracts for wet nurses survive on the papyri of Roman Egypt, and they inform us about this common practice in antiquity. Wet nurses were both free women and slaves, their period of service was usually two years, and if they violated their contracts, they were required to pay back in full and could be fined. Contracts often stipulate, "So long as she is duly paid she shall take proper care both of herself and of the child, not injuring her milk nor sleeping with a man nor becoming pregnant." These stipulations arose from the ancients' belief that breast milk was formed from menstrual blood, which was not shed during pregnancy.

Breast-feeding is rarely portrayed in Greek art other than on *kourotrophic* (nursing) figurines (see cat. 25). The image of the exposed breast suggested vulnerability and so was reserved for raped, wounded, insane, or murdered women.

On infant feeding, see Wickes 1953; Fildes 1986, esp. 17–25. On baby feeders, see Kern 1957; B. Sparkes and L. Talcott, *Black and Plain Pottery of the 6th, 5th, and 4th Centuries B.C.*, The Athenian Agora 12 (Princeton, 1970), 161–162; Bartsocas 1978; Collin-Bouffier 1999. For the term *bombylios*, see L. Vuillard and F. Blondé, "Sur quelques vases présents dans la *Collection Hippocratique*: Confrontation des données littéraires et archéologiques," *BCH* 116 (1992), 104–107, 114–117. For the terracotta in Geneva, see Gourevitch and Chamay 1992. For prehistoric examples, see A. D. Lacaille, "Infant Feeding-Bottles in Prehistoric Times," *Proceedings of the Royal Society of Medicine* 43 (1950), 565–568. On wet nursing, see Fildes 1988, 1–25. On bladder stone, see Makler 1980. On nursing contracts, see K. R. Bradley, "Sexual Regulations in the Wet-Nursing Contracts from Roman Egypt," *Klio* 62 (1980), 321–325. For images of breast-feeding, see Bonfante 1997.

30

30
Mycenaean Feeder

This simple, side-spouted jar with a basket handle is decorated with a painted black band at its greatest diameter. This shape is first documented in Mycenanean pottery in the Late Helladic IIB period and probably derives from a Middle Helladic version.

> Late Helladic III A2 (Furumark shape 160),
> ca. 1350 B.C.E.
> H. WITH HANDLE 10.5
> Haverford, Pennsylvania, Haverford College,
> Collection of Greek Antiquities
> Bequest of Ernest Allen, EA-1989-24

PUBLISHED: A. H. Ashmead, *Haverford College Collection of Classical Antiquities: The Bequest of Ernest Allen* (Philadelphia, 1999), 1–2, fig. 2.

On Mycenaean feeders, see P. A. Mountjoy, *Mycenaean Pottery: An Introduction* (Oxford, 1993); Y. Tzedakis and H. Martlew, *Minoans and Mycenaeans: Flavours of Their Time*, National Archaeological Museum exhib. cat. (Athens, 1999), 166, 169, no. 158 (feeding bottle from Midea).

31
Corinthian Feeder

(see also color illus. p. 176)

This feeder is more elaborate than the preceding example. It has two loop handles (one horizontal, one vertical) and a sieve with twenty-five holes over the fill opening. It is decorated with a band of

meander around the sieve and in the handle zone, and rays around the base of the spout.

> Late Corinthian II, ca. 550–500 B.C.E.
> H. WITH HANDLE 5.6; DIAM. 6.1
> Columbia, University of Missouri-Columbia,
> Museum of Art and Archaeology, 59.55

PUBLISHED: *CVA* University of Missouri 1 USA 36, 11 no. 24, pls. 11,5–7.

For other Late Corinthian examples, see H. Payne, *Necrocorinthia: A Study of Corinthian Art in the Archaic Period* (Oxford, 1931), 335–336. For a similarly decorated feeder in Heidelberg (inv. 148), see *CVA* Heidelberg 1 Germany 10, pl. 19,10. A fourth-century example from a child's grave at Corinth can be found in *Corinth* 13 (1964), 281, no. 449-1, pl. 71.

31

33

32

32
Feeder in the Form of a Pig

On this feeder in the shape of a pig, the spout protrudes like a tail from the rear of the animal. It is also furnished with two lug handles, pierced for suspension above the child's cradle. The ivy decoration on the pig's back may allude to Dionysos and the vase's possible contents: wine.

> Sicilian, Randazzo Group: Ivy Series,
> ca. 450 B.C.E.
> H. 4.9; L. 9.9
> The Cleveland Museum of Art
> Gift of Leo Mildenberg, 1975.91
> Ex Collection Züsl, Basel

PUBLISHED: *CVA* Cleveland 2 USA 35, 60, pls. 105,3–4.

For other Sicilian pig vases, see B. Heldring, *Sicilian Plastic Vases* (Utrecht, 1981).

33
Feeder in the Form of a Pomegranate

This plain, black-glazed feeder has a less tapering spout and a more prominent ring handle. What makes it distinctive is its serrated opening, which resembles the open corolla of a pomegranate, a fruit that in antiquity symbolized fertility on account of its many seeds. It also had close associations with Hades, because Persephone's eating of this fruit doomed her to spend part of every year in the underworld. It is possible that this feeder, which looks unused, was a funerary gift for a young child.

> South Italian, fourth–third century B.C.E.
> H. 10; DIAM. 9
> Chapel Hill, The University of North
> Carolina, Ackland Art Museum
> Gift of Henry and Sara Immerwahr, 91.93

PUBLISHED: C. R. Mack, *Classical Art from Carolina Collections* (Columbia, S.C., 1974), 31, no. 43.

For earlier pomegranate-shaped vases, see S. A. Immerwahr, "The Pomegranate Vase: Its Origins and Continuity," *Hesperia* 58 (1989), 397–410. For another black-glazed feeder with a serrated rim, see *CVA* Altenburg 3 Germany 19, pls. 116,17–18. For the symbolism of the pomegranate, see F. Muthmann, *Der Granatapfel: Symbol des Lebens in der alten Welt* (Bern, 1982).

34

Seated Old Man Offering Grapes to a Girl

A balding old man with white hair and beard and wrinkled forehead sits on a four-legged stool holding out a bunch of grapes in his right hand to a small girl standing across from him. She gestures with her right hand that she is eager to accept the gift, just as a child might do today when offered candy or some other sweet. Her left arm remains bent at her waist. He wears a mantle and holds a pomegranate on his lap in his left hand. Perhaps the girl was meant to choose from grandpa which sweet she wanted.

This is one of several scenes often involving more than one figure that give us intimate glimpses into everyday life. Many of them, like this one and cat. 61, were made in Boiotia at the end of the Archaic period. It is unclear what their purpose was: grave gifts, votives, and toys have all been discussed as possibilities.

> Tanagra terracotta figurine, Boiotian, first quarter of the fifth century B.C.E.
> H. 11
> Boston, Museum of Fine Arts
> Catharine Page Perkins Fund, 97.350

PUBLISHED: G. H. Chase, "Eight Terracottas in the Museum of Fine Arts, Boston," in *Festschrift für James Loeb* (Munich, 1930), 47, fig. 7 and 49–50; G. M. A. Richter, *The Furniture of the Greeks, Etruscans, and Romans*, 2d ed. (London, 1966), 47 and fig. 268; M. B. Comstock and C. C. Vermeule III, *Greek, Etruscan, and Roman Art: The Classical Collections of the Museum of Fine Arts, Boston*, rev. ed. (Boston, 1972), 51 and 70, fig. 59.

For these groups, see R. Higgins, *Greek Terracottas* (London, 1967), 77; Higgins 1986, 84–92.

34

36a

36
Woman and Children

On one side of this oil or perfume container is a striking picture of a woman with two male children. The smaller child is perched on her left hand and sleeps with his head and hands resting on her shoulder. The other stands at her side, clutching her chiton with his left hand and holding a pointed object down in his right (a dagger or a stick for trundling a toy hoop?). Both look apprehensively to the left, highlighted by the way the woman has drawn back her right hand to her chin. A *kalathos* (wool basket) sits on the ground to the right, and a *sakkos* hangs on the wall in the back, indicating that we are inside the *gynaikeion* (women's quarters). The woman's stylish hairdo, pulled up in back in a *krobyllos* and held in place by fillet,

suggests that she is not a servant but the children's mother.

Several other vases show a similarly posed mother and sleeping child, including a white-ground calyx-krater by the same painter and a red-figure skyphos by the Euaichme Painter. On the latter the woman is labeled Astyoche and stands across from her father, Aktor. Astyoche bore Ares two sons, who later led the Minyans to Troy. The lack of inscriptions and adult male on the *alabastron*, as well as the somewhat different gesture of the woman, indicate that this scene should not be interpreted as showing these mythological figures; rather, it is an everyday scene.

The picture on the other side of a seated youth engaged in conversation with a woman in chiton and mantle holding a mirror may or may not be connected with the first picture. Possibly they are the couple of the house, which would mean that the woman with the children is a servant rather than the mother. Or does it depict the husband visiting a brothel? This would mean that the woman with children in the other scene is the mother and might explain her apprehensive gesture.

Attic red-figure alabastron,
attributed to the Villa Giulia Painter,
ca. 460–450 B.C.E.
H. 18.3; D. 6.1
Providence, Rhode Island School of Design,
Museum of Art
Museum Appropriations and Special Gift,
25.088
From Greece
Ex Collection E. P. Warren

PUBLISHED: *ARV*² 624,88; *BAdd*² 271; *CVA* Providence 1 USA 2, pl. 22,3; D. M. Buitron, *Attic Vase Painting in New England Collections* (Cambridge, Mass., 1972), 122–123, no. 67; I. Wehgartner, *Attisch weissgrundige Keramik* (Mainz, 1983), 40 and pl. 6,4; *LIMC* 2 (1984), 938, no. 3.
For the white-ground calyx-krater: Reggio di Calabria, Museo Nazionale 12393: *ARV*² 619,11 bis; *BAdd*² 270; Wehgartner (supra), pls. 6,1–2; *LIMC* 2 (1984), pl. 687, Astyoche 2. For the skyphos: Boston, Museum of Fine Arts, 01.8097: *ARV*² 785,2; *Para* 218; *BAdd*² 289; Wehgartner (supra), pl. 6,3; *LIMC* 2 (1984), pl. 687, Astyoche 1.

36b

37

37
Baby Learning to Crawl or Walk
(see also color illus. p. 72)

Family pictures are rare in Greek vase painting, and this intimate picture of father (or paidagogos) and mother (or nurse) encouraging a baby boy to crawl or walk is unique. The mother, dressed in a peplos, stands on the right leaning over slightly at the waist with both hands out to encourage the boy forward. He lies in the center of the picture, supporting his raised torso on both arms, as he looks up and makes eye contact with his mother, thereby heightening the drama of the moment. The bearded and mantled father stands on the left, supporting himself with a staff in the right hand. He looks on but is not directly involved with the action. Greek men typically play a far less active and frequent role with children in Greek art than females, indicating that although they cared for their children, it was in a more removed fashion than is the case with most fathers today. The sakkos hanging on the wall in the background indicates an interior setting, probably the gynaikeion (women's quarters).

The picture of a mantled youth holding out a *phiale* on the back of the vase is not connected with the main picture.

Attic red-figure pelike, attributed to the Manner of the Washing Painter,
ca. 430–420 B.C.E.
H. 18.5
London, The British Museum, E 396
From Kamiros

PUBLISHED: *ARV*² 1134,6; I. Jenkins, *Greek and Roman Life* (London, 1986), 33, fig. 39; Garland 1990, 123, fig. 10; V. Sabetai, "The Washing Painter: A Contribution to the Wedding and Genre Iconography in the Second Half of the Fifth Century B.C." (Ph.D. diss., University of Cincinnati, 1993), 69 and pl. 72.

38
Crawling Baby
(see also color illus. p. 37)

This miniature bronze statuette of a crawling baby is startlingly naturalistic, particularly as it was made in the second millennium. The infant is nude, so probably male, and around six months of age. The proportions of his chubby body are realistic, and he is placed in a pose that was carefully observed by the Minoan sculptor. He is on all fours but raises his round head and cocks it to his right as if his attention is attracted by something above. A millennium later, crawling babies appear in exactly the same pose on Athenian vases (cats. 37, 117). The little lips in low relief are curved into a slight smile, the pug nose protrudes slightly from the middle of the face, and the eyes are formed by deep cavities in which a trace of the iris is incised.

This bronze was reputedly found in the Dictaean Cave on Crete, where Sir Arthur Evans excavated in 1896 before he began his famous work at Knossos. Located in central Crete above Psychro, this cave was the place where Rhea (see cat. 4) hid her infant son Zeus, according to the account of Hesiod (*Theogony* 481–484). It contained votive offerings ranging in date from Middle Minoan to Roman, so the possibility has been suggested that the bronze is Roman.

Arguments for a Late Minoan date for this unique bronze are its rough finish, the nature of the alloy of bronze and tin, and the shape of the baby's head, which has no precedent in Roman art. Close stylistic

38

parallels are the little ivory babies from Palaikastro whose heads are also nearly as wide as their shoulders and whose small round ears likewise protrude (see Rutter, figs. 8–9, p. 38).

Bronze statuette, solid cast, Late Minoan I, ca. 1550–1450 B.C.E.

H. 2.8; L. 4.8

Oxford, The University of Oxford, Ashmolean Museum

Gift of Sir Arthur J. Evans, 1938.1162

From the Dictaean Cave, Crete; bought by Evans from J. Mitsotakis in 1908

PUBLISHED: J. Boardman, *The Cretan Collection in Oxford: The Dictaean Cave and Iron Age Crete* (Oxford, 1961), 8, 11 no. 22, pl. 3; D. Mitten and S. Doeringer, *Master Bronzes from the Classical World*, exhib. cat. (Cambridge, Mass., 1967), 31, no. 6; S. Hood, *The Arts in Prehistoric Greece* (Harmondsworth, England, 1978), 112, fig. 98; Rühfel 1984a, 14–16, fig. 1; C. Verlinden, *Les statuettes anthropomorphes crétoises en bronze et en plomb du IIIe millénaire au VIIe siècle av. J.-C.*, Archaeologia Transatlantica 4 (Providence, 1984), 83, 191 no. 38, pl. 19; E. Sapouna-Sakellarakis, *Die bronzenen Menschenfiguren auf Kreta und in der Ägäis*, Prähistorische Bronzefunde I, no. 5 (Stuttgart, 1995), 33–34, no. 49, pl. 12.

On the Dictaean cave, see L. V. Watrous, *The Cave Sanctuary of Zeus at Psychro: A Study of Extra-Urban Sanctuaries in Minoan and Early Iron Age Crete*, Aegaeum 15 (Liège, 1996). For the Palaikastro ivories, see Rühfel 1984a, 15–16, figs. 2–3.

39

39
Group of Three Sleeping Children

This small, charming group of three young children huddled together reminds one of just how quickly the seemingly endless energy of toddlers can give way to sleep so deep that it can be hard to wake them. Although clothed in short tunics, they huddle together for warmth, just like a litter of puppies. Their similar ages and appearances suggest that they may be triplets.

Multiple births, especially ones that survived, were far less common in antiquity and seemed to have been well received for the most part.

Sleeping children and sleeping Erotes became popular subjects in the Hellenistic period, when artists became interested in different states of being. A similar group in marble is known, although the children are nude and lie in a nest propped among tree branches.

Bronze statuette, Hellenistic

H. 2.4; GREATEST DIMENSION 5.3

Boston, Museum of Fine Arts

James Fund and by Special Contribution, 10.170

Possibly from Sicily

PUBLISHED: Klein 1932, pl. 7b; M. B. Comstock and C. C. Vermeule, *Greek, Roman, and Etruscan Bronzes in the Museum of Fine Arts, Boston* (Boston, 1971), 80–81, no. 84; C. C. Vermeule and M. B. Comstock, *Sculpture in Stone and Bronze:*

Additions to the Collections of Greek, Etruscan, and Roman Art, 1971–1988, in the Museum of Fine Arts, Boston (Boston, 1988), 119.

For multiple births, see Dasen 1997, 49–63. For the marble group, see Rome, Vatican: G. Lippold, *Die Skulpturen des Vaticanischen Museums*, vol. 3, part 2 (Berlin, 1956), 150 and pl. 71. See also M. Söldner, *Untersuchungen zu liegenden Eroten in der hellenistischen und römischen Kunst* (Frankfurt, 1986), 343 and 570–571 n. 1421.

40

Seated Infant Girl with Outstretched Arms

This toddler sits with left leg bent up, the other lying on the ground before her. She stretches her arms out to the sides (the end of her right one is broken off) and turns her head right while looking up in order to gain attention quickly from someone older. Her chiton, which is girded above her waist, clings to her body, revealing her chubby, baby proportions, most noticeably her belly and navel. She wears a braid around her coiffure.

This impatient infant is rendered in a pose typical for those not yet able to walk who want to be taken care of immediately. A marble sculpture from Agrai in Athens depicts a girl in a similar pose.

> Tanagra terracotta figurine, Attic, ca. 330–310 B.C.E.
> H. 5.8
> Boston, Museum of Fine Arts
> Anonymous Gift, 02.38

PUBLISHED: Klein 1932, 7 and pl. 7e; J. J. Herrmann, Jr., *In the Shadow of the Acropolis: Popular and Private Art in 4th-Century Athens* (Worcester, Mass., 1984), 59, no 80.

For the Agrai statue, Athens, National Archaeological Museum, 696; Rühfel 1984a, 223–224, fig. 93 and 347, n. 154 with earlier bibliography and for the pose.

41

Child on Potty Stool

While adult Greeks had chamber pots and urinals (see cat. 66), upper-class toddlers had use of ceramic potty chairs, as seen on this *chous*. The baby sits in a deep bowl mounted on a tall conical base; his legs protrude from an opening in the side of the bowl. The baby is looking to the left and waving a club-shaped rattle, perhaps in an effort to get the attention of an adult. He is flanked by other belongings: a miniature chous at the left and a roller propped up against the wall at the right.

This vase painting is one of three extant depictions of the *lasana*, or potty seat. The others appear on vases of ca. 460 B.C.E.:

40

41

the baby stretching forth both arms and even his right leg. They gaze at each other in a manner that suggests intimacy and attachment; they are absorbed with each other and oblivious to the outside world. Heightening the effect of a peephole into the women's quarters is the small size of the tondo and its wide white-ground surround.

A petite and delicate *kylix* with special wishbone-shaped handles, this cup was made in one of the finest ceramic studios of Classical Athens, that of the potter Sotades. It forms a pair with a similar cup that was found together with it, along with seven other Sotadean vases, in a burial in Athens in 1890. Both of these tiny cups mix techniques (white-ground and coral red) and feature scenes of domestic life; the second cup shows a woman spinning her top. This unusually rich tomb is thought to be that of a wealthy young woman who may have died soon after marriage and so did not enjoy the duties and joys of motherhood so charmingly depicted on this funerary vase.

Attic red-figure and white-ground stemless kylix, attributed to the Sotades Painter Workshop, ca. 460 B.C.E.
H. 3; DIAM. 12.7
Brussels, Musées royaux d'Art et d'Histoire, A 890
From Athens

PUBLISHED: ARV² 771,1; BAdd² 287; CVA Brussels 1 Belgium 1, pl. 1,1; Klein 1932, frontispiece; Rühfel 1984b, 34, fig. 18; L. Burn, "Honey Pots: Three White-Ground Cups by the Sotades Painter," AntK 28 (1985), 100–102, pls. 25,1 and 27,7; B. A. Sparkes, *The Red and the Black* (London, 1996), 77, fig. III:9; Lewis 2002, 8 fig. 0.3.

For the tomb context and the second Brussels cup signed by the potter Hegesiboulos (A 891), see ARV² 771,2; BAdd² 287; Burn (supra) pls. 25,2 and 27,8.

a red-figure *lekythos* in Berlin and a stemless cup in Brussels (see cat. 42). On both of these the mother is present. She is no doubt excluded on the chous as these small wine jugs were made for children and rarely show adults.

An original potty stool was found in a sixth-century well in the Athenian Agora (P18010) and is dated to 580 B.C.E. on the basis of its painted decoration of birds and beasts. It consists of a rimmed bowl with a cutout section for the child's legs and a circular opening in the seat. It has been suggested that the receptacle was supported on two metal rods inserted in the lower part of the stand. It could then be removed by withdrawing the rods.

Attic red-figure chous, ca. 440–430 B.C.E.
H. 11.
London, The British Museum, 1910.6-15.4

PUBLISHED: D. B. Thompson, *The Athenian Agora: An Ancient Shopping Center* (Princeton, 1971), fig. 39; Jenkins 1986, 32, fig. 37; Garland 1990, 161, fig. 21; Fittà 1997, 75, fig. 136.

For the Berlin lekythos (F 2209), see ARV² 1587, 2 (top). For the Brussels cup (A 890), see ARV² 771, 1.

42
Baby on Stool with Mother

Given the rarity of scenes in Greek vase painting in which parents (as opposed to nurses or teachers) interact with their children, this charming vignette is particularly revealing in the way that mother and baby interact. It shows a well-dressed Athenian citizen wife seated on a diphros (stool) facing her infant child, who sits squirming in his high chair, which may do double duty as a potty stool (see cat. 41). Each figure reaches out to the other, the mother calmly extending her right hand,

42

43

artist began to draw a beard, perhaps out of habit, but then changed his mind.

The reverse shows the messenger god Hermes with his traveler's cap and winged boots in a similar pose to that of the father on the obverse. He is listening to a satyr, seated on a rock, playing a boxlike musical instrument. Behind him is another satyr, who is aroused and looking away. Peeping out from beyond the rock is the forepart of a kneeling goat. The satyrs' mouths are open as if singing, and all figures are wreathed.

The pelike is a shape particularly associated with scenes of craftsmen, salesmen, and other *banausic* or mundane lucrative activities. Ten black-figure and five red-figure pelikai are attributed to the hand of the Eucharides Painter, who also produced a number of Panathenaic prize amphoras.

Attic black-figure pelike, attributed to the Eucharides Painter, ca. 500 B.C.E.
H. 40
Oxford, The University of Oxford, Ashmolean Museum, G 247
From Rhodes

PUBLISHED: *ABV* 396,21 and 696; *Para* 173; *BAdd²* 104; *CVA* Oxford 2 Great Britain 9, pls. 8,7–8; Lacey 1968, fig. 20; Bazant 1985, pl. 36, no. 59; M. Vickers, *Ancient Greek Pottery* (Oxford, 1999), 35, no. 23.

For the Agora shoemaker's shop, see D. B. Thompson, "The House of Simon the Shoemaker," *Archaeology* 13 (1960), 234–240. For the lekane, see B. A. Sparkes and L. Talcott, *Black and Plain Pottery of the 6th, 5th, and 4th Centuries B.C.*, The Athenian Agora 12 (Princeton, 1970), 211–216, pls. 81–87. For the shoemaker scene on the unattributed neck-amphora in Boston (01.8035), see *CVA* Boston 1 USA 14, pl. 37. For the scene of satyrs and Hermes on the reverse, see T. Hadzisteliou-Price, "'To Be or Not To Be' on an Attic Black-Figure Pelike," *AJA* 75 (1971), 431–434. For the association of the pelike with banausoi, see H. A. Shapiro, "Correlating Shape and Subject: The Case of the Archaic Pelike," in J. H. Oakley et al., eds, *Athenian Potters and Painters* (Oxford, 1997), 63–70. On pelikai by the Eucharides Painter, see E. M. Langridge, "The Eucharides Painter and His Place in the Athenian Potters' Quarter" (Ph.D. diss., Princeton University, 1993), 378–384. See also cat. 48.

43
Boy at Shoemaker's
(see also color illus. p. 100)

In ancient Greece, boys would have need of footwear for the first time when they left the *oikos* and went off to school, that is, at about the age of seven. At that age an Athenian boy's father or paidagogos would have marched him down to the Agora (marketplace) to the shoemaker's shop to have a pair of sandals custom made. In the southwest corner of the Athenian Agora a house clearly belonging to a shoemaker named Simon has been excavated, and it may once have resembled the scene on the obverse of this vase, known as a *pelike*.

Here we see an unusual genre scene set in a shoemaker's shop, as indicated by the knife rack at the upper left. The half-draped, bearded shoemaker sits on a stool at the left and concentrates on following the outline of the boy's right foot as he guides his knife through a piece of leather set on a wooden block painted in added white. His customer, a young boy dressed in a *himation*, stands on a three-legged table and steadies himself on his left foot by laying his right hand on the head of the shoemaker. Below the table is a large two-handled basin of a type known as a *lekane*, which may have held water for wetting the leather. At the right and seen from the back is another bearded man dressed in a himation. He leans on his staff in front of a folding stool with added white bosses, observing the proceedings. Both bearded men wear wreaths, and a leafy tendril appears in the background.

It is generally assumed that the man at the right is the boy's father, although there are no comparable scenes except a neck-amphora in Boston (01.8035) that shows a young woman in place of the boy. Because she has prominent breasts, she is probably considerably older than the boy in our scene and is no doubt receiving sandals prior to her marriage, when she too will leave home for the first time. The incised line on the boy's chin suggests that the

Am I not right in thinking that a good
education is one that improves both the
mind and the body?

> Plato, *Laws*

The best provision for the journey towards
old age is education.

> Aristotle, *Diogenes Laertius* 5.21

T HE ancient Greeks valued education
as much as we do today, but theirs
differed from ours in its emphases. Since
Mycenaean times, training in athletics and
music had been considered an important
component of any elite boy's upbringing.
Military training began for boys in Sparta
at the age of twelve, when they took up
residence in a communal barracks. Education varied according to location, class,
and sex. While the Spartan *agoge* (system of
education) stressed obedience and
courage, the aim of the Athenians was to
produce the *kaloskagathos*, literally a beautiful and good man. While the children of
aristocrats learned athletics, music,
reading, writing, and rhetoric, the sons of
peasants were apprenticed to their fathers
at an early age. Girls at all levels of society
were usually taught only to spin and weave,
cook, and perform other domestic tasks.

We know most about education at
Athens, where it was not organized by the
city-state but was a matter of private enterprise and so depended upon the will of the
family. It began in the home with the
paidagogos, or male tutor, who was usually a
slave. He acted as the boy's guardian and
accompanied him outside the house for his
lessons with specialists. Of these teachers
(*didaskaloi*) there were three types: the
grammatistes (reading and writing teacher),
the *kitharistes* (music teacher), and the
paidotribes (the physical education instructor). At the age of seven the Athenian boy
went to school to learn to write, first with a
stylus and wax tablet, later with ink and a

44a

papyrus scroll. He also learned by heart
epic poetry, according to Plato: "When the
children have learned their letters and are
beginning to understand the written word
as well as the spoken, they are made to
learn by heart the famous poets, whose
works contain sound advice and good
stories, as well as praise of the heroes of
old, so that the child is inspired to imitate
them" (*Protagoras* 325 E). Training in music
was considered important for a well-edu-
cated gentleman. Again according to Plato:
"The kitharistes teaches the boys to play
the lyre and then to sing lyric songs to their
own accompaniment. In this way they
become more cultured, more controlled
and better balanced people, and their
behavior is all the better for it" (*Protagoras*
326 A).

A sound and healthy body was another
important aspect of Athenian education.
At about the age of twelve boys went to the
palaistra, where they learned to run, jump,
wrestle, box, throw the discus, and hurl the
javelin. Greek boys exercised naked and
cleaned their sweaty bodies by applying oil
and scraping it off with a *strigil* (see cat. 55).

Although informal gathering places,
like Plato's Academy outside the city of
Athens, were common, formal schools
were rare. Nonetheless, Herodotus (6.27)
mentions the collapse of the roof of a
school that resulted in the death of more
than one hundred children, which suggests
that some large educational buildings
existed in the fifth century.

For a general discussion of education, see Beck
1964; Barrow 1976; Cribore 2001. For images,
see Beck 1975. For the Spartan agoge, see
Kennell 1995.

44
School Scenes
(*see also color illus. p. 66*)

The prolific early-fifth-century cup
painter Douris made a specialty of education scenes, which appear on eight of his
kylixes, or stemmed drinking cups. This
kylix is the most famous, and one of only
a few that depict actual school scenes.
These are identifiable by the schoolmaster,

OVERLEAF

CAT. 46a Girls Going to School (?), Attic red-figure
kylix, attributed to the Painter of Bologna 417, ca.
460 B.C.E. New York, The Metropolitan Museum of
Art, Rogers Fund, 1906

44b

44c

who is seated in a backed chair (klismos) as shown in the center on the obverse of this cup. He is holding open a scroll on which is inscribed hexameter verse, presumably the lines being recited by the boy standing before him. The lines are

ΜΟΙΣΑΜΟΙ
ΑΦΙΣΚΑΜΑΝΔΡΟΝ
ΕΥΡΩΝΑΡΧΟΜΑΙ
ΑΕΙΝΔΕΝ

and are best understood as Μοισα μοι— ἀμφὶ Σκάμανδρον εὔρροον ἄρχομ᾽ ἀείδειν—. "Muse to me . . . I begin to sing of wide-flowing Scamander."

Behind him a music lesson is taking place, with both teacher and student seated on stools and holding lyres. At the far right is the paidagogos, identifiable by his staff, who has accompanied the boys to school and waits while they complete their lessons. In the background hang kylixes, lyres, a flute case, and a footed basket.

On the opposite side, seated on a stool, is the hypodidaskalos or assistant teacher, who holds a tablet and stylus with a student standing patiently before him. Behind him another music lesson is taking place, this time in singing to the aulos, or double flute. Another paidagogos sits waiting at the far right. In the background hang more accoutrements of the schoolroom: writing cases, lyre, knucklebone sack, and a mysterious cross-shaped object, possibly some sort of tuning device.

The interior of the cup shows a youth in the palaistra, his right leg propped up on a stool, presumably binding his sandal. In the background are a laver, a sponge and aryballos, and a walking stick. Thus this cup references the all-around training of an Athenian youth in athletics, music, and grammar.

Attic red-figure kylix, signed by Douris, ca. 490–480 B.C.E.
H. 11.5; DIAM. 28.4; W. 36.2
Berlin, Staatliche Museen, Antikensammlung, F 2285
From Cervetri

PUBLISHED: ARV² 431–432, 48 and 1653; Para 374; BAdd² 237; J. D. Beazley, "Hymn to Hermes," AJA 52 (1948) 337–338, no.2; CVA Berlin 2 Germany 21, pls. 77–78; Immerwahr

45a

1964, 18–19, no. 1; Beck 1975, pls. 10,53–54 and 30,168; Rühfel 1984b, 34–35 fig. 24a, 50–51 fig. 24b; Booth 1985; D. Buitron-Oliver, Douris: A Master-Painter of Athenian Red-Figure Vases (Mainz, 1995), 78, no. 88 and pl. 58; Cribiore 2001, 29 and figs. 1–2.

For the book roll, see Immerwahr 1964, Immerwahr 1973; E. Pöhlmann, "Die Notenschrift in der Überlieferung der griechischen Bühnenmusik," Würzburger Jahrbücher für die Altertumswissenschaft N.F. 2 (1976), 53–73; H. R. Immerwahr, Attic Script: A Survey (Oxford, 1990), 99.

45
Courting Scenes
(see also color illus. p. 84, 101–102)

At first glance the images on this cup look like boys attending music lessons. In the tondo it appears that a modestly draped youth holding his tortoise-shell lyre has

just arrived. He stands before a partially draped, bearded man, who leans on his knotty walking stick, and a cushioned stool completes the scene. On the exterior four boys are seated on their stools, and their lyres hang on the wall above their heads. Before each boy is a draped, bearded man, again leaning on his walking stick. Could each of these men be a kitharistes, and the singleton at the far right on each side a paidagogos who has accompanied his charges to their music lessons?

In fact subtle clues suggest that these are male courting scenes. The most telling is the presence of hares, which were common love gifts of men to young boys. On one side a man is handing a hare to the seated boy, while on the other side a hare sits calmly on the boy's lap. The division of the scene into couples is also an indication of male courtship. Hanging on the wall in the middle of each scene on the exterior is

45b

45c

a sack of knucklebones and palaistra equipment (sponge and aryballos). The latter suggests that the men have just come from the exercise ground, which was a popular spot for meeting boys. The aristocratic nature of male courtship is indicated here by the conspicuous elite attributes, such as the walking sticks and musical instruments.

Attic red-figure kylix, signed by Douris, attributed to Python as potter, ca. 480 B.C.E.
H. 11.9; DIAM. 31.2;
W. WITH HANDLES 38.8
Malibu, Calif., The J. Paul Getty Museum, 86.AE.290
Ex Collection Molly and Walter Bareiss

PUBLISHED: *Para* 375, 51bis; BAdd² 237; D. Buitron-Oliver, *Douris: A Master-Painter of Athenian Red-Figure Vases* (Mainz, 1995), pl. 61, no. 93; *CVA* Getty 8 USA 33, pls. 438–439; Schnapp 1997, fig. 32.

For hares as love gifts of older men to younger boys, see Koch-Harnack 1983, 63–89; M. Bouvier, *Le Lièvre dans l'antiquité* (Lyons, 2000).

46
Girls Going to School (?)
(see also color illus. p. 243)

This kylix, used for wine at the all-male symposium, is decorated on the interior with a unique scene involving two tall, well-dressed females. The first, who wears a *sakkos* (snood), grabs the wrist of the other, who looks reluctant to come along. The latter is holding a writing case with a stylus tucked beneath the strings, the only

attribute in this scene. The exterior, which shows three pairs of conversing girls per side, has more in the way of objects hanging in the background: *alabastron*, wreath, sandals, writing box, fillet, and pairs of castanets.

One scholar has labeled the scene in the tondo "girl being conducted reluctantly to school." This interpretation is based on comparison with more common scenes of boys going to school with their paidagogoi. Given the attribute carried by the girl, it is not an unreasonable reading of the scene. Because other Attic vase paintings show women reading, one might conclude that they went to school, although no actual school scenes with girls exist. Females, if they learned to read and write, did so within the confines of the oikos.

Only one category of women had lessons outside the house, and these were *hetairai*, or courtesans, who were often well educated (see cats. 58–59). The castanets are traditional attributes of Greek courtesans, and so these women should probably not be identified as citizen daughters. Also, the manner in which fully draped women are paired with less covered ones on the exterior suggests a parody of male courting scenes (see cat. 45). Because these scenes appear on a man's drinking vessel, they were probably intended to be humorous and entertaining rather than representative of everyday life.

Attic red-figure kylix, attributed to the Painter of Bologna 417, ca. 460 B.C.E.
H. 15.1; DIAM. 36.5; W. AT HANDLES 45.7
New York, The Metropolitan Museum of Art Rogers Fund, 1906, 06.1021.167

PUBLISHED: ARV² 908, 13; *Para* 430; BAdd² 304; Klein 1932, pl. 29B; G. M. A. Richter and L. F. Hall, *Red-Figured Athenian Vases in the Metropolitan Museum of Art* (New Haven, 1936), 107–108, no. 78, pl. 80; Beck 1975, 56 no. 350, pl. 69; Golden 1990, 73, fig. 11.

For the Painter of Bologna 417, see D. von Bothmer, "A Cup in Berne," *Hefte des archäologischen Seminars der Universität Bern* 7 (1981), 37–43, pls. 8–10. For the education of girls, see Pomeroy 1975; Cribiore 2001, 74–101.

46a

46b

46c

47

Boy with Seated Paidagogos

A bearded paidagogos with a mantle around his lower body and over his right shoulder sits on a block stool writing on a tablet set upon his knees. His balding head, snub nose, and deeply furrowed forehead give him the appearance of a Silen, evidence that the group to which this piece belongs was influenced by earlier ones of Papposilenos and the baby Dionysos (see cat. 8). The portraits of philosophers, particularly those of Socrates, are also not far removed. The tutor turns his head slightly to his right to see if the very young naked boy standing next to him is attentive or not. The attention of young children can easily wander, particularly when it comes to schoolwork, as he is undoubtedly aware.

Thanks to terracotta figurines such as this one, we learn that the paidagogos could also help children with instruction. This aspect of their duties is not mentioned in the literary sources.

Tanagra figurine, ca. 375–350 B.C.E.
H. 12.4
New York, The Metropolitan Museum of Art
Richard A. van Avery Gift Fund, 1923, 23.259

PUBLISHED: Klein 1932, 29 and pl. 28c; G. M. A. Richter, *Handbook of the Greek Collection* (Cambridge, Mass., 1953), 128, 310 n. 63, and pl. 109c; Bieber 1961, 141 n. 49 and fig. 588; K. Schefold, "Sokratische Wolkenverehrer," *AntK* 2 (1959), 23, 25, and pl. 14,3; Beck 1975, fig. 73; L. Moretti, "La trasformazione della società: La scuola, il ginnasio, l'efebia," in *Storia e civiltà dei Greci* 8 (1977), 471 and pl. 16c; Harten 1999, 287, n. 1339, 292–298, 306 n. 1434, 315 n. 1483, 316 n. 1491, 323, 346, and 418 no. Tc 2a.

For this type, see Schulze 1998, 47, and Harten 1999, 292–298.

48

Youth Writing

The interior of this red-figure cup gives the viewer a glimpse of what may be a schoolboy hard at work. He sits on a wooden stool and wears his *himation* so as to leave his right arm free to write. His wooden writing case is open on his lap, braced with his left hand. With his right hand he holds a stylus poised to make an impression in the wax. The writing case is divided into five sections rather like our spiral notebooks. The object at the right may be a chest for storing scrolls, which are occasionally depicted in school scenes. If this is an excerpt from a school scene, rather than a lone schoolboy doing homework, then the seated figure is most likely a young assistant teacher (hypodidaskalos), perhaps correcting a student's writing.

While scenes of boys reading and writing are fairly common on Athenian vases, other subjects such as mathematics do not occur. It has been suggested that the importance of literacy and writing in the young Athenian democracy accounts for the popularity of these school scenes on Attic vases. The Eucharides Painter, to whom this vase is attributed, illustrated another tondo with a seated boy reading a book.

Attic red-figure kylix, attributed to the
Eucharides Painter, ca. 480 B.C.E.
H. 7.4; DIAM. 21.2; W. 27.5
Philadelphia, University of Pennsylvania,
Museum of Archaeology and Anthropology,
MS 4842
From Orvieto

PUBLISHED: *ARV²* 231, 82; *BAdd²* 200; *Museum Journal* 4 (1913), 156–157, no. 10, fig. 134; *The Birth of Democracy*, exhib. cat. (Athens, 1993), 145, fig. 24.2; *Expedition: Bulletin of the Museum of the University of Pennsylvania* 36 (1994), 2–3, and A12.

The other cup by the Eucharides Painter is Vatican, Musei Vaticani, Astarita 656; see *ARV²* 231, 83.

48

53a

53b

54

53
Papyrus with Writing

A copying exercise is written on the back of an account sheet. The first four lines give three hexameters, each from a different mythological story, written by the teacher.

Translation (Daniel): "Althaia killed Meleagros with the pitiless firebrand. Polydeukes prevailed over Amykos, the chief of the Bebrykes. Perseus lopped off the head of the direful Medusa."

On the fifth line the student begins to copy the teacher's text but fails to complete the assignment. Below, he signs his name: Eutychides, son of Kalopos.

Graeco-Egyptian, third century C.E.
H. 9.3; W. 11.5
Ann Arbor, The University of Michigan, Harlan Hatcher Graduate Library, Papyrology Collection, P. Mich. Inv. 4953

PUBLISHED: R. W. Daniel, "P.Mich: Inv. 4953: A School Poem on Mythology," ZPE 49 (1982), 43–44 and pl. IC; Cribiore 1996, 206, no. 138.

54
Boy Boxers (?)

Boys received athletic training in the palaistra and competed in athletic contests at religious festivals. On this *chous* two nude boys are sparring in the palaistra, indicated by the turnposts flanking them. Because they wear wreaths, they might be taking part in a festival contest.

A late source defines a contest known as the *Limnomachai* as "the boys boxing at the place called Limnai" (Hesychius), and this may have taken place at the Anthesteria in honor of Dionysos. This chous may be further evidence for the contest, but in general athletic scenes are rare on small choes. Turnposts do appear on several.

This image of sparring boys calls to mind the Bronze Age fresco from Akrotiri that depicts boys boxing (see Rutter, fig. 25, p. 45).

Attic red-figure chous, ca. 420 B.C.E.
H. 8; DIAM. 6.8
Boston, Museum of Fine Arts
Catharine Page Perkins Fund, 95.53
From Athens
Ex Collections A. van Branteghem;
E. P. Warren

PUBLISHED: Hoorn 1951, 111, no. 368, fig. 132; Green 1971, 196, fig. 3d; Beck 1975, pl. 38, no. 205; Rühfel 1984b, 147, fig. 83.

55

55
Athlete

A young athlete sits amid his athletic equipment on the earthen ground of the palaistra. To his left are a large discus and a pickaxe used to loosen the soil for wrestling. Below are two black jumping weights (halteres). This equipment indicates that he is a pentathlete. The pentathlon is an event consisting of five contests: running, jumping, throwing the discus, hurling the javelin, and wrestling. That he is also a boxer is indicated by the rawhide thong that he is in the process of winding around his upraised left hand and wrist. Tied up with a red string in the background are his personal hygiene implements: a sponge, an aryballos (round oil flask), and a strigil for scraping off the oil, indicated by a thin curved black line. Beyond him to the left are painted the words Epidromos kalos (Epidromos is beautiful). This inscription used on other vases by the same painter gives the unknown

artist his nickname, the Epidromos Painter.

This image, perfectly adapted to the tondo of a kylix, portrays the ideal Greek youth—handsome, muscular, all-round athlete, well-kept body. Much of his young life has been spent in the palaistra, trained by his paidotribes, honing his athletic skills, competing with boys his age, and basking in the praise of older male admirers. His boldly foreshortened legs frame his taut abdomen, the muscles delineated in dilute glaze. His head has the short hair of an athlete, and delicate features, although at this time Greek artists are still painting the traditional frontal eye in the profile face. Clearly he has not yet spent much time in the ring; the Greeks considered boxing the most injurious of all their sports, and it often resulted in facial deformities.

Attic red-figure kylix, attributed to the Epidromos Painter, ca. 520–500 B.C.E.
H. 9.5; DIAM. 19.6
Hanover, N.H., Dartmouth College, Hood Museum of Art

Gift of Mr. and Mrs. Ray Winfield Smith, Class of 1918, C.1970.35
Ex Collection Ray W. Smith, Dublin, New Hampshire

PUBLISHED: ARV² 117,6; BAdd² 174; C. Boulter, "Fifth-century Attic Red Figure at Corinth," Hesperia 49 (1980), 296–297, pl. 77c; S. Laser, Sport und Spiel: Archeologia Homerica (Göttingen, 1987), 41, fig. 9; Numismatica e antichità classiche, Quaderni ticinese 16 (1987), 82, pl. 11.19; J. Neils, Goddess and Polis: The Panathenaic Festival in Ancient Athens (Hanover, N.H., 1992), 75 and 161 no. 27.

On the Epidromos Painter, see ARV² 117–118, 1577, and 1687; BAdd² 174; for Greek boxing, see M. B. Poliakoff, Combat Sports in the Ancient World: Competition, Violence, and Culture (New Haven, 1987), 68–88.

56
A Riding Lesson

A young boy attempts to mount a horse, possibly for the first time, as indicated by his awkward pose—right leg hooked over the horse's back, left foot facing the wrong direction, and both arms arranged so as to pull himself up. He looks toward a bearded, balding man, probably his father, who steadies him by placing his right hand on the boy's back. It seems that the horse senses the rider's insecurity and is himself therefore tense, as indicated by his slightly raised head. Or the posture may be because the youth is tugging at the reins, although none are visible. A mantled youth, possibly an older brother, stands on the right looking on.

Boys, particularly those of the upper classes, learned to ride at a young age so that they could compete at various sporting events in equestrian competitions and later in life hunt or ride around their estate or to town for pleasure or business. Plato (*Laws* VII 794c) suggests that they began at six, about the age of the boy on this vessel. Boy jockeys are often pictured racing in Greek art, either in the midst of the race or slowly led forward as victors. Later in life some of these young riders became members of the Athenian cavalry, an elite military unit. This unique picture shows a much earlier moment.

Mantled figures, a standard subject for the reverses of Classical vases, decorate the other side.

> Attic red-figure column-krater, attributed to the Naples Painter, ca. 440 B.C.E.
> H. 32.4
> London, The British Museum, E 485
> From Nola

PUBLISHED: *ARV²* 1098,32 and 1683; *BAdd²* 328; Klein 1932, pl. 14b; J. K. Anderson, *Ancient Greek Horsemanship* (Berkeley, 1961), pl. 18a; Beck 1975, pl. 40, 213; Rühfel 1984b, 55, fig. 30.

For boy riders, see Rühfel 1984b, 55–59.

56

57
Seated Youth with Theater Mask

Seated on a rock, this lad turns his head slightly to his left and looks pensively down, perhaps thinking about the festival he has just taken part in. A thick fillet, with a ball attachment by his forehead atop a wreath, encircles his head. His cloak covers his lower right arm and drapes down along his side. In his right hand he holds a theater mask, probably one used by an actor playing the role of a young man.

This figurine belongs to a large group of similarly wreathed youths from this time who stand or sit, and often hold theater masks; sometimes they bear other objects, such as balls, bags, or writing tablets. The masks and festive dress clearly indicate the figure's participation in a festival of Dionsyos. His reflective mood gives a sense of the seriousness of his role.

57

Tanagra terracotta figurine, Boiotian, first quarter of the third century B.C.E.
H. 14.8
New York, The Metropolitan Museum of Art
Gift of Mrs. Charles S. Sargent and Mrs. Arthur L. Devens, in memory of their mother, Mrs. James W. Markoe, 1962, 62.68.1

UNPUBLISHED: For this group, see Uhlenbrock 1990, 114, no. 7. For seated boys, see Rühfel 1984a, 200–201. For the mask, see T. B. L. Webster, *Monuments Illustrating New Comedy*, 3d ed., rev. and enlarged by J. R. Green and A. Seeberg, *BICS* suppl. 50 (London, 1995), vol. 1, 16–25. Richard Green suggests in a letter to Joan R. Mertens that the mask may be of the Panchrestos type, no. 10 in the list by Pollux: Webster (supra), 16–17.

58
Girl Learning to Dance

Dancing girls were a popular source of entertainment for men, and these girls often performed at the symposium. They were normally from the lower classes or slaves, and many also served as hetairai. A dancing instructor stands on the right with her left hand atop an upright *narthex* (a staff of fennel used to help keep time as well as enforce instruction) and gestures with her right hand to guide the girl. The teacher wears *chiton*, mantle, necklace, disk earring, and diadem. Meanwhile, the nude young girl dances vigorously, with crossstep, her hands held out together in front. Her hair is tied up in a ponytail in back, and she wears a disk earring and crossgirt apparatus. The reason for the latter is unclear, although it may have been a support or worn to make the girl's nudity more provocative. The fillet hanging in the background indicates an interior setting.

The Phiale Painter was an artist who took a particular interest in depicting dancing girls, showing them during training as well as while performing. Several of his *lekythoi* show a woman instructing a girl, as is the case on this vase. Different steps are performed by others of the painter's girls, and they can be clothed or partially clothed. In some cases male customers are present, as well as flute players.

58

Attic red-figure lekythos, attributed to the Phiale Painter, ca. 440–435 B.C.E.
H. 37.7; DIAM. OF MOUTH 6.5;
DIAM. OF BASE 7.1
Brunswick, Maine, Bowdoin College Museum of Art
Gift of Edward Perry Warren, Esq., Honorary Degree, 1926, 1913.011
From Gela

PUBLISHED: ARV² 1021,118; *Para* 441; BAdd² 316; *AJA* 37 (1933), 401, fig. 3; K. Herbert, *Ancient Art in Bowdoin College: A Descriptive Catalogue of the Warren and Other Collections* (Cambridge, Mass., 1964), pl. 25,2; D. M. Buitron, *Attic Vase Painting in New England Collections* (Cambridge, Mass., 1972), 137, no. 75; J. H. Oakley, *The Phiale Painter* (Mainz, 1990), 37–38, 85, no. 118 and pls. 96a–b.

For dancing girls, see J. D. Beazley, "Narthex," *AJA* 37 (1933), 400–403; H. Verhoogen, "Une leçon de danse," *Bulletin des Musées royaux d'Art et d'Histoire* 28 (1956), 5–16; L. B. Lawler, *The Dance in Ancient Greece* (London, 1964), 127–138; M. Robertson, "A Muffled Dancer and Others," in A. Cambitoglou, ed., *Studies in Honour of Arthur Dale Trendall* (Sydney, 1979), 129–134; Oakley (supra), 37–40 and 97; Rühfel 1984b, 41–45; V. Liventhal, "What Goes on Among Women? The Setting of Some Attic Vase Paintings of the Fifth Century B.C.," *Analecta Romana Instituti Danici* 14 (1985), 37–52.

59a

59b

59
Girl Dancing to Flute Music

The training of the girl dancer (see cat. 58) is the prelude to the performance shown on this *pelike*. A dancing girl wearing only a headband jumps high in the air, her left leg bent back. Apparently kicking one's backside while jumping was part of this dance, which is illustrated elsewhere. Turning, she looks back at a woman in chiton and mantle who provides the music by playing an aulos (double flute). The dancer works the *krotala* (castanets), whose clapping further emphasizes the rhythm of the music. These agile and well-trained entertainers were very popular.

A domestic scene of woolworking decorates the other side of the vessel. A seated woman spins wool on the left, while another holds up a skein of wool in one hand and a *kalathos* (wool basket) down in the other. Thus the two sides of this pelike show two different aspects of a girl's life—providing entertainment and making textiles.

Attic red-figure pelike, attributed to the
Earlier Mannerists, ca. 460 B.C.E.
H. 30.3; DIAM. 21.4; DIAM. OF MOUTH
14.7; DIAM. OF BASE 16.5
Stanford, Stanford University, Iris and
B. Gerald Cantor Center for Visual Arts
Gift of Mrs. Jane L. Stanford, 17410

PUBLISHED: *Para* 393; *BAdd*² 263; *AJA* 69 (1965), 64 and pl. 17, figs. 4–5; Beck 1975, 76, fig. 376.

60
Standing Girl with Tiara and Tambourine

A teenaged girl, whose breasts indicate that she has recently reached puberty, stands in a ceremonial costume consisting of a high-belted blue chiton, earrings, and a tall tiara that sits atop her melon-coiffure and is tied with ribbons or loops of hair. With her left hand she holds a large tambourine (*tympanon*) upright on the ground before her; her right arm is bent near her waist. She smiles and poses as if for a camera. In her case she is best perceived as about to go off to a festival, perhaps one of Dionysos.

> Tanagra terracotta figurine, Attic, ca. 325 B.C.E.
> H. 13.3
> Boston, Museum of Fine Arts
> Museum Purchase by Contribution, 01.7860
> From Aegina

PUBLISHED: Klein 1932, 17 and pl. 20a; J. J. Herrmann, Jr., *In the Shadow of the Acropolis: Popular and Private Art in 4th-Century Athens* (Worcester, Mass., 1984), 10, 53, and 59–60, no 81.

60

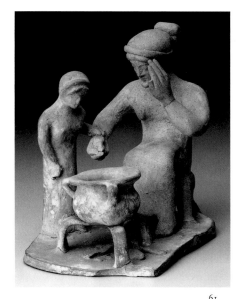

61

61
Woman Teaching Girl to Cook
(see also color illus. p. 112)

Greek girls learned to cook from the older females in the house, as we know from literary sources, but this may be the only known representation of such a lesson. A *chytra*, the common kettle for heating water and soup, sits on a tripod base atop a fire. This vase is unusual in that it has three handles instead of the single handle typical of this shape. Behind the cooking implements sits a woman on a *diphros*, or simple stool, who leans over to place the small object (herbs or spices?) that she holds out in her right hand into the pot. She raises the other hand to warn the girl standing near her to be careful. Although the girl has her hand on the woman's right arm, she bends over a little too far to look into the pot at what will probably be soup. Both figures wear chiton and *sakkos*.

This terracotta group (see also cat. 34) provides a vivid scene from everyday life, as do a number of other late Archaic Boiotian terracottas.

> Tanagra terracotta figurine, Boiotian, first quarter of the fifth century B.C.E.
> H. 10.7
> Boston, Museum of Fine Arts
> Museum Purchase by Contribution, 01.7788

PUBLISHED: Klein 1932, pl. 23d; G. H. Chase, "Eight Terracottas in the Museum of Fine Arts, Boston," in *Festschrift für James Loeb* (Munich, 1930), 46 fig. 3, 48, and 50; B. A. Sparkes and

L. Talcott, *Pots and Pans of Classical Athens* (Princeton, 1958), fig. 41; B. A. Sparkes, "The Greek Kitchen," *JHS* 82 (1962), 136 no. 70; C. C. Vermeule and M. B. Comstock, *Greek, Etruscan, and Roman Art: The Classical Collections of the Museum of Fine Arts, Boston*, rev. ed. (Boston, 1972), 51 and 70, fig. 59; Beck 1975, 56 and fig. 425; Higgins 1986, 87–88, fig. 92; Rühfel 1984a, 36–37, fig. 20, and 181 n. 61.

For the Greek kitchen, see Sparkes (supra), 121–137.

62
Visit to a Brothel (?)
(see also color illus. p. 99)

Painted on the body of this *hydria* is a problematic scene involving three standing males and a seated woman. The woman, draped in her himation and wearing a sakkos on her head, sits on a diphros holding a mirror. An alabastron hangs on the wall in the background. Confronting her is a young boy enveloped in his mantle. Next comes a bearded, half-draped man leaning on his walking stick and holding a leather or cloth sack, presumably a coin purse. A sponge and strigil, the equipment of athletes (see cats. 44–45 and 55), hang in the field behind him. Last comes another, older, boy, likewise enveloped in his mantle and so almost a twin, except in size, to the younger boy.

The most conspicuous and unusual aspect of this painting is the columned structure in which the woman sits receiving the younger boy. It consists of a fluted Aeolic column supporting an entablature of triglyphs and metopes, a plain architrave, and above, in black, regulae with guttae. Architecture of any kind is exceedingly rare on Attic vases and must be significant in this scene. The artist has made a clear distinction between the indoors, or women's area, and the outdoors, the domain of the older males. Although this could be a domestic scene and has been interpreted as such ("a vignette of family life, perhaps a henpecked husband trying to appease his wife with money?"), the money pouch is usually represented in scenes where a man is about to buy a woman's favors. Thus it seems likely that

64c

64d

ularly onerous for this boy, who had probably already worked all day.

Near the krater is the signature of
Hieron, the potter who made this vessel
and signed over fifty vases, most of them
by Makron. This may be his earliest signature. Makron painted servant boys underneath the handles of three other cups, one
of which is posed similarly to the sleeping
boy on this cup.

> Attic red-figure kylix, attributed to Makron
> and signed by Hieron as potter,
> ca. 490–480 B.C.E.
> H. 14; DIAM. 33.2; W. AT HANDLES 42.8
> Private Collection, New England
> Ex Collection E. Borowski

PUBLISHED: K. Schauenburg, "Herakles bei
Pholos zu zwei frührotfigurigen Schalen," AM
86 (1971), 51 and pls. 38–41.1; D. Bothmer,
"Notes on Makron," in D. C. Kurtz and B. A.
Sparkes, eds., The Eye of Greece: Studies in the Art
of Athens (Cambridge, 1982), 31, where he
notes that the fragment, Florence PD 317 (ARV²
467,120), joins the lower center of the scene on
side A; N. Leipen, Glimpses of Excellence: A Selection
of Greek Vases and Bronzes from the Elie Borowski
Collection (Toronto, 1984), 13–14, no. 10; N.
Kunisch, Makron (Mainz, 1997), 6, 28, 50, 65 fig.
28, 71, 80, 82, 112, 114, 165 no. 47 and pl. 21.

For the pose of the sleeping child, see D. von
Bothmer, "A Bronze Oinochoe in New York,"
in G. Kopcke and M. B. Moore, eds., Studies in
Classical Art and Archaeology: A Tribute to Peter von
Blanckenhagen (Locust Valley, N.Y., 1979), 66–67.
The other cups are Gotha, Schlossmuseum Ava
94 (ARV² 467,119; Para 378; Kunisch [supra],
pl. 100); New York, The Metropolitan Museum
of Art 20.246 (ARV² 467,118; Para 378; BAdd² 245;
Kunisch [supra], pl. 130), and Centre Island,
private (Kunisch [supra], pl. 81, 241), which has
the sleeping boy.

65
Serving Boy

Children were a common source of labor
in ancient Greece, and one of the most
common occupations for slave boys was
to serve men at the symposium. Frequently
the boys are shown standing by or making
ready to fill the empty drinking cups of the
symposiasts. Such a youth is pictured on
this oinochoe. He strides quickly to the

right, a ladle in his left hand and an oinochoe of exactly the same shape as this vessel in his right. A wreath in added red encircles his blond hair. He is probably off to the mixing bowl to refill his empty jug.

This vase and cat. 76 form a pair and were probably found together in the same tomb. They share the same trademark on the underside of the foot. The style of painting is close to that of the Berlin Painter, and they may well be copies of this master's work by the Harrow Painter, a lesser artist who was named after another oinochoe at Harrow showing a boy with hoop.

Attic red-figure oinochoe, attributed to the Harrow Painter, ca. 470 B.C.E.
H. WITH HANDLE 22.9; H. WITHOUT HANDLE 18.8; GREATEST DIAM. OF MOUTH 8.4; DIAM. OF BASE 7.4
Tampa Museum of Art
Joseph Veach Noble Collection, 1986.072

PUBLISHED: ARV² 1635,13bis and 1705,78bis; Para 345; BAdd² 197; H. Bloesch, "Varianten," in M. Rohde-Liegle et al., eds., Gestalt und Geschichte: Festschrift Karl Schefold, zu seinem 60 Geburtstag am 26 Jan. 1965, AntK suppl. 4 (Bern, 1967), 86, figs. 6–7, and 88; Münchner Jahrbuch der bildenden Kunst 27 (1976), 34, fig. 7; S. P. Murray, Collecting the Classical Past: Antiquities from the Joseph Veach Noble Collection (Tampa, 1985), 45, no. 65; J. M. Padgett, "The Geras Painter: An Athenian Eccentric and His Associates" (Ph.D. diss., Harvard University, 1989), 150, 155–156, and 196–197, no. H 78bis; M. Robertson, The Art of Vase-Painting in Classical Athens (Cambridge, 1992), 127–128, fig. 131; P. J. Russell, Ceramics and Society: Making and Marketing Ancient Greek Pottery (Tampa, 1994), cover and 33–34, no. 14.

For the Harrow Painter, see Robertson (supra), 127–128; Padgett (supra), 149–205.

66

66
Boy Serving a Reveler
(see also color illus. p. 148)

The Greek expression ἀμίδα παί (boy, a chamber pot) recorded in Athenaeus's Deipnosophistai (1:17d) must have been heard often at the Greek symposium as men drank a surfeit of wine. On this wine vase (chous) we find a visualization of this expression as a young slave holds an amis, or pot, into which a wreathed komast (reveler) with a bulging belly is urinating. Although this painting is surely meant to be amusing, it probably accurately reflects the existence of young slaves who were forced to cater to all their masters' needs. This boy not only holds the urinal but also carries the man's dinner basket over his shoulder and his knotty walking stick in his left hand. He is also patiently listening to the song being belted out by this drunken reveler with his open mouth. On other Attic vases, boys ladle out wine at the symposium and hold the heads of the symposiasts who have imbibed too much and are vomiting (see Golden, fig. 1, p. 17). As often on choes, a wreathed chous sits on the ground, mirroring the shape of the vessel itself.

The Greek word for child, pais, can also mean slave, and in Greek art it is often difficult to distinguish children from slaves, as both can be shown nude and of small stature. Because this boy is not wearing a banqueting wreath and is laden down with gear, he is almost certainly a slave.

The Oionokles Painter, named for the kalos name on four of his Nolan amphoras,

65

67

67
Captive Black Youth

This highly polished little statuette is in fact a hollow box whose cover slid into a groove on the underside of its square plinth. On top of the plinth crouches a black youth, his ankles shackled. His distinctive ethnic features include tightly curled hair radiating in rows from the top of the head, a broad nose, and thick lips. His left ear may be deliberately pierced, and he wears a belt around his waist. A compact figure, he holds his arms close to his body and his knees directly under his chin. The precise modeling of the youth's bony body, especially his ribs, suggests malnutrition.

Dark stone is often deliberately used for images of blacks, and their crouching form can be used for a variety of utilitarian objects from a bronze inkwell (perhaps chosen because of the color of ink) to a terracotta rattle (discovered in a child's grave in Roman Corinth). This use of blacks as utilitarian objects no doubt deliberately relates to the subservient position held by them—and other foreigners—in Greek society. This youth may well be a slave who is being punished for some form of disobedience.

Black steatite statuette, hollow, Hellenistic, second century B.C.E.
H. 9.3
Boston, Museum of Fine Arts
Henry Lillie Pierce Fund, 01.8210
From Corinth
Ex Collection E. P. Warren

PUBLISHED: F. M. Snowden, Jr., *Blacks in Antiquity: Ethiopians in the Graeco-Roman Experience* (Cambridge, Mass., 1970), 28 and 72, fig. 42; M. B. Comstock and C. C. Vermeule, *Sculpture in Stone: The Greek, Roman, and Etruscan Collections in the Museum of Fine Arts, Boston* (Boston, 1976), no. 112; Pinney and Ridgway 1979, 184–185, no. 89.

For a list of blacks carved in dark stone, see R. M. Schneider, *Bunte Barbaren: Orientalenstatuen aus farbigem Marmor in der römischen Repräsentationskunst* (Worms, 1986), 156–157 n. 1180. For the inkwell and the rattle, see J. Vercoutter et al., *The Image of the Black in Western Art* (New York, 1976), figs. 309 and 302.

was an Early Classical painter of smaller vases, but thus far this is the only chous attributed to him. This vase indicates that he had a sense of humor and could adapt the decoration to the function of the vessel.

Attic red-figure chous, attributed to the Oionokles Painter, ca. 470 B.C.E.
H. 23; DIAM. 18.6; DIAM. OF FOOT 12.3
Malibu, Calif., The J. Paul Getty Museum, 86.AE.237
Ex Collection Walter and Molly Bareiss

PUBLISHED: E. R. Knauer, "οὐ γὰρ ἦν ἁμίς: A Chous by the Oionokles Painter," *Greek Vases in the J. Paul Getty Museum* 3 (Malibu, Calif., 1986), 91–100; K. Vierneisel and B. Kaeser, *Kunst der Schale, Kultur des Trinkens* (Munich, 1990), 298,

fig. 48,16; B. Sparkes, *The Red and the Black* (London, 1996), 88, fig. III.18; CVA Getty 7 USA 32, 41–42, no. 38, pl. 365; A. Schäfer, *Unterhaltung beim griechischen Symposion* (Mainz, 1997), pl. 27.3; B. Cohen and H. A. Shapiro, "The Use and Abuse of Athenian Vases," in A. J. Clark and J. Gaunt, eds., *Essays in Honor of Dietrich von Bothmer* (Amsterdam, 2002), 87–88, pl. 22a.

On the term *pais*, see Golden 1985. On the Oionokles Painter, see E. D. Serbeti, "The Oionokles Painter," *Boreas* 12 (1989), 17–46.

73

74

73
Doll

(see also color illus. p. 15)

This doll wears a short chiton that has red
bands filled with short dashes, esses,
chevrons, and dotted saltires. Her long hair
is painted black.

> Corinthian terracotta doll,
> early fifth century B.C.E.
> H. 12.3
> New York, The Metropolitan Museum of Art
> Rogers Fund, 1944, 44.11.8

PUBLISHED: New York: Parke-Bernet Galleries,
Estate of the Late J. P. Morgan II, 22–25 March
1944, 25, lot no. 109.

74
Doll

> Boiotian terracotta doll,
> mid-fifth century B.C.E.
> H. 12.6; W. 4.55
> Princeton, New Jersey, Princeton University
> Art Museum
> Museum Purchase and Exchange,
> y1947-205

PUBLISHED: Pinney and Ridgway 1979,
244–245, no. 119; Reilly 1997, 157, fig. 34.

75

75
Boy Wheeling His Toy Roller

As children grew old enough to walk alone they would be given mechanical toys that could be pushed or pulled. The toy roller is one of the most ubiquitous playthings of male toddlers in Greek art, appearing on grave stelai, funerary vases, and dozens of choes (see cats. 122, 115, 97, and 101, respectively). Made of wood and called a *hamax*, according to Aristophanes (*Clouds* 879–880), this roller consisted of a stick attached to an axle with two wheels side by side. A box or simply a platform (as here) could be positioned between the wheels for giving rides to objects like choes, pet animals, or one's playmates.

Here we see a young boy giving a chous a turn on his roller. It is lashed on by a crossed cord. Behind him is another chous resting on a small table. Both in the boy's hand and on the table are small red objects, possibly grapes.

The vase is inscribed with the word KALOS (beautiful).

Attic red-figure chous (mouth missing), ca. 425 B.C.E.
PRES. H. 7.2; DIAM. 6.51
Brunswick, Maine,
Bowdoin College Museum of Art
Gift of Edward Perry Warren, Esq.,
Honorary Degree, 1926, 1915.038
Ex Collection Augustus Ready

PUBLISHED: Hoorn 1951, 115 no. 397, fig. 89.
For the hamax see Klein 1932, 13–14; Hoorn 1951, 44; Beck 1975, 45, nos. 277–281, pl. 54; Rühfel 1984a, 117–118, 123, 180, 328 n. 117 and 339 n. 319; May 1992, 74; Hamilton 1992, 72, 91, 105–106, and 117.

76
Serving Boy Holding Tray and Hoop

A serving boy runs right while looking back. Balanced between his left shoulder and hand is a serving tray with food and possibly a cover. In his other hand he holds a toy hoop and the rod used to trundle it. A wreath and added red encircles his head.

If it were not for the serving tray, the hoop and pose of the boy, who appears to be running away from someone, would identify him as Ganymede fleeing Zeus (see cat. 15). The gods pursuing their loves are sometimes depicted individually on two vases, rather than together on the same. This *oinochoe* is part of a pair, but the figure on the other oinochoe (see cat. 65) is clearly a serving boy, which indicates that the boy here is one as well.

Similar scenes are found earlier in the tondo of a cup by the Colmar Painter in Oxford and on a *skyphos* in Athens. In these cases the tray is completely covered, and the boy trundles the hoop rather than carrying it.

Attic red-figure oinochoe, attributed to the Harrow Painter, ca. 460 B.C.E.
H. WITH HANDLE 24.3; H. WITHOUT HANDLE 19.5; DIAM. OF MOUTH 9.2; DIAM. OF BASE 6.9
Tampa Museum of Art
Joseph Veach Noble Collection, 1986.073

PUBLISHED: *ARV*² 1635–1636,13ter and 1705,78ter; *Para* 345; *BAdd*² 197; H. Bloesch, "Varianten," in M. Rohde-Liegle et al., eds., *Gestalt und Geschichte: Festschrift Karl Schefold zu seinem 60 Geburtstag am 26 Jan. 1965*, AntK suppl. 4 (Bern, 1967), 88, figs. 6–7; *Münchner Jahrbuch der bildenden Kunst* 27 (1976), 34, figs. 5–6; S. P. Murray, *Collecting the Past: Antiquities from the Joseph Veach Noble Collection* (Tampa, 1985), 45, no. 66; J. M. Padgett, "The Geras Painter: An Athenian Eccentric and His Associates" (Ph.D. diss., Harvard University, 1989), 150, 155–156,

76

and 197, no. H 78ter; P. J. Russell, *Ceramics and Society: Making and Marketing Ancient Greek Pottery* (Tampa, 1994), back cover and 34, no. 15.

For the Harrow Painter, see also cat. 65. For the hoop, see cat. 15. For the cup: Oxford, Ashmolean Museum, 1886.587 (300): ARV^2 357,69; *Para* 363; $BAdd^2$ 221; *CVA* Oxford 1 Great Britain 3, pl. 1,8; J. Boardman, *Athenian Red Figure Vases: The Archaic Period* (London, 1975), fig. 236. For the skyphos: Athens, National Archaeological Museum, 14705; ARV^2 403,37; *BCH* 125:1 (2001), 101, fig. 13.

TOPS

The top (*strobilos, strombus, rombus, bembix*) was a common toy for both children and women in ancient Greece. They were made out of a variety of materials, including bronze, stone, glass, and lead, but wood and terracotta were the most common. There are two main types. The "twirler" or "teetodum" is characterized by a wooden stem on top for spinning the toy. The other, the "whipping top," was more popular. It has a cylindrical body atop a short, conical pointed base (see cat. 78), often with grooves on the sides. To spin the top, one struck it with a whip (*mastix*).

The earliest tops come from the end of the Geometric period, the late eighth century. Several have been found in sanctuaries, where they were dedicated as votives, a practice supported by literary evidence— for example, a poem from the Palatine Anthology (VI, 309) dating to the third century, in which they are dedicated to Hermes (see cat. 16). Although the literary sources do not preserve the rules for any specific game using tops, the depictions in ancient art (e.g., cat. 77) indicate that competitions existed.

For tops, see Harcourt-Smith 1929; *EAA* 3 (1961), s.v. giocattolo, 907 (J. Dörig); Trendall and Schneider-Hermann 1975, 269; Schmidt 1977, 39–44; Gould 1980; K. Braun and T. E. Haevernick, *Bemalte Keramik und Glas aus dem Kabirenheiligtum bei Theben*, vol. 4 (Berlin, 1981), 36–37; R. Holler, *Kreisel* (Munich, 1989). See also J. H. Oakley, "The Bosanquet Painter," in J. H. Oakley et al., eds., *Athenian Potters and Painters: The Conference Proceedings* (Oxford, 1997), 246–247.

77

77
Women Spinning Tops

Two females (mother and daughter?) are actively whipping the tops spinning on the ground between them. The older, left-hand woman, wearing chiton, mantle, and *sakkos*, stands with feet apart, her weight on her front leg. She holds the whip's rod at shoulder level, indicating that her arm is recoiling after just having struck the top. The other arm is covered with drapery. The younger woman, in chiton and mantle, is in exactly the same pose but shown from the back. The tip of the whip's rod is visible by her left shoulder. The viewer is placed in the midst of the action of some type of contest, the rules for which we don't know.

As is often the case with figures of women on Classical vases, it is not possible to tell the younger woman's exact age. She may be a teenager or older.

Attic red-figure squat lekythos, ca. 440–430 B.C.E.
H. RESTORED 17; DIAM. OF BASE 8.3
New York, The Metropolitan Museum of Art Gift of Samuel G. Ward, 1875, 75.2.9
Possibly from Greece

PUBLISHED: *AJA* 11 (1907), 420–422, fig. 4; McClees 1925, 44, fig. 5.3; *Münchener Jahrbuch der bildenden Kunst* 8 (1913), 88, fig. 5; *Monuments Piot* 29 (1927–1928), 115–116, fig. 4; Schmidt 1977, pl. 1; Gould 1980, 43, fig. 1.

78

78
Top

This toy is composed of a cylindrical body above a pointed conical base. The upper part is decorated on the outside by four panels alternating between black-silhouetted upright palmettes and water birds going left. There is a groove near the top. The conical base has three sets of two closely spaced horizontal lines. The surface on top has a large black dot in the middle surrounded at the outer edge by two black lines, the one farthest away being thicker.

Similar tops have been found at the Kabirion near Thebes, where they were dedicated to *Pais*, one of the divinities associated with this mystery cult. Some are decorated in a fashion similar to this toy; others have scenes of children playing.

Boiotian terracotta,
ca. fourth century B.C.E.
H. 9.4; DIAM. 6.8
Boston, Museum of Fine Arts
Henry Lillie Pierce Fund, 99.536
Possibly from Kabirion near Thebes

PUBLISHED: Klein 1932, 17 and pl. 18b.
For similar types with a mention of this top, see P. Wolters and G. Bruns, *Das Kabirenheiligtum bei Theben*, vol. 1 (Berlin, 1940), 123–124; Dörig (supra "Tops"), 907; and Braun and Haevernick (supra "Tops"), 36.

79
Boys Playing Ball

The ancient Greeks had a variety of ball games. Shown here is one called passé-boule, which was played by both boys and girls. The object was to throw the ball through a round hole in an upright board planted on the ground. Here an older boy, his right arm raised, is about to pitch the ball, while his younger opponent crouches on the other side of the wicket.

Four other Attic red-figure vase paintings representing this game are extant. A pig-head *rhyton* in Beirut shows a similar scene combined with other pairs of athletic boys in the *palaistra*. A pyxis in New York depicts a pair of girls in similar poses juxtaposed with a scene of girls playing knucklebones, but the setting is indoors. A small lekythos in Berlin features a single child kneeling before the board. Finally, an *aryballos* once in the Elgin collection shows a boy playing passé-boule with Eros on one side and boys and a toy cart on the other. All of these vases date from the latter half of the fifth century, when depictions of children's games reached their height in Greek art.

Attic red-figure chous, ca. 425 B.C.E.
H. 13.4; DIAM. OF FOOT 7.4
New York, The Metropolitan Museum of Art
Fletcher Fund, 1925, 25.78.48

PUBLISHED: Klein 1932, pl. 20E; Hoorn 1951, 159 no. 758, fig. 282; Beck 1975, 52, pl. 61,313; Schmidt 1977, 26–27.

On ballplaying in general, see Harris 1972, 75–111; May 2002, 92–99. On passé-boule, see Schmidt 1977, 26. For the rhyton (Beirut, National Museum, 123), see Lezzi-Hafter 1988, no. 268, pls. 176a–c. For girls playing, see Beck 1975, pl. 61,311 (New York, The Metropolitan Museum of Art, 06.1021.119). For Eros and a youth playing the game, see Beck 1975, pl. 61,312.

79

80
Girl Balancing a Stick

The game of balancing a stick on the end of one's finger while moving requires agility and control. It is not often represented in Greek art, and usually females are shown practicing it. On this lekythos a well-dressed woman in chiton, bracelets, earring, and cross-girt apparatus, with her hair tied up in back, moves to the right, lifting her dress with her left hand as she steps forward. Her eyes focus on the stick that she balances on the tip of her right hand, and she bends over slightly at the waist to help her control. The picture gives a real sense of the effort needed to play this game.

This subject is usually found on vases painted by contemporaries of the Meidias Painter. In most cases the figure is shown moving, and the hand can be either palm up or palm down. Often other females are shown, sometimes playing with other toys. A woman on a white-ground lekythos in Lecce by the Lupoli Painter moves in a fashion similar to the one here while balancing a stick, as does the girl *Paidia* (the personification of play) on a pyxis also in the Manner of the Meidias Painter.

Attic red-figure lekythos, attributed to the Manner of the Meidias Painter,
ca. 420 B.C.E.
H. 16.51; DIAM. 6.99
The Minneapolis Institute of Arts
The Miscellaneous Works of Art Fund,
57.41.1
Ex Collection Elgin

PUBLISHED: ARV² 1326,74; *The Minneapolis Institute of Arts Bulletin* (July–Sept. 1959), 14–15, fig. 8.

For this game, see G. M. A. Richter and L. F. Hall, *Red-Figured Athenian Vases in the Metropolitan Museum of Art* (New Haven, 1936), 203 n. 7; C. H. E. Haspels, "A Fragmentary Onos in the Allard Pierson Museum," *BABesch* 29 (1954), 25–30; A. Lezzi-Hafter, *Der Schuwalow-Maler: Eine Kannenwerkstatt der Parthenonzeit* (Mainz, 1976), 85, n. 317. For the white-ground lekythos, see Lecce, Museo Provinciale Sigismondo Castromediano, 566; M. Bernardini, *I vasi attici del Museo Provinciale di Lecce* (Galatina, Italy, 1981), 39; F. Felten, *Thanatos- und Kleophonmaler: Weiss-*

80

grundige und rotfigurige Vasenmalerei der Parthenonzeit (Munich, 1971), pl. 31,4; J. H. Oakley, *Picturing Death in Classical Athens: The Evidence of the White Lekythoi* (Cambridge, 2003), fig. 4. For the pyxis, see New York, The Metropolitan Museum of Art, 09.221.40; ARV² 1328,99; *Para* 479; BAdd² 364–365; Klein 1932, pl. 24c; Richter and Hall (supra), pls. 159,161 and 178,161; Beck 1975, pl. 64,330.

81
Girl Juggling

Females of various ages are often represented juggling in fifth-century Attic vase painting. This game of dexterity appears to have been a common and pleasant pastime for them while in the *gynaikeion*. Normally the jugglers are shown seated in an interior setting, and often a *kalathos* (wool basket) sits nearby. What exactly they juggle is mostly unclear. Sometimes it appears to be apples or some other nearly circular fruit. Apples were symbols of love and fertility and so appropriate objects for unmarried girls. At other times the juggled objects may be balls of wool, especially when the setting indicates wool working, or balls made of some other material. On some vases the balls are actually shown on top of the kalathos, indicating that they are probably wool.

What the female juggles on this pyxis is also unclear—are they apples, as has been suggested, or are they balls of wool? An interior setting is indicted both by a column and by the wreath and the sandals—one shown from the top, the other in profile—that hang in the background. Five females are shown. The first of the pair to the right of the column sits on a *diphros* juggling three circular objects. The female standing opposite her holds out another one in her hand, as does the similarly rendered female before another seated woman in the next pair of figures. In both cases a kalathos with golden-colored wool spilling over its rim sits on the ground between the seated and standing female. Completing the frieze is a female holding a mirror and standing before a diphros that has a large pillow decorated with black stripes. All the females wear chiton and mantle, but only the juggling woman's mantle does not cover her torso.

The pyxis, probably known in antiquity as a *kylichnis*, was used to hold female cosmetics, incense, and small objects like jewelry. Domestic scenes of women, such as this one, represent an appropriate subject for such a vessel. There are several other white-ground pyxides by the Painter of London D 12, including some of type A.

81

The figures and objects on these white-ground pyxides are often similar to those here.

Attic white-ground type A pyxis, attributed to the Painter of London D 12,
ca. 460 B.C.E.
H. 12; H. TO RIM 8.5; DIAM. OF RIM 8.3; DIAM. OF BODY 11.5; DIAM. OF BASE 7.7
Toledo, Ohio, Toledo Museum of Art
Purchase with Funds from the Libbey Endowment, Gift of Edward Drummond Libbey, 63.29

PUBLISHED: ARV² 1675,94bis; Para 434; BAdd² 308; *Bulletin of the Museum of Fine Arts, Boston* 67 (1969), 81 and 84–85, fig. 11–13; CVA Toledo 1 USA 17, pls. 58,1–4 and 60,1; S. Roberts, *The Attic Pyxis* (Chicago, 1978), 78–83 and pl. 54,2; W. G. Moon, ed., *Ancient Greek Art and Iconography* (Madison, Wis., 1983), 216, fig. 14.14; E. Gazda, ed., *The Villa of the Mysteries in Pompeii: Ancient Ritual—Modern Muse* (Ann Arbor, Mich., 2000), 230–231, no. 98.

For apples, see A. R. Littlewood, "The Symbolism of the Apple in Greek and Roman Literature," *HSCP* 72 (1968), 147–181; M. K. Brazda, *Zur Bedeutung des Apfels in der antiken Kultur* (Bonn, 1977); and J. H. Oakley, *The Phiale Painter* (Mainz, 1990), 98. For the sandals, see C. Weiss, "Vasi a forma di scarpa de produzione attica, ionica e della Magna Grecia," in G. Rizza, ed., *I vasi attici ed altre ceramiche coeve in Sicilia*, vol. 1, *Cronoache di Archeologia* 29 (1990), 155–169. For white-ground pyxides, see J. R. Mertens, *Attic White-Ground: Its Development on Shapes Other Than Lekythoi* (New York, 1977), 137; and I. Wehgartner, *Attisch weissgrundige Keramik* (Mainz, 1983), 136–149. For what the women juggle, see S. Karouzo, "Vases from Odos Pandrosou," *JHS* 64 (1945), 42; V. Sabetai, "The Washing Painter: A Contribution to the Wedding and Genre Iconography in the Second Half of the Fifth Century B.C." (Ph.D. diss., University of Cincinnati, 1993), 82–84.

84
Girl and Satyr Playing Ephedrismos

This oil flask is one of the earliest extant
vases to show a girl playing ephedrismos.
She is being carried on the back of a satyr,
recognizable by his balding head and the
tip of his tail that appears beyond the girl's
drapery. In the traditional pose he has
hoisted her up by her bent right leg, and
she covers his eyes with her hands. Their
closely enmeshed forms are deliberately
contrasted by the artist: the satyr is nude
and hunched over, while the girl is draped
in chiton and mantle and seems to float; he
is blinded and she stares straight ahead.
Because mortal women do not usually
consort with satyrs, she is probably a
maenad, and her short cropped hair supports this interpretation.

Attic red-figure lekythos, attributed to the
Ephedrismos Painter, ca. 470–460 B.C.E.
H. 24.5
Malibu, Calif., The J. Paul Getty Museum,
71.AE.444

PUBLISHED: F. Brommer, "Huckepack," *Getty-
MusJ* 6–7 (1978–1979), 139–146, fig. 1; F.
Brommer, "Satyrspielvasen," *Greek Vases in the
J. Paul Getty Museum*, vol. 1 (Malibu, Calif., 1983),
119, no. 345; V. Paul-Zinserling, *Der Jena-Maler
und sein Kreis* (Mainz, 1994), pl. 2,4; Scheffer
(supra "Ephedrismos"), 174, fig. 3; *LIMC* 8
(1997), s.v. Mainades, 788 no. 67, pl. 540.

KNUCKLEBONES

Winning in the boys' contest for pretty
     handwriting
Konnaros was awarded eighty
     knucklebones.
     Greek Anthology 6.308

Knucklebones, known in Greek as *astragaloi*, are the asymmetrical tarsal bones
of the hind leg of an animal, usually a
sheep or a goat (see cat. 88), which were
used as gaming pieces and for divination
throughout the ancient Mediterranean.
When thrown they can land on one of four
sides that are given numerical values like
dice. The concave side had the value of
four, the opposite, convex, side a value of
three, the narrower, indented, side a value
of six, and its opposite, fuller, side a value

84

of one. Thus opposite, sides add up to seven, just as on modern dice. Different combinations of throws were given names, such as the lucky Venus throw, when all four sides appear in a single throw of four astragaloi, or the Chian throw, when each bone registers one, the most unlucky throw of all. Various combinations could supply answers in a divinatory practice known as *astragalomanteia*.

A variety of games were played with these bones and their counterparts made of precious stone, ivory, metal (see cat. 89), and glass (see cat. 90). One, called "five stones" or *pentelithoi*, was played primarily by women (see cat. 85) and is similar to jacks. According to Pollux (IX, 126), "The knucklebones are thrown up into the air and an attempt is made to catch them on the back of your hand. If you are only partly successful, you have to pick up the knucklebones which have fallen on the ground, without dropping the ones already on your hand."

Children often are depicted clutching a sack filled with their knucklebones (see cat. 87). In Attic vase painting young boys are shown in settings with their knucklebone sacks, which are either net (see cat. 45) or leather with a flap (see cat. 104), hanging in the background. The Greek term *phormiskos* is often used for these sacks and their ceramic counterparts, which have a windowlike opening. Special molded vases in the form of enlarged knucklebones were particularly appropriate containers for astragaloi.

That children could become very possessive and competitive about their knucklebones is indicated in both literature and art. In the *Iliad* (23.88) Patroklos mentions losing at knucklebones as a child and becoming so enraged that he killed a companion. Some Hellenistic group statues show children biting each other over their knucklebones.

On knucklebones in general, see H. L. Enegren, "Four Astralgali in the Gustavianum," *Boreas* 22 (1993), 89–94. On knucklebone games, see Schmidt 1977, 44–56; May 1992, 100–105; U. Schädler, "Spielen mit Astragalen," *JdI* 111 (1996), 61–73; and cat. 86. For representations

85a

85b

of children playing knucklebones, see Beck 1975, pl. 67. For the phormiskos, see E. Hatzivassiliou, "The Attic Phormiskos: Problems of Origin and Function," *BICS* 45 (2001), 113–148. For fighting children, see A. Herrmann, "The Biter: A Late Hellenistic Astragal Player," in G. Kopcke and M. B. Moore, eds., *Studies in Classical Art and Archaeology: A Tribute to Peter Heinrich von Blanckenhagen* (Locust Valley, N.Y., 1979), 163–173, pls. 46–48. For sculptural versions of boy knucklebone players, see L. Beschi, "Gli 'Astragalizontes' di un Policleto," *Prospettiva* 15 (1978), 4–12.

85
Girls Playing Knucklebones

This group sculpture shows two crouching girls set on separate rectangular bases. They assume a similar pose, with left foot planted firmly on the ground and right foot pulled behind, and so the bodies were probably cast in the same mold. Their heads, arms, and drapery were cast separately and added, and details like the wavy hair were reworked after casting. They have assumed the traditional poses of knucklebone players. The one at the left, dressed only in a chiton, holds a sack in her left hand against her leg, while she is probably picking up her knucklebones with her outstretched right hand. Her partner, wearing chiton and mantle, is holding her right hand out with palm down, while her left arm, enveloped in the drapery, rests on

her left thigh. They appear to be playing pentelithoi, although no knucklebones are preserved.

Although these figures are sometimes referred to as women because of their breasts, Greek artists often gave girls prominent breasts simply in order to distinguish them from males, not as an indicator of age. In Hellenistic marble versions of a female knucklebone player seated on the ground, the drapery has actually slipped down the left arm, revealing the breast.

Tanagra terracotta figurines,
fourth century B.C.E.
H. 12.3 and 11.8
Boston, Museum of Fine Arts
Museum Purchase by Contribution,
01.7799 and 01.7798
Allegedly from Tanagra
Ex Collection Edward P. Warren

PUBLISHED: Uhlenbrock 1990, 118–119, nos. 1–12.

For a similar terracotta from Cyrenaica, see L. Burn and R. Higgins, *Catalogue of the Terracottas in the Department of Greek and Roman Antiquities, British Museum*, vol. 3 (London, 2001), 235 no. 2748, pl. 122. For the marble versions of a female knucklebone player, see F. Souchal, "Variations sur un thème de sculpture antique: 'La Joueuse d'osselets,'" *Gazette des Beaux Arts* 57 (1961), 257–272.

86
Boys Playing Knucklebones

(see also color illus. p. 263)

Three youths with knucklebones are shown in the midst of a contest. A variety of games were played by boys and women with these anklebones of sheep and goats (see cats. 88–90), and sometimes it is not certain which game is depicted. The boys on this vase may be playing *eis omillan*, the goal of which was to knock your opponents' knucklebones out of the center of a defined circular playing field by throwing your knucklebones at them. The youth squatting in the middle appears to be placing a knucklebone firmly down with his right hand, while holding several others in his left. Another youth on the right has just made a throw, for his knucklebone is shown in midair, as if having just been released from his open left hand. With the other hand he points in the direction of his goal. A third youth on the left looks back toward the thrower while holding onto his knucklebone.

Another possibility is that the boys are playing *pleistobolinda*. In this game, values were assigned to the different sides of the bone, similar to dice, and they were thrown on the ground. The player with the highest score captured the bones of the other players. Normally, however, only two contestants play this game.

All three youths wear wreath and headband. Their realistic squatting poses give viewers the sense that they are seeing a true snapshot of children's play in action. One of the finest depictions of knucklebone players in ancient Greek art, this scene is well suited to the chous.

> Attic red-figure chous, attributed to the Group of Boston 10.190, ca. 420 B.C.E.
> H. 17.3; DIAM. 13.7; DIAM. OF MOUTH 8.55; DIAM. OF BASE 9.1
> Malibu, Calif., The J. Paul Getty Museum, 96.AE.28
> Ex Collections Falcioni; Tyszkiewicz; Béhague; Fleischman

PUBLISHED: *ARV²* 1318,3; *Mélanges d'archéologie et d'histoire* 14 (1894), pl. 4; *BWPr* 77 (1920), 5; B. Schröder, *Der Sport im Altertum* (Berlin, 1927), 82, fig. 13; Hoorn 1951, 177, no. 884; J. Dörig, "Tarentinische Knochelspielerinnen," *Museum*

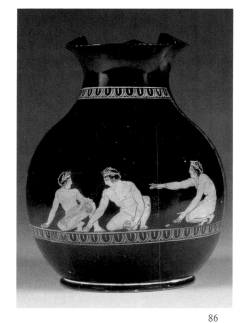

86

Helveticum 16 (1959), 32 n. 16 and 34, fig. 3; Sotheby's (Monaco), 5 December 1987, 126–127, lot 147; L. Burn, *The Meidias Painter* (Oxford, 1987), 86 and 102, no. B 3; Hamilton 1992, 205, no. 884; M. True and K. Hamma, eds., *A Passion for Antiquities: Ancient Art from the Collection of Barbara and Lawrence Fleischman* (Malibu, Calif., 1994), 101–102, no. 42.

For choes, see cats. 95–101. For the games of eis omillan and pleistobolinda, see especially Schmidt 1977, 45–49 and 53–54. For a similarly posed figure, see cat. 114.

87
Seated Girl with Bag

A stiffly posed girl sits on a block base, holding a red-brown sack-shaped bag by her waist with her right hand. Almost certainly it contains knucklebones. With her left hand she grabs the pink chiton she wears, which is girded high beneath her breasts. Shoes or slippers cover her feet. Her red hair is tied up in piles of locks on top of her head, a style known as the *lampadion*, as well as in balls of locks at the sides.

There are several variations on this type, which feature different hairstyles, and instead of a bag, the girls can hold a writing tablet, book roll, wreath, or bird, among other things.

> Tanagra terracotta figurine, Attic, first half of the third century B.C.E.
> H. 13.4
> Boston, Museum of Fine Arts
> Museum Purchase by Contribution, 01.7841

PUBLISHED: Klein 1932, pl. 19a.

For Tanagra figurines of seated girls, see D. B. Thompson, "The Origin of Tanagras," *AJA* 70 (1966), 59; Rühfel 1984a, 197–200; G. Zimmer and I. Kriseleit, *Bürgerwelten: Hellenistische Tonfiguren und Nachschöpfungen im 19. Jh.* (Berlin, 1994), 102–104, no. 22. For the hairstyle, see cat. 109.

87

88
Four Knucklebones

Bone astragaloi have been found in archae-ological contexts (graves, sanctuaries, domestic quarters, and caves) throughout the ancient Mediterranean, Near East, and Anatolia, dating as far back as the Neolithic period. By far the largest number of bone astragaloi excavated is the 23,000 from the Corycian cave near Delphi where Pan and the Nymphs were worshiped. Many of these were worked by either planing or perforating them, filling them with lead, and inscribing them with Greek letters or abbreviations of names (for example, Herakles, Thetis, Achilles, Ajax, Nyx). It has been suggested that this vast number of knucklebones represents the dedications of boys and girls on the occasion of coming of age, when they would conse-crate their playthings to a deity.

> Bone astragaloi
> L. 3.1, 2.7, 4.6, and 3
> Columbia, University of Missouri, Columbia, Museum of Art and Archaeology, TA 70 B4, 70 B5, 72 B26, 72 B27
> From Tel Anafa

For the knucklebones from the Corycian cave, see P. Amandry, "Os et coquilles," *L'Antre corycien* 2, BCH suppl. 9 (1984), 347–378.

88

89, left, and 90

89
Bronze Knucklebone

Bronze versions of knucklebones come in all sizes, from the natural goat or sheep size as here to much enlarged ones with handles that probably functioned as weights. Bronze knucklebones have been found at sanctuaries such as those of Hera at Perachora and Demeter and Persephone on Acrocorinth, and they were certainly votive offerings.

> Bronze astragalos, Hellenistic, second to first century B.C.E.
> H. 1.9; L. 4.5; D. 1.9
> Malibu, Calif., The J. Paul Getty Museum
> Gift of Arthur Silver, 81.AC.5

90
Glass Knucklebone

Knucklebones were fashioned out of a number of precious materials, including glass, gemstones, silver, and gold. Glass *skeuomorphs*—ornaments or designs repre-senting utensils or implements—have been found at the Kabeirion at Thebes and in Archaic levels at the Artemision at Ephesos.

> Glass astragalos, first century B.C.E./C.E.
> L. 1.8
> Malibu, Calif., The J. Paul Getty Museum
> Gift of Nicolas Koutoulakis, 79.AF.171

For finds of astragaloi from Greek sanctuaries, see D. S. Reese, "Worked Astragali," in J. W. and M. C. Shaw, eds., *Kommos IV: The Greek Sanctuary* (Princeton, 2000), 398–401. For a unique silver-covered knucklebone from the Idaian Cave on Crete, see J. A. Sakellarakis, "Some Geometric

and Archaic Votives from the Idaian Cave," in R. Hägg, ed., *Early Greek Cult Practice* (Stockholm, 1988), 188–189, figs. 25–28.

For her grasshopper, the nightingale of the
  fields, and her
cicada, dweller in the oak, Myro made a
  common tomb,
a girl shedding a maiden's tear. For Hades,
  hard to dissuade, took away both her
  play things.
  Hellenistic epigram by Anyte
  (A.P. 7.190)

According to the ample evidence of painted
vases and grave stelai, the most popular
pets of Greek children were birds, dogs,
cocks, hares, goats, and deer. Wealthy
aristocratic youths had more exotic pets,
like cheetahs or monkeys, and for older
boys racehorses and hunting hounds were
highly desired. Cocks and hares are often
represented on Athenian vases as love gifts
of older men to handsome young boys.
Ancient children did not always share our
sensitivity toward animals; a popular Hellenistic genre sculpture is a young boy
strangling a goose.

For children's pets see Klein 1932, 10–13;
Beck 1975, 49–50 nos. 296–310, pls. 58–60.
For animals on funerary monuments, see
D. Woysch-Méautis, *La représentation des animaux
et des êtres fabuleux sur les monuments funéraires grecs:
De l'epoque archaïque à la fin du IVᵉ siècle av. J.-C.*
(Lausanne, 1982). On cheetahs and other cats,
see Ashmead 1968. For the boy strangling the
goose, see Bieber 1961, 81–82, fig. 285.

91
Boy with His Pet Bird

If artistic representations are any indication, birds were the favorite pets of children, male and female. On this vase a
toddler tempts his pet bird with a *streptos*
cake. The bird is sitting calmly on a stool
on which the boy supports himself. Behind
him another amusement of boys, a roller
(see cat. 75), rests against the wall.

Among the birds with which children
are shown playing on Attic vases, one finds
swans, geese, ducks, cocks, and doves. The
bones of birds have also been found in
children's graves.

91

Attic red-figure chous, ca. 425–420 B.C.E.
H. 9; DIAM. 7.1
Boston, Museum of Fine Arts
Henry Lillie Pierce Fund, 01.8086
From Athens
Ex Collection E. P. Warren

PUBLISHED: Klein 1932, pl. 11A; Deubner 1932,
pl. 30,2; Hoorn 1951, 112, no. 377, fig. 363;
Beck 1975, pl. 58, no. 300; Rühfel 1984b, 145,
fig. 82 left.

On birds as pets, see J. Pollard, *Birds in Greek
Life and Myth* (London, 1977), 135–140. For bird
bones in graves, see AM 18 (1893), 175.

92
Girl with Toy Roller Chasing Bird
(see also color illus. p. 147)

Girls on choes are rare. Here we see one in
rapid motion, dashing to the right with an
upright roller in her right hand. She seems
to be running toward a large bird seated at
right, its head raised skyward. She wears
her hair tied up in a knot on her head and
is wearing a chiton and himation.

Attic red-figure chous, ca. 420 B.C.E.
H. 6.3
Worcester, Mass., Worcester Art Museum
Bequest of Sarah C. Garver, 1931.56
Probably purchased in Greece

PUBLISHED: Hoorn 1951, 193, no. 994, fig. 272.

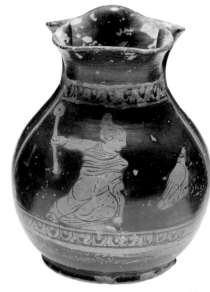

92

93
Youth with His Cat

Greek children had many of the standard types of pets we have today, including cats, dogs, and birds, as well as oddities like the weasel. Not only are children shown playing with pets in Greek art, but sometimes animals have been found in children's graves. Domestic cats, as on this lekythos, are not often depicted. More common is the spotted hunting leopard, or cheetah (*acinonyx iubatus*), which was imported from the East. It was apparently a popular pet with aristocratic youths, particularly in the first half of the fifth century.

This picture shows a mantled and wreathed youth standing cross-legged and leaning over to the right. In his right hand he holds out a piece of red meat to entice the cat to climb farther up the knotted staff he holds upright with his left hand. The sponge, aryballos, and *strigil* that hang in the background indicate that the setting is the palaistra.

Identifying the breeds of birds and animals in vase paintings is notoriously difficult, because vase painters were not normally concerned with accurately depicting the details of different breeds. The cat on this vase has been thought to resemble most closely the Abyssinian shorthair, the Egyptian domestic cat that was imported into Athens. A *pelike* in Philadelphia shows a spotted leopard climbing up a staff in a manner similar to the cat here.

Attic red-figure lekythos, attributed to the Eucharides Painter, ca. 490 B.C.E.
H. 33.1; DIAM. OF MOUTH 7.2;
DIAM. OF BASE 7.2
Private Collection
Ex Collection Christos G. Bastis

PUBLISHED: D. von Bothmer, *Antiquities from the Collection of Christos G. Bastis* (Mainz, 1987), 283, fig. 165; Sotheby's (N.Y.), 9 December 1999, 158-9, lot 138.

For cats, see A. Ashmead, "Greek Cats: Exotic Pets Kept by Rich Youths in Fifth-century Athens, as Portrayed on Greek Vases," *Expedition* 20, no. 3 (spring 1978), 38–47. For the Philadelphia pelike: Philadelphia, University Museum MS 399; Ashmead (supra), 39, fig. 2. For the

Eucharides Painter, see E. M. Langridge, "The Eucharides Painter and His Place in the Athenian Potters' Quarter" (Ph.D. diss., Princeton University, 1993). For cheetahs as love gifts, see Koch-Harnack 1983, 105–115.

93

94
Children at a Cockfight

Cockfighting was a popular spectator sport in antiquity, as it is still today in many cultures. It is often depicted in Greek art as the pastime of young boys or even toddlers, as in this charming terracotta group in Baltimore. In the center of the symmetrical composition the two cocks are sparring, with the fighter at the left ascendant over his opponent. The outcome is clearly reflected in the poses and facial expressions of the cocks' owners. The half-draped boy at the left is clapping his hands in glee and smiling as he crouches behind and encourages his winning cock. The boy at the right slumps over a wooden box, supporting his head with his right hand and tearful at the unfavorable outcome for his pet. In the center is preserved the lower, draped body of a female, probably a girl companion.

The coroplast who made this figurine delighted in the chubby bodies of the toddlers, the folds of the drapery, the tousled locks of hair, and especially the contrasting facial expressions. The sophisticated composition perhaps suggests influence from larger stone sculpture, such as the marble group in Istanbul in which two Erotes are depicted with their pet roosters. Such lighthearted, playful themes in Greek sculpture were common in the later Hellenistic period and have often been termed rococo in style.

Cocks were certainly chosen as pets to bring out the pugnacious spirit in boys, but there was an erotic as well as an agonistic side to cocks in ancient Greece. These birds were love gifts of older men to young boys, and the Trojan prince Ganymede is often depicted with one given to him by Zeus. They were also favored domestic pets, as one can see on the numerous depictions of them on Athenian choes.

Late Hellenistic terracotta figurine, second to first century B.C.E.
H. 10.9; W. 14
Baltimore, The Walters Art Museum, 48.1714
Found in Samsun (ancient Amisos) in 1912
Ex Collection Dikran Kelekian

PUBLISHED: D. K. Hill, "Greek Cock Fighting," BWalt 2 (1949), no. 3; Bieber 1961, 137, fig. 540; P. Bruneau, "Le motif des coqs affrontés dans l'imagerie antique," BCH 89 (1965), 104, fig. 14; E. L. Reeder, Hellenistic Art in the Walters Art Gallery (Baltimore, 1988), 79, fig. 66, and 183–184, no. 90; Uhlenbrock 1990, 150–151, no. 37; Salza Prina Ricotti 1995, 31, fig. 23.

On cockfighting, see A. Dundes, ed., The Cockfight: A Casebook (Madison, Wis., 1994). For the marble group in Istanbul (no. 554), see Bruneau (supra), 112–113, no. 76, fig. 22. For cocks as love gifts, see Koch-Harnack 1983, 97–105.

Krobylos is the same age as the locks of
    his hair
which the four-year-old shore for Phoibos
    the lyre-player,
and therewith did the son of Hegesidikos
    sacrifice
a fighting cock and a cheese pie. Oh
    Apollo,
bring up Krobylos to perfect manhood
    holding your hands over his home
    and his possessions.

Theodoridas, *Greek Anthology* VI.155

THIS epigram tells us that on the occasion of his first haircut a four-year-old boy dedicated not only his locks of hair but also a rooster and a rich cheese pastry to the god Apollo. Many such occasions from birth to coming of age punctuated the life of a Greek child; every transition demanded an appropriate ritual act. In addition to dedicating their toys, which have been found at sanctuaries (see cats. 78 and 88), Greek children were the recipients of cult paraphernalia in the form of small vases. The most common type is the *chous* (cats. 95–101), a special shape of *oinochoe*, or wine jug, which was used by children at the Anthesteria, a festival of the god of wine, Dionysos. Small *kraters* or *krateriskoi* (see Neils, fig. 11, p. 152) commemorated the ritual of girls at sanctuaries of Artemis. Boy athletes at the Panathenaia, a quadrennial festival in honor of Athena in her eponymous city, could earn large prize amphoras filled with olive oil (see Neils, fig. 14, p. 154). All these specialty vases

bear imagery of children and constitute an important source of information about their roles in religious festivals.

Children also took part in adult rituals, either as acolytes or assistants to the officiating priest or priestess, or as family members. They are regularly depicted on votive reliefs attending family visits to sanctuaries and on funerary vases and stelai mourning the dead. The contents of children's graves (cats. 118–119) inform us eloquently about what they valued most in their abbreviated lives. Their own early deaths are beautifully commemorated on smaller-scale grave stelai (cats. 122–126), a body of artworks that represent some of the finest expressions of Greek sculptors.

CHOES

More than one thousand of the small wine vessels we call *choes* (sing. *chous*) are extant. Most were produced in Athens in the late fifth century, but the vessel was imitated in other parts of the Greek world as well. The basic shape consists of a globular body with a continuous curve from the lip to a ring foot, trefoil mouth, and a vertical handle extending from lip to body. Choes come in all sizes and techniques, and their decoration is quite varied. The technique of decoration is normally red-figure; black-figure, white-ground, and Six's technique (see cat. 95) are also used. On the vases from the end of the fifth century, added colors are frequently applied.

In general, the larger the chous, the older the child depicted on it (see cats. 79 and 86, larger choes with older boys). Because much of the imagery of choes relates to the lives of children, they represent an important class of evidence for the study of Greek childhood, whether or not they can be associated with the Anthesteria, a three-day Athenian wine festival held in honor of Dionysos. The second day of this festival, called Choes, involved a drinking contest of the new wine for adults. The first to drain his chous (the full-size version holds 3.2 liters) of wine was crowned victor and awarded a full

wineskin. Miniature versions of these vessels were made for children and represent the full range of their activities, from crawling to horseracing. The majority of the children are male, but girls do appear (see cat. 92). Many of the small-scale or miniature choes have been found in children's graves in Athens and probably represent gifts to children who died before they could participate in the festival.

Much of the imagery of the choes is self-referential. Thus one often sees a chous in the scene (for example, cats. 75 and 96) or bunches of grapes, which refer to the vessel's function as a wine jug. In addition to wine, a variety of cakes seem to have been specially made for the festival and are often depicted on the choes in the hands of children. The cakes come in three shapes: *omphalos* (round with a central knob and divided into wedges, see cat. 101); *streptos* (long and twisted like a baguette, see cat. 91); and *pyramis* (pyramid-shaped).

On choes, see Hoorn 1951; Bazant 1975; Stern 1978; Rühfel 1984b, 128–174; Hamilton 1992.

95

96

97a

95
Boy with Dog
(see also color illus. p. 146)

A youth is shown training his dog. He holds aloft a treat (meat or grapes), and the dog rises onto its hind legs. The dog is standing on the top of a two-stepped base; the youth places his left foot on the lower step. Boys with their pet dogs are a common theme on Attic choes.

The so-called Six's technique of decorating vases consists of adding color, here white, on top of the black slip, and incising the details. It is a quick painting technique that was usually used on smaller vases, a number of which are choes.

> Attic red-figure miniature chous, Six's technique, ca. 420 B.C.E.
> H. 5.7; DIAM. 4.4
> Cambridge, Harvard University Art Museums, Arthur M. Sackler Museum Loan from Estate of Donald Upham and Mrs. R. U. Hunter, 24.1908

PUBLISHED: Klein 1932, pl. 26b; *CVA Fogg 1 USA* 8, 38, pl. 20,16; Hoorn 1951, 119, no. 438 and fig. 324.

Another chous with a boy training a dog is Karlsruhe, Badisches Landesmuseum W 271; see Hoorn 1951, fig. 323. On Six's technique, see J. Grossman, "Six's Technique at the Getty," *Greek Vases in the J. Paul Getty Museum* 5 (1993), 13–26.

96
Crawling Baby
(see also color illus. p. 146)

A chubby nude baby is crawling to the left toward a chous that rests on the ground. He wears a string of amulets across his chest. Crawling infants provide a popular subject for Attic choes, and they are often shown edging toward some object, bird, or pet.

> Attic red-figure chous, attributed to the Crawling Boy Workshop, ca. 420 B.C.E.
> H. 7.6; DIAM. 5.5; DIAM. OF FOOT 4.2
> Princeton, N.J., Princeton University Art Museum
> Museum Purchase, Caroline G. Mather Fund, y1953-22
> Ex Collection Franz von Matsch, Vienna

PUBLISHED: Hoorn 1951, 192 no. 988; *CVA Vienna* 1 Germany 5, Matsch pl. 8,9; F. F. Jones, "A Miniature Jug," *Record of the Art Museum, Princeton University* 12 (1953), 37; Green 1971, 216 no. 3.

On crawling babies, see Rühfel 1984b, 163–168. A chous in Athens (National Archaeological Museum 1556) with two male babies and two choes on the ground appears to be by the same hand; see Deubner 1932, pl. 29,1, and Hoorn 1951, 66, no. 51.

97
Boy and Cart
(see also color illus. p. 16)

On this small wine jug a chubby toddler is wheeling a cart to the right as his cloak flutters out behind him. He also wears a headband and bracelet. In his right hand he holds a globular chous in added yellow, while in his cart rests another one in added white. The white jug is more elongated and has what looks like an animal's head as its mouth. A bunch of grapes in added color, now largely lost, hangs on the central shoulder of the vase, as an indicator of its contents.

On choes young boys are often shown giving rides to their small wine jugs, either

97b

on their toy rollers or strapped to their dogs. They probably received these toys as well as miniature jugs as presents during the wine festival of the Anthesteria.

Attic red-figure chous with added color, ca. 400 B.C.E.
H. 7.2; DIAM. 5.8; DIAM. OF FOOT 3.7
Bryn Mawr, Pa., Bryn Mawr College, Ella Riegel Memorial Study Collection
Gift of Charles K. Williams, 1975, P-2159

PUBLISHED: Pinney and Ridgway 1979, 104–105, no. 49 (C. Lyons); Hamilton 1992, fig. 8.

For choes with animal attributes, see Hoorn 1951, no. 615, fig. 80. For boys giving rides to their choes, see Hoorn 1951, figs. 89–94 (carts), 96–97 (dogs).

99a

98

98
Boy Riding Fawn

A male baby, rendered in white, rides a galloping fawn to the right. He is wearing a white band in his curly hair and bracelets on his right wrist and ankle. This jewelry is rendered in relief, as is the amulet on his chest. Sprigs of olive grow up from the ground, and an ivy vine decorates the neck of the vessel.

Attic red-figure chous, ca. 400 B.C.E.
H. 8.9; DIAM. 5.8
Providence, Rhode Island School of Design, Museum of Art
Museum Appropriations Fund, 25.067

PUBLISHED: Klein 1932, pl. 13b; *CVA* Providence 1 USA 2, pl. 24,3; Hoorn 1951, 178 no. 891.

For other choes with boys riding deer, see Hoorn 1951, nos. 97, 203, 317, and 782; *ArchDelt* 18, no. 2 (1963), pl. 32,4; *ArchDelt* 23, no. 2 (1968), pl. 27c. Deer also pull children's carts: Hoorn 1951, nos. 13, 105, 182, and 960. Perhaps the child on the fawn was inspired by earlier choes showing young Silens riding these wild creatures; see Hoorn 1951, nos. 339 and 633.

99
Boy in Goat-Drawn Chariot
(see also color illus. p. 147)

> The children, placing purple reins upon
>   you, goat,
> And a noseband about your shaggy mouth,
> Train you in horse racing around the god's
>   temple
> To make you carry them gently for your
>   pleasure.
>> Hellenistic epigram by Anyte
>> (trans. K. Gutzwiller)

A boy wearing a long belted charioteer's gown and holding a *kentron* (goad), drives his chariot to the left. It is drawn by two galloping goats, the far one white, the near one brown in the color of the clay. The near goat wears a breastband decorated with white balls. Ahead of the goat runs another

99b

boy, who is holding the reins in his left hand and a chous in his right. He wears only an ivy wreath on his head, a string of amulets across his chest, and a *chlamys* draped over his arms.

An ivy vine decorates the neck of this and many other choes. It is certainly a reference to the contents, as it is associated with the wine god, Dionysos.

Attic red-figure chous with added color, ca. 400 B.C.E.
H. 9.9; DIAM. OF FOOT 5.1
New York, The Metropolitan Museum of Art
Rogers Fund, 1921, 21.88.80

PUBLISHED: Klein 1932, pl. 13c; Hoorn 1951, 159, no. 755.

100

101

100
Dionysiac Procession

This chous is unique in its large number of figures (six) and its iconography, which has been interpreted as a children's parody of the *hieros gamos*, which took place during the Anthesteria. At the right is an elderly man seated on a *klismos* in an ivy-canopied cart. Because he holds a *kantharos* and a *thyrsos*, he can be identified as the god of wine, Dionysos. Behind him are five youths on foot. The first is stepping onto the back of the cart and reaches out his hand to the next. These two are draped, and the second is often misinterpreted as female. The last three youths are nude and are carrying a T-shaped object on a long base; from the arms of the crossbar hang barely visible fillets rendered in dilute glaze.

This strange object has been subject to various identifications: a standard, perhaps of Dionysos's ship; a plowshare; a maypole or tree; a *kottabos* stand. Of these, the last is the most likely except that the stand lacks the requisite plate at the middle of its shaft. Perhaps it is intended to be another accoutrement of the nocturnal symposium, a lampstand? Such T-shaped stands often

have pendant hooks on either side of the central support. This reading is also supported by the fact that in numerous other vase paintings of Dionysos in procession, he is accompanied by satyrs carrying torches. The torches, like the lampstand, would serve as an indication of a nocturnal symposium.

Although this vase probably does not allude to the sacred marriage of Dionysos and the *Basilinna*, the wife of the Archon Basileus, it may parody the processions that took place during the Anthesteria, when revelers rode in vehicles and abused the bystanders (Plato, *Laws* I 637 B).

> Attic red-figure chous, ca. 450 B.C.E.
> H. 7.4; DIAM. OF FOOT 4.5
> New York, The Metropolitan Museum of Art
> Fletcher Fund, 24.97.34

PUBLISHED: Deubner 1932, 104–110, pls. 11,2–4; Klein 1932, pl. 26d; Hoorn 1951, 159, no. 757; *LIMC* 3 (1986), s.v. Dionysos, no. 825, pl. 398; J. Reilly, "Standards, Maypoles, and Sacred Trees," *AA* (1994), 499–505.

For a chous with a similar ivy-bedecked cart, cf. Paris, Musée du Louvre, 93: May 1992, 75 fig. 60.

101
Two Boys
(see also color illus. p. 146)

Two nude boys are facing each other. The one at the left is running forward with an omphalos cake balanced on his outstretched right hand. He seems to be handing it to the other boy, who stands calmly, holding forth his roller. Both wear added white fillets around their heads. Cakes were an integral part of Greek festivals and must have been much appreciated by children. As such they are frequently depicted in various forms on Attic choes.

> Attic red-figure chous, ca. 420–410 B.C.E.
> H. 14.4; DIAM. 10.6; DIAM. OF FOOT 7.2
> Princeton, N.J., Princeton University Art
> Museum
> Bequest of Professor George Rowley,
> y1962-13

PUBLISHED: Hamilton 1992, 185, fig. 18.

Possibly by the same hand is a chous with two boys playing ball in Athens, National Archaeological Museum, 1555: Hoorn 1951, 66, no. 50 and fig. 255.

102a   102b   102c

102

Girl on Swing

(see also color illus. p. 6)

On the body of this *lekythos* from South
Italy, a woman is pushing a young girl in a
swing. Both are wearing belted *chitons*,
necklaces and bracelets, and distinctive
crowns with upright spikes. Directly below
the swing is a young boy, half-draped and
seated on an altar. He holds what looks
like a *strigil*, and hanging below the edge
of the altar are a pomegranate and a fillet.
Behind the altar is an Ionic column, and
beyond that stands the god Hermes. He is

recognizable by his attributes: *petasos*, or
traveler's cap; laced boots; and *kerykeion*.

Although the rare images of girls on
swings in Greek art may look like mere
genre scenes, most of them probably
represent a religious ritual known as the
Aiora ("the swing"). In this rite, girls are
placed on swings in memory of a girl
named Erigone, who hanged herself after
the murder of her father. It is clearly a rite
of expiation, for the suicide of Erigone set
off a spate of girls hanging themselves that
could be stopped only by the establish-
ment of this cult. The sanctuary setting of
the scene on this vase, indicated by the

altar and column, illustrates that swinging
was a religious ritual among the Greeks of
southern Italy as well.

Eros pushing a girl on a swing appears
on a fourth-century Campanian red-figure
hydria in Milan and an Apulian *skyphos* in
the British Museum.

Apulian red-figure lekythos, associated with
the work of the Lecce Painter, ca. 400–375
B.C.E.
RESTORED H. 28.6; DIAM. 4.2
New York, The Metropolitan Museum of Art
Rogers Fund, 1913, 13.232.3
Ex Collection P. Hartwig

PUBLISHED: *RVAp* suppl. 1, 15, no. 235a; Klein 1932, pl. 23A; Beck 1975, pl. 57, no. 293; M. E. Mayo and K. Hamma, *The Art of South Italy: Vases from Magna Graecia, an Exhibition* (Richmond, Va., 1982), 93, no. 23.

For other South Italian vases with girls on swings, see K. Schauenburg, "Erotenspiele 1. Teil," *Antike Welt* 7 (1976), 43, 46 fig. 15 (London, The British Museum, skyphos), and 51 n. 79.

103
Girl with Box
(see also color illus. p. 138)

This life-sized standing figure of a young woman, missing its head and lower right arm, is an impressive work of Late Classical sculpture whose original context is unknown, thus making her identification difficult. The Kimbell girl (named for the museum in which she resides) is standing in a contrapposto pose, with her weight on her right leg. Her left arm is bent, and cradled within it is a square box with raised lid. Her long chiton is girt high, just below her small breasts, and is secured with shoulder cords that cross over her back. The drapery shows traces of at least six horizontal press folds, rendered as thin grooves, especially along her projecting left leg.

At first glance the Kimbell girl resembles the servant in the famous Hegeso grave relief who hands her seated mistress her box of jewels. However, a closer parallel for this figure is the frontally depicted servant girl in the Kallisto stele who holds the jewelry box at chest level. These comparisons might suggest that the Kimbell statue is a servant figure once attached to a funerary monument. Although such monuments can be nearly carved in the round, they usually show clear traces of scarring on the back where they were once attached to the background of the *naiskos*. The Kimbell statue is so finished in the back that it suggests a figure in the round, and so may represent an image of a temple attendant dedicated in a sanctuary. A later example of such a type is the so-called Anzio girl in Rome, who holds an offering tray in preparation for sacrifice.

103

Late Classical marble statue,
ca. 340–330 B.C.E.
H. 116.9; W. 47; D. 26.7
Fort Worth, Kimbell Art Museum
Foundation Acquisition, 1972, AP 72.3
Ex Collection Elie Borowski, Basel

PUBLISHED: Kimbell Art Museum, *Catalogue of the Collection* (Fort Worth, 1972), 4–6; Kimbell Art Museum, *Handbook of the Collection* (Fort Worth, 1981), 9; C. C. Vermeule, *Greek and Roman Sculpture in America: Masterpieces in Public Collections in the United States and Canada* (Malibu, Calif., 1981), 111, pl. 11; Kimbell Art Museum, *In Pursuit of Quality: An Illustrated History of the Art and Architecture* (New York, 1987), 108; *AA* (1997), 381–382, figs. 9–10.

For the Hegeso (Athens, National Archaeological Museum, 3624) and Kallisto (Athens, National Archaeological Museum, 732) stelai, see B. S. Ridgway, *Fourth-Century Styles in Greek Sculpture* (Madison, Wis., 1997), pls. 38 and 40. For shoulder cords, see E. B. Harrison, "The Shoulder-Cord of Themis," *Festschrift für Frank Brommer* (Mainz, 1977), 155–161, pls. 42–43. For the Anzio girl (Rome, Palazzo Massimo, 50170), see Bieber 1961, figs. 97–100.

106a

106
Sacrifice Scene

The reverse of this Early Classical amphora again shows a boy acolyte, but this time in the sanctuary in the presence of the priest. The sanctuary is indicated by the flaming, bloodstained altar in the center. The youth, wreathed and half-draped, stands frontally at the left and holds an oinochoe in his right hand. He extends his open left hand over the altar. At the right, a wreathed and bearded man draped in his *himation* stands in profile looking at the boy. In his left hand he clutches what appears to be a bunch of grapes, while in his right he holds the handle of a stemless cup from which red wine is overflowing onto the altar. Wine libations usually follow animal sacrifice, the wine being used to quench the fire after it has consumed the flesh. The cup with two high handles known as a kantharos is associated with Dionysos, as are grapes, and so it seems that the priest and his assistant are making an offering to the wine god.

This interpretation is perhaps borne out by the image on the obverse of the vase: the death of Orpheus. The musician, his lyre fallen to the ground below, is being impaled by a Thracian woman, maddened by Dionysos. Thus the human sacrifice on one side is equated with the pouring of the wine, which can be regarded as a type of sacrifice *(thusia)*, on the other. These two images are also deliberately contrasted: the former is a barbaric, foreign killing taking place in the mythological realm, while the latter represents the contemporary civilized practice of Greek ritual. The one is perpetrated by a crazed, out-of-control female, while the other is carried out by a calm, dignified male.

Attic red-figure neck-amphora, attributed to the Niobid Painter, ca. 460 B.C.E.
H. 53.2
Brooklyn Museum of Art
Museum Collection Fund, 59.34
From Vulci

PUBLISHED: *ARV*² 604, 57, and 1701; *Para* 395; *BAdd*² 267; E. M. Mylonas, "The Niobid Painter: A Neck-Amphora in the Brooklyn Museum Collection," *Brooklyn Annual* 1 (1959–1960), 16–24; The Brooklyn Museum, *Brief Guide to the Department of Egyptian and Classical Art* (Brooklyn, N.Y., 1974), 70–73.

On sacrifice to Dionysos see D. Obbink, "Dionysus Poured Out: Ancient and Modern Theories of Sacrifice and Cultural Formation," in T. H. Carpenter and C. A. Faraone, eds., *Masks of Dionysus* (Ithaca, N.Y., 1993), 65–86.

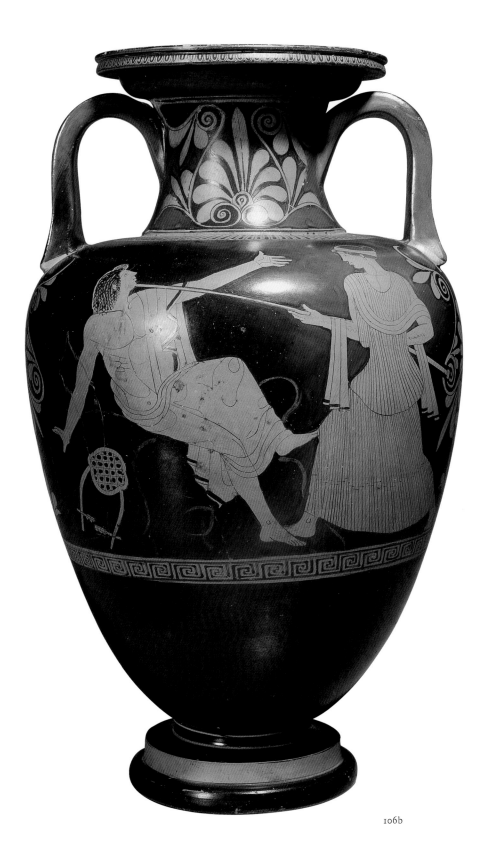

106b

107
Kanephoros (Basket Carrier)

This simple clay figurine consisting of a
square base and a standing frontal figure is
one of many representing the ritual basket
bearer, or *kanephoros*. A female of indeter-
minate age wearing a mantle symmetrically
over both shoulders stands with her arms
raised. On her head she is balancing a
kanoun (see cat. 105).

In public cult ceremonies a virgin girl
from an aristocratic family was specially
chosen to carry the sacrificial basket. In
his play *Lysistrata* Aristophanes uses the
phrase "pure as an Athenian kanephoros"
(1314–1315), and it was probably the last
honorific office an Athenian girl held
before marriage. Many representations of
cult processions painted on Greek vases
show the kanephoros with basket on her
head leading the way to the altar (see Neils,
fig. 21, p. 158). Girls acting as kanephoroi
are also depicted at the head of the Panathenaic procession on the sculpted frieze
of the Parthenon. The contents of the
kanoun are not usually depicted, but it held
barley to attract the animal to the altar and
a knife to kill it.

Small clay reproductions of these
three-handled baskets have been found in
Athenian graves, as have figurines of
kanephoroi. Both no doubt served to comfort the deceased by reminding her of the
important religious role of girls, one she
may have been too young to attain before
her death.

Attic terracotta mold-made figurine,
ca. 440–420 B.C.E.
H. 20.7
Munich, Staatliche Antikensammlungen und
Glyptothek, inv. no. Schoen 154
Possibly from Athens

PUBLISHED: R. Lullies, *Eine Sammlung griechischer Kleinkunst* (Munich, 1955) pl. 60; Reeder
1995, 235–236, no. 60.

For a similar kanephoros in Munich with
associated grave goods, see Hamdorf 1996, 50,
fig. 50. For kanephoroi on the Parthenon frieze,
see Neils 2001, 154–158.

107

108

108

Four Kanephoroi

(see also color illus. p. 283)

This terracotta figurine preserves three of
its four figures; the one at the right is
mostly missing. Except for the positions of
their arms, the figures are similarly posed
with their weight shifted onto their left
legs. Each wears the Doric woolen *peplos*
and a headband with hair parted in the
middle of the forehead. Atop their heads
each carries a low kanoun, the contents of
which are partially visible. Barley is clearly
seen in the basket borne by the first girl,
who steadies it with her right hand while
her left clasps that of the next kanephoros.
The next three hold their baskets with their
left hands, while their right arms hang at
their sides.

    This group of four frontal girls in con-
trapposto poses with baskets on their
heads recalls the famous caryatids or Porch
of the Maidens of the so-called Erechtheion
on the Athenian Acropolis. They too have
been identified as kanephoroi serving
Athena in the Panathenaic procession.

    Tarantine terracotta mold-made figurine,
    ca. 450–425 B.C.E.
    H. 25.2
    Amsterdam, Allard Pierson Museum, 1159
    From Taranto

PUBLISHED: R. A. Lunsingh Scheurleer, *Grieken
in het klein* exhib. cat. (Amsterdam, 1986), 7, no.
69; Jurriaans-Helle 2002, 33 fig. 65, 43 no. 106.

109

Seated Girl with Tambourine and Wreath

(see also color illus. p. 78)

An alert girl in festive costume sits frontally
on a block seat, her left leg crossing
slightly beneath the upright right leg, her
head turned to her right as she smiles. She
wears a chiton girded beneath her chest
and a mantle that is wrapped around her
lower left arm and hand. In her right hand
she holds a wreath and tambourine by her
leg, indicating that she has taken or will
take part in a festive ceremony, perhaps
one connected with the worship of Cybele
or Dionysos. Her hair is tied up in piles of
locks on top of her head, a style known as
the *lampadion*, or "little torch," because the
piles resemble the flames of a torch.

    Tanagra terracotta figurine, Boiotian, last
    quarter of the fourth century B.C.E.
    H. 12.5
    Boston, Museum of Fine Arts
    James Fund and by Special Contribution,
    10.230

PUBLISHED: Klein 1932, 32 and pl. 32c;
Uhlenbrock 1990, 51, 109, and 117, no. 10.
    For Tanagra figurines of seated girls, see
D. B. Thompson, "The Origin of Tanagras," *AJA*
70 (1966), 59.

109

110a

110

**Preparations for the Bride's Wedding
Bath**

(see also color illus. p. 140)

The wedding marked the transition for
women to adulthood, and young girls and
boys participated in various parts of this
ritual. On the night before the wedding
feast the bride took her ritual bath, the
water for which normally came from an
important local water source. In Athens
this was the Enneakrounos, the fountain
house for the Kallirrhoe Spring, and the
water was carried in a special ritual vase
known as the *loutrophoros*, which had two
forms—the *loutrophoros-hydria*, as here,
with three handles and normally associated with females, and the *loutrophoros-
amphora*, with two and associated with
males. These vessels were also used to
mark the tombs of those who died unmarried. The procession to obtain this water
(*loutrophoreia*) occurs already on seventh-
century Proto-Attic vases but is most
common on fifth-century red-figure vases,
when greater emphasis was placed on
wedding imagery. The water purified the
bride for the ritual and was thought to aid
in fertility.

110b

The bride is depicted in the center of the front side carrying a large loutrophoros-hydria decorated with red ribbons. She is dressed in chiton and mantle, and the ends of her hair are enclosed in a small bag at the back. Before her a woman walks forward, looking back and holding a wreath out in her left hand. Behind the bride comes another woman, who holds a long, lit torch, indicating that it is night. Underneath the right handle is a young boy in mantle playing the *auloi*. He leads the procession, as he does in other depictions of this event. His instrument is supported at the mouth by a *phorbeia*—a head band. Beneath the other handle a girl carrying two wreaths follows along in the procession, indicating that females of various ages took part in this event too. Behind her comes another woman carrying a torch, followed by one holding a basket that may contain clean clothes for the bride. She gestures back, giving the impression that the procession continues unbroken around the vessel. A wreath hangs behind her in the background.

A shortened version of the same scene is found on the vessel's neck—a bride carrying a large loutrophoros-hydria, followed by two women, one of whom carries a torch, the other a wreath. Other depictions of the loutrophoreia provide further details. Often a young girl rather than the bride carries the vessel, as on a loutrophoros in Karlsruhe that also shows a female dancer, an altar, and a herm before the house, and the Enneakrounos springhouse.

> Attic red-figure loutrophoros-hydria, attributed to the Pan Painter, ca. 470 B.C.E.
> H. 39.8; W. 38.7; DIAM. OF MOUTH 7.9; DIAM. OF BASE 7.9
> Houston, The Museum of Fine Arts
> Gift of Miss Annette Finnigan, 37.10

PUBLISHED: ARV² 554,79; BAdd² 258; H. Hoffmann, *Ten Centuries That Shaped the West: Greek and Roman Art in Texas Collections* (Mainz, 1970), 398–401, no. 181; Reeder 1995, 161–163, no. 22.

For the wedding, see Oakley and Sinos 1993, especially 15–16, and figs. 16–19 for the Karlsruhe loutrophoros; A.-M. Vérilhac and C. Vial, *Le mariage grec du VIe siècle av. J.-C. à l'époque d'Auguste*, BCH suppl. 32 (Paris, 1998).

III

III
Grave Memorial with Family Scene
(see also color illus. p. 187)

Five members of an Athenian household are depicted on this gravestone, which reproduces in marble the shape of the common earthenware, white-ground vase used for funerary purposes (see cats. 113, 115, 116, and 117). Its top and base are missing, but the figured scene, along with its inscriptions, is intact. At the far right is a bearded, and so older, man wearing a himation and leaning on his staff, once painted but now lost. His name, Timophon, is inscribed above his head, and he is shaking hands with a standing woman in the center. Labeled Lysistrate, she is dressed in a chiton and himation that she clasps with her left hand at shoulder level. Below her outstretched right hand is a girl, facing right, labeled Kleippe. She is certainly the daughter of this couple, who bid each other farewell with the traditional handshake, known in Greek as *dexiosis*.

At the far left stands a woman in simpler dress holding a newborn infant, wrapped in a cloth and wearing a pointed bonnet. She is clearly the nurse, as her name is not inscribed, nor is that of the newborn, who is probably not yet old enough to have been given a name. Their presence suggests that the woman Lysistrate died in childbirth and that this monument commemorates her passing. A similar lekythos with identical names inscribed by the same hand almost certainly belongs to the same funerary complex. The pair probably once served as pendants at opposite ends of the terrace wall delineating the family precinct.

> Attic marble lekythos, Later Classical, ca. 400–375 B.C.E.
> H. 53.7
> The Cleveland Museum of Art
> Gift of J. H. Wade, 1925.1342

PUBLISHED: CAT 3.745; B. Schmaltz, *Untersuchungen zu den attischen Marmorlekythen* (Berlin, 1970), 131, A 134; Bieber 1961, 9, fig. 2; Hadzisteliou-Price 1978, 52, no. 550, fig. 40; J. Bergemann, *Demos und Thanatos: Untersuchungen zum Wertsystem der Polis im Spiegel der attischen Grabreliefs des 4. Jahrhunderts v. Chr. und zur Funktion der gleichzeitigen Grabbauten* (Munich, 1997), 210 and pl. 4,3; Schulze 1998, 109 no. A G 59.

For nurses with infants on funerary lekythoi, see Schulze 1998, 29–32, pl. 8. For the pendant in Columbia, Missouri (79.143), see CAT 3.746.

112

Family Funeral Scene

(see also color illus. of cat. 112a–b, p. 166)

This funerary vase, with the only known
depiction of the corpse being placed into
the coffin, gives us one of the most remarkable pictures of ancient funerary rites.
Among the participants is a young girl,
demonstrating once again that children
were involved in various parts of the funerary ritual. The primary action takes place
on the front of the vessel, where the
shrouded body of a man is gently lowered
into a wooden coffin that has the form of a
footed chest. The inscription above the
bearded man, who holds onto the upper
part of the body, can be read as *lab[ē] me
lit(o)ta[ta]*—hold me very gently. Behind
him a woman, perhaps the deceased's
mother or wife, reaches toward him in a
gesture of mourning. Two other women
aid in lowering the body at the other end of
the coffin. Each wears chiton and mantle,
as do all the women on this vase, and their
hair is tattered from mourning. Behind
them are two bearded men. The first
reaches out toward the corpse, the other
raises his left hand in the gesture of valediction, a farewell given to the dead made
almost exclusively by males. Over his left
shoulder he holds an axe, indicating that
he is the carpenter who will close the
coffin's lid, once the corpse is in place.
Beside him a woman bends over to pick up
a funerary basket loaded with lekythoi.
This is the earliest known representation of
the funerary basket. She will bring it to the
grave (see cat. 116 and Oakley, figs. 7, 10,
and 13, pp. 167, 169, 173). A shield hangs
on the wall above the coffin, suggesting
that the action takes place in the *andron*, the
main room of the house. The two lit lamps
indicate that it is still dark outside. The
function of the three disk-shaped objects
hanging above is uncertain.

The second group of figures appears
behind the carpenter. Central is the old
man seated on a *diphros*, who mourns
vociferously, bending over at the waist and
holding his right arm up toward his head.
Only traces of his white hair remain. He is
comforted by a young girl, perhaps his
granddaughter, who stands before him
with both hands extended toward his lap.

112b

Behind him stands a crying woman, who
reaches up to dab away her tears with her
right hand while holding an *alabastron* up
in the other. She is comforted in turn by the
woman standing before her, who places her
left hand on the crying woman's shoulder.
These family members are shown in a moment of great grief.

The third and final group consists of
two short men walking toward a woman
who stands beside a diphros. The first
carries a hydria on his shoulder, while the
other holds a hemispherical vessel whose
contents are not possible to identify with
certainty. They may be understood as

preparing for the *perideipnon*, the funerary feast that took place later that day after the deceased was buried; the *prosphagma*, a sacrifice made either at home before the procession to the grave or after it at the grave; or the *aponimma*, water poured into a pit west of the grave after burial, followed by a prayer.

The Sappho Painter produced several other interesting funeral pictures (see Oakley, fig. 3, p. 165), and he liked to write inscriptions. Often, as also the case with many on this vase, they are nonsense (the letters do not form identifiable words), although some of them can be read, like the inscription by the corpse's head.

Bail-handled oinochoai are a special type of Attic funerary vessel. Those with pictures are all black-figure and date to the first quarter of the fifth century, but the shape continued to be made in black-gloss down into the fourth century. The bail-handle in the form of a rope suggests that the vessel was used for carrying liquid, most likely water, but not for pouring it.

Attic black-figure bail-handled oinochoe, attributed to the Sappho Painter, ca. 500–490 B.C.E.
H. 37.3; H. WITHOUT HANDLE 30.7; DIAM. OF MOUTH 13.9; DIAM. OF BASE 11.5
Brunswick, Maine, Bowdoin College Museum of Art
Museum Purchase with funds from the Adela Wood Smith Trust in memory of Harry de Forest Smith, 1891; 1984.023
Ex Collection Gillet, Lausanne

PUBLISHED: *Para* 247; *BAdd*² 126–127; D. C. Kurtz and J. Boardman, *Greek Burial Customs* (London, 1971), 149 and pls. 37–38; *CAH* plates to vol. 4, 168, nos. 218a–c; *AJA* 95 (1991), 635, fig. 4; H. Laxander, *Individuum und Gemeinschaft im Fest: Untersuchungen zu attischen Darstellungen von Festgeschehen im 6. und frühen 5. Jahrhundert v. Chr.* (Münster, Germany, 2000), pls. 68,1–4; *AntK* 45 (2002), pls. 3,1–2; J. H. Oakley, "Bail-Oinochoai," forthcoming.

For the Sappho Painter, see C. Jubier, "Les peintres de Sappho et de Diosphos, structure d'atelier," in M.-C. V. Puig et al., eds., *Céramique et peinture grecques: Modes d'emploi* (Paris, 1999),

112c

181–186; C. Jubier, "De l'usage des pseudo-inscriptions chez le peintre de Sappho, du signe du sens," *Métis*, forthcoming; and S. Weber, "Sappho- und Diosphos-Maler: Studien zur attischen spätest-schwarzfigurigen Keramik" (Ph.D. diss., Johannes Gutenberg-Universität, Mainz), 2000. For other vases of this shape, see Oakley (supra).

WHITE LEKYTHOI

During the fifth century a special type of funerary vase, the white or white-ground lekythos, was made in Athens. An oil or perfume container, it was placed in and on the tomb, as well as around the bier, during the *prothesis* (laying out of the corpse for viewing). The technique of decoration consisted of a white slip used to cover much of the vase's body and shoulder, on top of which were painted figures and ornament. The earliest white lekythoi had black-figure decoration and, later, figures in outline. Between 470 and 400, however, polychrome washes were used to color most of the areas between the outlines, and when we speak of white or white-ground lekythoi, we normally mean by convention the polychrome ones.

Three major types of subjects decorated these vessels: domestic scenes; the mythological ministers of death—Charon, Hermes, and Hypnos and Thanatos (sleep and death); and a visit to the grave. A smaller group shows the prothesis. These subjects and the more than two thousand white lekythoi that are preserved make these vessels the most important source for funerary imagery from Classical Greece.

113
Youth and Girl Visiting a Tomb
(see also color illus. p. 168)

Children of all ages participated in Greek funerary ritual, including the visit to the grave when gifts were offered and the tomb was decorated. This lekythos has one of the earliest depictions of this scene on white lekythoi, a subject that after the middle of the century became the predominant one on this special class of funerary vases. The grave is marked with a white mound *(tymbos)* atop a base. An upright stele with rounded finial stands either atop the mound or behind it; the Greek conventions of drawing at this time do not allow us to distinguish which is the case. The black circles on the mound's base have been variously interpreted as ornament, air holes, places for offerings, or drainage holes.

113

To the left a teenage youth places a fillet, the most common offering, on the tomb, while a younger girl on the right holds up an alabastron in her left hand and offers a flower with her right. The brighter white ("second or added white") used for the girl's skin and the grave monument is common on early white lekythoi. Because both children make offerings at the tomb, neither is likely to represent the deceased making an epiphany at the tomb, as is the case on other white lekythoi. Children making offerings at the tomb is not a common subject but was probably a normal practice in Greece when parents died young.

Attic white-ground lekythos, attributed to the Painter of Athens 1826, ca. 460 B.C.E.
H. 24.7; DIAM. 8.9; DIAM. OF MOUTH 5.1; DIAM. OF BASE 4.8
Malibu, Calif., The J. Paul Getty Museum, 86.AE.253
Ex Collection Bareiss 105

PUBLISHED: ARV² 746,5bis; Para 413; BAdd² 284; S. B. Matheson and J. J. Pollitt, *Greek Vases at Yale* (New Haven, 1975), 79–80, no. 63; N. Nakayama, *Untersuchung der auf weissgrundigen Lekythen dargestellten Grabmaeler* (Freiburg, Germany, 1982), 182, no. GH-1–3; D. C. Kurtz, "Two Athenian White-ground Lekythoi," *Greek Vases in the J. Paul Getty Museum* 4 (OPA 5 [1989]), 113 n. 1 and 129, fig. 7; *CVA* Malibu 7 U.S.A. 32, pls. 383, 384,1–2, and 386,5–6 and fig. 30.

For scenes of a visit to the grave and for the black dots on the base, see most recently J. H. Oakley, *Picturing Death in Classical Athens: The Evidence of the White Lekythoi* (Cambridge, 2003).

114
A Boy Led by Hermes to Charon, and Boys Playing Knucklebones at the Grave
(see also color illus. p. 173)

This remarkable red-figure funerary vase has two scenes clearly influenced by those on contemporary white-ground lekythoi. On one side is the only known red-figure depiction of Charon. He sits perched in his boat on the left side, supporting himself with his oar. Most of the white for his beard and hair is lost, and he wears his typical attire of *exomis* (garment with one shoulder bare) and rustic cap. Hermes approaches him from the right, reaching back toward a youth who holds a bag in his left hand. Most likely the pouch contains knucklebones, a favorite toy of Greek boys (see cats. 85–90, preceded by "Knucklebones" introduction). The boy is the

114a

114b

deceased whom Charon will ferry across the water to Hades. This is a subject found almost exclusively on white lekythoi.

Boys playing knucklebones decorate the vase's other side. The central youth, who stands resting his chin on his left hand, lost in thought, may very well be the deceased, possibly the youth in the scene with Charon. Meanwhile, a youth on the left squats to pick up a knucklebone to add to the pile he clutches in his left hand. Although it is not certain what the youth on the right does, he is probably poised to cast a knucklebone. A visit to the grave was the most popular scene on white lekythoi, and although none shows a game of knucklebones, others do combine the former activities of the deceased with a picture of the grave, as seems to be the case here.

Black-figure Panathenaic amphorae were filled with olive oil and given as prizes to the victors of the Greater Panathenaic games (see Neils, fig. 14, p. 154). Red-figure vases imitating their shape, such as this vessel, are much rarer. Sometimes the subjects painted on them are related to the festival, other times not, but this is the only example with funerary iconography. Most likely it was placed in or on a boy's tomb, indicating either that he was a past winner in the games, or that he died before he reached the age to compete in them.

Attic red-figure amphora of Panathenaic shape, attributed to the Kleophon Painter, ca. 430 B.C.E.
PRES. H. TO TOP OF HANDLE 49.1;
DIAM. 31
Québec City, Musée national des beaux-arts du Québec, Purchase, 66.230
Ex Collection V. Diniakopoulos

PUBLISHED: J. H. Oakley, "Charon on an Attic Red-figure Amphora of Panathenaic Shape: A Masterpiece by the Kleophon Painter in Quebec," in M. Bentz and N. Eschbach, eds., *Panathenaïka: Symposion zu den Panathenäischen Preisamphoren, Rauischholzhausen 25.11–9.11 1998* (Mainz, 2001), 137–143 and pls. 38–39.

For red-figured amphorae of Panatheniac shape, see most recently the list given by J. Neils, J. H. Oakley, and H. A. Shapiro in Bentz and Eschbach (supra), 199–202, and the articles by Oakley (supra), Lezzi-Hafter (pp. 131–135), and Shapiro (pp. 119–124) in the same volume. For the iconography of white-ground lekythoi, see J. H. Oakley, *Picturing Death in Classical Athens: The Evidence of the White Lekythoi* (Cambridge, 2003).

115
Charon, Mother, and Baby Boy
(see also color illus. pp. 162, 174)

One of the most touching of all farewell scenes in Greek vase painting, this image underscores the sadness of losing a child. Charon, the old ferryman who transported the shades of the dead across the water to the underworld, is a frequent subject on

115a

115b

white-ground lekythoi. Here, as on several other lekythoi, Charon's cargo will be a young child rather than the more commonly shown youth or woman (mature males are rare). Standing on a rock, a nude young boy with long flowing hair in a headband waits holding the pole of his toy roller in his left hand. His body faces Charon's ship, which is moored on the right, as he turns to look at his mother behind him, extending his arm in a poignant gesture of farewell. She stands motionless, wrapped in her mantle, gazing down upon her lost son.

Charon holds a pole upright in his left hand and stands patiently in the boat, only the front half of which is shown. He gestures with his right hand ever so slightly to indicate that it is time to go. This and his downward gaze suggest that he is sympathetic to the situation, a quality he does not always exhibit in other depictions, although he does on other white lekythoi by this artist. The exomis and rustic cap are Charon's typical attire.

Boys are often shown with toy rollers in other media, particularly on carved gravestones (see cat. 122) and on Attic red-figure choes (see cats. 97 and 101). They were given as gifts to young boys at the Diasia (festival for Zeus and Dionysos) and possibly the Anthesteria (Dionysiac festival). Sometimes there is a platform or box atop the wheel or wheels, as here, and other times not. The size varies, and some were pushed instead of rolled. On other white lekythoi toy rollers are occasionally shown in the hands of a boy standing at the grave (see Oakley, fig. 13, p. 173), and a metal example has been found in a child's grave (see Oakley, fig. 21, p. 182). Most toy rollers, however, were made of wood and have long since perished. Equivalent to modern toy trucks or cars, they provided hours of amusement for Greek toddlers.

Attic white-ground lekythos, attributed to the Painter of Munich 2335, ca. 430 B.C.E.
H. 31.9; DIAM. OF MOUTH 6.4;
DIAM. OF BASE 6.6
New York, The Metropolitan Museum of Art
Rogers Fund, 1909, 09.221.44
From Greece

PUBLISHED: ARV² 1168,128; BAdd² 338; D. C. Kurtz, *Athenian White Lekythoi: Patterns and Painters* (Oxford, 1975), pl. 42,1; Rühfel 1984a, 116, fig. 47a; LIMC 3 (1986), s.v. Charon I, 213 no. 13 and pl. 169 (C. Sourvinou-Inwood); J. Boardman, *Athenian Red-figure Vases: The Classical Period: A Handbook* (London, 1989), fig. 268.

For scenes of Charon, see most recently J. H. Oakley, *Picturing Death in Classical Athens: The Evidence of the White Lekythoi* (Cambridge, 2003), with a list of known examples. See also LIMC 3 (1986), s.v. Charon I, 210–225 (C. Sourvinou-Inwood); C. Sourvinou-Inwood, *"Reading" Greek Death: To the End of the Classical Period* (Oxford, 1995), 303–361; and F. Díez de Velasco, *Los caminos de la muerte* (Madrid, 1995), 42–57.

For the toy rollers, see Klein 1932, 13–14; Hoorn 1951, 44; Schmidt 1977, 97–102; Rühfel 1984a, 117–118, 123, 180, 328 n. 117, and 339 n. 319; Hamilton 1992, 72, 91, 105–106, and 117; CAT 6.145 with a list of gravestones showing them, and 1.144.

116
Mother and Maid at Child's Tomb
(see also color illus. p. 172)

In this unique image a baby boy sits on top of a short grave stele with four-step base decorated with fillets, supporting himself with extended arms while looking off to the right. He is able to sit up but not yet stand. Only a few other white lekythoi depict small figures atop the grave shaft, one of which in Athens shows a seated mother offering grapes to a baby boy. These figures, like the toddler on this vase, are not sculpture atop the tomb or living visitors; rather they represent the deceased occupant(s) of the tomb, a baby boy in the case of this lekythos.

From the right an Ethiopian maid approaches, carrying a funeral basket with fillets on her head and an alabastron in her left hand. Her pug nose and short hair and her stooped pose indicate her race and servile status, respectively. Only one other white lekythos in Berlin has a similar figure. On the other side of the grave stands a woman enveloped in her mantle, staring straight ahead at the tomb. She is probably the mother of the dead boy, here to mourn, or she may also be dead, having died in childbirth—identifying the deceased in grave scenes has long been problematical. The *sakkos* hanging up behind her recalls those found in household scenes, reminding the viewer of the dead boy's and possibly the dead mother's former home while viewing their new home, the tomb.

Another lekythos by the Thanatos Painter (see Oakley, fig. 8, p. 168), probably from the same grave, shows a young girl holding a doll at a tomb. This suggests that both of these vases may have come from a child's grave.

Attic white-ground lekythos, attributed to the Thanatos Painter, ca. 440 B.C.E.
H. 25.7; DIAM. OF MOUTH 5.1;
DIAM. OF BASE 5.8
Atlanta, Emory University,
Michael C. Carlos Museum
Carlos Collection of Ancient Greek Art,
1999.11.1
Ex Collections William G. Helis, Jr., New Orleans; Claude Hankes-Drielsma, London

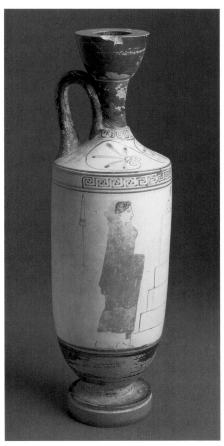

116a

116b

116c

117

PUBLISHED: ARV² 1230,44; BAdd² 351; H. A. Shapiro, Art, Myth, and Culture: Greek Vases from Southern Collections (New Orleans, 1981), 112–113, no. 44; Sotheby's (New York), 14 December 1993, lot 28; Reeder 1995, 223–224, no. 54.

For scenes of the visit to the grave, see cat. 113. For small figures atop stelae, see most recently J. H. Oakley, Picturing Death in Classical Athens: The Evidence of the White Lekythoi (Cambridge, 2003), with a list of known examples. The Athens lekythos is by the Sabouroff Painter: Athens, National Archaeological Museum, 1815; ARV² 845,169; BAdd² 297; G. G. Kavvadias, O Zographos tou Sabouroff (Athens, 2000), pl. 176. The Berlin lekythos is by the Bosanquet Painter: Staatliche Museen, Antikensammlung Inv. 3291; ARV² 1227,9; BAdd² 350; W. Reizler, Weissgrundige attische Lekythen (Munich, 1914), pl. 25.

117
Mother and Child at Grave
(see also color illus. p. 171)

A tymbos with a red ribbon tied around it marks the tomb of the young boy who is shown crawling on the grave's steps. Urged on by his mother, who stands on the right with her hands held out, palms up, he attempts to raise himself by pushing up with his arms. This tender moment of motherly encouragement is intensified by the direct eye contact they maintain. In many cases it is not possible to identify who the deceased is in these popular scenes of a visit to the grave, but because graveyards were not the place where children learned to walk, the baby must be the tomb's occupant, as is possibly the mother as well, if she had died in childbirth. The combination of a household scene with the visit to the grave is not uncommon on white lekythoi at this time and signals the past and the present, and the deceased's old home and new home.

About twenty white lekythoi show children at the grave, several of whom are babies that crawl or make ready to walk on or by the tomb. They all date from the last thirty years of the fifth century, at a time when Athenians were keenly aware of the importance of the next generation, because so many male warriors were being killed in the Peloponnesian War. Only on one other contemporary white lekythos does the mother interact with the baby as here. In this case she appears to entice the baby boy with a piece of fruit.

Attic white-ground lekythos, attributed to the Bird Painter, ca. 430 B.C.E.
H. 20
Munich, Staatliche Antikensammlungen und Glyptothek, 7619
From Greece

PUBLISHED: ARV² 1233,18; BAdd² 352; J. D. Beazley, Attic White Lekythoi (Oxford, 1938), pl. 6,2; Rühfel 1984a, 112, figs. 45a–b. For scenes of children at the tomb, see most recently J. H. Oakley, Picturing Death in Classical Athens: The Evidence of the White Lekythoi (Cambridge, 2003), with a list of known examples. For the other lekythos, Once Frankfurt Market, see ARV2 1236,2; Auktion Helbing, 11–13 Mai 1937, pl. 14,217; photo—Beazley Archive.

118
Child's Tomb Group
(see also color illus. p. 176)

This child's tomb group consists of eleven miniature earthenware objects and a bronze mirror. The miniature vessels are an olpe or jug, a bucketlike dipper with vertical handle, and a mesomphalos phiale (one with a central knob) with fluted walls. Terracotta toys include a cubic die with painted dots, a spherical ball or marble, and a female doll's head. A truncated biconical spindle whorl reflects the domestic sphere, as does what looks to be a miniature cake of the long streptos type (see cat. 91). The function of the terracotta ring is uncertain, as is the terracotta footed object. The bronze disk would originally have had a highly polished surface for reflection. Finally, there are two animal statuettes, a cock and a horse. The nature of these grave goods—in particular the mirror, doll's head, and spindle whorl—indicate that the occupant of the grave was a young girl.

Apulian, earthenware and bronze (mirror), fourth century B.C.E.

Jug: H. 6.4; Dipper: H. 3.5; Mirror: DIAM. 13.3; Spindle whorl: H. 2.54; Die: L. 1.9; Cake: L. 5.4; Cup: DIAM. 5.7; Ball: DIAM. 1.6; Ring: DIAM. OF OUTER RIM 5.4; Cock statuette: H. 11.4; Horse statuette: H. 9.2

Newark, N.J., The Newark Museum Eugene Schaefer Collection, Gift of Mrs. Eugene Schaefer, 1950, 50.212, 50.292, 50.367.A–C, 50.638–640, 50.647, 50.649–650, 50.720–721

PUBLISHED: *The Newark Museum* n.s. 3, no. 2 (spring 1951), 11, fig. 14; Pinney and Ridgway 1979, 248–249, no. 121.

For examples of excavated grave goods from earlier child burials in South Italy and Sicily, see B. D. Wescoat, ed., *Syracuse, the Fairest Greek City* (Atlanta, 1989), 113–118, nos. 37–48 (Tomb 121, Giardino Spagna, ca. 500); G. Pugliese Carratelli, ed., *The Western Greeks*, exhib. cat. (Milan, 1998), 224–225 (Tomb 102 at Braida Vaglio Basilicata, Potenza, ca. 500).

119
Child's Tomb Group (?)

Although their archaeological context is lost, all four of these miniature Xenon vases probably came from a child's tomb, for miniature vases are often found in children's graves. The group is a drinking set—gifts from adults for the child's afterlife. The *nestoris*, a native Italian shape, is a jar used for liquids, the oinochoe is a pouring jug, and the skyphos is a drinking cup.

Xenon is a South Italian ware that cannot be classified as either purely Greek or native Italian. It is characterized by red decoration, both figures and pattern, on black gloss.

> a. Xenon miniature nestoris,
> fourth century B.C.E.
> H. 6.4
> Tampa Museum of Art
> Joseph Veach Noble Collection, 1986.118

On one side of the body between the handles is a running meander with one line

above and two below, and on the other is a vine pattern.

> b. Xenon miniature oinochoe,
> fourth century B.C.E.
> H. 6.0
> Tampa Museum of Art
> Joseph Veach Noble Collection, 1986.119

This vase is decorated with rays on the shoulder above a laurel wreath between lines on the body.

> c. Xenon miniature skyphos,
> fourth century B.C.E.
> H. 5.5
> Tampa Museum of Art
> Joseph Veach Noble Collection, 1986.120

This skyphos is decorated with a chevron pattern beneath the rim in the handle zone, and a vine pattern between lines on the body.

> d. Xenon miniature nestoris,
> fourth century B.C.E.
> H. 6.4
> Tampa Museum of Art
> Joseph Veach Noble Collection, 1986.117

This vase is decorated with a wave above two lines on the shoulder between the handles.

PUBLISHED: M. E. Mayo and K. Hamma, *The Art of South Italy: Vases from Magna Graecia. An Exhibition* (Richmond, Va., 1982), 304, no. 159; S. P. Murray, *Collecting the Classical Past: Antiquities from the Joseph Veach Noble Collection* (Tampa, 1985), 50, nos. 115–118.

For miniature vessels, see cat. 118.

118

120

Child's Bracelet

This small bracelet consists of a hoop
formed from a strip having a pair of ropes
along each edge with a row of granulated
lozenges on the body. At each end is a
hinge fastening held in place by a molded
strip. The size of the bracelet indicates that
it was for a child, and although the archaeological context is not known, it probably
was found in a child's grave.

> Gold bracelet, Eastern Mediterranean,
> late fourth or third century B.C.E.
> DIAM. 3.48; WT. 5.8g
> Bloomington, Indiana University Art
> Museum
> Burton Y. Berry Collection,
> 69.88.16

PUBLISHED: W. Rudolph and E. Rudolph,
Ancient Jewelry from the Collection of Burton Y. Berry
(Bloomington, Ind., 1973), 66–67, no. 50c.

121 a, b, from left

121

Pair of Child's Snake Bracelets

The snake was the most popular form of
bracelet in ancient Greece, as indicated by
preserved examples and renditions in
Greek art. It should not be a surprise, therefore, that this type occurs in children's
jewelry, for the snake is an apotropaic and
chthonic motif, as illustrated in Euripides'
play *Ion* (1427–1432), in which Ion's
mother, Creusa, places golden snakes
around the baby's neck before exposing
him.

The form of this snake bracelet emphasizes the golden hoop band, which has a
scale pattern between raised molding on
the outside and ends in the form of
abstracted snake heads. The holes in the
heads may have been used for fastening
threads. The emphasis on abstract, linear,
two-dimensional form represented here is
typical of Late Hellenistic jewelry and
contrasts with other, particularly earlier,
snake bracelets that feature the coiled

nature of the reptile, the band formed to
wrap several times around the wearer's
arm. The dimensions of these bracelets
suggest that they may be children's
bracelets, although they border on the size
suitable for a small adult.

> Gold bracelets, Eastern Mediterranean
> (Egypt?), ca. 100 B.C.E.–100 C.E.
> a. DIAM. 5.2–5.4; W. OF HOOP 0.8;
> TH. OF HOOP 0.15; WT. 30.17g
> b. DIAM. 5.35–5.5; W. OF HOOP 0.85;
> TH. OF HOOP 0.15; WT. 23.82g
> Bloomington, Indiana University Art
> Museum
> Burton Y. Berry Collection, 76.95.114.A–B

PUBLISHED: W. Rudolph, *A Golden Legacy:*
Ancient Jewelry from the Burton Y. Berry Collection
(Bloomington, Ind., 1995), 189–190, no. 44.

GRAVESTONES

During the late fifth century and the fourth (ca. 430–317), a variety of stone gravestones marked the family plots along the main thoroughfares leading out of the city of Athens and various Attic *demes*. These markers included naiskoi with painted or sculpted figures, stelai with and without figural decoration, and marble vases, primarily lekythoi (see cat. 111) and loutrophoroi. About a third of the gravestones depicted children, and some showed only a child, thereby indicating that they were intended for children's graves. These are some of the most moving images of Greek children.

For children on grave stelai, see essay by Oakley, this volume.

122
Gravestone of the Boy Mnesikles
(see also color illus. p. 181)

This gravestone of Pentelic marble commemorates a three- to five-year-old boy called Mnesikles, whose name is inscribed on the lower part of the pediment that crowns the shaft (ΜΝΗΣΙΚΛΕΗΣ). Only the central *acroterion* atop the pediment remains. The boy is nude, with an *apiculate* (ending in a short point) headband, and he carries a mantle with his left hand over his left shoulder, both common motifs on children's gravestones. In his right he clutches the pole of his toy roller, a common attribute of very young boys and pictured elsewhere in this exhibition on Attic vases (see cats. 75, 101, and 115). The lower part of the pole between his legs and the section connecting to the wheel are not visible, suggesting that these details were originally painted, as were probably the straps of his sandals, of which only the soles remain. The sculptor has realistically rendered the squat proportions and pudgy, unarticulated musculature of a toddler, as well as the child's hairstyle, with short corkscrew locks covering the top of the back of the neck. The boy's face, however, is like that of an adult.

Single children represent a common subject for classical gravestones, and normally they are shown with toys and pets,

122

reflecting their world rather than their parents'. This imagery suggests that the parents, who chose the tombstone, wanted to remember their lost children as happy, playful tots, not as the adults they would never become. Similar figures are found on several other gravestones, indicating that this type may have been mass-produced.

> Attic Pentelic marble grave stele,
> ca. 400–350 B.C.E.
> H. 66.5; W. 27.5
> Princeton, N.J., Princeton University Art Museum
> Fowler McCormick, Class of 1921, Museum Purchase Fund, y1986–87
> From Attica

PUBLISHED: *Record of the Art Museum, Princeton University* 46, no. 1 (1987), 45 and 47; Hamilton 1992, 92 n. 28 and fig. 6; B. S. Ridgway and J. M. Berkin, *Greek Sculpture in the Art Museum, Princeton University: Greek Originals, Roman Copies, and Variants* (Princeton, 1994), 12–15, no. 2; CAT 0.928; B. S. Ridgway, *Fourth-Century Styles in Greek Sculpture* (Madison, Wis., 1997), 164–165 and pl. 36.

Mnesikles was also the name of the architect of the Propylaea, the Periclean gateway to the Athenian Acropolis, but there is no certain connection between this child and the architect. For children on grave stelai, see the article by Oakley in this volume, with bibliography. For other tombstones with a boy and toy roller, see

Paris, Musée de Louvre MND 1869 (CAT 0.926); Athens, Piraeus Museum 262 (CAT 0.927), and Athens, National Museum (CAT 0.929).

123
Gravestone of the Boy Apolexis

A nude boy, preserved from the buttocks up, stands in profile to the right. He holds up what may be a small bird or pouch of knucklebones in his left hand and stares intently at it. What he holds down in his right hand is uncertain. It may be the handle of a cart, or he may be touching the snout of a dog, most of whose body is lost. Birds and dogs are the most common combination of pets on children's gravestones (see cat. 124). Both his round face and the slightly fatty flesh are typical of preteen boys, and the braid running down the middle of his head likewise marks him as a child (see cats. 125 and 126).

This finely carved and sensitive rendering reflects very much the style of the Parthenon sculptures and is a good example of a *Bildfeldstele*—that is, one with a recessed figural panel, which in this case takes the form of an aedicula of a naiskos also carved in relief. On the naiskos's architrave below the pediment is inscribed the boy's name: Apolexis (ΑΠΟΛΗΞΙΣ). It is not an uncommon one in Attica.

> Attic Pentelic marble grave stele,
> ca. 400–375 B.C.E.
> H. 45.8; W. 35.9; D. 8.3
> Bloomington, Indiana University Art Museum
> V. G. Simkhovitch Collection, 63.105.33

PUBLISHED: CAT 0.705; *IG* II², 10711a; A. Calinescu, *Of Gods and Mortals: Ancient Art from the V. G. Simkhovitch Collection* (Bloomington, Ind., 1987), 6–7, fig. 5; W. Rudolph and A. Calinescu, *Ancient Art from the V. G. Simkhovitch Collection* (Bloomington, Ind., 1988), 32–33, no. 12; A. Scholl, *Die attischen Bildfeldstelen des 4. Jhs. v. Chr.: Untersuchungen zu den kleinformatigen Grabreliefs im spätklassischen Athen*, AM suppl. 17 (Berlin, 1996), 118, 320, no. 361, and pl. 33,1.

124

124

Gravestone of the Girl Melisto

(see also color illus. p. xviii)

This charming young girl of six to eight years old is happily engrossed with her playthings, her pleasure evident in the broad, happy smile upon her face. She stands in a three-quarter view to the right, with head nearly in profile, right leg drawn back. In her right hand she holds a bird toward which a Maltese dog with curled tail jumps, balancing itself on its hind legs. This is a common motif on children's gravestones. In her left hand the girl holds a small female figurine without clothes, arms, or the lower part of the legs. Recently it has been suggested that this is not a doll but a votive offering to ensure the girl's health, but this seems unlikely because of her age, the context, and the way that she stares at the figure with such affection (see cats. 68 and 72–74). She wears a belted chiton underneath a mantle, and several small holes in the background by her hair suggest that a metal *stephane* (marriage crown) once decorated her head.

Inscribed on the narrow architrave beneath the pediment of the naiskos is her name: Melisto daughter of Ktesikrates

from the deme of Potamios (ΜΕΛΙΣΤΩ ΚΤΗΣΙΚΡΑΤΟΥΣ ΠΟΤΑΜΙΟΥ). Potamios was not far from Brauron, and the girl's hairstyle—central part with locks combed straight back and ending in curls over the ears—is reminiscent of that found on statues of *arktoi* ("bears"), girls who served Artemis in her sanctuary at Brauron (see Neils, fig. 12, p. 152). These statues may have influenced the sculptor of this stele. Traces remain of an egg-and-dart pattern painted on the molding above the inscription.

> Attic marble grave stele, ca. 340 B.C.E.
> H. 95.5; W. 49.2
> Cambridge, Harvard University Art Museums, Arthur M. Sackler Museum Alpheus Hyatt Purchasing and Gifts for Special Uses Funds in memory of Katherine Brewster Taylor, as a tribute to her many years at the Fogg Museum, 1961.86

PUBLISHED: SEG 22.181; *Ars Antiqua III*, 29 April 1961, lot no. 22, pl. 9; J. G. Pedley, "An Attic Grave Stele in the Fogg Art Museum," HSCP 69 (1965), 259–267; D. Woysch-Méautis, *La représentation des animaux et des êtres fabuleux sur les monuments funéraires grecs: De l'époque archaïque à la fin du IVᵉ siècle av. J.-C.* (Lausanne, 1982), 119, no. 184 and pl. 27,184; Rühfel 1984a, 176–177, fig. 73; O. Cavalier, "Une stèle attique classique au Musée Calvet d'Avignon," RLouvre, 1988, 288, fig. 8; C. C. Vermeule and A. Brauer, *Stone Sculptures: The Greek, Roman, and Etruscan Collections of the Harvard University Art Museums* (Cambridge, Mass., 1990), 40, no. 24; CAT 0.915; Reilly 1997, 157–158, fig. 36.

125

Gravestone of the Girl Demainete

(see also color illus. p. 183)

The young girl Demainete, daughter of Prokles, stands nearly frontally in a naiskos composed of an *anta* to either side crowned by a shallow architrave with her name (ΔΗΜΑΙΝΕΤΗ ΠΡΟΚΛΟΥΣ) inscribed on it below a roof whose *sima* has three *antefixes*. Dressed in a mantle and short-sleeved chiton that is girded above the waist and with shoulder cords, she smiles and bows her head down to look at the small, now headless, bird that she holds up in her right hand. The details of her feet are not

carved; rather, they remain blocklike, and there is a possible trace of a sole beneath her left foot, suggesting that she may have worn shoes or sandals. Running down the middle of her head is a braid that helps to keep her curly hair in place. Both boys and girls wore this hairstyle. Her left arm is covered by her mantle.

On the left stands a slave girl, as indicated by her short stature, her long-sleeved chiton—the *chiton cheirodotos*—and her shortly cropped hair. She holds a larger bird in her hands at her waist, possibly a duck or partridge, and looks up toward the girl. Sometimes adult servants are rendered diminutively, their size indicative not of age but of their servile status, but the shoulder cords suggest in this case that the servant is a child also. The rendering of her left foot indicates that she may, likewise, have worn shoes or sandals.

Birds were commonly depicted with children on gravestones, but usually there is only one. They were apparently perceived by the ancients as appropriate playthings for the dead, possibly because they, like the souls of the dead, were able to traverse

125

the air, thereby suggesting that they could accompany the dead to their new world. Fond of her small pet, this girl with her broad-faced, wide-eyed, smiling countenance must have left her parents with the image of a happy, playful child, just as did the girls on several other similar stelai.

Attic Pentelic marble grave stele,
ca. 310 B.C.E.
H. 96.5; W. 47.5; D. 15
Malibu, Calif., The J. Paul Getty Museum,
75.AA.63

PUBLISHED: *Recent Acquisitions of Antiquities: The J. Paul Getty Museum* (Malibu, Calif., 1976), 3, no. 2; SEG 33.222; CAT 0.909; M. J. Osbourne and S. B. Byrne, eds., *A Lexicon of Greek Personal Names*, vol. 2 (Oxford, 1994), 103, no. 10, s.v. Demainete, and 381, no. 59, s.v. Prokles; J. B. Grossman, *Greek Funerary Sculpture: Catalogue of the Collections at the Getty Villa* (Malibu, Calif., 2001), 69–70, no. 24.

For similar tombstones, see Athens, National Archaeological Museum, 895 (CAT 0.912); Athens, National Archaeological Museum, 892 + 3659 (CAT 0.911), and Athens, National Archaeological Museum, 2102 (CAT 0.890).

126

Gravestone of the Girl Apollonia
(see also color illus. p. 190)

The architrave atop the antae of this naiskos gives the name of the girl depicted: Apollonia the daughter of Aristandros and Thebageneia (ΑΠΟΛΛΟΝΙΑ ΑΡΙΣΤΑΝΔΡΟΥ ΚΑΙ ΘΗΒΑΓΕΝΕΙΑΣ). In a sleeveless chiton girt above the waist, mantle, and sandals, she stands nearly frontally, turning slightly to her right. With her right hand she reaches up to stroke the dove seated on a rectangular stele, and she holds a round fruit, probably a pomegranate, in her left hand. Both the dove and pomegranate are associated with Persephone, queen of the underworld, symbols that further associate the girl with the realm of death.

The bodily proportions of this still somewhat scrawny preteen are not that of an adult: her hands are large, she is tall and thin, and there is no sign that her breasts have started to develop. The central braid

running down the center of her head is a hairstyle worn by children and also featured on the gravestone of Demainete (cat. 125).

This is one of the finest of the very few Hellenistic gravestones from Athens. It was influenced by classical prototypes, but the grave monument has features common to other Hellenistic gravestones, such as the rectangular stele. The affection shown for the pet on the well-defined, three-quarter-view face of the girl makes this a touching memorial for a daughter who died well before her time. This image surely would have reminded her parents of the affection she once had for them. The four holes, two above on the antae, the others on the top corners of the field, were for metal pegs that held wreaths, fillets, and other gifts left at the tomb.

Attic marble grave stele (with polychrome),
ca. 100 B.C.E.
H. 112.4; W. 63.5; D. 20
Malibu, Calif., The J. Paul Getty Museum,
74.AA.13

PUBLISHED: *The J. Paul Getty Museum Guidebook* (Malibu, Calif., 1975), 31; Vermeule 202, no. 167; S. Lymeropoulos, *Untersuchungen zu den nachklassischen Attischen Grabreliefs unter besonderer Berücksichtigung der Kaiserzeit* (Hamburg, 1985), no. G1; I. Spiliopoulou-Donderer, "Das Grabrelief der Apollonia im J. Paul Getty Museum," in *Roman Funerary Monuments in the J. Paul Getty Museum*, vol. 1 (Malibu, Calif., 1990), 5–14; SEG 40.229; M. J. Osbourne and S. G. Byrne, eds., *A Lexicon of Greek Personal Names*, vol. 2 (Oxford, 1994), 44, s.v. Apollonia, and 51, s.v. Aristandros; J. B. Grossman, "Hellenistic Sculpted Funerary Monuments from the Athenian Agora," in O. Palagia and W. Coulson, eds., *Regional Schools in Hellenistic Sculpture: Proceedings of an International Conference Held at the American School of Classical Studies at Athens, March 15–17, 1996* (Oxford, 1998), 79–80 and fig. 11; D. W. von Moock, *Die figürlichen Grabstelen Attikas in der Kaiserzeit: Studien zur Vebreitung, Chronologie, Typologie und Ikonographie* (Mainz, 1998), 27 n. 328, 35, 52 n. 635, 78 n. 928–929, and 170, no. 450; J. B. Grossman, *Greek Funerary Sculpture: Catalogue of the Collections at the Getty Villa* (Malibu, Calif., 2001), 95–97, no. 35. B. S. Ridgway, *Hellenistic Sculpture III: The Styles of ca. 100–31 B.C.* (Madison, Wis., 2002), 217, pls. 96a–b.

For doves, see D. Woysch-Méautis, *La représentation des animaux et des êtres fabuleux sur les monuments funéraires grec de l'époque archaïque à la fin du IVe siècle av. J.-C.* (Lausanne, 1982), 50–51. For pomegranates, see F. Muthmann, *Der Granatapfel: Symbol des Lebens in der alten Welt* (Bern, 1982), 77–99, for the fruit's funerary uses.

126

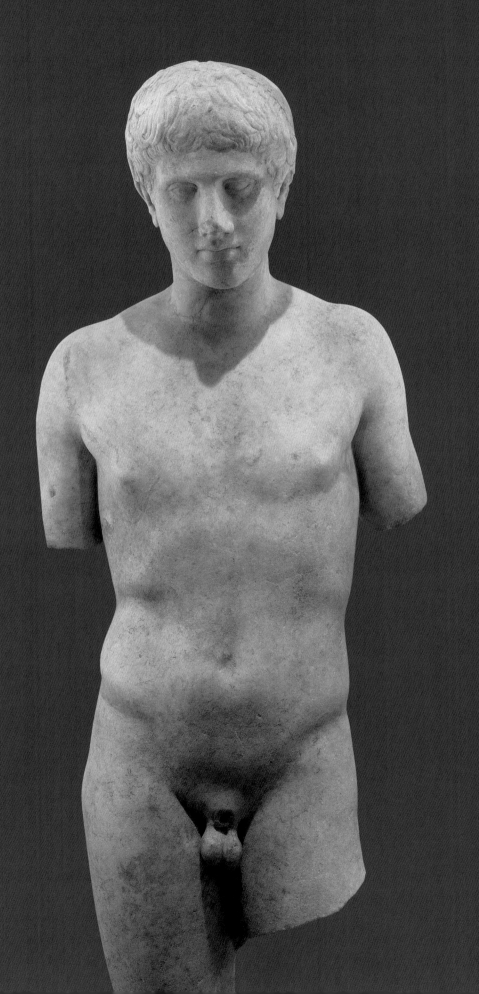

ADOLESCENCE was certainly far different in antiquity from what it is today. Not only did children come of age much earlier, but adult status was not legally defined; rather it varied according to class and gender. For lower-class Greeks and slave children the marking of life's transitions was probably a luxury they could not afford. Already at a young age these children, male and female, worked alongside adults in the household, the workshop, the stables, and the fields (see cats. 61–66).

The wealthy or elite Greek boy enjoyed a long adolescence involving a gradual acculturation to the civic and social responsibilities that marked the adult male's public life. At the age of sixteen the Athenian youth was officially admitted to the *phratry*, or clan, though a symbolic hair-cutting ritual. In his eighteenth year he was enrolled in his family's *deme*, or township, as an Athenian citizen and acquired voting rights and obligations. At this point he was required to fulfill two years of military service as an *ephebe*, a period during which, for the first time, he spent time away from his family and among his peers. Thus an Athenian boy had an extended period during which he was prepared to take on the public responsibilities of his adult life.

A Greek woman had a considerably shorter and more private childhood than a man. Her transition to adulthood occurred at marriage, which took place as early as the age of fourteen or fifteen, often with a man twice her age. The transition was also a physical one, from the household of her childhood to that of her new husband (see cat. 110), so rather than gaining independence she simply exchanged masters. Her completion of this transition was effected by the birth of a child, preferably male. Only at this point did she became a *gyne* or woman.

For the transition to adulthood, see Garland 1990, 163–198; Beaumont 2000.

For the marriage age of Athenian girls, see Ingalls 2001, who argues that only the most elite married early.

127
Youth

An introspective mood characterizes this statue of an adolescent boy, the style of which is derived from that of the famous Argive sculptor Polykleitos. Although the body's lower arms and legs are missing, his stance can be reconstructed. He bears his weight on his straight right leg, and his left leg is bent at the knee and drawn back slightly, thus creating a contrapposto shift in the hips. His arms are lowered at his sides. His head is turned slightly, giving him a serious, pensive look. His body type is that of a young athlete; note in particular the prominent iliac crest. His hair is short and curly in the style of the late fifth-century Polykleitan athletes.

This statue is a Roman copy either of a work by the master sculptor of Polykleitos himself or by one of his followers, and was probably carved in Greece in the Hadrianic period. It was later altered into a figure of Eros by the addition of wings on the back; the cuttings are still visible. With its delicate facial features and young athletic body, this marble youth captures the Greek male ideal of a thoughtful mind in a healthy body. On the verge of adulthood, he is poised to compete equally in athletic competitions or on the battlefield.

> Marble statue, Roman copy of a Greek original of ca. 430 B.C.E.
> H. 92.7
> Pittsburgh, Carnegie Museum of Art
> AODA Purchase Fund, 1971, 71.16
> Allegedly found near Olympia

PUBLISHED: D. T. Owsley, *Carnegie Magazine* 46 (1972), 16–22; C. C. Vermeule *Greek and Roman Sculpture in America* (Berkeley, 1981), 52, no. 25 (with earlier bibliography); B. S. Ridgway, *Fifth*

127

Century Styles in Greek Sculpture (Princeton, 1981), 216 no. 3, figs. 138–141.

For Polykleitos see C. C. Vermeule, *Polykleitos* (Boston, 1969); H. Beck et al., eds., *Polyklet, Der Bildhauer der griechischen Klassik*, exhib. cat. (Frankfurt, 1990); W. G. Moon, ed., *Polykleitos, the Doryphoros, and Tradition* (Madison, Wis., 1995).

128
Bridal Scenes

The preparation of the bride is one of the most common wedding scenes on Attic vases, and the attention focused on the bride underscores the importance of this event, because it represents her transition to adulthood and to a new home. The *lebes gamikos*, or wedding bowl, was a special ritual vase used in connection with the wedding, although its exact function is unknown. Primarily decorated with wedding imagery, the vase survives in two variants, one with a high stand, as in this vase, the other without. Three scenes decorate this vessel. On one side a seated woman, probably the bride, sits on a

OVERLEAF

CAT. 127 Youth, marble statue, Roman copy of a Greek original of ca. 430 B.C.E. Pittsburgh, Carnegie Museum of Art, AODA Purchase Fund

128a   128b

klismos looking at herself in the mirror, flanked by two females. The taller one on the left may by the *nympheutria* (woman responsible for adorning the bride), while the shorter one may be a teenaged girl (a sister?).

A similar three-figured composition is found on the other side. In this case the woman, the bride, is seated to the left. She may have just received a wooden casket from the woman in *peplos* standing before her, who looks down at her, gesturing with both hands. Another woman stands frontally behind the bride, turning to gesture with her right hand toward the other standing woman. This may be another scene of adornment, but more likely it is meant to recall the *epaulia*, the day after the wedding night when the bride received friends and relatives bringing gifts to her new home.

Underneath the handles on either side is a flying winged woman. These figures have been variously interpreted as Nikai (Victories) or underworld deities. Speaking for the latter interpretation is the altar beneath the figure underneath the right handle, because we know that some chthonic deities had to be propitiated before the wedding (Aeschylus, *Eumenides* 834–836).

Running around the conical stand is a mythological narrative frieze, with Peleus pursuing the sea nymph Thetis to the right.

She moves toward her father, the old man Nereus, while behind Peleus one of her companions flees, holding a floral in her right hand. The small dolphin between the companion and Nereus secures their identities as water divinities, for normally Peleus is shown having already closed with Thetis (cat. 14b), rather than still in hot pursuit as here. He has the traveler's attire of *chlamys*, *petasos* (hanging from his neck), and traveler's sandals, and he carries two spears in his right hand.

Pursuit scenes can be a metaphor for courtship, so that the bride in this case is subtly likened to Thetis. Thus the imagery on the vase represents three stages in the wedding, ranging from the beginning to the end: courtship, preparations for the wedding day, and the final day of the ritual. A similar program is found on one of the finest of all wedding vases, the *epinetron* (knee and lower thigh guard for woolworking) by the Eretria Painter.

> Attic red-figure lebes gamikos,
> ca. 440 B.C.E.
> H. 56.8; H. WITH LID 64.2; DIAM. 23.9
> Oxford, The University of Mississippi, University Museums
> David Moore Robinson Collection
> From a cemetery near Vari in Attica

PUBLISHED: *CVA* Robinson Collection 2 USA 6, 36–38 and pls. 50–51; D. Robinson, "A New Lebes Gamikos with a Possible Representation of Apollo and Daphne," *AJA* 40 (1936), 507–519, figs. 1–4; Reeder 1995, 229–231, no. 57.

For the lebes gamikos, see M. Sgourou, "Attic Lebetes Gamikoi" (Ph.D. diss., University of Cincinnati, 1994); and M. Sgourou, "Lebetes Gamikoi: O Gamos kai e attike kerameike paragoge ton klasikon chronon," in J. H. Oakley et al., eds., *Athenian Potters and Painters: The Conference Proceedings* (Oxford, 1997), 71–83. For the epinetron: Athens, National Museum 1629: *ARV*² 1250–1251,34 and 1688; *Para* 469; *BAdd*² 354; Lezzi-Hafter 1988, pls. 168–169; Oakley and Sinos 1993, figs. 128–130.

Abbreviations

AA
Archäologischer Anzeiger

AAA
Archaiologika Analekta ex Athenon
(Athens Annals of Archaeology)

ABL
C. H. E. Haspels, *Attic Black-Figured Lekythoi*
(Paris, 1936)

ABV
J. D. Beazley, *Attic Black-Figure Vase-Painters*
(Oxford, 1956)

AJA
American Journal of Archaeology

AJAH
American Journal of Ancient History

AM
Mitteilungen des Deutschen Archäologischen
Instituts, Athenische Abteilung

AncSoc
Ancient Society

AncW
The Ancient World

AntCl
L'antiquité classique

AntK
Antike Kunst

ArchDelt
Archaiologikon Deltion

ArchEph
Archaiologike Ephemeris

ArchReports
Archaeological Reports

ARV^2
J. D. Beazley, *Attic Red-Figure Vase-Painters*,
2d ed. (Oxford, 1963)

BABesch
Bulletin antieke beschaving: Annual Papers on
Classical Archaeology

BAdd^2
T. H. Carpenter, *Beazley Addenda*, 2d ed.
(Oxford, 1989)

BAGB
Bulletin de l'Association Guillaume Budé (Paris)

BAR-IS
British Archaeological Reports, International Series

BCH
Bulletin de correspondance hellénique

BICS
Bulletin of the Institute of Classical Studies of the
University of London

BSA
Annual of the British School at Athens

BWalt
Bulletin of the Walters Art Gallery

BWPr
Winckelmannsprogramm der archäologischen
Gesellschaft zu Berlin

CAF
Congrès archéologique de France

CAH
Cambridge Ancient History

C & M
Classica and Mediævalia: Revue danoise d'histoire
et de philologie publiée par la Société danoise pour
les études anciennes et médiévales (Copenhagen)

CAT
C. Clairmont, Classical Attic Tombstones
(Kilchberg, Switzerland, 1993)

CEG 1
P. A. Hansen, Carmina epigraphica graeca saecu-
lorum VIII–V a. Chr. n (Berlin, 1983)

CEG 2
P. A. Hansen, Carmina epigraphica graeca saeculi
IV a. Chr. n (Berlin, 1989)

CJ
Classical Journal

CMS
Corpus der minoischen und mykenischen Siegel

CQ
Classical Quarterly

CVA
Corpus Vasorum Antiquorum

EAA
Enciclopedia dell'arte antica, classica e orientale
(Rome, 1958–1984)

EJA
European Journal of Archaeology

EMC
Echos du monde classique / Classical views

FGrH
F. Jacoby, Fragmente der griechischen Historiker
(Berlin, 1923–1958)

G&R
Greece and Rome (Oxford)

GBA
Gazette des beaux Arts

GettyMusJ
The J. Paul Getty Museum Journal

HSCP
Harvard Studies in Classical Philology

IG
Inscriptiones Graecae

JdI
Jahrbuch des deutschen archäologischen Instituts

JHS
Journal of Hellenic Studies

JIES
Journal of Indo-European Studies

JWalt
Journal of the Walters Art Gallery

LEC
Les études classiques

LIMC
Lexicon Iconographicum, Mythologiae Classicae
(Zurich, 1981–1997)

OJA
Oxford Journal of Archaeology

OPA
Occasional Papers on Antiquities

Para
J. D. Beazley, Paralipomena (Oxford, 1971)

PCG
Poetae Comici Graeci

PZ
Prähistorische Zeitschrift

RhM
Rheinisches Museum für Philologie

RLouvre
La revue du Louvre et des musées de France

RVAp
A. D. Trendall and A. Cambitoglou, The Red-
Figured Vases of Apulia (Oxford, 1978–1982)

SEG
Supplementum Epigraphicum Graecum

SIMA
Studies in Mediterranean Archaeology

TAPA
Transactions of the American Philological
Association

ZPE
Zeitschrift für Papyrologie und Epigraphik

BIBLIOGRAPHY

ARIÈS, P. 1962. *Centuries of Childhood: A Social History of Family Life*. Trans. Robert Baldick. London.

ASHMEAD, A. 1978. "Greek Cats: Exotic Pets Kept by Rich Youths in Fifth Century B.C. Athens, as Portrayed on Greek Vases." *Expedition* 20, no. 1: 38–47.

BARROW, R. 1976. *Greek and Roman Education*. Basingstoke, England.

BARTSOCAS, C. 1978. "Ancient Greek Feeding-bottles." *Transactions and Studies of the College of Physicians of Philadelphia* 45: 297–327.

BAZANT, J. 1975. "The Iconography of the Choes Reconsidered." *Listy Filologicke* 98: 72–78.

———. 1985. *Les Citoyens sur les vases athéniens*. Prague.

BEAUMONT, L. 1994. "Constructing a Methodology for the Interpretation of Childhood Age in Classical Athenian Iconography." *Archaeological Review from Cambridge* 13, no. 2: 81–96.

———. 1995. "Mythological Childhood: A Male Preserve? An Interpretation of Classical Athenian Iconography in Its Socio-Historical Context." *BSA* 90: 339–361.

———. 1998. "Born Old or Never Young? Femininity, Childhood, and the Goddesses of Ancient Greece." In S. Blundell and M. Williamson, eds., *The Sacred and the Feminine in Ancient Greece*, 71–95. London.

———. 2000. "The Social Status and Artistic Representations of 'Adolescence' in Fifth Century Athens." In Sofaer Derevenski 2000, 39–50.

BECK, F. A. G. 1964. *Greek Education, 450–350 B.C.* New York.

———. 1975. *Album of Greek Education: The Greeks at School and at Play*. Sydney.

BEER, C. 1987. "Comparative Votive Religion: The Evidence of Children in Cyprus, Greece, and Etruria." In T. Linders and G. Nordquist, eds., *Gifts to the Gods*, Boreas 15: 21–29.

———. 1994. *Temple-Boys: A Study of Cypriote Votive Sculpture*. Jonsered, Sweden.

BERTMAN, S., ed. 1976. *The Conflict of Generations in Ancient Greece and Rome*. Amsterdam.

BIEBER, M. 1961. *The Sculpture of the Hellenistic Age*. Rev. ed. New York.

BILLIGMEIER, J.-C. 1985. "Studies on the Family in the Aegean Bronze Age and in Homer." *Trends in History* 3: 9–18.

BOAK, A. E. R. 1921. "Greek and Coptic School Tablets at the University of Michigan." *Classical Philology* 16: 189–194.

BONFANTE, L. 1997. "Nursing Mothers in Classical Art." In A. O. Koloski-Ostrow and C. L. Lyons, eds., *Naked Truths: Women, Sexuality, and Gender in Classical Art and Archaeology*, 174–196. London.

BOOTH, A. D. 1985. "Douris' Cup and the Stages of Schooling in Classical Athens." *EMC* 29: 274–280.

BRELICH, A. 1969. *Paides e Parthenoi*. Rome.

BREMMER, J. N. 1999. "Fosterage, Kinship, and the Circulation of Children in Ancient Greece." *Dialogos* 6: 1–20.

BRULÉ, P. 1987. *La Fille d'Athènes: La religion des filles à Athènes à l'époque classique: Mythes, cultes et société*. Paris.

BRYANT, A. A. 1907. "Boyhood and Youth in the Days of Aristophanes." *HSCP* 18: 73–122.

BURKERT, W. 1985. *Greek Religion: Archaic and Classical*. Oxford.

CALAME, C. 1994. *Choruses of Young Women in Ancient Greece: Their Morphology, Religious Role, and Social Function*. Trans. Derek Collins and Janice Orion. Lanham, Md.

COLE, S. G. 1984. "The Social Function of Rituals of Maturation: The Koureion and the Arkteia." *ZPE* 55: 233–244.

————. 1998. "Domesticating Artemis." In S. Blundell and M. Williamson, eds., *The Sacred and the Feminine in Ancient Greece*, 27–43. London.

COLLIN-BOUFFIER, S. 1999. "Des vases pour les enfants." In M.-C. Villanueva Puig et al., eds., *Céramique et peinture grècques: Modes d'emploi*, 91–96. Paris.

COLÓN, A. R., with P. A. COLÓN. 2001. *A History of Children: A Socio-Cultural Survey Across Millennia*. Westport, Conn.

COX, C. A. 1988. "Sibling Relationships in Classical Athens: Brother-Sister Ties." *Journal of Family History* 13, no. 4: 377–395.

————. 1998. *Household Interests: Property, Marriage Strategies, and Family Dynamics in Ancient Athens*. Princeton.

CRIBIORE, R. 1996. *Writing, Teachers, and Students in Graeco-Roman Egypt*. American Studies in Papyrology 36. Atlanta.

————. 2001. *Gymnastics of the Mind: Greek Education in Hellenistic and Roman Egypt*. Princeton.

CUNNINGHAM, H. 1998. "Histories of Childhood." *American Historical Review* 103: 1195–1208.

DAKORONIA, F., AND L. GOUNAROPOULOU. 1992. "Artemiskult auf einem Weihrelief aus Archinos bei Lamia." *AM* 107: 217–227.

DASEN, V. 1997. "Multiple Births in Graeco-Roman Antiquity." *OJA* 16: 49–63.

————. 2001. "Dix ans de travaux sur l'enfance." *Annales de Démographie historique* 2001–2002: 5–100.

DAVIS, E. 1986. "Youth and Age in the Thera Frescoes." *AJA* 90: 399–406.

DEMAND, N. 1994. *Birth, Death, and Motherhood in Classical Greece*. Baltimore.

DEMAUSE, L. 1974. *The History of Childhood*. New York.

DEUBNER, L. 1932. *Attische Feste*. Berlin.

DIETRICH, B. C. 1961. "A Rite of Swinging During the Anthesteria." *Hermes* 89: 36–50.

DILLON, M. 2000. "Did Parthenoi Attend the Olympic Games? Girls and Women Competing, Spectating, and Carrying Out Cult Roles at Greek Religious Festivals." *Hermes* 128: 457–480.

————. 2002. *Girls and Women in Classical Greek Religion*. London.

DONNAY, G. 1997. "L'Arrhéphorie: Initiation ou rite civique? Un cas d'école." *Kernos* 10: 177–205.

DÖRIG, J. 1958. "Von griechischen Puppen." *AntK* 1: 41–52.

ELDERKIN, K. 1930. "Jointed Dolls in Antiquity." *AJA* 34: 455–479.

ENGELS, D. 1980. "The Problem of Female Infanticide in the Graeco-Roman World." *Classical Philology* 75: 112–120.

FARAONE, C. A. 2003. "Playing the Bear and Fawn for Artemis: Female Initiation or Substitute Sacrifice?" In D. Dodds and C. A. Faraone, eds., *Initiation in Ancient Greek Rituals and Narratives: New Critical Perspectives*. London.

FILDES, V. A. 1986. *Breasts, Bottles, and Babies: A History of Infant Feeding*. Edinburgh.

————. 1988. *Wet Nursing: A History from Antiquity to the Present*. Oxford.

FITTÀ, M. 1997. *Giochi e giocattoli nell'antichità*. Milan.

FOLEY, H., ed. 1994. *The Homeric Hymn to Demeter: Translation, Commentary, and Interpretive Essays*. Princeton.

FRENCH, V. 1977. "History of the Child's Influence: Ancient Mediterranean Civilizations." In R. Q. Bell and L. V. Harper, eds., *Child Effects on Adults*, 3–29. Hillsdale, N.J.

GARLAND, R. 1985. *The Greek Way of Death*. Ithaca, N.Y.

————. 1990. *The Greek Way of Life: From Conception to Old Age*. Ithaca, N.Y.

GATES, C. 1992. "Art for Children in Mycenaean Greece." In R. Laffineur and J. L. Crowley, eds., *EIKON: Aegean Bronze Age Iconography: Shaping a Methodology*. Aegaeum 8: 161–171. Liège.

GEAGAN, D. J. 1994. "Children in Athenian Dedicatory Monuments." *Boeotia antique* 4: 163–173.

GERMAIN, L. R. F. 1975. "L'exposition des enfants nouveau-nés dans la Grèce ancienne: Aspects sociologiques." *Recueils de la Société Jean Bodin* 35: 211–242.

GOLDEN, M. 1981. "Demography and the Exposure of Girls at Athens." *Phoenix* 35: 316–331.

————. 1985. "Pais, 'child' and 'slave.'" *AntCl* 54: 91–104.

————. 1986. "Names and Naming at Athens: Three Studies." *EMC* 5: 245–269.

————. 1990. *Children and Childhood in Classical Athens*. Baltimore.

————. 1995. "Baby Talk and Child Language in Ancient Greece." In F. de Martino and A. H. Sommerstein, eds., *Lo spettacolo delle voci*, 11–34. Bari, Italy.

————. 1997. "Change or Continuity? Children and Childhood in Hellenistic Historiography." In M. Golden and P. Toohey, eds., *Inventing Ancient Culture: Historicism, Periodization, and the Ancient World*, 176–191. London.

GOULD, D. W. 1980. "The Uncertain Fate of a Princely Diversion: An Historical Survey of Tops." *Expedition* 22, no. 3: 43–47.

GOUREVITCH, D., AND J. CHAMAY. 1992. "Femme nourrissant son enfant au biberon." *AntK* 35, no. 1: 78–81, pl. 19.

GREEN, R. 1971. "Choes of the Later Fifth Century." *BSA* 66: 189–228, pls. 30–33.

HADZISTELIOU-PRICE, T. 1978. *Kourotrophos: Cults and Representations of the Greek Nursing Deities*. Leiden.

HÄGG, R., ED. In press. *The Child in Greek Cult*. Acta Atheniensia 8.

HAM, G. L. 1999. "The Choes and Anthesteria Reconsidered: Male Maturation Rites and the Peloponnesian Wars." In Padilla 1999, 201–218.

HAMDORF, F. W. 1996. *Hauch des Prometheus: Meisterwerke in Ton*. Munich.

HAMILTON, R. 1984. "Sources for the Athenian Amphidromia." *Greek, Roman, and Byzantine Studies* 25: 243–251.

————. 1989. "Alkman the Athenian Arkteia." *Hesperia* 58: 449–453.

————. 1992. *Choes and Anthesteria: Athenian Iconography and Ritual*. Ann Arbor, Mich.

HANI, J. 1978. "La fête athénienne de l'Aiora et le symbolisme de la balançoire." *Revue des études grecques* 91: 107–122.

HARCOURT-SMITH, C. 1929. "Whip-Tops." *JHS* 49: 217–219.

HARRIS, H. A. 1972. *Sport in Greece and Rome*. Ithaca, N.Y.

HARRIS, W. V. 1982. "The Theoretical Possibility of Extensive Infanticide in the Graeco-Roman World." *CQ* 32: 114–116.

HARRISON, E. B. 1988. "Greek Sculpted Coiffures and Ritual Haircuts." In R. Hägg et al., eds., *Early Greek Cult Practice: Proceedings of the Fifth International Symposium at the Swedish Institute at Athens, 26–29 June 1986*, 247–254. Stockholm.

HARTEN, T. 1999. *Paidagogos: Der Pädagoge in der griechischen Kunst*. Kiel, Germany.

HIBLER, R. W. 1988. *Life and Learning in Ancient Athens*. Lanham, Md.

HIGGINS, R. 1986. *Tanagra and the Figurines*. London.

HIRSCH-DYCZEK, O. 1983. *Les Représentations des enfants sur les stèles funéraires attiques*. Warsaw.

HOORN, G. VAN. 1909. *De Vita atque Cultu Puerorum Monumentis Antiquis Explanato*. Amsterdam.

———. 1951. *Choes and Anthesteria*. Leiden.

HOUBY-NIELSEN, S. 2000. "Child Burials in Ancient Athens." In Sofaer Derevenski 2000, 151–166.

HRDY, S. B. 1999. *Mother Nature: A History of Mothers, Infants, and Natural Selection*. New York.

HUMPHREYS, S. 1978. *Anthropology and the Greeks*. London.

———. 1983. *The Family, Women, and Death: Comparative Studies*. London.

HUYS, M. 1996. "The Spartan Practice of Selective Infanticide and Its Parallels in Ancient Utopian Tradition." *AncSoc* 27: 47–74.

IMMERWAHR, H. R. 1964. "Book Rolls on Attic Vases." In C. Henderson, Jr., ed., *Classical, Mediaeval, and Renaissance Studies in Honor of Berthold Louis Ullman*, vol. 1, 17–48. Rome.

———. 1973. "More Book Rolls on Attic Vases." *AntK* 16: 143–147.

INGALLS, W. B. 1998. "Attitudes Towards Children in the Iliad." *EMC* 17: 13–34.

———. 2000. "Ritual Performance as Training for Daughters in Archaic Greece." *Phoenix* 54: 1–20.

———. 2001. "PAIDA NEAN MALISTA: When Did Athenian Girls Really Marry?" *Mouseion* 1: 17–29.

JEANMAIRE, H. 1939. *Couroi et Courètes: Essai sur l'éducation spartiate et les rites d'adolescense dans l'antiquité hellénique*. Lille.

JENKINS, I. 1986. *Greek and Roman Life*. Cambridge, Mass.

JENKINS, I., AND S. BIRD. 1982. *An Athenian Childhood*. London.

JOHNSTON, S. I. 2001. "Charming Children: The Use of the Child in Ancient Divination." *Arethusa* 34: 97–117.

JURRIAANS-HELLE, G., ED. 2001. *Jong in de oudheid*. Allard Pierson Museum exhib. cat. Amsterdam.

KAHIL, L. 1965. "Autour de l'Artémis attique," *AntK* 8: 20–33, pls. 7–10.

———. 1977. "L'Artémis de Brauron: Rites et mystère." *AntK* 20: 86–98.

———. 1983. "Mythological Repertoire of Brauron." In W. G. Moon, ed., *Ancient Greek Art and Iconography*, 231–244. Madison, Wis.

KARRAS, M., AND J. WIESEHÖFER. 1981. *Kindheit und Jugend in der Antike: Eine Bibliographie*. Bonn.

KEARNS, E. 1989. *The Heroes of Attica*. London.

KENNELL, N. M. 1995. *The Gymnasium of Virtue: Education and Culture in Ancient Sparta*. Chapel Hill, N.C.

KERN, J. H. C. 1957. "An Attic Feeding Bottle of the 4th Century B.C. in Leyden." *Mnemosyne* 10: 16–21.

KLEIN, A. E. 1932. *Child Life in Greek Art*. New York.

KOCH-HARNACK, G. 1983. *Knabenliebe und Tiergeschenke: Ihre Bedeutung im päderastischen Erziehungssystem Athens*. Berlin.

KOLIADES, M. G. 1988. *Die Jugend im Athen der klassischen Zeit*. Frankfurt.

KURTZ, D. C., AND J. BOARDMAN. 1971. *Greek Burial Customs*. Ithaca, N.Y.

LAAGER, J. 1957. *Geburt und Kindheit des Gottes in der griechischen Mythologie*. Winterthur, Switzerland.

LACEY, W. K. 1968. *The Family in Classical Greece*. Ithaca, N.Y.

LARSON, J. 1995. *Greek Heroine Cults*. Madison, Wis.

LEE, D. R. 1919. *Child-Life, Adolescence, and Marriage in Greek New Comedy and in the Comedies of Plautus: A Study of the Relations Represented as Existing Between Parents and Their Children*. Madison, Wis.

LEWIS, S. 2002. *The Athenian Woman*. London.

LEZZI-HAFTER, A. 1988. *Der Eretria-Maler*. Mainz.

LONSDALE, S. H. 1993. *Dance and Ritual Play in Greek Religion*. Baltimore.

MAKLER, P. T. 1980. "New Information on Nutrition in Ancient Greece." *Klio* 62: 317–319.

MARINATOS, S. 1968. "Aiora." *Antichthon* 2: 1–14.

MARROU, H. I. 1964. *A History of Education in Antiquity*. Trans. George Lamb. New York.

MASSAR, N. 1995. "Images de la famille sur les vases attiques à figures rouges à l'époque classique (480–430 av. J.-C.)." *Annales d'histoire de l'art et d'archeologie* 17: 27–38.

MAY, R., ET AL. 1992. *Jouer dans l'Antiquité*. Musée d'Archéologie Méditerranéenne exhib. cat. Marseille.

MCCLEES, H. 1925. *The Daily Life of the Greeks and Romans as Illustrated in the Classical Collections*. Metropolitan Museum of Art. New York.

MORRIS, I. 1987. *Burial and Ancient Society: The Rise of the Greek City-State*. Cambridge.

MÜHLBAUER, K. R., and T. Miller. 1988. "Spielzeug und Kult: Zur religiösen und kultischen Bedeutung von Kinderspielzeug in der griechischen Antike." *AJAH* 13, no. 2: 154–169, figs. 1–20.

MÜLLER, C. 1990. *Kindheit und Jugend in der griechischen Frühzeit: Eine Studie zur pädagogischen Bedeutung von Riten und Kulten*. Giessen, Germany.

NEILS, J., ED. 1996. *Worshipping Athena: Panathenaia and Parthenon*. Madison, Wis.

———. 2001. *The Parthenon Frieze*. New York.

OAKLEY, J., AND R. SINOS. 1993. *The Wedding in Ancient Athens*. Madison, Wis.

OLDENZIEL, R. 1987. "The Historiography of Infanticide in Antiquity: A Literature Stillborn." In J. Blok and P. Mason, eds., *Sexual Asymmetry: Studies in Ancient Society*, 87–90. Amsterdam.

OLSEN, B. A. 1998. "Women, Children, and the Family in the Late Aegean Bronze Age: Differences in Minoan and Mycenaean Constructions of Gender." *World Archaeology* 29: 380–392.

PADILLA, M. W., ED. 1999. *Rites of Passage in Ancient Greece: Literature, Religion, Society*. Lewisburg, Pa.

PALAGIA, O. 1995. "Akropolis Museum 581: A Family at the Apaturia?" *AJA* 64: 493–501, pls. 114–116.

PARADISO, A. 1988. "L'Agregation du nouveau-né au foyer familial: Les Amphidromies." *Dialogues d'histoire ancienne* 14: 203–218.

PARKE, H. W. 1977. *Festivals of the Athenians*. London.

PATTERSON. C. B. 1998. *The Family in Greek History*. Cambridge, Mass.

PERCY, W. A. III. 1996. *Pederasty and Pedagogy in Archaic Greece*. Champaign-Urbana, Ill.

PERLMAN, P. 1989. "Acting the She-Bear for Artemis." *Arethusa* 22: 111–133.

PINGIATOGLOU, S. 1981. *Eileithyia*. Würzburg, Germany.

PINNEY, G. F., AND B. S. RIDGWAY. 1979. *Aspects of Ancient Greece*. Allentown Art Museum exhib. cat. Allentown, Pa.

POLLITT, J. J. 1986. *Art in the Hellenistic Age.* Cambridge.

POMEROY, S. B. 1975. "Technikai kai Mousikai: The Education of Women in the Fourth Century and in the Hellenistic Period." *AJAH* 2: 51–68.

———. 1984. *Women in Hellenistic Egypt: From Alexander to Cleopatra.* New York.

———. 1997. *Families in Classical and Hellenistic Greece: Representations and Realities.* Oxford.

RAFTOPOULOU, E. G. 2001. *Figurines enfantines du Musée National d'Athènes.* Munich.

REEDER, E. D. 1995. *Pandora: Women in Classical Greece.* Princeton.

REILLY, J. 1997. "Naked and Limbless: Learning About the Feminine Body in Ancient Athens." In A. O. Koloski-Ostrow and C. L. Lyons, eds., *Naked Truths: Women, Sexuality, and Gender in Classical Art and Archaeology,* 154–173. London.

REINSBERG, C. 1993. *Ehe, Hetärentum und Knabenliebe im antiken Griechenland.* Munich.

ROBERTSON, N. 1983. "The Riddle of the Arrhephoria at Athens." *HSCP* 87: 241–288.

ROCCOS, L. 1995. "The Kanephoros and Her Festival Mantle in Greek Art." *AJA* 99, no. 4: 641–666.

ROSEMANN, G. 1993. *Spielzeug der Antike: Austellung des Hessischen Puppenmuseums, 4.7–31.10 1993.* Hanau-Wilhelmsbad, Germany.

ROSOKOKI, A. 1995. *Die Erigone des Eratosthenes.* Heidelberg.

RÜHFEL, H. 1984a. *Das Kind in der griechischen Kunst von der minoisch-mykenischen Zeit bis zum Hellenismus.* Mainz.

———. 1984b. *Kinderleben im klassischen Athen: Bilder auf klassischen Vasen.* Mainz.

SALZA PRINA RICOTTI, E. 1995. *Giochi e giocattoli.* Rome.

SAVAGE, C. A. 1907. *The Athenian Family: A Sociological and Legal Study, Based Chiefly on the Works of the Attic Orators.* Baltimore.

SCANLON, T. F. 1984. "The Footrace of the Heraia at Olympia." *AncW* 9: 77–90.

———. 1990. "Race or Chase at the Arkteia of Attica?" *Nikephoros* 3: 73–120.

SCHLÖRB-VIERNEISEL, B. 1964. "Zwei klassische Kindergraeber im Kerameikos." *AM* 79: 85–104.

SCHMIDT, E. 1971. *Spielzeug und Spiele der Kinder im klassischen Altertum.* Meiningen, Germany.

SCHMIDT, M. 1983. "Hephaistos Lebt-Untersuchungen zur Frage der Behandlung behinderter Kinder in der Antike." *Hephaistos* 5–6: 133–161.

SCHMIDT, R. 1977. *Darstellung von Kinderspielzeug und Kinderspiel in der griechischen Kunst.* Vienna.

SCHNAPP, A. 1997. "Images of Young People in the Greek City-State." In G. Levi and J.-C. Schmitt, eds., *A History of Young People in the West,* 12–50. Cambridge, Mass.

SCHULZE, H. 1998. *Ammen und Pädagogen: Sklavinnen und Sklaven als Erzieher in der antiken Kunst und Gesellschaft.* Mainz.

SCOTT, E. 1999. *The Archaeology of Infancy and Infant Death.* Oxford.

SERWINT, N. 1993. "The Female Athletic Costume at the Heraia and Prenuptial Initiation Rites." *AJA* 97: 403–422.

SHAPIRO, H. A. 1981. "Courtship Scenes in Attic Vase-Painting," *AJA* 85: 133–143, pls. 24–28.

———. 1995. "The Cult of Heroines: Kekrops' Daughters." In Reeder 1995, 39–48.

SIMON, E. 1983. *Festivals of Attica.* Madison, Wis.

SISSA, G. 1996. "The Family in Ancient Athens (Fifth and Fourth Century BC)." In A. Burguière et al., eds., *A History of the Family,* 194–227. Cambridge.

SLATER, P. 1968. *The Glory of Hera: Greek Mythology and the Greek Family.* Boston.

SOFAER DEREVENSKI, J., ED. 2000. *Children and Material Culture.* London.

SOURVINOU-INWOOD, C. 1988. *Studies in Girls' Transitions: Aspects of the Arkteia and Age Representation in Attic Iconography.* Athens.

———. 1990. "Ancient Rites and Modern Constructs: On the Brauronian Bears Again." *BICS* 37: 1–14.

SPRAGUE, R. K. 1984. "Plato and Children's Games." In D. E. Gerber, ed., *Greek Poetry and Philosophy,* 275–284. Chico, Calif.

STEHLE, E. 2001. "The Good Daughter: Mothers' Tutelage in Erinna's *Distaff* and Fourth-Century Epitaphs." In A. Lardinois and L. M. McClure, eds., *Making Silence Speak: Women's Voices in Greek Literature and Society,* 179–200. Princeton.

STERN, M. 1978. "Kinderkännchen zum Choenfest," *Castrum Peregrini* 132, no. 3: 27–37.

STRAUSS, B. S. 1993. *Fathers and Sons in Athens: Ideology and Society in the Era of the Peloponnesian War.* Princeton.

SUTTON, R. F. 2003. "Family Portraits: Recognizing the *Oikos* on Attic Red-figure Pottery." In A. Chapin, ed., *Charis: Essays in Honor of Sara A. Immerwahr,* Hesperia supple 33.

TAZELAAR, C. M. 1967. "Paides kai Epheboi: Some Notes on the Spartan Stages of Youth." *Mnemosyne* 20: 127–153.

THOMPSON, D. B. 1982. "A Dove for Dione." *Studies in Athenian Architecture, Sculpture, and Topography.* Hesperia suppl. 20: 155–162, pls. 23–27.

TOO, Y. L., ED. 2001. *Education in Greek and Roman Antiquity.* Leiden.

TRENDALL, A. D., AND G. SCHNEIDER-HERMANN. 1975. "Eros with a Whipping-Top on an Apulian Pelike." *BABesch* 2: 267–282.

TRESS, D. M. 1997. "Aristotle's Child: Development Through Genesis, Oikos, and Polis." *Ancient Philosophy* 17: 63–84.

UHLENBROCK, J. P. 1990. *The Coroplast's Art: Greek Terracottas of the Hellenistic World.* College Art Gallery, The College at New Paltz, State University of New York, exhib. cat. New Rochelle, N.Y.

VANHOVE, D., ED. 1992. *Le Sport dans la Grèce antique: Du jeu à la compétition.* Palais des Beaux-Arts exhib. cat. Brussels.

VAN STRATEN, F. T. 1995. *Hierà kalá: Images of Animal Sacrifice in Archaic and Classical Greece.* Leiden.

VOLLKOMMER, R. 2000. "Mythological Children in Archaic Art: On the Problem of Age Differentiation for Small Children." In G. R. Tsetskhladze et al., eds., *Periplous: Papers on Classical Art and Archaeology Presented to Sir John Boardman,* 371–382. New York.

VORSTER, C. 1983. *Griechische Kinderstatuen.* Cologne.

WÆRN, I. 1960. "Greek Lullabies." *Eranos* 58: 1–8.

WEBSTER, T. B. L. 1969. *Everyday Life in Classical Athens.* London.

WICKES, I. G. 1953. "A History of Infant Feeding." Part 1, "Primitive Peoples, Ancient Works, Renaissance Writers." *Archives of Disease in Childhood* 28: 151–158.

WILLIAMS, D. 2000. "Of Geometric Toys, Symbols and Votives." In G. R. Tsetskhladze et al., eds., *Periplous: Papers on Classical Art and Archaeology Presented to Sir John Boardman,* 388–396. London.

GLOSSARY

aetion—foundation legend

ageneios (pl. *ageneioi*)—literally, beardless; age designation for young men

agoge—educational system for Spartan boys

agora—marketplace

Aiora—(1) a festival at Athens commemorating Erigone; (2) swing

akroterion—decoration at the corners of a *pediment*

alabastron—slender, cylindrical oil or perfume vase

amis—chamber pot

Amphidromia—a family festival in Athens during which a newborn infant was officially incorporated into the household and carried by its nurse around the hearth

amphora—a pot with two vertical handles used for holding wine, olive oil, or other liquids and foods

andron—main dining and entertaining room in a Greek house

anta (pl. *antae*)—the slightly thickened ends of the walls in Greek and Roman buildings

antefix—decorative plaques on the edges of a roof that serve to cover the ends and joint of the roofing tiles

Anthesteria—three-day festival of Dionysos celebrated in the spring; the second day, named Choes, involved drinking parties, with competition in the draining of a *chous*

Apatouria—feast during which fathers officially enrolled their children as members of the *phratry*

apobates—armed men who jump from a moving chariot

architrave—a horizontal beam forming the lowest element of the entablature, which rested directly on the capitals of the columns and *antae*

Archon Basileus—annual ruler at Athens in charge of religious matters

arete—virtue, excellence, goodness, manly diginity

Arkteia—a female ritual chiefly at Brauron, in celebration of Artemis, that marked a change in biological status for girls

arktos (pl. *arkteia*)—"bear"; the girls in the *Arkteia* ritual were called "little bears" and performed ritual acts in a bearlike manner

arrephoros (pl. *arrephoroi*)—literally, bearer of secret things; a ritual position held by girls between the ages of seven and eleven chosen by the *Archon Basileus* to serve Athena Polias. The girls lived on the Acropolis assisting the priestess of Athena Polias in ritual duties, including the weaving of the *peplos*

aryballos—small oil or perfume vessel with a pointed conical or round body and short and narrow neck

astragaloi—the knucklebones of sheep and goats used to play games

Attic—from Attica, the region surrounding the city of Athens

aulos—the Greek double flute

baskania—beads and pendants on a child's necklace meant to be protective against malice

bibasis—Spartan dance, practiced by both men and women, wherein the feet touch the buttocks

Bildfeldstele—a *stele* with a sunken rectangular picture field

brephos—embryo, foetus, or newborn

chernips—the water used to purify and cleanse hands before sacrifice

chiton—a long tunic dress of linen, usually worn by women

chiton cheirodotos—*chiton* with long sleeves, worn by slaves and other servants

chlamys—cloak worn by young men, horsemen, and soldiers, normally fastened by a brooch at the shoulder

choregos (pl. *choregoi*)—rich citizen responsible for paying for the training of a chorus for festival competitions

chous (pl. *choes*)—a form of *oinochoe* with trefoil mouth, used especially during the *Anthesteria*

chytra—kettle

cista—box, basket, or casket, often cylindrical in shape

coroplast—craftsperson specializing in molding *terracotta* or clay, particularly into figurines

deme—township in Athens and Attica; the basic administrative unit

dexiosis—handshake of right hands, frequently depicted on grave *stelai* taking place between the deceased and living family members

didaskalos—teacher

dike—justice; law; right; a lawful action raised against a transgressor

diphros—a backless chair or stool

drachma—Greek silver coin

eidolon (pl. *eidola*)—image representing the soul

eispnelas—literally, one who inspires love; an older youth acting as both lover and mentor to a younger boy

ekphora—funerary procession from the dead person's home to the graveyard

endyma—burial shroud around a corpse

ephebos (pl. *epheboi*)—a boy who has reached puberty, who in Athens entered a two-year period of military training

ephedrismos—game similar to piggy-back

epiblema—loose cloth placed over the corpse during burial

erastes—literally, lover; the older man in a Greek homosexual relationship

eromenos—literally, beloved; the younger male in a Greek homosexual relationship

exomis—Greek tunic without sleeves often worn by fishermen and other outdoorsmen, as well as manual laborers

extispicy—the foretelling of the future by examination of the entrails of a sacrificial animal

genethlia—gifts given on the birthday (genethliacon)

genos—family group descending from the same ancestor

geranos—"crane" dance, celebrating the rescue of the fourteen Athenian youths and maidens from the Cretan labyrinth

grammatistes—teacher in charge of reading and writing

gynaikeion—women's quarters in a Greek house

halteres—jumping weights

hamaxis (or *trochos*)—toy roller

hebe—puberty, traditionally set at fourteen

Heraia—festival in honor of the goddess Hera

herm—stone pillar used to mark crossroads and boundaries, having a head, usually of Hermes, an upright phallus carved at the front, and square pegs extending out from the shoulders

hetaira—literally, female companion; euphemism for prostitutes of various categories

hieros gamos—sacred marriage of male and female divinities that promotes peace and fecundity

himation—mantle, long cloak

homoioi—"equals," a term that Spartan citizens with full rights used to describe themselves

hoplite—heavily armed foot soldier

hydria—vessel with three handles, one vertical and two horizontal, for transporting water

hypodidaskalos—assistant teacher

kalathos—wool basket

kalos—literally, beautiful, good, or moral; kalos inscriptions praised the beauty of youths on many Attic vases

kandys—gown worn by the Medes and Persians over their trousers and other garments

kanephoros (pl. *kanephoroi*)—literally, basket bearer; a position held by prominent young women who carried baskets or vessels in religious processions

kanoun—a basket used in sacrificial rites

kantharos—high-handled drinking cup

kerykeion—messenger's wand often carried by Hermes

kithara—a stringed musical instrument similar to the lyre but with a square or angular wooden casing instead of the round shell casing of the lyre

kitharistes—music teacher

kline—couch and bed

klismos—chair with curved back

kore (pl. *korai*)—literally, maiden; a term used for an Archaic marble statue of a young woman

koreion—sacrifice at the *Koureion* that involved the cutting of a young man's hair

kottabos—game played by casting wine dregs either to sink small objects in a liquid-filled container or to dislodge a small metal disk from the top of a pole

Koureion—a ritual for adolescent boys formally registering them into their family's *phratry*, as well as marking a change in biological status akin to the female ritual *Arkteia*

kouros (pl. *kouroi*)—literally, young man; term applied to an Archaic statue of a standing youth, generally nude with left leg advanced

kourotrophos—(1) protector of young children; (2) figurine that shows an infant or young child in the care of an adult woman

krater—mixing bowl in which wine was mixed with water

krateriskoi—literally, little *kraters*; small pedestaled bowls that were dedicated to Artemis during the *Arkteia* festival at Brauron

krotalon (pl. *krotala*)—castanet

kylix—drinking cup with a high stem and two horizontal handles just under the rim

kyrios—the adult male citizen who headed the household

lagobalon—hunting club, especially for hares

lampadion—literally, little torch; hairstyle with locks of hair piled up on top of the head so as to resemble the flames of a torch flickering back

larnax (pl. *larnakes*)—coffer, box, chest

lasana—toddler's potty chair

lekanis—low, rather flat dish with a cover

lekythos—oil or perfume vessel, normally with a cylindrical body, narrow neck, and single vertical handle running between the mouth and shoulder

loutrophoreia—procession to obtain water for the bride's wedding bath

loutrophoros (pl. *loutrophoroi*)—tall, slender vessel with narrow neck and two or three handles, used to carry bath water for weddings and to mark the tombs of the unmarried

maenads—female companions of Dionysos

maia—midwife

miasma—stain, defilement, pollution

naiskos—small to medium-sized nichelike enclosed architectural construction

narthex—staff of fennel used by dance instructors to keep time and enforce instruction

nothos (pl. *nothoi*)—bastard

nymphe (pl. nymphai)—bride; nymph

nympheutria—bridesmaid

oikos—house, household

oimoi—"woe is me!"

oinochoe—wine jug with a vertical handle

omphalos—(1) the navel; (2) mound-shaped stone representing the geographical center of Delphi

omphalos cake—round cake with central knob, divided into sections

othonai—chinstraps used during burial to hold the corpse's jaw shut

paidagogos—tutor, a guardian and guide of boys who was often a trustworthy slave

paidarion—child who can walk and talk, or little slave

paidia—child's play

paidion—nurseling or young slave

paidiskos—a young boy

paidonomos—literally, boyherd; the official immediately responsible for groups of Spartan boys

paidotribes—physical education teacher

pais (pl. paides)— child; slave

pais amphithaleis—young boy with both parents living

palaistra—building with a central courtyard used for exercising and practicing athletics

Panathenaia—annual Athenian festival for Athena, with a Greater Panathenaia held every fourth year

parochos—groom's best man

parthenaia—songs sung by maidens to the flute with dancing

parthenos (pl. parthenoi)—virgin; marriageable woman not yet married

pediment—triangular area at the ends of a building with a pitched roof that often contains sculpture

pedophoros—one carrying a child

pelike—variation of the one-piece amphora whose greatest diameter is set below the middle of the vessel

peplophoros—one wearing a peplos

peplos—woolen dress worn by women

petasos—broad-brimmed hat often worn by travelers

phiale—shallow libation bowl occasionally used for drinking

phorbeia—headband to support the aulos at the mouth

phormiskos—leather sack used for holding astragaloi

phratry (pl. phratries)—hereditary association found in Athens and many other Greek city-states

pithos—large storage vessel

Plynteria—an Athenian festival during which the ancient image of Athena Polias was undressed and washed by women

polis—Greek city-state

polos—conical hat often worn by fertility goddesses in the Near East and Greece

prokephalaiai—pillows used on funerary couch to prop the corpse's head

prothesis—lying-in-state of the body, during which relatives pay their last respects

pyrrhic—an ancient Greek martial dance

pyxis—woman's jewelry and cosmetics container

rhyton—drinking vessel often ending in the shape of the head of an animal

sakkos—sack or bag used to cover the hair of women; snood

satyrs—male companions of Dionysos who are bestial in appearance and actions

sima—gutter

skaphe—a hollow vessel, tub, trough, basin, bowl

skyphos—deep, stemless drinking cup with two handles

splanchna—viscera, innards

stadion—(1) one length of a running track; (2) sprint race one stadion long

stele (pl. stelai)—upright rectangular marble slab, often with relief decoration or inscription

stephane—crown; bridal crown

stoa—all-purpose Greek building type having the form of an open colonnade

stoichedon—writing style with letters in a grid-pattern system of placement

streptos—baguette-shaped cake

strigil—implement used by athletes to scrape the oil, sweat, and dirt from their bodies after exercise

Styx—river that separates the world of the living from that of the dead; Charon, the ferryman, takes souls across it

symposion—Greek drinking party following the main meal, replete with games and various other types of entertainment, including sexual

syssition (pl. syssitia)—one of the public mess companies in Sparta to which Spartan males were apportioned

terracotta—fired clay object

Thesmophoria—women's festival in honor of Demeter, common to all Greeks

tokos—birth, time of delivery; offspring, child, son

tondo—round, interior area in the center of a kylix that is frequently decorated

trapeza—table, base, counter

trochos (or hamaxis)—toy roller

trophos—nurse

tymbos—mound of earth covering the grave

CONTRIBUTORS

Jenifer Neils is Ruth Coulter Heede Professor of Art History at Case Western Reserve University.

John H. Oakley is chairman of the Department of Classical Studies, Chancellor Professor, and Forrest D. Murden Jr. Professor at the College of William and Mary.

Lesley A. Beaumont is assistant professor at the University of Sydney and former assistant director of the British School of Archaeology in Athens.

Helene Foley is professor of classics at Barnard College, Columbia University.

Mark Golden is professor of classics at the University of Winnipeg.

Katherine Hart is the Barbara C. and Harvey P. Hood 1918 Curator of Academic Programming at the Hood Museum of Art, Dartmouth College.

Jill Korbin is professor of anthropology and director of the childhood studies program at Case Western Reserve University.

Jeremy Rutter is Sherman Fairchild Professor of the Humanities at Dartmouth College and teaches Greek archaeology in the Classics Department.

H. A. Shapiro is the W. H. Collins Vickers Professor of Archaeology and chairman of the Classics Department at Johns Hopkins University.

Photo Credits

Copyright Notices

INDEX

Aphrodite, 16, 89, 116, 119, 126–127, 128, 137n49, 141, 153, 204, 208

Aphrodite Holding Her Children Himeros and Eros, 140–141, 141

Apollo, 14, 87, 116, 117, 128, 154, 155, 161n63, 204

apprenticeships, 18

Apulia, 114, 150, 169, 176, 179, 209

Arcadia, 211

Archaic period, 3, 4, 13–29, 60–65; childhood in, 13–29, 14–26, 60–65, 60–64, 85–111, 85–106, 113–136, 112–135, 139–161, 138–159, 163–194, 162–188, 209, 210, 216, 216, 225–238, 226–237, 244, 257, 258, 264–281, 265–281. See also specific artists, forms, iconography, regions, and subjects

Archanes, 38

Archestrate, 134, 134

Archippos, Son of Dion, 189, 189

Argolid, 46

Ariadne, 89, 95, 95, 109nn37,56

Ariès, Phillipe, 2, 5n3, 16

Aristophanes, 15, 99, 102, 123, 151, 178; Clouds, 25, 107, 264, 269; Lysistrata, 118, 139, 149, 294; Thesmophoriazusae, 146; Wasps, 107

Aristotle, 1, 14, 15, 19, 22, 24, 27n23, 144, 163, 178, 244

Arkteia, 151–152, 153

arktoi, 151, 152

arrhephoroi, 15, 18, 42, 149–152, 151

Artemis, 15, 61, 77, 78, 87, 116, 117, 128, 135, 142, 143, 145, 151–152, 153, 157, 178, 200, 202, 284

Artemis and Apollo Threaten Tityos as He Seizes Their Mother Leto, 117, 117

aryballos, 180, 246, 247; Corinthian, 154–155, 155

Asklepios, 78

Askoid Feeding Bottle, 36, 36

Astyanax, 69, 71, 82nn27,28, 189

Athanasia, 143

Athena, 15, 16, 17, 18, 62–63, 82n19, 87, 89, 92, 94, 97, 109n37, 143, 150–151, 153, 159, 204, 206–207, 208, 212, 284, 295; birth of, 62–63, 116, 206–207

Athena and the Daughters of Kekrops, 150, 150

Athena Ergane, 118

Athens, 3, 14, 16, 93–95, 143, 164, 176, 177; Archaic and Classical periods, 13–29, 60–77, 96–107; father-son relationship in, 96–107, 108n1; plague, 181; politics, 67–68, 178

athletics, 17, 18–19, 63, 153; Archaic and Classical, 17–21, 67, 310; education, 65, 67, 244, 252–254; girls, 20–21, 154; rituals, 153–154

Attica, 46, 96, 98, 167, 181

Attic vase painting. See vases

augury, 158–159

Aulode Contest for Boys, 154, 155

Ayia Triadha, 41, 42

B

Baby Boy Grapples with a Goose, 79, 79

Baby Learning to Crawl or Walk, 71–72, 72, 237, 237

Baby on Stool with Mother, 240, 241

Baby Opheltes, 142, 142

Bassai, 73, 75

bastards (nothoi), 21–22

bell-krater: Apulian red-figure, 114; Attic red-figure, 93, 94, 125, 158, 158

belly amphora, Attic black-figure, 61, 61

Bird Painter, work attributed to, 170–171, 171

birds, 36, 73–74, 75, 234, 280; death and, 73–74, 167, 180–183, 189–190, 265, 305–308

birth, 16–17, 19, 21, 114–117, 222; death in child-birth, 3, 143, 163, 185–187, 191, 222–223, 296; first childbirth, 114; gender and, 16–17; mother-daughter relationship, 114–117; rituals, 143–145. See also birth scenes

Birth of Athena, 62–63, 116, 116, 206–207, 207

Birth of Erichthonios, 89, 89

Birth of Erichthonios and Eos Chasing Kephalos, 88, 89, 143, 143, 208, 208, 209

Birth of Helen, The, 115, 209, 209

birth scenes, 62–63, 114–117, 114–117; Athena, 62–63, 116, 116, 206–207, 207; Erichthonios, 89, 89 ; Helen, 114, 114, 115, 209, 209

Bithynia, 179

Black Fury Group, work attributed to, 150

Boiotia, 12, 13, 46, 48, 61, 78, 113, 120, 141, 157, 233, 255, 257, 266, 268, 271

bone astragaloi, 279, 279

Boreas Painter, work attributed to, 68–69

Boxing Boys, 45, 45

boy(s), 8, 10, 14; adolescent, 76–77, 97–103, 310–311; in Aegean prehistory, 38, 40–45, 48, 56n73, 57n86; in Archaic and Classical periods, 16–20, 24–26, 62, 63–65, 72, 75, 85–111, 114, 165, 168, 191, 222, 230, 244; education of, 17, 18, 19–20, 24, 65–67, 244, 249, 257–258; father-son relationship, 85–111, 84–106; favored, 16–17, 24, 76; in Hellenistic period, 77, 80, 81; music, 22, 154–156; names, 21, 144; pederasty, 4, 8, 20, 22, 63, 99, 102, 110; rituals, 15, 102–103, 141–142, 144–147, 153–159, 284, 285–287, 291–293; Spartan, 19–21; transition to adult-hood, 143, 145, 153–154, 310–311

Boy and Cart, 15, 16, 145, 285, 285, 286

Boy and Girl with Female Chorus, 157, 157

Boy Assisting Sick Man, 16, 17

Boy at Shoemaker's, 99, 100, 242, 242

Boy Boxers (?), 252, 252

Boy Carrying Piglet and Basket, 158, 158, 291, 291

Boy in Goat-Drawn Chariot, 145, 147, 286, 286

Boy Led by Hermes to Charon, and Boys Playing Knucklebones at the Grave, A, 173, 173, 299, 299, 300, 300

Boy Riding Fawn, 286, 286

Boys' Dancing Competition, 154–155, 155

Boy Serving a Reveler, 145, 147, 148, 261, 261, 262

Boy Slave, 80, 81

Boys Playing Ball, 271, 271

Boys Playing Knucklebones, 146, 263, 264, 278, 278

Boy Wheeling His Toy Roller, 269, 269

Boy with Dog, 145, 146, 285, 285

Boy with His Pet Bird, 280, 280

Boy with Hoop and Stick in the Family Home, 75, 76

Boy with Lyre at an Altar, 290, 290

Boy with Seated Paidagogos, 249, 249

bracelets, 177, 177, 304, 304

Brauron, 77, 78, 117, 143, 149, 150, 151, 152, 157, 200

Bridal Scenes, 310, 311, 312

Bride and Her Mother Make Prenuptial Offerings to Aphrodite, 126, 127

Bronze Age, 2, 4, 14, 32, 34, 35, 49, 50n2, 224, 224, 230; Early, 32, 33–34; Late, 31–32, 35, 44, 46, 49, 224; Middle, 32, 34, 35, 36–37

Bronze Knucklebone, 279, 279

bronze statues and statuettes, 21, 38, 81, 200; Aegean prehistoric, 36–37, 37, 38, 225, 225, 237–238, 237; Archaic and Classical, 20, 21, 154, 176; Hellenistic, 58, 59, 142, 204, 204, 205, 213, 213, 238, 238

Bronze Stylus, 250, 250

bronze toys, 181–182, 182

Brygos Painter, work attributed to, 17, 18

bull-jumping, 42–43, 55n57

burial: Aegean prehistoric, 33, 34–36, 41, 46, 48, 50n7, 52nn18,20,26,27, 57n88; Archaic and Classical periods, 22–24, 61, 63–65, 72–77, 82n25, 105–107, 113, 130–135, 163–194, 222–223, 296–308; of children, 174–179; Geometric periods, 155–157, 164, 166, 176, 177, 178; larnakes, 48; methods and types, 167, 176. See also death; grave(s)

C

cakes, 146

Callimachus, 149; Hymn of Artemis, 116

calyx-krater: Apulian red-figure, 150, 150; Attic red-figure, 71, 71, 88, 89, 105, 118, 122, 122, 143, 208, 208, 209; Lucanian red-figure, 23, 217, 217, 218

Captive Black Youth, 262, 262

Cassandra, 121

Castor and Pollux, 21

catalogue, 195–312, 197–311; children in myth, 198, 204–220, 203–219; education, 198–199, 244–262, 243–262; household (oikos), 198, 222–242, 221–242; ritual, 199, 284–308, 283–308; statues of young children, 197, 198, 200–201, 200–201; toys and games, 199, 264–282, 263–282